The Ultimate Imperative

# The
# Ultimate
# Imperative

An Interpretation **of Christian Ethics**

Ronald H. Stone

The Pilgrim Press
Cleveland, Ohio

The Pilgrim Press, Cleveland, Ohio 44115
© 1999 by Ronald H. Stone

Earlier versions of newly edited and revised materials appeared in the
following publications and permission to reproduce them here is grate-
fully acknowledged:

*Christian Realism and Peace Making* (Nashville: Abingdon Press, 1988),
86–101, for discussion of just war theory. • *The Ecumenist* 2 (April–
June 1995): 19–22 for discussion of "Truth and the CIA." • *Horizons
in Biblical Theology* 10 (December 1988): 51–66, reworked into chapter 7.
• *Laval Theologíque et Philosophique* 44 (June 1988): 157–64, reworked
as chapter 3 and used in concept of justice. • *Reformed Urban Ethics*
(Pittsburgh: Mellen Research Press, 1991), for discussion of concept of
justice and a conception of "A Christian Ethic of American Politics."
• Portions of *Reformed Faith and Politics* (Lanham, Md.: University
Press of America, 1983) were adapted into "A Christian Ethic of
American Politics." • Paul Tillich's essay from *Pulpit Digest* 34, no. 194
(June 1954), is used by permission of the estate of Paul Tillich.

Biblical quotations, unless otherwise noted, are from the New Revised
Standard Version of the Bible, © 1989 by the Division of Christian
Education of the National Council of Churches of Christ in the
U.S.A., and are used by permission

Printed in the United States of America on acid-free paper

05 04 03 02 01 99   5 4 3 2 1

Library of Congress Cataloging-in-Publication Data

Stone, Ronald H.
    The ultimate imperative : an interpretation of Christian ethics /
Ronald H. Stone.
        p. cm.
    Includes bibliographical references and index.
    ISBN 0-8298-1330-6 (pbk. : alk. paper)
    1. Christian ethics.  2. Love—Religious aspects—Christianity.
I. Title.
BJ1251.S865   1999
241—dc21                                              98-50596
                                                        CIP

*To Bebb Wheeler Stone,*
*companion in the ethics of life*

# Contents

# Preface

Christian ethics for the church starts with Jesus' own ethic of love of God and of neighbor. The rest is commentary, for better or worse. Jesus as a Jew presupposed the history of the moral traditions of Israel and particularly the Ten Commandments. As we in the church teach the Ten Commandments to our children in church confirmation courses, we affirm their development of the requirements to love God and to love the neighbor. We attempt in the church, by teaching, example, and practice, to influence the Christian conscience toward appropriate behavior in God's world.

Ethics derived from the love commandments and the Ten Commandments is expressed in principles that serve as moral guidelines for Christian life. Ethics is not all of life, although it is relevant to the decisions of human life. Ethics is not a theory of human psychology or a theory of society, although it uses such theories. Ethics is different from politics. Christian ethics reflects on the moral traditions and practices of the church and from such reflection suggests guidelines or moral principles for today. The ethic developed in this book is loyal to scripture and church tradition, but its authority rests in its persuasiveness to those who honor these traditions and desire to live socially relevant Christian lives in the contemporary world.

My involvements in writing and teaching have emphasized the social dimensions of life more than the inner-personal or biological, and so the bulk of this book, part 3, focuses on social issues. Many of the more personal issues are discussed in part 2, but even there the exposition of the biblical imperatives tends to emphasize social ethics. The experiential sources of this study are life in the church and action in society. I was nurtured in liberal-evangelical Methodism. As a young man I preached on a sustained basis for the first time in the United Church of Christ and then edited that denomination's journal *Social Action*. Most of my adult years of worship, as a layman, were in interdenominational churches—the Riverside Church in New York City and the Community of Reconciliation in Pittsburgh. Twenty years ago I returned to the Presbyterian denomination of my grandparents and my interracial neighborhood congregation of East Liberty Presbyterian Church. My seminary students, although ecumenical, are mostly from the Presbyterian and Methodist Churches, and I teach from both Reformed and Methodist traditions. My actions in society have been mainly in the struggles for racial and economic justice, political ethics, and peacemaking in international relations. All of these activities have led me to organizing, writing, and personal physical actions, as this volume reveals.

Although many interpretations of Christian ethics are investigated in this study, the predominant influences of John Calvin and Reinhold Niebuhr are obvious. Their serious involvements with scripture and moral traditions of the church and their deep engagements with the social problematics of their times make them the best representatives of this principled-engaged Christian ethic. There are, of course, problems with their ethics, as there are unresolved issues with the ethic presented here, but their preservation of the essence of Christian ethics, while promoting Christian social reform, overrides their well-known weaknesses.

I began teaching ethics in a summer school at Morningside College in 1964. I remember arriving late for the start of the session because I had been arrested for occupying the South African embassy protesting the threatened death sentence of Nelson Mandela. More than thirty years later, gains in justice have been won, and this book explains how I see the subject of Christian ethics after teaching it at four universities, three colleges, and two seminaries. It necessarily has the tone of presentation for the college educated or those in college. I hope it still has the passion of that 1964 occupation of the South African embassy and some of its relevance.

Chapter 3, "Nurtured in Community and Seeking Justice," contains a reworked presentation from two previous writings on justice. My book *Reformed Urban Ethics* (San Francisco: Mellen Research Press, 1991) and the essay "Paulus and Gustavo: Religious Socialism and Liberation Theology," in *Laval Théologique et Philosophique* 44 (June 1988), have been drawn on for the discussion of justice. In chapter 5, "Concern for the Other," the discussion of killing in war draws heavily on the chapter "The Justifiable War Tradition" in my book *Christian Realism and Peace Making* (Nashville: Abingdon Press, 1988). Also, the discussion on "Truth and the CIA" is from my essay of the same title in *The Ecumenist* 2 (April–June 1995). Chapter 7 is an edited version of "The Distinction between Personal and Public Morality," from *Horizons in Biblical Theology* 10 (December 1988). The section on Calvin and the concluding pages of chapter 8 are from my *Reformed Urban Ethics*, as is a rewritten, expanded version of chapter 9. The chapter "Political Apathy" draws on my previous writings in *Reformed Faith and Politics* (Washington: University Press of America, 1983), *Reformed Urban Ethics*, and *Church and Society* (September/October 1996).

*The Ultimate Imperative* began as the inaugural lecture for the John Witherspoon Professorship in Christian Ethics at Pittsburgh Theological Seminary in 1992. Most of my previous books had been intellectual biographies, or studies in international relations or religion-and-society issues. The lecture forced me to arrange the priorities in Christian ethics, and that project developed into this relatively systematic Christian ethic.

My thanks go to the board of directors and president of Pittsburgh Theological Seminary for the sabbatical to write the book and for the John Witherspoon Chair of Christian Ethics, which initiated the process. I owe special thanks to Mrs. Sheryl Gilliland, who found this as her first book project on becoming faculty secretary at the seminary. The work of my research assistant, Ms. Anita Sattler, improved the punctuation of the book and the accuracy of the endnotes greatly. The gracious thoroughness of editors Tim Staveteig and Ed Huddleston and copyeditor Craig Kirkpatrick polished the manuscript to its present level, and I owe them my most sincere thanks.

# Part
## One
# Foundations

# An Interpretation
# of Christian Ethics

The study of Christian ethics is a worldwide activity transcending all national and cultural boundaries. The study group may meet in Iraq, reflecting almost two thousand years of Christian presence, or in a tribe newly introduced to Christianity within the last decade, but in either case the will of the transcendent, eternal God is sought. In its more pure forms, Christian ethics is studied. In its more material forms, it shapes the institutions at which it is studied. Whether the institution is a basic Christian community of poor peasants in El Salvador or a graduate seminar at Harvard Divinity School, the institutions have been shaped by Christian ethics as much as they have studied Christian ethics.

Beyond the shaping of Christian communities and Christian graduate schools, the Christian ethic has shaped institutions that are generally regarded as secular or set apart from the sacred. The democratic constitutionalism of James Madison and the market economy of Adam Smith reflect their origins in the moral philosophy of Presbyterian Scotland that was explicitly taught in the eighteenth-century classrooms of the College of New Jersey and the University of Glasgow. In addition to these direct offsprings of Christian ethics, its indirect world-changing influence can be seen in the revolution of the Congregationalist Sun Yat-sen, who led the overthrow of imperial China, and in the Roman Catholic overthrow of Marcos's dictatorial regime in the Philippines. So inquiry into the depths of Christian ethics requires an examination of Christian community itself and a study of the worldwide effects of Christian ethics.

The depths of Christian ethics and claims for its universality are rooted not in the institutions of market capitalism and democratic constitutionalism but in the institution of the Christian church. Around the world, the scriptures are examined daily by the church for moral guidance. Not philosophers, but ordinary people—workers, the unemployed, businesspeople, and grassroots clergy people—are looking for the truth of Christian ethics. In so searching they are primarily seeking not rules, but the will of God. John Wesley, another eighteenth-century thinker, said that the will of God is not separable from

God, but is God. When you know the will of God, you know God. Of course, another claim for the *universality* of the Christian ethics is just this—the will of God, the creator, sustainer, and redeemer of the universe.

The ethic constitutive of God's will would be the universal ethic. It would, by definition, be the ethic beyond multicultural pluralism, beyond gender differences, and beyond ideological taint. Can we locate such an ethic? We cannot create a pure method, for it would be subject to the relativities of pluralistic centers, gender differences, and subtle ideological preferences. But if we cannot create a new method, we can look where such a claim is made and examine it. The scriptures of the three historical monotheistic religions contain such an ethic. Here, at the beginnings of monotheism and universalism, the ethic or way of life is named *love*.

Love appears as the motif of Hosea's prophecy. God's nature is to love, and God loves even when Israel, like a wandering spouse, seeks fulfillment elsewhere. It erupts in the passionate Song of Solomon as the insatiable longing of the lover for the beloved. In its various forms it drives Israel to propagate and also to seek covenant community. It is more basic than law, it is reality, it is in the nature of the Divine. But it appears as commandment also, for Israel has forgotten and has been led from the way, forgetting what is central. In the Code of Holiness we are reminded: "You shall not take vengeance or bear a grudge against any of your people, but you shall love your neighbor as yourself: I am the Lord" (Lev. 19:18).

Quoting this mandate half a millennium later, Paul said: "For the whole law is summed up in a single command, 'You shall love your neighbor as yourself'" (Gal. 5:14). The Gospel writers, not knowing of Paul's summary, put the tradition a little differently, incorporating the Shema tradition from Deuteronomy 6:4–5: "Hear, O Israel: The Lord is our God, the Lord alone. You shall love the Lord your God with all your heart, and with all your soul, and with all your might."

In Mark 12, Luke 10, and Matthew 22, this great commandment is joined with the concern for the neighbor as it was in Exodus in the Ten Commandments. Here it is in summary: "You shall love your God with all your heart, and with all your soul, and with all your mind. This is the greatest and first commandment. And a second is like it, you shall love your neighbor as yourself. On these two commandments hang all the law and the prophets" (Matt. 22:37–40).

Paul concludes his great hymn to love: "Faith, hope, love, these three abide, but the greatest of these is love" (1 Cor. 13:13). John also pushes love into ultimacy: "Love is from God, everyone who loves is born of God and knows God" (1 John 4:7). "God is love, and those who abide in love abide in God, and God abides in them" (1 John 4:16). "The commandment we have from God is this: those who love God must love their brothers and sisters also" (1 John 4:21).

So here we have it: the understanding of Christian ethics as a love ethic is secured. The love referred to uses the same word, *ahab* in Hebrew or *agape* in Greek, for love of the Divine and love of the human. Neither the Old Testament nor the New Testament permits love to be exempt from the conflicts of life. They both discuss love in terms of reality. In the same chapter in John, for example, love becomes specific: "Those who say, 'I love God,' and hate their brothers or sisters, are liars; for those who do not love a brother or sister whom they have seen, cannot love God whom they have not seen" (1 John 4:20).

This Johannine correspondence was written in a profound crisis of faith. Conflict between synagogue and church was very real. John says that if you do not love your brother and sister you are a liar if you claim to love God. Love takes on meaning. It means the fulfilling of all the commandments. It means telling those who do not actively love that their profession of Christian faith is a *lie*. Tenderheartedness is required, but in a sinful world this means opposition to the sinful world and addressing as liars those Christians who do not demonstrate love. As a young student pastor, the first time my neighbors ever called me a communist was when I applied this meaning in my home church to race relations in the United States and interpreted love as active service for racial justice. Race continued to be the divisive issue. As a young professor in a seminary, I was asked to debate the business manager about suspending all construction, including the new chapel, to support the demands of African Americans to be included in trade union guilds. In my pride, I think I won the debate, but of course I lost the issue and the approval of the then president. I managed to survive his tenure in office without ever receiving an invitation to meet him, anywhere. Love seeks practical expression and intermediary principles or guidelines: confront lethargy in the church, practice racial justice, treat everyone as one—"Your neighbor as yourself," Jesus said—and this means *equally*. The book of Acts expresses love thusly: "It was distributed to each as any had need." Love drives toward expression in moral law, and moral law underlies the civil law as applied moral law under the conditions of sin. Imagine the conflicts ahead as we try to realize greater equality and more justice in our hierarchical, racially divided church and society.

The dangers of stressing love as the center of Christian ethics is that it could be expressed sentimentally and simplistically. But the parables of Jesus and the stories of his life and conflicts engage love in feeding, teaching, healing, and religious-political conflicts.

The honest sermon on love does not leave everyone feeling good as much as it leaves people feeling convicted. It reveals humanity as liars in need of truth, as well as encouraging the perfection of life in love. Likewise, love as moral teaching is summary: it does not stand alone but is the means of interpreting the moral principles it expresses.

## ETHICS AND HERMENEUTICS

This study is one approach to Christian ethics. There are other perspectives. A survey[1] or a history[2] of Christian ethics should try to cover most of these other perspectives. Broad coverage is available and valuable, but here a relatively systematic proposal is presented. This constructive work requires several choices among the options available in Christian ethics. A brief

survey of these choices will place this ethic and its choices within the context
of several types.

The most recent book by Edward L. Long Jr. stresses the importance of
the hermeneutics (the art of interpretation) of scripture in Christian ethics.[3]
The ethic developed here agrees with the importance of both scripture and
its interpretation that Long emphasizes. He is able to identify seven types of
hermeneutics and recognizes that each type has a contribution to make in some
aspect or aspects of the church's broad life. The first type involves focusing on
particular texts. While recognizing that there are both sophisticated and simple
(even fundamentalist) interpretations of texts, Long is persuaded that perspectives larger than those of particular texts must be considered for ethics. Second,
the study of the origins of particular ethical concepts in scripture has become
very sophisticated, but the questions of genealogy or origins of moral insights
are insufficient grounding for contemporary moral judgment.[4] The third type of
interpretation that Long discusses is that of "controlling concepts." Here he
recognizes the centrality of "love" ethics and *justice* hermeneutics to mainline
Christians.[5] The fourth type has to do with emphasizing the development of
moral teaching in scripture. Like the study of origins, the hermeneutic of development is useful but not controlling, because the interpretation of scripture in
early formulations of morals may be as profound as that in later formulations.
There is no need to presuppose moral progress in our hermeneutical presuppositions. The fifth type relies on the church context for the meaning and
interpretation of scripture. He notes that a sixth form of hermeneutics, that of
suspicion, has been used effectively by feminist scholarship. It has successfully
revealed male bias, misogyny, and patriarchal presuppositions of scripture. Yet
Long wants to avoid any one hermeneutic becoming more of a "controlling idea
than a hermeneutic of suspicion."[6] The final category he mentions is that of
"tutored responsiveness," which is a religious interpretation responding to scripture in a personal or communal existential affirmation of meaning. This ethic
within his seven types is an ethic of controlling concepts of love and justice in
the context of community and church. These choices are grounded in the
assumption that in terms of ethics, they are the dominant biblical norms.
Beyond the terms used by Long, the particular importance for ethics of the Ten
Commandments and Jesus' teaching is grounded in their centrality to the life of
the Christian community.

## MODELS OF ETHICS

Beyond interpretation of scripture, the ethic presented in this book has a
structure that can be analyzed in relationship to other alternatives. To place
this ethic in context is to consider it as a type of religious ethic or as a model
of ethical discourse alongside other models.

H. Richard Niebuhr, in his posthumously published volume *The
Responsible Self*, has noted the emergence of the term, symbol, or concept of
responsibility. The rise of the term "responsibility" as a primary category for

moral self-understanding is rooted, Niebuhr thinks, in certain characteristics of our general knowledge of humanity in the twentieth century. The word "responsibility" is supplanting the words "duty," "good," "law," "virtue," and "morality" in moral discourse, and this displacement is not merely a shift in vocabulary. Rather, the symbol of responsibility links contemporary patterns of meaning and current notions of motivation in a general model of what moral action means today.

Niebuhr's attempt in *The Responsible Self* is to analyze moral discourse and to discover what the patterns of moral life are. There is more prescription in this volume than he seems to be willing to confess—that is, he is arguing for the adoption of a model and not simply noting that it has arrived. He believes that human behavior exhibits the quality of responsiveness as he describes it, but he also knows that he is attempting to displace two other models of moral life from their claims to primal recognition.

*instead of God as maker?*

A symbol that has proven very fruitful in the past is humanity as maker. Cannot the model of humanity as artist, technician, or fashioner be adapted to moral life? Aristotle begins his *Ethics* with the statement "Every art and every inquiry and similarly every action and pursuit is thought to aim at some good." People act toward ends, and they act to fashion themselves into goals or ends. In light of this model, humans act purposively to mold themselves and their actions so as to realize ends. By acting for ends, humanity the maker shapes itself.

This image of the maker supports all ethical theories regarded as teleological—i.e., theories that determine what ought to be done by reference to the goal or *telos* being desired. There is a degree of necessity for this type of thinking. H. Richard Niebuhr wrote:

> When we are dealing with this human nature of ours, in ourselves and in others, as administrators of our private realms of body and mind or as directors of social enterprises—from families seeking happiness to international societies seeking peace—we cannot fail to ask: "At what long—or short—range state of affairs are we aiming, and what are the immediate steps that must be taken toward the attainment of the possible goal?"[7]

Those who have used this image have not agreed on the best ends to pursue. They have disagreed on the means to be used even when agreeing on goals. They have exhibited wide disagreement on what constitutes the human nature that is to be shaped. These disagreements, however, have reflected agreement on the nature of personal existence. Humanity makes itself and its environment in light of chosen goals.

A second model of the moral life that has dominated ethics is the model of the citizen. Life is not art, for human nature is not clay to be molded. Human sentiments and passions are more like citizens to be ruled than clay to be molded. The human builder can reject inadequate material, but we have been given ourselves and our communities. Niebuhr raises the question

"What use would it have been had Socrates designed for himself that happy life which Aristotle described?"[8] We cannot select our destiny; the most we can do is decide by which rules we will conduct ourselves. Life is more like politics, the art of the possible, than like the design and construction of a cathedral. We are confronted with prescriptions, rules, mores, laws, and the influence of communal pressures. We can only ask to which laws we will assent and against which laws we will rebel.

Contemporary religion across the United States relates itself very closely to this principled model of the moral life. The church understands itself in thousands of places as the guardian of the moral law. The moral law is seen as revealed by God and is often compared in popular pulpit rhetoric to the law of nature. As the law of gravity forces objects to return to earth and is ignored only at considerable risk to the one who defies it, so the laws protecting family, for example, hold the society together and result in the near destruction of those who violate them.

To a considerable degree, Christianity is bound to this model as long as it holds to its scriptures. Matthew viewed Jesus as the eschatological giver of laws to those receiving grace. Paul wrestled with the issues of conflicting laws throughout his life. The basic human dilemma for much of orthodox Protestantism is how a rebellious humanity, which has from the Garden of Eden violated the law and the covenants, can be saved from the wrath of a righteous God. The human story from Genesis through Romans is seen through a model of jurisprudence with the image of the unworthy citizen of God's realm as a dominating motif.

The primordial nature of the mythology of humanity as law abider is witnessed to in the genesis myths of Greek, Mesopotamian, and Hebrew culture. The cosmos reflects the ordering of humanity's world and the gods who direct the cosmos also direct humanity.

The model has illuminated moral experience in primitive and contemporary culture. Tyranny and democracy both shape the life of their community by appeals to law and order. It has helped us in making complex decisions, and the roles of both Solon and Kant in the cultural experience of the West give evidence of its power.

Debates between the representatives of the teleological and deontological schools have not been conclusive. For those who focus on ends, rules are utilitarian in character; they are guides to the desired ends. The deontologists can insist, however, that only the life lived according to right standards is good. The moral life is not to be suspended for some future end. (The end probably will not be unambiguously achieved, anyway.) The right life is demanded in the present. The deontologists or formalists have their strongest representatives in a primitive monotheism with a revealed morality or in the skillful philosophic hands of an R. M. Hare or an Immanuel Kant. It is very hard to refute the utilitarians when we are discussing questions of practical social morality and polity. The question is alive, however, in issues of the conflict between conscience and tactics in Christians who agonize over breaking laws to achieve desirable ends. The laws in question may be the laws they perceive to be grounded in their religious faith or the laws of the broader community. The widespread failure of government in the twentieth century reduces the attraction of humanity as citizen.

The inadequacies of the previously discussed images permit us to consider the advantages of the image of humanity as answerer. This is the implied image behind the emphasis on responsibility. We are engaged in dialogue with other selves, and we form ourselves by responding to other selves and by reacting to their perceptions. Humanity exists in reacting to stimuli.

Humanity is now writing its history not so much in terms of the ideals and laws of previous societies as in terms of how those societies responded to challenges in their environments. The older images have not lost their meaning, but they are being replaced by an emphasis on interaction.

The understanding of moral agents as responsive beings who answer actions exerted on themselves with acts in accordance with their interpretations of the actions illumines aspects of conduct that the previous emphases on citizen or maker obscured. This understanding is not completely new. It is prefigured in Aristotle's notion of the mean that defines virtue or in his emphasis on the fitting act. Elements of Stoicism, naturalism, and Marxism also reflect aspects of this ethic. H. Richard Niebuhr argues that this model is more helpful in containing the Hebraic-prophetic traditions than the legal model.

Practical life also reflects the pattern of responsive action in the testing and breaking of societies and persons. Suffering, either social or personal, calls forth a response that shapes the ethos of the community and the character of the individual. Ideals, goals, and laws play a role in shaping a country's response to emergency, but the response in action itself shapes the life and self-definition of the community.

The differences among the three models of moral actions are perceived in their central concepts of the *good*, the *right*, and the *fitting*.[9] The ethical question is not simply "What is my end?" or "What is my duty?" but rather first "What is going on?" The fitting action, the one that fits the total interaction as response and anticipation of further response, is the only action that can contribute maximally to the good and is the only action that can be said to be right.

Niebuhr defines his understanding of responsibility as an image of the moral life. The idea or pattern of responsibility, then, may be defined summarily and abstractly as the idea of agents' actions as a response to actions exerted on them in accordance with their interpretation of the latter actions and with their expectation of a response to their response; and all of this occurs in a continuous community of agents.[10]

This response ethic of H. Richard Niebuhr was much more profound than the situation ethics of the debates of the 1960s. It brought in the full range of moral theory and was interpreted in the context of a world created and sustained by God. It worked well—particularly in the hands of as skillful a moral philosopher as Niebuhr. Its reception by women moral thinkers[11] would develop and eventually, in a transmuted form, appear decades later in the moral philosophy of Carol Gilligan, who emphasized how women's decision making differed from men's.

Gradually, however, as religious illiteracy in the church grew to the point where the moral rules and principles were unknown, the dialogue of Christian moral thinkers weakened. Failures in church school, the influx of new uninformed members into the church, and the complexities of a secularizing culture meant that the presuppositions for Christian moral dialogue were absent. Furthermore, the responsiveness of the model—its conversational consideration of all complexities—lacked the force for change of either a goal-oriented ethic or a principle-guided ethic.

At the end of the twentieth century, one of the most thorough of the Christian ethicists of ecology and technology, Ian Barbour, is, in the full consideration of H. Richard Niebuhr's model, opting for a central role of values or end-oriented ethics.[12] He cannot abandon any of the three types of ethics, but he finally gives the weight of his preference to the ethics of the good rather than the *right* or the *responsible*. Social policy, he argues, needs the choice of values as a central consideration, and this may be particularly true of technological trends that affect the future.[13] *The Ultimate Imperative*, because of the need for recovery of the Christian presuppositions of ethics, the weight of biblical preference for ethics of love, justice, and commandments, and less of an emphasis on values and more on politics in shaping the future, leans toward an emphasis on ethics of right principles. It corrects this emphasis with values or end-oriented ethics, and with responsiveness to dialogue as needed to fulfill love, justice, and community.

The final comparative discussion that concludes this section responds to Edward L. Long Jr.'s survey of the field.[14] Long followed H. Richard Niebuhr in dividing the field into (1) deliberative motifs, (2) prescriptive motifs from Bible, tradition, command or context, and (3) relational motifs. The ethic presented here is within the prescriptive motif of the Bible and of tradition. Then, in regard to the application or implementation of the ethic, Long considered three forms of implementation: (1) the institutional motif in law, order, and institutions; (2) the operational motif in terms of power; and (3) the intentional motif in separatism and renewal, sects, and particular causes. Although this ethic expresses itself in all three of the implementation strategies, its primary weight is on institutional renewal as seen by Calvin for church and state and on social action in light of power considerations as seen operationally by Reinhold Niebuhr, Paul Tillich, and Martin Luther King Jr.[15]

The choices that I have made in developing this ethic have resulted from constant life in Methodist, Presbyterian, and United Church of Christ churches, academic preparation enthusiastically affirmed, and an ongoing practice of reform-oriented social action in a democratic society. These experiences have produced an ethic characterized by a hermeneutic of Bible and tradition rooted in love primarily, justice socially, and community necessarily.

This ethic is expressed in principles or a prescriptive understanding of ethics and is made operational in power and in institutions.

## THREE CLASSICAL EXAMPLES

A brief foray into church history will illustrate the love ethic. Augustine in the fifth century summarized Christianity as faith, hope, and love. Faith expressed trust in God as understood by Christian doctrine. Hope was that God's loving power would be victorious over the sin of history. In his handbook of faith, Augustine makes clear the interdependence of faith, hope, and love, and the preeminence of love. *Love* for Augustine is the seeking of union with God, and in seeking this union we can love rightly the things of the world. In seeking the union with the good, worldly objects are not to be ultimately loved, but we can love the divine substance in them. We can love others and ourselves rightly and thereby love God as the divine loving ground of everything. The highest calling of human life would be to contemplate God and enjoy God in God's own self. However, those in the world with power may serve God rightly as judges and as soldiers. They are to work in the world as duty commands, serving as judges with more mercy than pagans because of love and defending the innocent with armed forces if necessary. War made Augustine profoundly sorrowful, but it could be engaged in as a last resort out of love to defend the innocent or to right a wrong, but never out of pride or selfishness, or for an unjust cause. From Augustine comes this classical Christian ethic, that love is all. "Love God and do as you will," but let us understand what you will do by means of principles. Love expresses principles, summarizes principles, and utilizes principles.

John Calvin places his political thought in his most systematic theological work, *The Institutes of the Christian Religion*. His political thought is a great synthesis of biblical teachings and political philosophy. For him, the moral law consists of the two commandments. The will of God is that God be worshiped by all and that "we mutually love one another." This moral law is for Calvin also the natural law that God has placed in human minds. All laws, by whatever people, that are directed to these ends need not be changed, even though they vary in details. The requirements of Jewish ceremonial law are set aside, as are various details of Jewish judicial law, but "the precepts and duties of love remain of perpetual obligation. . . . If this be true, certainly all nations are left at liberty to enact such laws as they shall find to be respectively expedient for them, provided they be framed according to that perpetual rule of love, so that, though they vary in form, they may have at the same end."[16]

Even though Calvin follows Luther in theology, Calvin, the former lawyer, retains a much higher view of moral teaching than does Luther, the former monk. Calvin's use of the Ten Commandments to guide the conscience of the Christian is more rigorously moral than Luther's reflection on them. This is the central difference between this study and Lehmann's ethics of the Ten Commandments. Although this study uses both Luther and Calvin, Calvin is usually preferred. Lehmann's fresh study[17] is a combination of commentary on Luther and Lehmann's own reasoning on recent moral issues. Surely it is better to get closer to scripture than to Martin Luther, or "Brother Martin," as Lehmann so endearingly calls him. Likewise, our day needs the moral prescriptiveness of an interpreted moralist like Calvin more than it needs the tendencies toward antinomianism lurking in Luther and Lehmann. These reservations about the posthumously published commentary of Lehmann on Luther's interpretation of the Ten Commandments must not obscure the importance of his intention. An emphasis on the Ten Commandments is now needed in the church. This study argues that the best framework for understanding Christian morality is as the moral principles rooted in the Ten Commandments and interpreted by the two great commandments of love. So, for Calvin, the moral law is love also expressed in natural law. It is expressed rationally through legislation varying from people to people. Here again we find Christian ethics universal, grounded in God's will, cognizant of social relativities, and committed to reforming action in the world.

John Witherspoon, the revolutionary clergyman and signatory of the Declaration of Independence, belonged to this same tradition. The basis of human conduct is the double love commandment. In his "Treatise on Generation," he wrote:

> The love of God is the first precept of the moral law, and the first duty of every intelligent creature; but it is easy to see that unless our love is fixed upon the true God, it is spurious and unprofitable . . . and [it] will certainly produce the most sincere and fervent love to all one's fellow-creatures.[18]

The principles of the moral law are impressed on the conscience and are discoverable by reason. The social work of the world is to be guided by reason in discovering its moral foundations. So, out of gratitude for God's work and love for the neighbor, Witherspoon reasons and publishes his advice on economic relations, just war theory, and the constitution of a new government for the free colonies.

Witherspoon did not neglect the church. He presided over his church's first general assembly and is known as the first moderator of the Presbyterian church. He did not neglect the scriptural basis of Christian ethics. He kept James Madison at Princeton for an extra year to teach him more Hebrew, as well as moral philosophy, but his own social ethic was love expressed in rational argument out of human moral wisdom. In political theory, this drew him particularly to reflect on Montesquieu. This is important for us to understand, because by the time Montesquieu's enlightenment political philosophy found its way into our constitution, it had already been run through this Calvinist filter of John Witherspoon, who taught it to James Madison.

The ethical tradition traced here is a prescriptive tradition. Ethics as a tradition in the Christian church is largely in a prescriptive mode. If we were unambiguously creatures of love and justice, Christian ethics could be presented as a description of the actions flowing from that state. However, because we are less than good, but human, our ethics is presented to us as a prescriptive tradition that shows us the good and the right. The most recent attempt to present Christian ethics as description falls into confusion. Nancy Duff tries to establish that Paul Lehmann's move to present the Ten Commandments as description was his attempt to avoid the destruction of human freedom by an "absolute or prescriptive nature of moral law." This was not his point at all; description can be as absolute as prescription, and context can be as binding as rules. But the problem is not only Duff's—it is Lehmann's as well. It is appropriate for Lehmann to present the Ten Commandments as "descriptive statements of what happens behaviorally in a world that God has made and has made fit for being human in,"[19] but it makes no sense to say that they are not prescriptions for human conduct. "Thou shall not murder" is prescriptive for human behavior in the moral traditions of the world and of the church. It is a needed bulwark against what humans have done since Cain murdered Abel.

## TWO MODERN EXAMPLES

Emil Brunner's *The Divine Imperative*, the best Protestant study of Christian ethics in the twentieth century, was published in 1932, on the eve of Adolf Hitler's assumption of power in Germany. Protestant ethics was necessarily locked in a death struggle with the Promethean, demonic spirit of National Socialist ideology. Both could not survive. Thanks be to God that Protestant ethics survived even though it was badly mauled by the twentieth-century state of nationalistic wars beginning in 1914. Brunner's Protestant direction was basically correct: ethics will never save us, only God's will can save us. We cannot find the good in our own autonomy; only God's command can tell us God's will. "But to be obedient to the will of God means: 'love your neighbour!' Hence the content of the commandment is not an abstract law, not a programme that can be known beforehand and codified, but it means a swift responsiveness to the needs of others, and action in accordance with their needs in their particular circumstances."[20]

We are not moved into Christian action by duty, but by inclination. As our purpose is in God, God's love moves us toward the concrete need of the neighbor. This is done only in the real world of actual neighbors, forces of corporate power, and nations surrounded by clouds of greed, ignorance, and racism. God's ethic is that of neighbor love, and all ethics is social ethics, although some ethical questions are more complicated than others by social realities. The universal law turns out to be God's will; other laws, whether the perceptions of natural law, moral law, or positive law, reveal the particularities of their human sources and their consequent relativities.

Christian ethics provides moral guidance for church life in its ecclesiastically organized forms and in its broader Christian life within other social institutions. These moral guidelines may properly be called moral principles. I would avoid, in the modern world, the term "moral law," because law implies sovereignty directly enforcing sanctions, and God's way permits more freedom than human authorities have managed to allow. The church possesses no powers of coercion in society, so moral principles, moral policy guidelines, and moral advice seem to be the best ways of speaking of the fruit of Christian ethics. The sources of moral policy guidelines or moral wisdom are of course the classical sources: the Bible, human history, human science, and theology all used critically under the guidance of the church in council.

The marvel of understanding God's command as loving the neighbor is that it equips us for the new encounter. As the Samaritan encountered the stranger on the road to Jericho, we can in our freedom see love's new meanings. Thus, confronting the ecological crisis, we learn that our neighbor involves the living nature of which we are a part. We cannot love our neighbor and pollute her well. Facing the ecological crisis, we must act newly and boldly. Isaiah called our attention to this twenty-eight centuries ago:

> The earth lies polluted under its inhabitants; for they have transgressed laws, violated the statutes, broken the everlasting covenant. Therefore a curse devours the earth, and its inhabitants suffer for their guilt; therefore the inhabitants of the earth dwindled, and few people are left. The wine dries up, the vine languishes, all the merry-hearted sigh. . . . The city of chaos is broken down, every house is shut up so that no one can enter. There is an outcry in the streets for lack of wine; all joy has reached its eventide; the gladness of the earth is banished. (Isa. 24:5–7; 10–11)

Neighbor love in its concreteness calls us to consider questions of ecology that were confronted by none of the theologians previously affirmed.

My own teacher of ethics, John C. Bennett, who died in 1995 at Pilgrim Place in Claremont, California, stood in this tradition also as a former liberal. His later Christian realist theology was impacted heavily by the wretched suffering of the world's poor and the articulation of their cries by the theologians of liberation. His last book was entitled *The Radical Imperative*.[21] The imperative was radical for Christians in two ways: it was a thorough critique of the world's institutions—political and economic—which left so many in misery; and it expressed God's love for the world and the human response to this love of total commitment, to the struggle for peace and justice. God's love requires, Bennett taught, a strategic response of human attention and work to correct the conditions of utter sorrow in which much of humanity lives. The parable of the Last Judgment, in which Christ is identified with the hungry and thirsty, identifies him now with more than a billion people, of whom many millions are Christians and more than twenty-five million are American poor, most of whom are Christians. John Bennett used to like to quote a lesser theologian, but a more important administrator, Pope John XXIII. In our world, "love is the motivation, justice is the goal."

Drawing on a recognition of God's aggressive love, the reality of human structured sin, the prophets' denunciation of injustice, Christ's love for the lost, the witness of the ecumenical church, and theological recognition of human agency in implementing or denying God's will, Bennett consistently called for thorough change in our exploitative ways of living. Bennett, who was president of Union Seminary, also learned through his bold wife's prodding that love of neighbor required the transformation of our patriarchal institutions and the provision of opportunities to women that they had not previously enjoyed. If this meant promoting brilliant women scholars ahead of men who had formally fulfilled the requirements for promotion, even if the women had not, so be it. Love and justice demanded action and risk. Love still does.

This is where *agape* comes in for our time in this place. It requires realism; there is no love without attention to the real sinful details of human existence that must be overcome by love. It also requires strategic and tactical attention for every possible victory of human liberation from thirst, hunger, imprisonment, and poverty. It requires neither moralistic whining about the world God allows us to live in nor utopian fantasies about a world that never was or will be historically. It requires action—the binding up of the wounds of the one in the ditch and enforcing safe travel on the road from Jericho to Jerusalem.

Theologically, ethics and theology are bound together in love. Because ethics is controlled by love, it is the metaprinciple, so theology must be controlled by love. God's nature is to love humans in loving communion with their neighbors. This love has a creative, driving, receiving trajectory. It is akin to sexual love; it is God seeking communion with human consciousness in the universe. It was Hosea's love story. The best theologies have a touch of eroticism. The medieval mystics Dame Julian of Norwich and Margery Kempe expressed this as a mystical erotic relationship with Christ. Contemporary theologian Sallie McFague describes God in the metaphor of the world's lover. This love seeks form for humans; Hosea's God paralleled love to a marriage. Marriage is a human structure intended to express love in justice and still on its way to justice. This pulsating, powerful, dangerous, divine love seeks to be expressed in ethics in terms of moral law or better moral principles in fitting with the divine creativity. Christian ethics then is theological at its core, is inevitably erotic, is often frightening, and is, in a sinful world, consistently radical. It expresses itself in principles and adjudicates the conflicts between principles with love. The trajectories of this love ethic are to sustain nature, achieve fairness in gender relations, protect and teach the children, reduce consumption, share to meet the needs of the poor, achieve participation in decisions by the greatest possible number of the affected, always reform the institutions, and, as much as possible, live peaceably with all. Such activity may not be rewarded on earth, but we are promised that it will be rewarded in heaven.

## SUMMARY

The ultimate imperative for Christian ethics expresses the universal will of God, which is an expression of the nature of God. This will of *agape* is that humans live in mutual regard for each other, taking care of the needs of the other. In this mutuality, all are lifted up to fulfill their human possibilities. Sometimes this love may call for self-sacrifice and sometimes it is represented by the drive of egos toward union, but its basic core meaning is the care and regard for the real needs of the other. In meeting the needs of the other in obedience to God, the potentiality of the self is released toward fulfillment. At some levels and at some times, the defense of the self is required to meet the requirements of the equality and mutuality of love. But the basic model is the development of the self through the centering of the self on God and service to the neighbor that produces self-fulfillment. Both *eros* and self-sacrifice for others are meanings of love, but neither is central, for the care of the other is central as God's care for humanity is central. The meaning of this ultimate imperative will become clearer in the exposition of its relationships to covenant, community, justice, the Ten Commandments, and the Christian public life.

The explanation of the ultimate imperative requires that many practices, theories, and examples be consulted. Two dominant voices are returned to often—those of John Calvin and Reinhold Niebuhr. Their essentially New Testament appropriation of love and its principles is expressed here in their characteristically socially realistic, reforming-action mode. Grounded in Christian community and the essence of biblical ethics, the Christian life is to be lived in public for God and the neighbor.

# A Particular Love as
## the Ultimate Imperative

To this point, the reflections on the essence of Christian ethics as the ultimate imperative have been derived from scripture, the history of Christian ethics, and the two recent examples of Brunner and Bennett. Although all have used the double love commandment as the foundation for their ethics, they have not meant exactly the same imperative. Any study of Christian love needs to stipulate its core meaning of love. The discussion may expand beyond the central meaning of love but it ought not contradict it.

## SO WHAT IS LOVE?

The explication of the meaning of love for Christian ethics is undertaken by analyzing several of the twentieth-century discussions of love that are of importance to the church's understanding of love.

### Walter Rauschenbusch

Walter Rauschenbusch, the leading interpreter of the social gospel in the early twentieth century, is recognized as having the "Kingdom of God" as his major concept. However, he could rise to lyrical passion in interpreting Christianity as a religion of love. For him, Paul summarized the Christian message in the thirteenth chapter of First Corinthians, and Rauschenbusch made it the motif of *Dare We Be Christians?*[1] This little book of 1914 was written as an inspiration and apology for Christianity. It is not an academic treatise that bears up under analysis. This, however, is the nature of much of the Christian literature written for ordinary people like the conflicted Corinthians. Aside from the hymnlike praise of love, its meaning is found in love as the force that brings human beings together.

Love is the social instinct, the power of special coherence, the *sine qua non* of human society. What was Paul requiring but the social solidarity of the

Corinthians when he called for them to assert their unity in Christ? "In demanding love he demands social solidarity."[2] Rauschenbusch holds to this meaning of love as that which calls people together as he discusses sexuality, family, parenthood, social amelioration, charity toward the helpless, treatment of minority groups, and patriotism. Love was the force that brought people together and formed society.[3] In this book, love by businesspeople was the force he called on to reform society, as he dismissed class divisiveness as separating that which should be united. The demand of love is universal, excluding no one.

Toward his conclusion Rauschenbusch moves from Pauline solidarity to Johannine theology: "God is love." He calls all Christians to affirm it and live it. The little volume does not reflect the sociological sophistication of his earlier work, *Christianity and the Social Crisis*,[4] which dealt realistically from a hopeful socialist perspective with class conflict. Nor does it reflect the theological development of the later volume *A Theology for the Social Gospel*,[5] but this later volume refers to the social portrait of love in *Dare We Be Christians?*, whereas the earlier volume interpreted Jesus' teaching of the virtue of love largely as social attraction and solidarity. "The fundamental virtue in the ethics of Jesus was love, because love is the society-making quality. Human life originates in love. It is love that holds together the basal human organization, the family. . . . Love creates fellowship."[6]

Rauschenbusch concentrates his theological reflection on the "Kingdom of God" and its reforming social implications. His discussions on the concept of God emphasize the reformation of the concept of God that occurs when it is undertaken by different social groups. His hopes are to democratize and make ethically relevant the concept of God. Consequently, most of his writing on the double love commandment is about the love of neighbor, and the imperative to love God does not receive equal emphasis. It should be noted that for Rauschenbusch the community defines the concept of God whereas love produces community.

## Ernst Troeltsch

Although writing at the same time, neither Rauschenbusch nor Ernst Troeltsch utilized the work of the other. Rauschenbusch might have raised Troeltsch's estimate of the prospects for a revival of social Christianity. Troeltsch would have dimmed some of Rauschenbusch's optimism. Troeltsch's *The Social Teaching of the Christian Churches* came to have great influence in the United States only after its English publication in 1931.[7] Both of the Niebuhr brothers had come under its influence much earlier, from its German editions. Rauschenbusch, who was the son of an immigrant German and who himself had studied in Germany, did not rely on Troeltsch's *Social Teaching*.

For Troeltsch, the essence of the Christian ethic by the end of the nineteenth century had come to mean four essential theses, all derived from the double love commandment. The first was the personalistic theism recognized in the unity of heart, mind, and soul oriented toward God. The second was the  social solidarity that in love embraces everyone and, grounded in metaphysical reality, overcomes competition, compulsion, reserve, and strife. The third was  the ethical orientation of "mutual recognition, confidence, and care for others" that resolves the inescapable issues of equality and inequality. Finally, the  fourth was the Christian ethos that produces charity to relieve the suffering of the world, which is inevitable. Beyond these four contributions is the vision and promise of overcoming life in the kingdom of God. The kingdom is for God to realize, but Christian life is also lived anticipatorily in it now.[8]

Before coming to his concluding theses, Troeltsch had ransacked nineteen centuries of Christian history, condensing it into a thousand-page text. What had begun as a religious idea of reality and ethics had in its evolution compromised with both the world and other philosophies. Such a compromise was necessary and fitting, and each age would need to work out its own compromises between the ethic of Jesus and its historical reality. Troeltsch's Lutheran Church was ill equipped to do so, and its reality cast a Teutonic gloom over his historical perspective.

Jesus' ethic or the gospel ethic seemed straightforward to Troeltsch. Jesus' inspiration was religious—it came from his relationship to God. Troeltsch's insistence on "the religious idea" is similar to the "spirituality" discussed later. The first concept is the Kingdom of God as meaning "the rule of God upon earth." Its date of completion is unknown, but probably soon. Jesus called followers to a purity of heart and a radical loyalty to God. This loyalty involved self-renunciation and a centering of life on God. The way was severe but not socially radical in Troeltsch's perspective. In emphasizing the "spirituality" of Jesus, he wrote, "To love one's neighbors, that is, that in intercourse with him we are to reveal to him or to arouse in him the Divine spirit of Love."[9]

Once he had established the religious devotional quality of Jesus and his call to discipleship, Troeltsch could then investigate the sociological characteristics of the "gospel ethic." Without wanting to deny a distinction between spirituality and political economy, it is wise to set aside some of Troeltsch's extreme statements. Jesus' ministry was brief and the records are fragmentary, but we need not agree with Troeltsch that Jesus did not fight oppression, did not found a church, and had no concept of the state. The conflicts of Jesus with authorities, the organization of the Twelve, and his political-religious execution all assert that Troeltsch had more to learn about Jesus. Of course, Troeltsch still had to go through World War I, see his church changed, and serve in a revolutionary government before his last thought on social order was written.

## Reinhold Niebuhr

These theses of the socially powerless Jesus, the compromise of gospel ethic with world and other systems of thought, the centrality of the love commandments, the need for a viable social ethic utilizing social philosophies, and the understanding of all this in relationship to the history of social philosophies had a forceful impact on Reinhold Niebuhr. These ideas of Troeltsch controlled Reinhold's ethic throughout his career. H. Richard Niebuhr interpreted Troeltsch's work in a typological method in *Christ and Culture*,[10] whereas Reinhold presented it in a linear model in his first book, *Does Civilization Need Religion?*[11] He then continued to rewrite this history of the ideal hopes and norms and of the reality for most of his career and in many of his books until he wrote *Man's Nature and His Communities*,[12] his last volume.

Reinhold Niebuhr was not centrally interested in exact definitions of ethical terms. He was more committed to writing and speaking so that people would be encouraged to perform compassionate acts. In his course on theological ethics, he explicated *agape* in terms of the considerations of Anders Nygren, M. C. D'Arcy, Søren Kierkegaard, and Emil Brunner while referring to the classical sources in scripture, Plato and Aristotle. In the end he found a middle position between theological liberalism, which he believed regarded *agape* as a human possibility, and Anders Nygren, who regarded it as a human impossibility.

For Niebuhr, *agape* is a vision of life that is obligatory on humanity, because it reflects human possibilities under grace. The rich young ruler who came to Jesus knew that beyond particular moral requirements there was a deeper commandment. The requirement of total commitment was too much. The disciples asked how anyone could be saved, and Jesus responded that salvation was possible only with God and not by human effort alone. *Agape* as an expression of love contained reference to the perfection of the unity of person in heart, mind, and spirit in relationship to God and to the harmonious relationship of one to the neighbor. Under conditions of existence, neither harmony with God nor harmony with neighbor was normally expected. Love as the ultimate rule of human relations is for Niebuhr a derivative of the complete faith and trust in God. The further extension of this theology to justice as a work of love is considered later in this volume.

## Anders Nygren

Anders Nygren, Lutheran bishop of Lund, contributed a sharp distinction between *agape* and *eros* to the twentieth-century discussions. In a profound survey of the history of the discussion of love in biblical, classical, and Christian sources, he concluded that *agape* was the central Christian idea. In its truest form in Martin Luther, *agape* as God's disinterested love for humanity was radically distinguished from *eros* as human love for the good. Love for Martin Luther and Nygren was not human love but divine love, which God poured through humanity as through a tube. Ideally, it had nothing to do with human striving or fulfilling of a law. This meaning of love ignored egocentricity or self-love. Only one loved by God and blessed could pass on this love.[13]

Metaphorically, *agape* flowed down from God's love to neighbor love and to love for God, and denied self-love; *eros* flowed up from self-love to love for God and to neighbor love, and ignored God's love. Now Nygren recognized these distinctions as ideal types or motifs that in many Christian thinkers and practices were mixed. But, to the greatest extent possible, he wanted to sharpen the contrast and to theologically overcome the Roman Catholic tradition that had, from Augustine until Martin Luther, mixed *agape* and *eros* under the motif of charity. The ideal types may be too ideal in their presentation. Are not most expressions of Christian love mixtures of grace, obligation, trust, and even unfaith? If God desires human response, is even divine love free of *eros*? But most of all, any type of Christian *agape* that attaches little emphasis to human love of God, as Nygren's schematic does,[14] is deficient, because this love of God is still the first commandment.

## Gene Outka

The realization that Nygren divided *agape* and *eros* too sharply requires that the understanding of *agape* be sought elsewhere. Gene Outka surveyed the literature on *agape* from 1930, the culmination of Nygren's research, to 1967, the date of Outka's dissertation defense at Yale, and refined his work with Basil Mitchell at Oxford in 1968–69. His work combines knowledge of continental theology, American Christian ethics, and British analytic philosophy. He succeeds in sharing the conceptual difficulties inherent in discussion of this love imperative.

Outka chose to restrict his work to concerns about *agape* as neighbor love, recognizing that such a choice exacted a price.[15] "*Agape* is a regard for the neighbor which in crucial respects is independent and unalterable."[16] He set out to analyze how *agape* is the requirement "to consider the interests of others and not simply his own."[17] The choice not to examine more fully the reference to love of God in the first commandment led to the neglect of obvious theological references in the texts he analyzed. An example is a very full paragraph of H. Richard Niebuhr's from *The Purpose of the Church and Its Ministry*,[18] in which Outka claims, "The richness of the meaning of neighbor regard is nicely exemplified."[19] But the text actually is referenced to the love of God and neighbor by Niebuhr on the preceding and following pages. One cannot explain Christian neighbor love without reference to the love of God and the meaning of Christ. Christian ethics without its theological context appears conceptually confused. The left tablet of the Ten Commandments presupposes the right tablet, and the second commandment depends on the first and on the theological context of the New Testament witness to Christ.

It seemed strange to find the Christian ethics of Reinhold Niebuhr discussed under the rubric of "self-sacrifice" in Outka's book, because Niebuhr never talked much at all about self-sacrifice in his ethics courses. His courses were more about the history of Christian ethics, power issues in society, relative natural law norms, criteria of justice, etc. The three-hundred-page book of his writings entitled *Love and Justice,* edited by D. B. Robertson, discusses love as the ideal of "pure disinterestedness,"[20] "an attitude of spirit without any prudential or selfish consideration,"[21] and "love in which each life affirms the interests of the other."[22]

Niebuhr does talk about sacrificial love as an ideal and also as a solvent in human affairs. As a Christian theologian, he sees Christ's acts in accepting the cross and initiating atonement as sacrificial love. So Niebuhr refers to sacrificial love as the pinnacle of love. For Niebuhr *agape* has qualities of ecstasy that define "the ultimate heroic possibilities of human existence (involving, of course, martyrdom)."[23]

But *agape* is also forgiving love in emulation of God and a universal sense of obligation that transcends particular obligations. We are obligated to love, which is the meaning of love affirmed by Outka as equal regard for the welfare of the other. Outka has discovered a dimension of love implied in Jesus' commandment, but in his neglect of the other dimensions in Niebuhr's interpretation he misses aspects of Christian *agape*. *Agape* includes self-sacrifice as in Christ or as in Martin Luther King Jr. and Dietrich Bonhoeffer in Niebuhr's and Outka's own history. Niebuhr was concerned that *agape* not be reduced simply to achievable good acts that liberals suggest to be the meaning of love. They may be loving, but they lack the profundity of *agape*. The differences between Niebuhr's broad Christological use of love and Outka's rather humanistic use of love include both theological and sociological differences. Another pivotal point is that Niebuhr understands love to be the overcoming of the cleavage between essence and existence. In love, the gap between what one is and what one ought to be is overcome. It is a commandment, but it is not literally fulfilled. The commandment itself shows that the separation is not overcome in history. The love imperative for Niebuhr is a religious symbol confronting egoism and promoting humility. We will not have the perfectly united self to be utterly directed to God with all our mind, heart, and soul. Nor will we love our neighbor perfectly with the same interest with which we serve ourselves. But still, to do so would be to realize the harmony of God. Yet, with the full religious message of the gospel, people in Christian community can and do produce moral fruit utilizing *agape* in family and social strategies of mutuality and forgiveness. So Niebuhr's understanding of love is both more religious and more communal than the relatively rationalistic, individualistic ethic[24] of Outka. In his presentation of most theologians' views in *Agape: An Ethical Analysis*, Outka suppresses their theology except for that of Karl Barth. In so doing, at least in the case of the Niebuhrs, he misses their meaning. But the sociological clash is even more acute. Niebuhr would have little else but scorn for the youthful Outka's social optimism. Outka wrote:

> The personal relations and perhaps also (or sometimes instead) the social order in which one finds oneself may be more amenable to a progressive realization of harmony and brotherhood than Kierkegaard and Niebuhr believe. While there is no strict guarantee that the appropriate response will be elicited, there should be no systematic refusal to hope, if not for perfection, then at least for continuous progress.[25]

He recognized that the conflict with Niebuhr was over different estimations of the human possibilities in history, and then he wrote, "Conflict may be increasingly channeled in non-violent directions, for example, and in any case is not as much of a fixed datum as Niebuhr appears to believe."[26]

Both Reinhold Niebuhr and Walter Rauschenbusch understood love at its base to be a drive for union or unity. Niebuhr expressed this more transcendentally and Rauschenbusch more immanently. They were both in the tradition of the social gospel, as Niebuhr affirmed in *An Interpretation of Christian Ethics*. The more recent Outka does not emphasize this harmony and seems not to be in this same tradition of the social gospel.

In summarizing the results of his analysis, Outka concludes that *agape* expresses "equal regard" for the other. The other is treated with an "active concern for the neighbor's well being" without undue emphasis on the particularity of the other.[27] All neighbors are equal in their relationship to God in their need for freedom and the meeting of basic human needs. This understanding of *agape* as equal regard carries over to Outka's understanding of justice, in which one finds egalitarian ideas of justice overlapping with *agape*. He does not intend to collapse the distinction between love and egalitarian justice. The goals of meeting needs equally may require unequal distributions, and different characteristics may be treated differently, but equal regard is required by justice. Outka's conclusions in his careful, analytic book are meager, but they point in helpful ways toward further development of the relationship of the norm of justice to *agape*.

## Paul Ramsey

The New Testament presents us with many uses of *agape*. It is from God for the world, the love of human beings toward God, and toward one another. Its context is the radically theistic context of the prophetic tradition culminating and transformed in Jesus Christ. Paul Ramsey was certainly correct when he explained that: "To be *in* the world with transforming power, the *agape* of Christ must be clearly understood as not *of* this world."[28] Such an insight shows again the need for consideration of *agape* in terms of revelation, paradox, and theism. Ramsey is correct in relating this revealed norm to the nature of humanity and showing it to be expressed in a radical revisioning of natural law. The dangers of the expressions of natural law are in the association of natural law with time-bound statements of natural law and in the neglect of the degree to which natural law reflects its historical context. Also, the conclusions of natural law theorists reveal the very relativity of the perceptions of natural law. So, in this attempt to explicate Christian ethics, love is related to a particular tradition of moral norms understood as both revelation and natural law in a particular communal context.

## CONCERNS ABOUT THIS LOVE TRADITION

The Ten Commandments are taken to be the most important summary statement of both Hebrew morality and Christian morality, and they are specifications of *agape*. Yet before the stipulated meaning of *agape* is finalized, voices from two traditions critical of the analysis so far need to be included: the feminist tradition and the African American nonviolent tradition.

## Sallie McFague

Sallie McFague's metaphorical theology expresses the Christian gospel as radical love. For her, love becomes the essence of theology expressed in her metaphorical trinity. The parenthood of God is expressed in *agape* that seeks the fulfillment of life as a mother nurtures and cares for the next generation. Love as *eros* is expressed as the second of the trinity that seeks union with humanity in God's body of the universe. God as *philia* seeks to express the companionship and friendship of the Divine with the world. McFague tends to find the double love commandment as incapable of achievement, but affirming its direction she expresses it in terms she regards as more adequate for a nuclear and ecologically threatened age. Each of the expressions of the trinity has its own characteristic ethic. That of the divine-universal parent is justice. Here the drive is for humans to model the loving presentation and fulfillment of life in concrete actions. The model of God as love expresses the understanding of God and humanity as healers working together to heal society and nature. Here McFague expresses the necessity of recognizing anger as characteristic of God's love and, by extension, human love.

> Healers and liberators must be tireless in their battle against the forces that bring disorder to the body, that enslave the spirit. . . . God as mother-creator feels the same anger and judges those harshly who deny life and nourishment to her children.[29]

The work of God as friend is to be with humanity in the world, and the human ethic is to accompany the other and not to betray life to the enemy. The friendship with God requires the struggle for justice and the identification with the suffering by the friends of the Friend of the World.

McFague playfully suggests the enrichment of our models of the Trinity. In her elevation of love to the center of her theology, she is faithful to the New Testament and especially to the Johannine emphases. The recognition that God's love can be expressed persuasively as divine parent, lover, and friend, each with its own developed ethical meaning, is a welcome joining of ethics with her theology. The theology of the Trinity in her care is ethical in its essence; expressed metaphorically it also has ethical consequences.

The political symbols for God in the older traditional theology—Father, King, Monarch, Creator—may have more of the Janus-faced character than McFague elaborates. In the words of Jesus, these symbols express love, not oppression or heteronomy. The preference for organic metaphors in much of her theology and the displacement of political-social metaphors like the Kingdom of God may not be as helpful to Christian thought as she thinks. Is it not the case that the threat of nuclear terror has been reduced by political choices and changes? Wise ecological choices, too, must be made politically before the organic death and responses themselves overwhelm politics. McFague is correct to recognize the need to include the material-organic in her theology, but she errs if this emphasis trivializes the political-social symbols.

McFague is also correct that theology articulates models of God and that metaphor is a large part of the building of such models. She is wise in adopting her middle way between fundamentalism about religious symbols and the cynical deconstruction of religious symbols. Christian realism in the spirit of Paul Tillich or Reinhold Niebuhr is closer to the reality pole than to the deconstructionist pole, because here the symbols express hypotheses about human nature that are verifiable in human experience. In our time, when one of the great human advances is the gender revolution, the need for McFague's symbols of love, parent, and friend for God can be accepted with less tentativeness than characterized her book.

## Barbara Hilkert Andolsen

Barbara Hilkert Andolsen's research into feminist ethics is a strong reminder that patriarchalism has haunted the tradition. From the nineteenth century, women have protested that they do not need counsel from male ethicists to sacrifice themselves. Margaret Farley represents the tradition in recognizing *agape* as full mutual love marked by gender equality.[30] Andolsen affirms *agape* as a norm applicable to all realms of life. I think she erred in regarding Niebuhr as following "in the footsteps of Nygren condemning self-love and emphasizing sacrifice as the primary historical manifestation of *agape*."[31] The textual evidence is clear that Niebuhr warns against egoism as corrupting mutuality. Christ as a religious symbol participates in sacrifice. Our old, weak, patriarchy-dependent selves need to be given up, but the goal of Niebuhr's ethic is fulfilled people living in as much mutuality as is possible under the limits of sin.

## Beverly Harrison

Beverly Harrison preceded Sallie McFague in using the term "radical love" to discuss passionate, engaged, embodied love in relational terms. She also made the point that anger is part of love. Anger reveals the connected relationality of the bearer of the anger. Harrison fears that Christians have nearly stamped out love and become boring because of their reluctance to express anger. For her, anger for her expresses caring and is "a sign of some resistance in ourselves to the moral quality of the social relations in which we are immersed."[32] Anger becomes both the recognition that change is needed and part of the energy needed to achieve the change. The model of God as a mother angry at the mistreatment of her children is a powerful image and one worthy of our acceptance as we enact our Christian ethics. Of course, one may mistakenly direct anger at the wrong source. The wise use of anger implies adequate analysis of the causes of anger. Anger itself may blind one to truth or energize a foolish cause. Anger, like passion, requires appropriately directed action.

## Mohandas Gandhi

The theory and practice of love in direct action for social change received new impetus in the twentieth century. Out of anger over servitude, oppression, and colonialism, Mohandas Gandhi was able to fashion organized force to impel the British to surrender India to its people. Combining the respect for life from his Jain-influenced Hindu traditions with the image of love from the Sermon on the Mount, he evolved a theory and practice of nonviolent action. By articulating just needs for change, negotiation, purification, disciplined suffering, and further negotiations, he organized the expression of love that moved the empire. From Gandhi's success in India, worldwide decolonization became the world's agenda. Massive nonviolent civil disobedience carried forth from India would eventually win civil rights for African Americans in the United States and be an important ingredient in the overthrow of communism and apartheid in the closing years of the century. Gandhi was impelled by *agape* as he learned it from Christian example and study. But the British justice in which he trained as a law student in London failed in India, and as an Indian he utilized love and strategy to force justice to cede power and become more just.

## Martin Luther King Jr.

Martin Luther King Jr., as an African American minister, grafted Gandhi's methods onto the African American church's own nonviolence and his Christian theological studies. In his life and thought, nonviolent direct action became *agape* in action. This certainly is correct. The church as a spiritual community ought not adopt the tools of violence for social change even though the world always presupposes violence. Nonviolent tactics are necessarily more loving and more in keeping with the nature of the church than tactics that employ violence to achieve their ends. The church cannot deny all violence to the world—particularly the violence of self or communal defense against violent attack—but it can and must teach that *agape* governs church tactics directly and nonchurch tactics indirectly. In its ecumenical discussions, the church, having learned that God is love, will have to insist that the religious utilization of violence for social or political change is a failure. If dialogue partners argue for violence for other than justifiable defense, the Christian criteria of *agape* will incline Christians to argue that the other religious tradition be amended. Christianity has amended its tradition in light of *agape*, and others can learn from that growth that *agape* governs methods as well as goals of religious life, and that crusade or fanatic religious mentality is outdated and wrong.

## OBJECTION TO LOVE AS THE CENTER

A major challenge to the centrality and prominence of the ethic of love was raised by Stanley Hauerwas. Hauerwas believed that the center of the concern about Christian ethics should be moved away from mainline Protestant-type social actions and toward actions more normally associated with Mennonite activist practices represented by the thought of John Yoder. Beyond Yoder, his preference for ethics seemed to follow more in the patterns of reasoned ethics or, in Edward L. Long Jr.'s terms, the deliberative motif in ethics of Aquinas and Aristotle. Furthermore, his interest in biblical ethics seemed to follow the stories or narratives more than the explicit ethical imperatives or commands.[33] Hauerwas's boast that he knew Aristotle's *Nicomachean Ethics* better than the New Testament[34] reveals his desire to supplant with alternatives the love ethic that has been so central.

Stanley Hauerwas reacted to the situationalist-principle debate of the 1960s by arguing against love as the primary, ethical category of Christianity. It is understandable that in a reaction to Joseph Fletcher's reductionism a polemical writer would overreact, but no late-twentieth-century thinker can dethrone love from the pinnacle of Christian ethics no matter how exaggerated the arguments. Hauerwas recognizes that "love has a prominent place in Jesus' teaching and preaching e.g., the 'great commandment' in the Gospels."[35]

How revealing it is that Hauerwas has nothing to say about the defining nature of love for Paul's ethics or the ethic of love in the Johannine literature. His essay is innocent of the knowledge of love in the Old Testament or the recognition that the Ten Commandments themselves are further specifications of the double love commandment. He ignores its centrality to Augustine, Calvin, Witherspoon, Brunner, and Bennett in his essay and attacks only weak representations of the love ethic of his own conjuring.

One naturally affirms Hauerwas's respect for reason, and the need for the category of justice, the need for arguments and analysis beyond the imperative and summary of love, but this respect creates no need to attack the ethical teaching of Jesus as sentimental, wrong, platitudinous, and without discipline or suffering.[36] One can respect the attempt to rearrange priorities in Christian ethics in Mennonite or Aristotelian directions, but the center of the tradition is too strong—it refuses to yield.

Some of Hauerwas's confusion is probably attributable to his not understanding that for Christian discourse the double love commandment has summarized and included the Ten Commandments. The First Catechism of the Presbyterian Church (U.S.A.), designed for third and fourth graders, asks the question: "What is the main point of these commandments?" The correct response is: "You shall love your God with all your heart, mind, and strength, and you shall love your neighbor as yourself."[37]

## SUMMARY

This running commentary on selective twentieth-century interpretations of *agape* in Christian ethics reveals certain convictions and trajectories. This interpretation is undertaken from a Christian Realist perspective rooted in John Calvin's sense that Christians and others need moral instruction. The love commandments require their theological roots—they are ultimate matters. We also need their practical illustration. The parable of the good Samaritan follows on the lawyer's recounting of the double love commandment. The lawyer needed to know who his neighbor was. It was the other encountered in need. The response was to care for and provide what the other needed. So *agape* is ultimate, universal, and particular with broad consequences.

To reduce each of these broad theories of love to a single (even if complex) insight is hazardous. Still, for summary, single emphases may be isolated:

Walter Rauschenbusch: *Agape* is the power that unites human society.

Ernst Troeltsch: *Agape* as personal-social theism produces charity and social harmony.

Reinhold Niebuhr: *Agape* is a transcendent requirement that is relevant to all immanent situations.

Anders Nygren: God's grace is best recognized when our inadequate human love is not equated with God's *agape*.

Gene Outka: Equal regard for the other and justice as equality are expressions of *agape*.

Paul Ramsey: *Agape* is expressed through other moral norms and nondistinctively Christian moral insights.

Sallie McFague: The meaning of *agape* is determinative for theology and shapes the meanings of *eros* and *philia*, and the three together are metaphors for the Trinity.

Beverly Harrison: *Agape* as radical love contains mutuality, anger, and friendship more completely than heretofore emphasized.

Mohandas Gandhi and Martin Luther King Jr.: *Agape* is expressed in different religious traditions and societies as a means of social change as well as a religious reality.

Our understanding of love is, as Jesus recognized, a summary of our total ethic. It is also that on which all our prophetic religion and moral guidelines depend. It governs religion and ethics. If a teaching cannot be reconciled with love, it is not Christian ethics. We recognize its source in the nature of God and God's will for humanity. Beyond these general guidelines that determine the shape of Christian ethics, it is the meeting of the particular needs of our encountered neighbor as if they were our own needs.

With the love of God for the world, the imperatives of loving God and the neighbor assumed, and the commands somewhat explicated, advancement into our study of Christian ethics is possible. After our beginning point of love, the second theme could be either justice or community. Love leads to both. But perhaps we cannot hear the demands of justice without some community support, so we will explore community first and then justice.

# Nurtured in Community and Seeking Justice

T he ultimacy of the love imperative does not mean that it stands alone. It is a summary of Christian ethics and an essential feature authenticated by the teaching of Jesus himself. But it is nurtured in community, founded in the nature of God, expressed in hope, and applied in a suffering world. Because of its uniting function, love implies community. Because it seeks the good of the neighbor, love leads to the seeking of justice. These discoveries of Christian community and the struggle for justice in the broader society require principles that express the trajectory and requirements of love.

Christian ethics is a reflective process presupposed by organized Christian moral life. The moral teachings of the church, whether they are taught in a communicant's class or expressed in a lobbying effort before governmental powers, presuppose processes of organization, thought and critical reflection. Telling a child that he ought to help prepare the family meal is a moral statement. Explaining why he ought to do so is the process of ethics. Sometimes moral statements are simply taught, but whenever the question of why we ought to do a particular thing arises, the process of ethical reflection has begun.

Most Christian morality is learned and internalized by people who participate in the life of the church. Through sermons, liturgies, prayers, hymns, classes, and discussions, the Christian ways of being moral are passed on from one generation to another. Christians learn morality from parents, peers, and the church. They simply pick it up as they grow up in the church. Usually, it is not debated; people simply learn a way of Christian morality as they learn other parts of church tradition.

Christians tend to think of their particular way of being moral as the Christian way, but when Christians from different moral traditions disagree about what ought to be done, the plurality of Christian ways of being moral becomes evident. Christian rules and customs are often held unreflectively. If debates break out over affirmative action, abortion, sexual mores, or foreign policy, Christians realize that they must reason at an ethical level—that is, at a level deeper than that of their immediately available moral positions. Also, as they engage life in a pluralistic world, it becomes clear that a way of Christian morality is one way among many options. As they give reasons for their ways of being moral, they are engaging in ethical reasoning.

Christian ethics means the same as moral theory or moral philosophy practiced by Christians. It is practiced both by individuals who identify themselves as Christians and by the church as it reasons about moral matters in committees, sessions, assemblies, synods, or boards. It involves the analysis of moral decisions made by Christian communities and individuals, and it moves beyond analysis of decisions actually made to reflection on how Christian lives and the life of the church should be shaped. It also recommends how the church in its organized life and in its scattered life should act in the world. These levels of analysis, critical reflection, and recommendation interpenetrate one another, and often the various levels are not at all clearly defined.

The subject matter of Christian ethics is vast. If Socrates and Jesus are posited as the primary sources of ethical reflection in the Western world, the complexity is at once apparent. Neither Socrates nor Jesus left us a text. They are both interpreted from the perspectives of followers after the martyrdoms of the original teachers. Jesus' teaching is shaped by the perspectives of the Gospel authors, and Socrates' teaching is shaped by Plato's purposes. Jesus' teaching runs from Matthew's construct of the Sermon on the Mount to conflict situations, to instruction intended for his closest disciples. Plato presents Socrates as engaging in inconclusive arguments about the meaning of the good in early dialogues, but he also presents him as a utopian visionary in *The Republic* and as one providing instruction for the enforcement of morality in *The Laws*.

Christian ethics in our time presupposes that human beings are often free enough to reason about their conduct and to choose what obligations they will undertake. This freedom is constrained by tradition, historical situation, and social pressures, but it is real. Determinism, whether assumed to be divine, social, historical, or biological, would ultimately make ethics only an illusion.

Freedom, even as it is presupposed in my choosing to write this sentence, implies responsibility. The author of the sentence is responsible for its structure. Analogously, the liver of a life is meaningfully responsible for that life. The sentence or the life presupposes shaping from the sources of life and the conditions of life, but the author, to a degree adequate for the assigning of blame or praise, is responsible.

Christian ethics is quite free and quite historical. It is very difficult to say anything truly novel in Christian ethics, because Christian ethics has been discussed and developed for twenty centuries by Christians reflecting on their lives. The insights are rearranged in each generation and to a degree by each thinker, but the people engaging in ethics draw on the tradition, and to the extent that they ignore the tradition their ethics is impoverished. As a person growing to maturity reworks the experiences of earlier life, so the church growing through history relearns and refashions its ethics out of its historical experience. As a critical process of reflection, Christian ethics owns its own history. It finds sorrowful chapters in that history, but it attempts to learn from that history and to continually reform itself for the contemporary task of guiding human life.

A creative-contemporary Christian ethic is characterized by a free, responsible approach to issues of life in a person conscious of God and characterized by faith, hope, and love. The person is bound in solidarity to the church and committed to acting realistically for the poor, the dispossessed and the suffering. Such an ethic is more reform-oriented than it is rebellious; it looks to reforming all of life so that it reflects the purposes of God. The autonomous self-oriented life lacks several of the characteristics of the life lived within the guidance of a Christian ethic. The life lived under a heteronomous law is also inadequate when viewed from the standpoint of Christian ethics. Neither law nor rebellion is particularly profound when examined by Christian ethics. Rather, Christian ethics seeks a life drawing on sources of divine guidance using customs, mores, and laws with freedom to shape the future toward greater fulfillment of God's order. Customs, mores, and laws are neither despised nor made sacred in Christian ethics.

The twentieth century has seen a proliferation of investigations into the history of Christian ethics. Since the publication of Ernst Troeltsch's *The Social Teaching of the Christian Churches*[1] in 1911, an explosion of specialized studies has deepened our insight into the complexity of the Christian ethical tradition. At this time, too much is known about the variety of Christian ethics to reduce it to any one central motif. Single-factor analyses of the Christian ethic that have placed various virtues at the apex of the ethic are refuted by the great proliferation of knowledge about the various forms of ethics that have been vitally Christian. The ethic cannot be defined solely as an ethic of *koinonia*, or of love, or of hope, or of commandment, or of situation. This complexity refutes Paul Lehmann's thesis that "In our thinking about Christian ethics everything depends upon the point of departure."[2] He argued very powerfully that the proper starting point was "the fact and nature of the Christian church," but on examination that fact and nature is itself pluralistic, and it is of course preceded by the teaching of the very Jewish Jesus.

The entire history of Christian ethics is relevant. Some moments are more relevant than others to the construction of the most appropriate ethic for our time. The writer of ethics must choose, but nothing may be excluded in principle, for the changing situations of the worldwide movement of Christians continually alter the importance of various motifs. Even the pluralistic motif approach of H. Richard Niebuhr in *Christ and Culture*[3] has been quickly superseded by the emergence of the new motifs of Christ in solidarity with the poor and Christ the liberator. It is evident in the closing decade of the twentieth century that the social teachings of the churches and other religious bodies have an immense impact on the social problems of our day.

## THE CHURCH COMMUNITY

Christian ethics is community ethics. Our ethics is derived from a particular group of people with a particular history of more than three thousand years of reflecting on humanity and what it ought to do. This history has a great variety of positions within it, and often it is very difficult to find the uniting themes. One of these themes, however, is that our conscience needs to be shaped, and in fact is shaped, by those whom we trust and relate to in religious community.

It seems appropriate to recognize that the church creates Christian ethics. It is the recognition of the social creation of humankind's artifacts, ideologies, and groups that makes this conclusion inevitable. From the very first, the church has, through its own processes of deliberation, tried to articulate what an adequate ethical response to Jesus Christ is in terms of its moral norms and behavior. Through the church, people have learned what the primary sources of Christian moral wisdom are; they have also developed their attitudes toward pagan practices and alternative philosophies in discussions in the church community. Communities create their own ethos, and the Christian community with its own memories has developed, through trial and error and through discussion, its own way of life.

Philosophers and academic theologians may miss the real point of contact between the Bible, particularly the Epistles, and the contemporary person in the church pew. The philosopher or academic theologian may think that the hermeneutical gap is bridged for the individual in the pew by existential angst or a sense of universal history, but the person who is really immersed in the church knows better. The real bridge is the church. Both in the Epistles to the new churches (e.g., Corinth) and in today's churches, the issues of finance, immorality, heresies, and parties in the church reappear as Christians try to be obedient to what they have heard. The ethics is developed in the community, communicated by the community, and reflected on today in the community. Christian ethics must be understood as church ethics or run the dangers of sociological naiveté, irrelevance to the Christian community, and foreignness to the history that it claims to continue.

The church, presupposed as the shaper of Christian ethics, contains the *koinonia* or the *ecclesiola in ecclesia* or the City of God. It is the communion of the saints oriented toward the reign of God trying to live a responsible life in the history in which it finds itself. This community cannot be simply identified with the institutional church, nor can it be severed from it. It is the community that serves to reform the institutional church and to move ahead of and leave the institutional church behind if it cannot reform it. It does not reject the institutional church, but it may in loyalty to the realm of God move so far ahead of the institutional church that the institutional church is tempted to reject it. The institutional church, though perhaps unable to achieve in its reality the ideals of the community, still creates the context in which the realm of God is nurtured and from which its members are enlisted. God works through the church to realize God's reign directly in the spiritual-moral lives of some Christians. These Christians understand them-selves thoroughly as disciples of Jesus, and their lives express this in moral fruit that the institutional church, and sometimes the secular world, can recognize. For others, the institutional church affects them as the dominant religious institution of their world. The tensions between those living in the realm of God and those living elsewhere in the church create much of the moral debate of the church. Other debates include several community debates. A given issue may give rise to input from the community of the Kingdom of God, other communities within the institutional church, and various other communities that are part of national society.

The recognition that the church is the creator of its ethics frees the church to stand in obedience to its true nature vis-à-vis the culture and the govern-ment. Acculturated forms of Christian ethics give the struggle away before it begins. If the primary role of the church is recognized as the molding of its own ethos, the possibility of the church choosing to oppose, retreat from, accommodate, transform, or rule a given culture or government is acknowl-edged. In the United States, because of its history, there is always the danger that the culture or government will make a vital Christian ethic nearly impos-sible. This impossibility is converted to a possibility when the creative self-conscious role of the church as a shaper of its own ethos is emphasized.

The "church community" as the bearer of Christian ethics means the rel-atively intimate group of people who share enough theological convictions to organize worship together. They usually also share rough agreement over polity or how their life together is organized. In most cases, these are "face-to-face" relationships in which the people know one another's names. In the larger churches, the intimacy among the whole declines, but in principle the people recognize common ultimate connections and principles of organiza-tion. There are also lesser connections to the universal church and to the history of the church. But these dimensions are less community-oriented. This church is not American society; it is much more united and intimate. The society is much more pluralistic and polytheistic in its commitments. Community is not society and society is not community. In the United States, Christians may have other communities. Sometimes they have communities in business organizations, social organizations, and neighborhoods. Moral for-mation may occur in any of these communities, but in the church it is of central concern. The church moral life is organized around love. When this love is sought in the larger society, it is called justice. American society does not at present possess widespread moral consensus, and so the church, while at the same time taking on aspects of the society, is distinguished from the society by its commitments to love and to justice. The church often learns from the society about moral insights, and it also contributes moral insights to the society. The church is not the only community in society, but for the Christian it is particularly the place where moral insight is developed.

Church communities seem to be weakening compared with what they were a generation ago. Church attendance has declined, and participation in face-to-face communities in general seems to be declining, in the United States. Robert D. Putnam attributes some of the decline to the presence of television in the society. Putnam, the Harvard professor of government who won fame for his essay on the decline of community, "Bowling Alone: America's Declining Social Capital," blames the decline on mass television, which is also influencing politics and religion. The isolated compulsive viewing of violence, sexuality, and imaginative lifestyles undercuts the very being together in conversation that morality-forming communities need. Moral life requires communal conversation.

Recognition of the church as the context for Christian ethics is in continuity with the knowledge that the beginnings of organized Hebrew ethics were in covenants. Since the Sinai beginnings of a distinctive ethos for the Hebrews, ethics or organized morality has been found in covenantal contexts. Hebrew ethics and its continuation in Christian ethics have been internalized in people bonded together and accepting moral stands derived from the nature of God. The major moral instruction of the Christian church has been derived from the Hebrew covenants of Exodus and Deuteronomy. The central meanings of those covenants have been the Ten Commandments. In a typical confirmation class, the major biblical content that the children are required to memorize is the Ten Commandments. The names of the books of the Bible and the Apostles' Creed are typically added, and the beatitudes of Jesus' Sermon on the Mount, another covenant teaching, and the two great commandments may also be added. In its rite of membership, then, the covenantal nature of the church is recognized, as is the covenantal nature of Christian ethics.

Our Bible places the Ten Commandments as high points of the covenantal legislation ascribed to Moses. This placement is, of course, the work of later editors. The commandments echo traces of Moses and Sinai and even the traditions of the Kenites who sheltered Moses. The Ten Commandments in both Exodus and Deuteronomy interrupt the flow of the narrative, but as portrayed as the Word of God spoken by Moses they claim in our Bible an authoritative role that overshadows more particularized covenant legislation. The interpretation of the church and its theologians that the Ten Commandments could stand by themselves as easily memorizable moral rules for the community reflects their separate origins.[4]

The covenants as historical outcomes of the uniting of peoples were not in themselves focused in nonhuman nature. However, the Hebrews also maintained traditions of prehistorical covenants with Noah and Abraham. The covenant with Noah and his dependents was also a covenant with nature. In emphasizing the historical covenants, care must be taken not to neglect this prehistorical binding of God's care to nature itself. Bernhard Anderson has called the covenant of Noah "the ecological covenant." George Kehm's interpretation has stressed that the great covenants do not annul but rather presuppose each other. In his words, "the later covenants include the commitments made in the earlier ones."[5] These warnings encourage contemporary ethicists to search out and emphasize signs of care for creation that may still be present in the historical covenants. For example, the explanations for the Sabbath in terms of rest for the land and the concluding injunctions against covetousness take on a moral force in the late twentieth century that we could not well discern in the earlier years of this same century.

Hebrew ethics was founded in these reformulations of covenants of people bonded together in solidarity with God. Three thousand years of historical experience has, of course, changed the context. The Old Testament covenants were moral, religious, and ritual rules, social ethics, and laws. The New Testament covenants were given in the context of the church, which was distanced from governmental rule. Later historical covenants like the Mayflower Compact united religious community and law, but the covenants of the Declaration of Independence and the Constitution of the United States of America took a more secular approach, leaving the explicitly religious covenants to the church. So today, U.S. Christians have two covenants, one in the church and one in government. Both covenants influence Christian conduct in the shared area of society. The church carries in the Old Testament covenant the teaching of its Ten Commandments, having dropped much of the other covenant legislation, whereas in society and government the struggle over the norms of this more secular covenant continues, and the role of religious input into that struggle is disputed.

## THE CHURCH COMMUNITY AND IMPERIAL SOCIETY

In the United States, approximately 265 million people are bound together by economics, politics, geography, and aspects of shared language, culture, and history. They participate in the society as both individuals and groups. If they are members of churches, as the majority are, they also participate through their churches. Within their churches they share polities, educational events, and socializing activities. The society of the American empire lacks the intensity of the community-building functions of the churches, but it also reflects powerful unifying values, experiences, and pressures. Through the various levels of government and corporate practices, American society is able to impose enough order to create a powerful empire.

The empire has been formed by subjugating native peoples of the North American continent, importing slaves to work as plantation hands and as servants, attracting immigrants to provide labor, promising a better life to populations seeking improvement, and providing a brilliant constitutional order derived from both secular and religious insights. The society exhibits a tumultuous, shifting mass in which groups are born, flourish, and expire to be replaced by other groups. The churches and the government, by virtue of the Constitution, share the society and provide depth and stability to the societal mix. The constitutional order is secular, the vitality of the churches gives the society a religious cast, and the societal functions vacillate between moral values derived from religious insights and those derived from secular values. Within the societal groups are included the corporations, which, imbibing the materialistic values of the society, exert great power and outweigh any direct influence of the church. They can compete with or dominate the government on selected issues vital to the corporations. The secular institutions of education also contribute values derived from their secular commitments and secular philosophies while sometimes allying with and supporting the ethics of the church as well.

This American society seems very religious when compared with European societies; it appears secularized when compared with India or Saudi Arabia. The term "ambiguity" is very important when considering American society. It is a society characterized by contrasts. On the religious side, it is popular to say that it is a post-Constantinian society. This is true if it means that the church cannot control society, but of course the Constantinian church did not control society either. The emperors were not subject to the church, and even Constantine's use of piety to influence society was neither more religious nor more cynical than competition among politicians for control of the American empire. The society is both very materialistic and very spiritualistic. The society demands a lot of freedom and is very conformist. The society hangs on to laissez-faire capitalism and socializes large areas of its life. It proclaims human rights and reflects racism in its institutions. It produces millionaires and encourages dreadful poverty. In its foreign policy, it proclaims national self-determination and exerts dominance around the world. It proclaims peace, but fights more wars than other countries. It supports both the world's best universities and terrible public schools existing in the shadows of those universities. These ambiguities produce a great deal of societal conflict as groups advance their own interests or attempt to influence the nation's direction. These comments about ambiguity are not meant to obscure the oligarchic character of American society, because the society, despite its turmoil, is governed in most of its major choices by a few thousand men, most of whom participate deeply in the establishment ethos of the republic.

The collapse of the Russian empire as the Soviet Union broke up was the last of the victories over other imperial competitors. The military defeats of the Japanese and German empires in World War II had left the United States supreme in the world, rivaled only by the Russian empire. The Japanese and German empires had weakened England and France so that their colonial empires rebelled successfully. The Austrian and Ottoman empires had vanished in World War I, and the United States had acquired the remnants of the Spanish empire at the end of the nineteenth century. The Brazilian and Mexican empires had succumbed earlier and lost out economically. Of course, Russia, China, and India are still empires presiding over polyglot peoples of different nationalities and languages, and Russia may still have further imperial remnants to shed.

When it gained social legitimacy, the church did so in the context of the Roman empire. Its first great theological council was convened by the emperor, so the church may naturally be as much at home in an empire exerting great influence as in a more modest nation-state. The church's theology since the fourth century has been articulated with one eye on the political-social realities of the empires. Other churches may express their ethics for life in nation-states, the dominant form of social organization in the world. The U.S. church will have to articulate its ethic with one eye on the imperial reality of the United States. But the U.S. church is disunited and particularized, and so the church ethos is fragmented. That fragmentation points ambiguously to the need for church unity but also to particularized expressions. While the National Council of Churches and the World Council of Churches speak to the society, the various denominations, local church councils, and local churches also speak to the society. Their voices express their particular convictions, and the society can expect to hear different accents from Mennonites and Roman Catholics. The society also needs and deserves to hear the particular groups translate their particular voices into the language of justice for the society. The purpose of all the churches is to teach and encourage humanity to love God with all their hearts, minds, and souls, and to realize the good of the neighbors through loving care for them. In the ambiguous empire of the United States, the second commandment is translated into the achievement of justice in the society. So the social goals of the church are vital piety and justice.

## JUSTICE

Justice means the good of the society. Since Plato and Aristotle, it has been taken as the central value or structure of the ethics of society. This broad meaning of justice as the aim of social ethics has absorbed the Hebrew meanings of righteousness and right relationships. In modern, liberal, market-oriented societies, justice has come to mean fair relationships for government, commerce, and society.

Justice is understood as an ideal or a future goal to strive for. Since Amos in the eighth century B.C.E., the Hebrew tradition and then the Jewish and Christian traditions have insisted that God is just. So Western society has urged that justice is constitutive of the way things are in their essence. The world was fashioned by justice, but in reality it exists outside of just relations. Both reform movements and revolutionary movements try to move the society in the direction of justice. Western religions and social thought have, at their best, understood justice to be a goal but its fulfillment to be a matter of eschatological hope.

In Christian ethics, justice is closely related to love. The greatest clarity is achieved if the two imperatives are distinguished and then related. Because of the closeness of their meanings and because both are regarded as essential to the meaning of the concept of God, they can be regarded as two meanings of the ultimate imperative. Humanity responds to the love of God with love for God and for the neighbor. The practical love of the neighbor is, in many dimensions, the seeking of justice. The neighbor is loved by being part of a more just society. We love the neighbor by seeing that the neighbor's wounds are healed, the neighbor is sheltered, the neighbor is protected, the neighbor is visited, and the neighbor is provided for in terms of concrete human needs.

Justice regarded as the good of society is perceived differently by different interested humans and groups of humans. Each person or group thinks of justice from their own perspective. A contemporary Christian understanding of justice sees it as the social arrangement under which all have the opportunity to flourish. Restrictions that thwart human flourishing, expressed in practices of oppressive classism, racism, and sexism, are the forces resisting justice. Justice means that each person has access to education, housing, food, health, and opportunities on an equal basis with all others. Such achievements, of course, mean the radical redistribution of power and resources. The world is governed by elites who reserve resources for themselves, their children, and their associates while restricting or denying access to others. The hierarchical injustices of Haiti and India are replicated in all other human societies in various degrees. So to speak of justice in a Western, Christian informed way carries into the meaning of justice dynamic change, whether reform or revolution. To a degree that, according to R. H. Tawney, is "still revolting," the destinies of individuals are determined by the opportunities for education and access to resources that are passed on from one generation to the next. So as we are to love our neighbor as ourselves, which is a meaning of justice, equality of consideration is demanded. Justice includes equality and until equality is achieved, justice is not yet achieved. All are equal recipients of God's love, but the expression of that love in life is thwarted by systems and by other individuals. Justice is present ontologically and eschatologically; historically, it is struggled for by those committed to it.

Theodore Parker, an abolitionist preacher engaged in the struggle to end slavery, captured this expression of justice when he said, "The arc of the moral universe is long, but it bends toward justice."[6]

## LIBERATION AND JUSTICE

Ismael Garcia's dissertation directed by James Gustafson has now been published as *Justice in Latin American Theology of Liberation*.[7] The focus of the work is on Hugo Assmann, José Míguez Bonino, Gustavo Gutiérrez, and José Porfirio Miranda. Gutiérrez is regarded as the classical figure of the movement, and his work is consulted most regularly in the book. The chapter entitled "The Centrality of Justice" argues that justice is the central concern of liberation theology. However, Garcia is forced to argue that although "justice is central to the reflection and practice of liberation theologians, they never present a clear statement of what they mean by this frequently used term."[8]

Garcia develops the argument that any formal definition of justice must come from the needs of the poor. Warnings are given against the dangers of any historical understanding of justice. Justice cannot be defined abstractly. Garcia admits, even in the conclusion, that the authors of liberation theology remain unclear about the meaning of justice, but that the elements necessary for a clear definition are available in their work. The elements may be there, but the process of clarifying the relationship among them would still be a quite abstract piece of work. Or perhaps they cannot be clarified without more analysis.

Throughout Garcia's book, the term "liberation," which is defined abstractly, dominates the term "justice." The work of liberation theology is focused mostly on the conceptual work of overthrowing injustice rather than on the work of building justice. Justice certainly presupposes order, and early liberation theology was not advocating order in any Latin American country in the 1970s. Hannah Arendt's distinction between the processes of fighting for freedom and structuring freedom is relevant here. Garcia may have been led to focus on justice because of the necessary fight against injustice.

Garcia's conclusion[9] discusses aspects of justice from a liberation perspective. They are:

1. Justice is based on each person's equality of worth.
2. Justice reflects humanity's social nature.
3. Justice is based on a criterion of need.
4. Justice means "the eradication of all those forms of inequality that enable some to exploit and dominate others."
5. All are entitled to economic well-being and political freedom.
6. Institutions that care for the poor deserve support in a just society.
7. Justice implies that rich nations help poor nations.
8. Well-being has a priority over freedom, given the historical struggles.
9. In the Latin American context, only some form of socialism will lead to justice.

As the relationship among these diverse elements remains unclarified, Garcia's liberation attempt to conceptualize justice fails. The perspective of Garcia is that "justice can only be properly defined in the activity of bringing it about in light of the concrete situations that limit its realization."[10]

This passion for the liberation process motivates Garcia's study and allows Jacques Maritain and other theorists who used natural law theory to define justice to be set aside. The natural law theory produced understandings of justice that informed Christian Democratic parties' reform efforts. But if reform has been overcome, Garcia argues, the process called for is liberation. If socialist liberation is not on the foreseeable horizon for most of Latin America, we are called back to look at alternative definitions of justice. For many countries, some of the more traditional definitions of justice may still be helpful. Nicaragua's need for justice may require different concepts than Argentina's present situation.

Lebacqz[11] finds the contributions of Miranda and Gutiérrez to a theory of justice in their staying close to a biblical meaning of righteousness. She explains that for Miranda and Gutiérrez, justice is real, right relationships. This requires special attention to the poor, for their situation must be altered. Justice is seen by their denunciations of injustice, particularly the injustices done to the poor of Latin America. The world is characterized by injustice; God's work is particularly the righting of the wrongs that oppress the poor.

The important contribution of Gutiérrez requires an understanding of the Peruvian context that his translated works do not provide. The social research of his institute is published in Peru in *Paginas*. The institute, Centro Bartolomé de las Casas, is located in Rimac, a *barriada* of Lima. Tillich suggested that the writings of socialism are unintelligible without a commitment to the social struggle reflected in socialism. Moreover, the writings of Gutiérrez are not intelligible without a commitment to solidarity with the poor to change their social situation. The poverty of Peru, which leads to starvation and exploitation, is the necessary context for understanding Gutiérrez's work.

A remarkable book by Curt Cadorette[12] is an introduction to the Peruvian poverty of which Gutiérrez writes. Cadorette makes clear to North American readers the context of the sharp contrast between the poverty of the poor Indians of Lima and the benefits of capitalism for the wealthy of Lima. Moreover, he puts meaning into the footnotes of Gutiérrez to Peruvian thinkers on whom Gutiérrez draws. For years, Gutiérrez taught a course based on José Carlos Mariategui's ideas of combining popular class insights with a theory of Peruvian society.[13] Similarly, Gutiérrez's friendship with and utilization of the Peruvian social-novelist José Mario Arguedas reveals the deeply indigenous quality of Gutiérrez's social thought.

Gutiérrez's work draws on these Peruvian thinkers and on current sociological-anthropological research, including the work of his own institute. His utilization of Marxist critiques of society is indigenous, drawing on a long history of Marxism's critical application to the society of Peru. In the immediate context, his work has to take account of the new reality of Christian base communities in which he has invested his life, the shifts in ecclesiastical politics, the realities of the threat from the *Sendero Luminoso* (Shining Path) guerrilla movement, the ever-present threat of military coup, the major players of international business, and the intervention by outside governmental agencies. Given the fluidity of these realities, Gutiérrez's realism may lead him to shift his emphasis while always looking for openings in the situation that may give his people, the poor, a chance to improve their lives.

Gutiérrez's writings on justice and revolution are within the perceptions of a radically unjust, repressive social situation. He writes of "institutionalized injustice" following the frequent use of it at the Puebla conference. One finds more references to institutionalized injustice than to institutionalized justice in his writings. One of his clearest paragraphs on justice states that the proclamation of Jesus of the reign of God is the proclaiming of a reign of justice and liberation. Justice for Gutiérrez is absolute. "The only justice is the one that assaults all the consequences and expressions of this cleavage in friendship. The only justice is the definitive justice that builds, starting right now, in our conflict-filled history, a kingdom in which God's love will be present and exploitation abolished."[14] Justice is used to denounce the present and as a perspective from which all oppressors will be overthrown. Liberation or the overthrow of the political-economic structures dominates the writing, rather than justice as something that the rulers could now deliver.

In his meditations on Job, Gutiérrez makes it clear that although justice is essential to the meaning of God, the meaning of God is not circumscribed by any theories of justice. Job has been freed in the end from "the temptation of imprisoning God in a narrow conception of justice."[15] The theology of retribution is abandoned, but the obligation of doing justice with God is affirmed. We seem to lack in Gutiérrez that which Karen Lebacqz and Ismael Garcia were looking for—"a theory of justice."

## Expectation and Justice

Justice was not the central theme of Paul Tillich's religious socialist polemic against capitalism when he was in Germany. He did not often judge capitalism by the criterion of justice; rather, he assumed that the contradictions within capitalism were going to destroy it. He regarded the spirit of capitalism as the proclamation of a self-sufficient finitude, and his basic argument with it was that it was not open to the experience of the unconditioned. Capitalism encouraged alienation, competition, and meaninglessness, and it was self-destructive. Justice became a central concept for Tillich in his American experience when the socialist cause, or at least the expression of it in the categories of the young Karl Marx, seemed irrelevant to the American social scene.

Three exceptions to the abovementioned generalization are Tillich's essays "Grundlinien des Religiösen Sozialismus" (1923)[16] and "Man and Society in Religious Socialism" (1943),[17] and his book *The Socialist Decision* (1933).[18] Neither the essays nor the book pushes the discussion of justice to the ontological depths of his later work. Neither essay uses the criterion of justice as a weapon with which to criticize society in the way Reinhold Niebuhr did in the same period. It could further be said that the Hegelian background is just below the surface in the 1923 work and that the 1943 essay is more reminiscent of the political philosophical discussion in England and America.

According to Tillich's 1943 essay, human nature bears the claim that every human being be recognized as a person.[19] There is a natural equality that is the equality of the right to express one's creativity—later he would say the power of being. "This is the ultimate criterion of justice."[20] Justice concedes to finitude that the contingent characteristics of human *existence* prevent absolute equality. But justice requires that accidental differences, by which Tillich meant sex, race, intelligence, strength, and birth, not infringe on *essential* equality. Therefore, all the structures that reinforce *essential* inequality are to be opposed. Fascism, monopolistic capitalism, and class-determined education all result in dehumanization, or the violation of the opportunity to express one's power of being, and therefore they are opposed to justice.

Justice plays an important role in Tillich's most profound socialist writing. *The Socialist Decision* was written under the pressures of reactionary seizure of power in Berlin by chancellor Franz von Papen and the romantic-revolutionary gains by the Nazis. Neither party in Tillich's analysis represented the claims of justice. They both appealed to myths of the origins of life and not to a future shaped by the critique of justice. Tillich argued for an understanding of socialism that would be religious in its respect for the origins of being and prophetic in its insistence on justice. The symbol of the future is "expectation." Expectation expresses the direction of humanity; it is the power of human transformation. Tillich finds the power of expectation in the longings of the proletariat to overcome the demonic conditions under which they survive. In the book, the discussion of expectation is elaborately developed. It is a powerful precursor to the later theologies of hope. This development of expectation, which is a presentation of eschatology in secular-autonomous terms, obscures the importance of justice in the argument, and yet justice, although not elaborated, is important. The call of the future is the call of justice. Justice is the demand arising in human consciousness that calls for the future to be different. Justice requires expectation; "justice is the true power of being."[21]

Justice means "the dignity of being free, of being the bearer of the fulfillment implied in the origin. This recognition of the equal dignity of the 'Thou' and the 'I' is justice."[22] Here, although not stated, is the definition of justice as the second commandment of Jesus: "Love your neighbor as yourself." To the religious reader, the trusting in expectation for the proletariat is similar to living as if one expected an answer in history to the daily prayer "Thy Kingdom come." Tillich's argument in the book depends on the proletariat and the proletariat's ability to understand the possibilities of transforming its historical situation. The book is committed to the possibilities of the proletariat. Of course, very few of the proletariat could have understood the book if they had read it, and Nazi suppression of the book in 1933 made the reading of it virtually impossible.

Beyond the justice rooted in the I-Thou encounter, Tillich speaks of justice as the consent to the social contract. Justice is therefore necessary to power as distinct from force. Consent to power, in the long run, depends on the recognition of justice. "Such consent is given because those who assent to the exercise of power consider the way in which the unified will is executed to be just. *The exercise of power appears to be just when all members of a society can acknowledge that their own will is contained in the will of the whole.*"[23]

Tillich perhaps overestimated the need for assent to a successful party's version of justice by other groups. The Nazis demonstrated the power of terror and force in dividing groups with alternative visions of justice competing for power. Tillich's hope in linking justice to power was to dissuade socialists from utopian politics of justice that neglected power. For him, "the problem of power proves to be the problem of a concrete justice."[24] In his perspective, the Social Democrats had failed to "exercise and consolidate" power when it had come to them. In his view, socialism had been stronger in elaborating justice than it had been in exercising power. The state depends on both justice and power, and effective politics required an understanding of their mutual dependence. Justice for Tillich in this 1932 writing was the movement toward the classless society and the planned economy. It was antithetical to both the revolutionary Nazis and the reactionary Junkers. It depended on the emergence of a tougher and more religious socialism. The failure of such a movement to emerge permitted the Nazis to win and to consolidate power without justice, and thus permitted barbarism to reign in Europe.

Tillich's 1954 work *Love, Power, and Justice* is his most systematic discussion of justice. Here he united reflection on justice with two concepts on which he had worked for years—love and power. He attempted to find a way between realists who would reduce justice to the meaning of power and idealists who would assert the demands of justice without reference to power. He sought to overcome dichotomies in Protestant ethics between justice and love without collapsing them into each other.

The method of Tillich's book may be confusing.[25] I would regard his method as conceptual analysis of basic categories of ethics and politics. Tillich asserts that such elaboration is the work of ontology. Consequently, what I would regard as conceptual analysis of terms that have ontological implications as well as other meanings, he calls ontological analysis. Also, much of the method is etymology, but Tillich in his search for "root" meanings of terms also regards this as ontology. This difference in naming the method Tillich uses does not vitiate the results for me. It does mean, however, that the following of Tillich's argument leaves the conclusion as to the relationship of love, power, and justice as one model reflecting several human, even political, decisions rather than seeing it as a conclusion necessarily rooted in the way things ultimately are. Tillich's Protestant principle forces him to agree with this conclusion.

"Justice is the form in which the power of being actualizes itself."[26] All beings drive toward self-transcendence in Tillich's ontology. This drive toward transcendence produces competition, and justice is the form that allows creativity to be expressed without destroying the whole.

Tillich's discussion of justice is complete only if the entire book is comprehended, and even reflection on the entire book leaves a sense of incompleteness. The understanding of justice is dynamic and relative to each society. The argument of the book is in movement and a few sentences indicate that Tillich knew it was not complete. Mark Thomas of Beloit College has engaged me in discussion regarding how we are to understand Tillich's text. After learning from his suggestions, it seems to me that the overarching principle of justice is love, and that love requires other principles, including the adequacy of any understanding of justice in its particular historical situation. Equality as the second subsidiary principle has both its expression in hierarchy, in which equals in rank are treated equally, and its democratic expression, in which all are recognized as equal in certain aspects of life. This equality is the recognition of the "demand to treat every person as a person." In a liberal society, the recognition of the principle of personality elevates liberty to the rank of "an essential principle of justice." If reflection on love is seen as central to justice, then the principle of solidarity, comradeship, or community is the context in which the unresolved tensions in the principles of equality and liberty are contained.

We can see the four principles of justice based on the ontology of love: (1) adequacy, (2) equality, (3) liberty expressing the reality of human personality, and (4) community.[27] All through the discussion of the principles of justice, Tillich can be seen analyzing the concepts as they appeared historically, but also stipulating his preferred meanings. The stipulations reflect his existentialist background and his protest against dehumanization.

Tillich applies the principles of justice at various levels of justice. He lists (1) the intrinsic level; (2) the tributive level, including the distributive, the attributive, and the retributive; and (3) the transforming level. The transforming level of justice is the level at which the biblical roots of Tillich's discussion of justice are most clear. Creative or transforming justice is the form of reuniting love that does what is necessary for the reunion of human beings. "Love does not do more than justice demands, but love is the ultimate principle of justice. Love reunites; justice preserves what is to be united. It is the form in which and through which love performs its work. Justice in its ultimate meaning is creative justice, and creative justice is the form of reunited love."[28]

The Hegelian background of Tillich's discussion of justice reaches through his entire thought, and the influence of Hegel is particularly strong in *Love, Power, and Justice*. Tillich's oft-repeated statement that the relationship between theology and politics was the driving force of Hegel's system applies only a little less accurately to Tillich himself.

## Love and Justice

Tillich recognized the need for a socialist ethic while promoting socialism, but he did not write such an ethic. Consequently, the concept of justice was underdeveloped in his most socialist period. Despite Garcia's claim for the centrality of justice in liberation theology, it is obscured there under the categories of liberation. Only in the older Tillich does it become a central concept and is it expressed as the form that allows life to flourish and not as a denunciation of the present. Tillich's discussion of justice can be read from his earlier commitments to passionate, religious socialism, but *Love, Power, and Justice* is not written that way. In Tillich, the formal presentation of justice, which the liberation theologians avoided, seems to lose its force of moral indignation regarding the present. In this book, particularly, the absence of the proletariat is felt. Tillich did not find a proletarian class in America, and the force of his socialism was lost. He did not use the special class of the poor as did liberation theology. His groups are national groups, not classes, in this writing. Tillich does not expect fulfillment in history; Gutiérrez demands social fulfillment and righteousness. It may be just this passionate zeal for overthrowing structures of injustice that prevented Gutiérrez from presenting an adequate formal definition of justice.

If the writings of Gutiérrez and Tillich are both too closely tied to socialist analysis to be immediately useful in the United States, where do we turn? Karen Lebacqz had opted for the liberation development of justice, particularly that of José Porfirio Miranda,[29] but that development collapsed with the failure of Marxist economics and the exposure of its ideologically based biblical interpretation. Her work would be improved by a consideration of democratic, mixed-economy views of justice. In particular, she should reconsider Reinhold Niebuhr's views. She found in Niebuhr a view of covenant similar to her own. She realized that Niebuhr "recognized the realities of injustice" and the need for realistic use of power, including force.[30]

Her critique was that liberation was not a primary theme for Niebuhr and that his separation of love and justice tended to relegate justice to a secondary status. She is correct that liberation was not a central theme for Niebuhr, but freedom and equality seemed to carry the same weight in his work. In his day, the major struggle in the African American community was "the freedom struggle," not liberation, and it seems that his essay "The Negro Minority and Its Fate in a Self-Righteous Nation"[31] caught the spirit of that movement. Already, "development" seems to be displacing "liberation" in the vocabulary of the poor countries, and terms are shifting rapidly. The distinction between love and justice seems both biblical and contemporary. Even in personal relations, the difference between being in love and dealing justly with others seems clear. Both are necessary, as is loving the neighbor, but they are not the same. Lebacqz's own enthusiasm for a cooperative economic experiment as representing her model of justice activity could have inclined her to study Niebuhr's deep commitments to an interracial economic cooperative in Mississippi from 1936 to the mid-1950s. If current "liberation ethics" does not seem to invalidate Niebuhr, a return to his examination of justice may deepen the discussion.

The key to understanding Niebuhr's ethic is the dialectic relationship between love and justice. Love for Niebuhr is the way people would live together if they were not selfish and if they consistently sought to fulfill the greatest good for their neighbors. Love is an outgoing acceptance of the other and a seeking of the other's good. The model of love for the other is the ethic of Jesus. Humanity lives under two commandments: to love God and to love the neighbor. The Greek word *agape* is used in both commandments and is translated "love." The love for God, however, is more an act of adoration and trust, whereas the love for humanity is understood in a decision to treat others as one would have oneself be treated. For Niebuhr, love describes both the motive for social action and the greatest possible state of mutuality between two people or among a group of people.

Justice in the sense of God's justice, or the perfect state of justice, would not differ greatly from love, but justice as Niebuhr usually uses it refers to a state of society in which the values of freedom and equality are fulfilled to the greatest degree possible under the given conditions. Justice depends on the interests of various individuals and groups in a community and on their capacity to agree on tolerable solutions to their inevitable conflicts. Justice refers both to the agreed-on rules for settling conflicts and to the more ideal standards that people, in their transcendence of the status quo in their communities, continually express.

Love refers to the possibilities for human mutuality that are always relevant to any social situation as inspiration and critique. Justice refers to the degree of love that can be achieved under the pressures of conflicting interests among people who pursue their own advantage at the cost of the greater social good. Love motivates the search for justice, and in history love reaches further than justice. Love cannot be substituted for justice in society, because people need rules for decisions to maintain their community life. Justice at its best utilizes power to enforce its judgments for social welfare; love at its best, for Niebuhr, is the willingness to sacrifice the self for the other.

Niebuhr is concerned with mining the philosophical traditions of Western thought so that principles of social wisdom can be reformulated for contemporary life. The notion that there are laws of any kind that can be relied on to furnish universal-eternal ideals for human society is rejected by Niebuhr. Scripture, reason, and nature do not provide universally valid concepts of justice for all time. Humanity in its freedom changes its communities. The double love commandment presupposes this freedom, but particular formulations of principles of justice reveal the particular historical contingencies of the formulators and must be revised in each new era. Of course, there is wisdom in the various expressions of the natural law traditions. Humanity continues to transform those societies by reference to standards beyond its present societies. However, humanity is not free to escape historical contingencies by reference to an eternal natural law. What was claimed as natural law by Thomas Aquinas or by eighteenth-century philosophers reveals that these laws were human-historical products, as were the positive laws of those periods.

The search and struggle for justice are endless, as is the quest for truth. As with truth, humanity both has it and cannot grasp it. If justice is the harmony that preserves the vitalities of the participants or the approximation of full human community under the conditions of sin, it is a transforming process that ought not be halted.[32] Because justice implies a balance or a harmony, it is not found without order in society. An order may be unjust if it maximizes force to gain consent to its existence. Most orders imply some approximation of justice; justice implies order. In the society Niebuhr usually comments on, Western democratic society, the principles relevant to a just order are primarily liberty, equality, and tolerance. These three principles can in certain expressions be in tension; in Niebuhr's understanding, they complement one another.

The understanding of justice, not only as an ideal but finally as a harmony reinforced by a balance of power, relates Niebuhr's ethic directly to politics. In a society in which important decisions are made through political action, to pursue justice means to engage in politics. The struggle for justice is the struggle for power, in part. Justice without power is a vague ideal; power without justice is either chaos or tyranny, depending on how it is organized. Given Niebuhr's understanding, politics is not strange ground for a Protestant social moralist; rather, it is a necessary field of study.

After his acceptance of the New Deal, Niebuhr's social ethic was articulated in terms relevant to the American political process. He no longer advocated a displacement of that system, although he often severely criticized it. He regarded most revolutionary rhetoric as irrelevant to the hard choices confronting the American public. There was nothing in his social ethic itself that eliminated the possibility of sanctioning revolution. Politics, not revolution or evolution, was the most effective instrument of obtaining justice in the United States, and so he remained a political activist making hard and often unpleasant choices between greater and lesser evils.

His ethic is controlled by love, and this has a sobering effect in one sense. Concrete human needs and lives take priority over conceptual schemes for a new society and over dreams that may be comforting but produce no results in political action.

The expression of the social ethics of Protestantism with which Niebuhr identifies his own thought most consistently is revolutionary Calvinism. Again and again he emphasizes that seventeenth-century Calvinism, particularly when mixed with sectarian radicalism, produced the greatest social fruits in the history of Protestantism. His words unequivocally indicate his own identification with militant Protestantism:

> Perhaps the most impressive social ethic of the churches of the Reformation was that which developed in seventeenth-century Calvinism. This form of Calvinism revealed itself in the struggles with Catholic princes in Scotland and Holland and in the Cromwellian revolution in England. It laid the foundations for a free society and for toleration in the religious sphere, without which a modern pluralistic national community would not be possible. . . . It is the only form of Protestant social ethic which I find congenial to present perplexities.[33]

Love is expressed socially through justice. The particular ways of achieving justice are evaluated in terms of pragmatic calculation. Niebuhr tended to write as a political pragmatist seeking political goods in light of his theological framework. He resisted defining justice, but rather wrote about the long process of thinking about it from Aristotle to his own contemporaries. Justice was defined by historically relative philosophies in particular historical movements. In contemporary America, it was pursued under the regulative principles of equality and liberty,[34] but even when Niebuhr wrote an essay on those principles of justice, he did not exactly define justice. His reluctance to define justice has drawn criticism from more precise academics,[35] but it left him free as a historical actor to shift as his perception of the historical agenda shifted.

## JUSTICE AND EQUALITY

If we choose to think of distributive justice as the relationships by which people agree to have the produce of a society distributed, what can we say about contemporary society? Liberal, democratic political theory is well represented in the book by S. I. Benn and R. S. Peters entitled *Social Principles and the Democratic State*,[36] published in the United States as *The Principles of Political Thought*. They argue that the declarations of equality in the Declaration of Independence (1776), the Declaration of the Rights of Man (1789), and the Universal Declaration of Human Rights (1948) are not meant in a descriptive, comparative sense. Nor do they believe that such declarations are meant to be universally prescriptive for the treatment of everyone. They mean that everyone covered by these declarations is to receive "equality of consideration." People are to be treated impartially. Relevant criteria of partiality are still needed. These authors incline toward Aristotle's understanding of justice that equals are to be treated equally.[37] Differences in treatment should be proportional to the degrees by which the persons differ relevantly. Of course, relevance is determined by self-interested parties and groups working out their arrangements. Equality has relevance to those things that are to be equalized. Our social arrangements represent the history of groups struggling to overcome inequalities that have oppressed them. Benn and Peters argue that the movement toward public standards of justice will require that the standards themselves be acceptable to the public and also predictable, flexible under special circumstances, and enforced with integrity.

The recognition that equality is so far from being realized demands a commitment to transforming justice. The public sense of justice needs to be continually corrected in favor of the poor, for whom the system does not produce a fair share of distribution.

John Rawls, in an early writing[38] previous to his publication of *A Theory of Justice*, argued that the outline of justice could be expressed in terms of two principles: (1) that everyone had an equal right to liberty compatible with the liberty of all, and (2) that inequalities were arbitrary or unjust unless they worked out for everyone's benefit and unless special benefits were accessible to anyone. This meant that justice was roughly synonymous with the idea of "fair play" and demanded the elimination of distinctions that were arbitrary or reserved to any special group. This philosophical theory[39] is similar to Reinhold Niebuhr's concept of justice[40] as the agreed-on system of distribution subject to the maximization of both liberty and equality.

The development of these principles will require ongoing discussion and struggle, but the contrast between justice and our social reality is obvious. R. H. Tawney's book *Equality*[41] was written for the United Kingdom over half a century ago. He found two fundamental blocks to equality in British society: inherited wealth and privileged education. His words about Britain in 1931 are distressingly true for us today. "The destiny of the individual is decided, to an extent which is somewhat less, indeed, than in the past, but which remains revolting, not by his personal quality, but by place in the social system, by position as a member of this stratum or that."[42]

One's destiny, to a distressing degree, is determined by the fact of birth to this or that family, carrying with it opportunities of wealth and education or lack of such opportunities. The inequality associated with birth is buttressed by the power positions of the advantaged families. Power and money have gradually drifted toward the elite families. In the 1770s, the top 1 percent of the rich families may have accrued 14.6 percent of the country's wealth. Their control has been reduced in depressions. It declined after the New Deal and the Great Depression, but by 1976 the top 1 percent owned 17.6 percent of the wealth, and by 1991 the top 1 percent owned more than 36 percent of the wealth.

G. William Domhoff in *Who Rules America?*[43] indicates that the upper class rules America. He defined this class as the top 0.5 percent of the population in terms of income. They are the families in the Social Register, the private preparatory schools, and the exclusive clubs—the ranks of the millionaires and their executives and lawyers. One percent of the population owns more than one-third of the wealth of the country. Thomas R. Dye's research described a smaller group of about five thousand persons who controlled half of the nation's resources. This number in 1976 was approximately 0.002 percent of the population.[44]

Larry Rasmussen described the decade of the 1980s as a period distinguished for the ransacking of natural resources in the United States while the public treasury was looted by the rich. In terms of both wealth and annual income, the wealthy increased their share of the national resources and the poor decreased their relative share. By 1997, the number of poor had increased to its highest number since 1964. Less than 1 million households at the top had more wealth than 84 million households, and the gap between the rich and the poor was increasing.[45]

The system of distribution benefits this elite and satisfies enough of the middle class for them to remain in place. Others tolerate it or suffer under it without sufficient power to change it. As privilege becomes more and more exaggerated, the authority of the system weakens. It becomes more clear that rational people would not have chosen such a system if they had been given a choice. So whether justice is taken as the revealed will of God or as the choice of covenanting people, it remains a norm and only sometimes an approximated reality.

The inequality associated with life in the United States is even more extreme on the world scene. So far in its historical existence, humanity has been characterized by inequality in social opportunities and material resources. Humanity reflects hierarchical tendencies that are occasionally alleviated by social reform movements providing for greater equality. The American values of individualism, material success, and free market economics have all reinforced the natural inequalities that evolve if not checked. Low taxes and minimal regulations on inheritance, combined with unequal educational opportunities, further exacerbate the natural inequalities of humans to produce great inequalities in the United States. American power in military, cultural, and economic terms further maximizes the U.S. advantage in the world, granting even more privilege to the elite in the United States and allied elites around the world, while reducing the power and opportunity of the masses in the United States and the world. The domestic inequality in the United States is also projected abroad, increasing through international relationships the natural and constructed inequalities among the world's population. So the whole world becomes organized with elites dominating and increasing their domination while their consumption threatens the ecological safety of human life and leaves a billion people in absolute poverty and hundreds of thousands poor to the extent of early death by starvation. These inequalities are further strengthened by the penalization of people on the basis of gender, race, or class characteristics.

The same powers of and pressures from elite groups minimize freedom for the world's peoples. The organization of the world into large corporations characterized by bureaucracy reinforces natural human tendencies toward conformity. As governments and corporations seek the capacity for mobility and adjustment to changing situations, they also seek and enforce conformity to the values they promulgate. Dissent against corporate or government directions is found particularly in two disorganized sectors—students and the poor. Here dissent can become somewhat organized. Also, where meaningful choices are politically allowed, freedom can be exercised in the ballot and dissent registered, but for most of society, rewards are correlated with conformity, and freedom is reduced.

There is also a tension between freedom and equality. Limits on freedom seem to be needed to reduce inequality, but the more major impediments to freedom are the many controls exercised by rationalizing, controlling conformity enforced by corporate and governmental structures for the benefit of the elite who control those structures. Even without sin, the hierarchical and conforming tendencies of humans in society would make the growth of justice improbable. However, the sin of sloth encourages humans not to protest or rebel against unjust structures. Sloth, particularly expressed in the refusal to be human by asserting one's right to be human and in acquiescence to a more domesticated-animal-like existence, facilitates exploitation by humans driven by two other sins. Human selfishness was the sin exposed and challenged by the Social Gospel movement. With the Social Gospel movement's success reflected in much of Franklin Delano Roosevelt's New Deal policies, the movement as a Christian protest faded. The Christian Realist inheritors of the Social Gospel movement stressed the sin of pride, which particularly characterized political life. Pride led to distortions in all of human life and particularly to the rabid defense of privilege by the victors in the social struggle. The prideful exertions of terrible modern power by business elites, fascists, and communists fueled the militant struggles over ideology and the imperial conflicts that characterized the twentieth century.

So justice confronts hierarchy and conformity strengthened by sloth, self-ishness, and pride. Justice is an ideal and is historically only an approximated reality. It is real both ontologically and theologically. For Christian social ethics, it is an eschatological promise grounded in the nature of God that one rigorously pursues because of the love imperative. Moreover, there are guidelines for living in right relationships and making justice in an unjust world. The classical Christian guidelines are given in the Hebrew Scriptures and are reinforced in church teaching as the Ten Commandments.

# Part
## Two
# Principles

# Loyalty to God

A s the tradition of the decalogue or Ten Commandments is absorbed by the church, the theocentric nature of Christian morality is stressed. There is no Christian morality without the central dependence on God. The God revealed is the "I am" of Moses' revelation, but God is more forcefully named as the liberating God. It is Yahweh, who brought Israel out of slavery, who sanctions these commandments. They are the principles of the God who has liberated the slaves, and they are the founding principles of God's nation.

## THE FIRST COMMANDMENT

Convenience of memorization has reduced the First Commandment to "Thou shall have no other gods before me." This shortened form fits the scholarly consensus that the Ten Commandments were related to the ten-digit human hand for easy reference. Still, that which is often relegated to an introduction is intricately connected with the injunction. Our First Commandment should read "I am the Lord your God, who brought you out of the land of Egypt, out of the house of slavery; you shall have no other gods before me" (Exod. 20:2–3).

Israel was founded in mighty acts of liberation. The specific enslaver is named—Egypt. This morality of the Ten Commandments is founded in the political action of immigration, escape from slavery, and the defeat of the oppressor. The conjunction of the identification of God with this political activity makes it impossible to study these commandments without a recognition of their community meanings and their covenant connections. Identity is found in the moral conventions of a group or in the character of an individual; here identity for former slaves is found in moral principles.

These moral principles reflect their religious foundations in the naming of God and in the denial of having other gods before God. Interpreters can speculate on whether "other gods before God" means the idolatry specifically of idol worship or, as some commentators interpret it, exaltation of other values over God. In a society dominated by idols, such as Egypt or Canaan, it must have referred first to avoidance of bringing idols before the presence of God as in the ark, tabernacles, or temple. As interpreted by Judaism, a strong polemic against the presence of idols in Jerusalem or in the temple evolved and was often challenged. Israel was not to revere idols even if the strongest polemics against idolatry were reserved for the later prophets Amos and Hosea. The First Commandment could always be appealed to, and often was, in order to support iconoclasm or the destruction of objects of religious reverence. Such tendencies would find strong expression in Judaism, in Islam, in Eastern Orthodox iconoclasts, and in periods of Protestant protest.

Martin Luther stressed the First Commandment as denouncing any value other than loyalty to God that captured the heart or center of a human being. Luther particularly criticized loyalty to wealth, which he regarded as worship of a deity called mammon.[1] Luther, following Augustine—as did Roman Catholicism—merged the First and Second Commandments so that false worship and false central values were seen as the same reality. From the perspective of ancient Israel or contemporary polytheistic societies, there seems to be ample room for preferring the distinction between "no other gods before me" and "no idols." The First Commandment names liberation, and rejects the gods of Egyptian slavery and, of course, specifically the divinity of Pharaoh, as deserving of a place before or even in the presence of the liberator God. The Second Commandment heightens the critique, reflecting perhaps a later date and a shift in religious consciousness, and ties it to covenant law. However, Luther's polemic against the idolatrous love of money or the god mammon must not be lost. Luther's evangelically warm interpretation of the First Commandment is in its call to complete love of God. Henry Sloane Coffin saw this as the central demand of the First Commandment.[2] It was to center the believer in commitment to God, which he interpreted Christologically. For him all dualisms in morality were overcome in this injunction. One could not be both polytheist and Hebrew or Christian. One could not confess love in family and life and yet try to order business by self-interest or international relations by power struggles. Coffin, the Calvinist, interpreted this commandment rather more as Luther than as Calvin, stressing the warmth and centering value orientations of the commandment.

John Calvin's exposition of the First Commandment, in the *Institutes of the Christian Religion*, is straightforward. The Lawgiver, who has freed Israel, demands proper worship, and therefore no other divinities or superstitions are to be honored. In harmony with Calvin's threefold use of the law, the human inability to so honor God has driven humanity to depend on Christ. Now, in the power of grace, humanity is instructed in what they in the covenant community are to do, which is to worship rightly and deny honor to other claimants for adoration. In his *Harmony*,[3] Calvin related major sections of scripture to this one commandment in two hundred pages of exposition, but in the *Institutes* he is brief, clear, and to the point. Because of God's knowledge, however, even the "recent thoughts of apostasy" must be cleaned from the conscience. In this commandment, Israel was given a manifesto that it has carried out and also betrayed. Christianity's Trinity has expressed this while striving to encompass the dynamism of the expression of the Divine. Modern and ancient polytheism have continued in alternative expressions. The First Commandment is still a shocking concentration of meaning from the viewpoint of a polytheistic society or even a disparate, pluralistic university. Where is the "unity" in a modern university, in modern society, or in modern families? It may be in the faith in a transcendent symbol of meaning symbolized in nonpluralistic worship, but the polytheism is always present in a culture's pluralism.

Paul Tillich found the essence of Protestantism in this principle. He called the bold insistence that only one God is to be worshiped, "The Protestant Principle."[4] All other values are to receive their value in relationship to this transcendent source of value. Only that on which all others depended could, for Tillich, be properly worshiped. He read the commandment as reflecting the Shema or the ancient Hebrew faith: "Hear, O Israel: The Lord is our God, the Lord alone," and its accompanying injunction, "You shall love the Lord your God with all your heart and with all your soul and with all your might" (Deut. 6:4–5).

So in the First Commandment, Tillich read absolute loyalty to *God the Creator*, and we must surely add *God the Liberator* if we are to catch its full significance. In terms of *The Protestant Principle*, it is this radical loyalty that properly identifies all other loyalties. Protestantism, if it remains loyal to this center, must protest loyalties in religion, politics, and economics that threaten to replace awe for the Creator-Liberator God. This understanding calls for protests and relations that guard against false centers. This particular genius of Protestantism is, of course, available to be shared by members of other religious communities who read the First Commandment in the same way.

This injunction, which was so radical for a people between the gods of Egypt and the gods of Canaan, can seem to be a triumph in culture. However, it challenged Pharaoh, the political deity of its day, so with any imagination and even with cautious interpretations, it was a radical challenge to culture. Tyrannies of mass marketing, controlling bureaucracies, and folk cultures are all subject to critique and are relativized. As Calvin warned, the First Commandment has implications for the secrets of our hearts. Luther's warning against the all-controlling god of money has never been more relevant.

## THE SECOND COMMANDMENT

The Second Commandment against making images of God or worshiping images is so close to the First Commandment that Roman Catholics and Lutherans have read them together. Other Protestants and Jews have separated them, thereby reinforcing the starkness of the injunctions against idolatry. Here at the forefront of our summary of moral principles is the concern for the integrity of worship and the honoring of God. The Ten Commandments and all Christian ethics in continuity with them have this concern for a theocentric character of Christian ethics grounded in authentic worship.

I have observed in both Hindu and Buddhist cultures how Christians, free from the idols of those traditions, dread them. In Bangkok, Christian visitors to Buddhist temples have expressed their nervousness in quiet mocking of the deities of those communities and the way of life they symbolize. In southern India I have visited with Christians who will not set foot in the great temples of the Hindu deities. In places in India now undergoing Hindu nationalism, Christians, Muslims, and other non-Hindus are denied access to temples. This intolerance is understandable; images of gods symbolize archetypes of religious-secular reality. They are awesome and they inspire both reverence and fear. The Hebrew rejection of idolatry was a radically distinguishing feature of its religious culture. Christianity and Islam inherited this distinctive feature attributed to Moses.[5]

The Christian adherence to this principle of ethics brought it into its life-and-death struggle with Rome. Idolatry, in the early church, was one of the central unforgivable sins.

The eventual compromise of the church in forgiving while disciplining idolaters led to reductions in severe church discipline in other areas as well. Eventually, with the victory over Roman paganism, the church would begin to compromise even with idolatry as defeated gods became saints and the cult of a mother of God appeared and found representation in art in churches. The struggle goes on.

The Christian ethic is not to be imposed on others, and Christians can tolerate others making images and worshiping them, or with them, or through them. Yet the making and worshiping of images, whether images of Lenin or Buddha, reflect whole systems of meaning that are foreign to Christians conscious of their debt to Hebrew covenant faith.

The lack of images in worship can, when combined with other strengths, encourage oral and written communication, hymnody, and a focus on humanity as bearing an image of God. At its deepest levels for Christians, the impossibility of pictures of God leads to a reverence for Jesus as the Christ whose physical appearance was never described.[6] Any images of Jesus are works of human imagination and, while perhaps not subject to the prohibitions of the Second Commandment, are best used infrequently and with a plurality of interpretations. Arguments about the color, gender, and class of Jesus as the bearer of the Divine run afoul of these early wise prohibitions against physical images of the Divine.

> You shall not make for yourself an idol, whether in the form of anything that is in heaven above, or that is on the earth beneath, or that is in the water under the earth. You shall not bow down to them or worship them; for I the Lord your God am a jealous God, punishing children for the

iniquity of parents, to the third and fourth generation of those who reject me, but showing steadfast love to the thousandth generation of those who love me and keep my commandments. (Exod. 20:4–6)

Are there limits to art and theology? It seems that to those communities who wish to stand honestly in continuity with the commandment tradition of Sinai, there is a limit. For those who would honor the Divine by words and the Word, a limit can be seen. Art in the church should go so far and then desist. There is one who should not be captured or turned into an image.

The reason given for the injunction against making and worshiping idols resides in the nature of God described here as jealous, wrathful, and loving. Perhaps not too much weight should be put on all these details, but they are intelligible. To create images of Yahweh would be to deny the mystery of Yahweh or of Yahweh's freedom. The community that would mold, carve, or paint Yahweh would not be Yahweh's community. The observation that punishment for betrayal of loyalty by parents extends for three or four generations seems obviously true. Those of us fortunate enough to remember or know our grandparents and great-grandparents see the consequences of their choices, styles, and characters repeated in ourselves. We know that to an inescapable degree some of our life will turn up in our grandchildren and great-grandchildren. It is hard to make sense of blessings to a thousand generations unless this is interpreted genetically. It is more probable that the alternative reading of "to thousands" retained in the Revised Standard Version and the King James Version should be preferred.

John Calvin's reading of God's blessings to thousands of generations contrasted God's overwhelming mercy against God's punishments for iniquities, which extended only to three or four generations.[7] It is important to note in this text that the references to jealousy and punishments are combined with *hesed*, meaning faithful, covenant love. This faithful, covenant love has its consequences as does the spurning of it. Love accepted or rejected has consequences. The metaphor of covenant love applies to marriage as well as to the founding realities of Israel, and so the metaphors of jealousy and consequences to future generations are quite apt. Calvin himself interpreted the Second Commandment in terms of Hosea's marriage, broken covenant, idolatry, and adultery images.[8]

This prohibition of images of the Divine represents a watershed in the history of religions. Energy is not to be put into fashioning of images of the Deity out of the wealth of the people. The only image of the Divine that is sanctioned is the people themselves. The later priestly source would identify the humans, male and female, as created in the image of God. The people themselves are to represent God in this world. The making of images of God out of animals, as the Hebrews were tempted to do in the creation of divine images of bulls or calves, is a double mistake. It denies God the proper image while missing the point of Hebrew faith of the Divine represented in humanity. Modern Christians, perhaps in little danger of actually forming images of God out of wood or clay, may still find the relevance of the Second Commandment in its implications of rendering human life fit to bear the image of God.[9]

## THE THIRD COMMANDMENT

The Third Commandment develops the loyalty demanded in the Second Commandment. As the Hebrews were enjoined against making images of God, so they were not to misuse the divine name. Walter Harrelson translated the Third Commandment as follows: "Thou shalt not lift up the name of Yahweh for mischief."[10] Like most contemporary exegetes, he regarded the additional phrase "for Yahweh will not hold the one guiltless who lifts up his name for mischief" as later commentary strengthening the force of the commandment.[11]

The consensus among scholars is that this commandment was an injunction separating Hebrew reverence for the divine name from widespread practices in the ancient world using the name of God in magic, sorcery, and curses.[12] Its primary force is to protect this glorious name from religious or pseudoreligious misuse.

Andrew Greeley and many other commentators have discussed how they were taught as children that they were not to swear or to use other "naughty" words. I can remember wondering as a child whether the words of the Third Commandment meant I couldn't use "damn" or "darn," or any words having to do with sexuality, in public. The usual translation forbidding the use of "God's name in vain" lent itself to this common trivialization. Obviously, committed believers would restrain themselves from cheapening the divine name by careless usage, but this principle means more than this obvious point. How little our common American cursing is understood as deeply painful to those who find their meaning in God's name or in the revelation of God's love in Jesus Christ. To use the divine name violently or spitefully or commonly causes pain in the heart of the believer.

The other common interpretation of the injunction is in reference to binding oaths taken in the name of God in transaction of life or in court. It seems to me that the profundity of the principle is missed if this interpretation is stressed. The Ninth Commandment guards against swearing falsely and is not needed this close to the central theological principles of the commandments. John Calvin interpreted it as referring to oaths, and others, including Henry Sloane Coffin and Martin Israel, have so interpreted it. Penalties against perjury could be seen to be reinforced by the second clause of the Ninth Commandment. H. G. G. Herklots found in it primarily an injunction against perjury.[13] Considerations of translation, theology, and the other injunction against perjury in the Ninth Commandment argue for regarding this commandment as a principle against misusing the divine name in its religious context.

The members of the covenant community were not to use God's name to accomplish evil. John Calvin stressed that they were to avoid levity in matters of faith and to take religious responsibility seriously. This seems appropriate today. However, the seriousness of this principle for modern Christian ethics is the forbidding of the use of ultimate religious resources for less than ultimate causes. Self-improvement schemes, programs of national interest, wars of conquest, and programs of special group interest are not to be blessed with God's name. God's name is holy, and we are to use it reverently and to glorify it.

This protection of the divine name is particularly an injunction for the religious community. If one is in a community that knows God's name, one is reverential in protecting it from association with lesser, partial values. God's good name has suffered, and people have been turned away from God by those followers who used God's name vainly to bless trivial causes.

God's name is misused to bless most of the mischief that humanity accomplishes. From wars to racism, evil actions have been given God's name. The evil has even been prosecuted more enthusiastically because of the association of God's name with evil actions. The religious leadership's insistence that God's name be restricted from evil application would be a major step toward God's will. Faithful religious communities can refrain from proclaiming God's blessing on evil projects and reserve God's name for the good.

Religious leaders must not use the shadow side of their religious power to exploit others sexually, financially, or emotionally. God's good name is tarnished whenever religious leaders betray this trust granted to them as servants of God.

So the implications of honoring God's name are far-reaching. The principle that one should not do mischief in God's name seems to be a simple one, but it means more than not cursing, or not perjuring oneself while under a religious oath; it is the steadfast refusal to convey the legitimacy of God's name on any action that harms God's people. It particularly echoes against the injustices of religious communities themselves. They know God's name and they must act rightly. Martin Luther found the greatest abuse of the Third Commandment "in spiritual matters when false preachers arise and present untruthful teachings as the Word of God."[14] There is probably no connection between true reverence and ethics that is more direct than this connection. The truly reverent or spiritual religious leader must continually guard worship and teaching from reverential betrayal of the true name of God.

The positive thrust of this principle is in the daily prayer of Christians taught by Jesus: "Hallowed be thy name."[15] It is in the deep reverence of this prayer that the seriousness of protecting the name from misuse is obvious and obligatory. In our day, we have tended to neglect the reverential and right reference to God's name. Before her death, Joy Davidman reminded us of it: "Habitually, day after day, we have taken God's name in vain. Let us, if we can, teach ourselves to take it in earnest. It is high time."[16] The honoring of the name of God is the best antidote to our dishonoring of it.

## THE FOURTH COMMANDMENT

The Fourth Commandment is a major theme of the entire Bible. "Remember the Sabbath day, to keep it holy" distinguished the Hebrews from their neighboring nations. It became a major bone of contention between Jesus and the religious authorities. Christians used it to distinguish themselves from Jews. Today it is still a matter of legal and social controversy.[17]

Even though the origins of the Sabbath are lost in the dimness of antiquity, there is wide agreement that it reflected a taboo against work on the seventh day. The word "Sabbath" means to cease or to desist, to abstain or to end. J. Morgenstern's speculation that the Sabbath originated in a primitive Semitic calendar may improve on Babylonian or other hypotheses concerning its origins, but it still remains only a possibility.[18] Some of the most interesting studies state that the Fourth Commandment had an early negative form. Nielsen renders it as "Thou shalt not do any work upon the Sabbath."[19] Harrelson prefers to use "Thou shalt not despise the Sabbath day."[20] By the time of the priestly editors of the Nehemiah court, however, the seventh day had become the revered Holy Day. If it had echoed a negative prohibition, it became a festival of Israel's freedom. So, in addition to having murky origins, the principle of honoring the Sabbath contains both the early negative connotations and the newer positive celebrative overtones.

Another issue regarding the Sabbath is the theological interpretation of why work is to cease. Exodus provides a different reason than Deuteronomy provides for refraining from work. Exodus 20:11 grounds the imperative in the argument that God rested on the seventh day after creating the world in six days. Without giving credence to any one-week theory of creation, we can appreciate the connection of the Sabbath by a priestly editor of Exodus with creation theology. Bonhoeffer responded to this with an affirmation that God gave this commandment to rest before anything was said about work.[21] Calvin permitted himself to become mystical about the Sabbath by interpreting it as resting in God so that God could be present in us. Here, the Sabbath, the distinctive religious day of Judaism, is grounded ontologically in assertions about creation itself. The need to rest and to rest in God is more true than anything suggested about creation in this connection. The second interpretation within the scriptures, given in Deuteronomy 5, does not relate the prohibition against work to the theology of creation, but to the theology of liberation. God brought Israel out of its servanthood to Egypt and commanded Israel to keep the Sabbath Day. It is ordered as a day of rest, with a special emphasis on resting by servants, because the people of Israel are to remember that they were servants. No one is to work—the servants, the animals, the sojourners, the children, or the masters. So the Fourth Commandment has two theological explanations: creation and liberation. Shorter versions of the commandment also appear in Exodus 34:21 and Exodus 35:2, without the theological elaboration that it had in perhaps its earliest formulation in Exodus 16:22–23.

The third ambiguity surrounding the principle of the Sabbath has to do with the fact that Christians abandoned the seventh-day prohibition. Jesus attended synagogue on the Sabbath, "as was his custom." He preached in the synagogues on the Sabbath, but many of his conflicts were over the Sabbath regulations. Jewish Christians seemed to maintain both the Sabbath and "the Lord's Day," or the first day of the week. Paul, the apostle to the non-Jewish world, neglected the Sabbath, and his congregations turned to the first day of the week to celebrate in their own gatherings the resurrection of Jesus Christ. From its early history, Christianity would be distinguished from Judaism by its worship on the first day of the week. The Islam world chose the sixth day, and Judaism would stay with the seventh. Early Christians probably observed the Lord's Day early in the morning and in their evening fellowship, but there is no indication that they tried to enforce injunctions against work on the first day of the week until much later. Paul regarded the observance of special days as superstition, and Athanasius made it plain that the Christians had no Sabbath. "We keep no Sabbaths; we keep the Lord's Day as a memorial of the beginning of the new creation."[22] Augustine, too, would resist transferring Jewish sabbatarian regulations to the first day of the week. Thus, the ambiguity is with us, because neither Jesus nor Paul instituted a no-work, first-day-of-the-week celebration. That distinction goes to the new convert Emperor Constantine, who, for his own mixed motives, proclaimed the first day of the week to be freed from many kinds of work and thereby instituted on the Christian worship day an imperial policy of regulation freeing the church to utilize the day.

In 789 c.e. Charlemagne enjoined all ordinary labor on the Sabbath, and since then various church councils have ruled on the Sabbath. Martin Luther understood the Fourth Commandment to be abrogated by the New Testament and yet urged the following of tradition regarding the first day. John Calvin, the Westminster Confession, and seventeenth-century Scotland all took Sabbath restrictions on the first day of the week with great seriousness. In the pre–Civil War period in the United States, movements to enforce Sabbath regulations produced a great many studies and social debates. In Europe, most all of the factories were shut down on Sundays by the early twentieth century.[23]

No contemporary Protestant theologian has claimed as much for the Fourth Commandment as Karl Barth. He places it first in the requirements of his ethics. It is for him a total commandment. He says, "The Sabbath commandment explains all the other commandments, or all the other forms of the one commandment. It is thus to be placed at their head."[24]

The difference between Barth's placing the Fourth Commandment first and this book's placing the love imperative first is obvious. For Barth, God commands renouncing of work on the Sabbath and, more important, a celebrative response to God on this day. Barth does not desire compulsory worship service but the free acceptance of worship on Sunday, so that the rest of the Sabbath has meaning and thanksgiving. He does not propose Sabbath rules to bind all Christians, but rather suggests directions that would enable Christians to learn God's command regarding the Sabbath.

First, Barth suggests that Sunday needs to be a day of both relaxation (or rest) and worship. Second, the Sabbath is to be celebrated in a joyous manner.

Third, Sunday or the Sabbath is not to be a day for isolation, but a community holiday. Finally, he urges that the direction of rest from work, worship, and joy of Sunday illuminate the days of work, which follow the first day.[25] Barth, however, avoids legalisms concerning the day; he knows of the sorrowful consequences of some of the sabbatarian laws enforced by Protestant predecessors. In his four guidelines, which he calls questions, guidance can be found.

In light of present unemployment of significant percentages in Christian-influenced industrial nations, which is accompanied by overemployment of elites, adjustments are needed. The need for meaningful work, as well as the need for rest, is recognized in the Sabbath commandment. Many of us can find in the commandment a requirement of limits or, to use Barth's term, an ethic of renouncing. We must not become all we can be, but we must become appropriately limited human beings. Others need help finding work so that they may live and, in terms of our subject, so that their Sundays are a day of rest from work. We are limited, and Sunday religiously proclaims this and is relevant to the whole week.

Sunday for Christians is a day for rest that needs to include healthy leisure activities, services of worship, a focus on family life, and times of meditation. Parents need, as part of their mentoring, to model Sunday in such a way that it becomes for them and their children the best day. It is a day for joy, for religious study, and for worship and togetherness in the communities of family and church. The Old Testament insistence that it be on the seventh day is gone, as is the penalty of death for its violation.[26] The sense, however, of a festival of religious, joyous freedom and rest remains as a penultimate imperative worth sacrificing for and worth fighting for with social or commercial forces that would infringe on these freedoms.

The meaning of leisure ultimately depends on our work and its place in our total life. In common usage, leisure is freedom from toil. It is the capacity to escape the restrictions of the duties of work. The meaning of leisure could be sought and defined in terms of contemplation, play, relaxation, aware passivity, or an inner attitude of taking it easy based on trust. It seems to me wiser to trust common usage and the dictionary tendency to define leisure as time free from duties or work. This humble definition permits us to realize that leisure may become a resource for either great happiness or great pain.

The writing of these paragraphs on leisure was an act of work—an act of work incidentally piled on top of my normal duties. One day as I wrote, I put pen aside to experience leisure. Across the street, the teenagers of Peabody High School were frantically doing exercises in the gym, and my mind wandered back to all those hours of exercise to which my young body had been subjected. On Saturday morning, as I exercised my freedom over my leisure by staying home and writing, I observed two cats enjoying the sun on a fence in our back yard. One cat was a huge gray tom. He reminded me of my boyhood pet, and as I sat there I fondled my past in my memory. One use of leisure time is thus to find ourselves free to treasure the ways in which life has been good to us. A few years ago, while my son played games with toy knights and

Vikings in his room, I sat in a rocker in our living room listening to music and contemplating the future. How should I respond to offers of positions at opposite ends of the country? Were these openings of quite different sorts the beckonings of a new future, or were they nothing more than normal temptations in a shifting and chaotic ecclesiastical-academic world? Our use of leisure over the weekend in question also involved a trip to a Pitt basketball game, which was to my son a promise of bold new things to come while for my wife and me it was more a memory of a time when organized school athletics had been important to us. She asked, amid the teenagers, "Do you want to go to a 'sock-hop' after the game?" We watched *Much Ado about Nothing* in a delightful TV performance and appreciated IBM's generosity in subjecting us to only infrequent, tasteful advertisements. At the same time, IBM's role in the computerized warfare in Laos flitted across our minds in the midst of their romantic ads.

It is my fate as a scholar to have my "leisure" (Greek *schole*, Latin *schola*) flow in and out of my work. At home, the threat to my being with my family is the abundance of books around the house waiting to be read. At the office the threat to reading and writing is conversations with students or fellow faculty members, or my own contemplation. Scholarship requires leisure as it requires discipline, and so there is a tendency in my mind to regard as duty only the meeting of classes and committees and the preparation that is absolutely required for the two. Students and faculty in a situation in which the nature of scholarship is understood therefore have abundant leisure even though their vocation requires more effort than they probably are capable of giving.

Thinking back to my days on the production line, I wonder—for that occupation also provided ample opportunity for contemplation—whether such work could in some sense be called leisure. I concluded not, because one was still at the beck and call of the production line. An alienating fantasizing occurs wherein the mind unused in production moves on in protest and in stupor to other tasks. The leisure of life occurred very obviously there during the coffee breaks and lunch breaks, but not on the job while one served the rhythms of the machine. The need or tendency of the workers to repress the day's work in alcoholic fellowship after the machines were stilled pointed to the sense that production as production largely for the welfare of the owners could not be regarded as healthy in any deep sense.

An ethic for leisure must also be an ethic for work. If the work is to be, as the Protestant reformers thought, a *vocation*, it must be transforming of the present to a more humane future. Leisure as rest from that work can become integrative of the purposes of that work. If one's work is a vocation before God, as before the Reformation only the roles of the clerics and the religious were vocations, then the young who are not yet working full-time and the elderly who have finished working full-time can in the use of their leisure continue the transforming activity of that work. In a world like ours, in which the gifts of technology are ambiguous, and in which many are hungry and illiterate, work and leisure must be united in loving service to be meaningful.

The formal writing in the theology of play has come out of the theologies of hope and the theologies of revolution in the main. This is profoundly as it should be, for it is in the service of transforming our present, out of respect for the past, into a better future that our work and leisure take on meaning. Leisure without hope is squandered. Work without love is distractive. Life without faith is a bore. Part of the seeking of the imperative to take leisure and to honor God is also to surrender or at least relax about the Protestant work ethic with its stern demands.

## BEYOND THE WORK ETHIC

In the United States, the heritage of the Reformed tradition of Christian ethics has merged in popular thinking with the work ethic. The work ethic has in turn helped shape the social mores of non-Reformed people who have come into the dominant ethos of the United States. As the United States economy made a smaller and smaller contribution to the total world economy in the decades of the 1970s and 1980s, the transfer of the work ethic through industrialization to non-Western societies became a reality. New questions about the dominance of the work ethic became apparent. The work ethic itself became an issue of political campaigns in the late twentieth century.

The speed of change in our society feeds on technological advances. These changes in our social environment create dispute over the values to be honored. The outcome of the debates over values and priorities furnishes the context for the next stage of change resulting from the application of technology. The work ethic is one of the structures of value choices that has been hotly debated. Within our homes and during our presidential elections, the clamor over the work ethic has arisen. A columnist, Joseph Kraft, referred to President Nixon's anti–New Deal budget as "The Work Ethic Budget."[27] The former secretary of defense and secretary of health, education, and welfare referred to the same cuts in welfare spending as reflecting the "voluntary ethic" and claimed that such an ethic is "as we all know, a very deep part of the Hebraic tradition. It is a foundation stone of the Judeo-Christian ethic. It is also a particularly American quality."[28] The work ethic issue emerges in a variety of contexts. In the struggle over immigration policy, Representative Dick Armey of Texas associated the work ethic with "most immigrants."[29] He seemed to mean that they would not become a burden to the welfare system, but that they would work hard and cheaply.

Hidden behind wages, working conditions, tax distribution, and welfare programs are ethical assumptions. The predominant organizing ethic in the United States has been an ethic associated with the Calvinist wing of Protestantism and the spirit of capitalism. This ethic has been variously labeled the Protestant ethic, the capitalist ethic, the work ethic, and, in Secretary Richardson's terminology, the voluntary ethic.

The work ethic has been associated with the rise of Protestant capitalism, and now forces as diverse as demands for increased leisure time for workers, longer life for all, and cultural protest by the youth have questioned its adequacy. National leaders, mistaking the subject of the work ethic for the related issue of whether people ought to work, joined the debate in defense of the work ethic.

Max Weber, a German economist and sociologist at the turn of the century, articulated a theory that the spirit of capitalism was reinforced by the Protestant ethic.[30] He thought that the ascetic, hardworking concentration on one's vocation to the neglect of other values was related to Protestantism. Furthermore, he thought that capitalism first flourished in Protestant areas of Europe. Today, all of his conclusions are matters of debate among sociologists; nevertheless, he created the concept of a work ethic, which meant that people found guarantees of meaning primarily through their work. In fact, he thought that in seventeenth-century Protestantism success in one's work was a sign of salvation for people who had no other worldly signs since Calvinism had abandoned most of the signs of salvation within Roman Catholicism.

R. H. Tawney, an English economist, added to the argument of Max Weber's *The Protestant Ethic and the Spirit of Capitalism* detailed studies of the relationship of Protestantism to capitalism in England. He found in the Puritan insistence on the responsibility of the individual a tendency to slip into the suggestion that society is not responsible. In teaching that God's realm is different from this world, the move could be made to the view that this world has almost no connection with God's realm. The ground for blaming poverty on vice was laid in the later developments of the Reformation. The harsh treatment of the poor characteristic of England from the late seventeenth century into Victorian times was related to the glorification of the economic virtues by Christians.

> In their emphasis on the moral duty of untiring activity, on work as an end in itself, on the evils of luxury and extravagance, on foresight and thrift, on moderation and self-discipline and rational calculation, they had created an ideal of Christian conduct, which canonized as an ethical principle the efficiency which economic theorists were preaching as a specific for social disorders. It was as captivating as it was novel. . . . The shrewd, calculating commercialism which tries all human relations by pecuniary standards, the acquisitiveness which cannot rest while there are competitors to be conquered or profits to be won, the love of social power and hunger for economic gain—these irrepressible appetites had evoked from time immemorial the warnings and denunciations of saints and sages. Plunged in the cleansing waters of later Puritanism, the qualities which less enlightened ages had denounced as social vices emerged as economic virtues. They emerged as mortal virtues as well. For the world exists not to be enjoyed, but to be conquered. Only its conqueror deserves the name of Christian. For such a philosophy, the question "What shall it profit a man?" carries no sting. In winning the world, he wins the salvation of his own soul as well.[31]

Today, the work ethic means the devotion to one's work to the neglect of other values. As inheritors of an American tradition heavily influenced by Calvinism, we have some of this work ethic in our minds even though confessionally we are Catholics, Jews, or Methodists.

To a remarkably high degree, we are creatures of our social history. Our individual selves in their freedom organize the data given in their social relationships. We mold, modify, and change our inheritance, but the data comes to us from this social-historical inheritance.

Defenders of the work ethic who are interested in maintaining the dignity of work would do better to defend an ethic that includes work. Critics of the work ethic who want to protest against tying all of life to a focus on work also need to explain just how they would define their own ethic for work. Certainly the counterculture's celebration of love was sentimental when it interpreted love as an "in-group celebration" with no responsibility for the larger world. Similarly, the establishment's dismissal of all who were too young, too old, disabled, or unemployed, because meaning and dignity depended on work, was cruel.

In her analysis of aging, Simone de Beauvoir points to the need for purposes that give life dignity continuing in old age. Only in devotion to individuals and groups, and by giving oneself to causes—social, political, or intellectual—can the passions that nurture life with dignity be found. Aging with dignity requires a life with dignity.

Her book *The Coming of Age* never uses the term "work ethic," but her analysis shows the price of that work ethic. "It is the meaning that men attribute to their life, it is their entire system of values that define the meaning and value of old age. The reverse applies: by the way in which a society behaves towards its old people it uncovers the naked, and often carefully hidden, truth about its real principles and aims."[32]

Western society reveals that it basically has looked on people as producers or as an ingredient in the means of production. When they are no longer able to work, they are brushed aside. "Society confesses that as far as it is concerned, profit is the only thing that counts, and that its 'humanism' is mere window dressing."[33] By the 1990s, political pressure from the elderly themselves was changing the economic situation.

Because we have allowed our ethic of production to become our controlling ethic, we have no meaning to give to the nonproducers. The young and the old feel that they do not belong. The young have to define themselves as future workers (note their answers to the question: What do you want to be?); the old define themselves as ex-workers. Simone de Beauvoir concluded her study by saying that only by changing our life can we really correct the way we brutalize the old. We cannot really change our life until we change the sense of meaning (the ethic) that we attach to our work. The growth of retirement plans, pensions, and social security in the 1980s changed the financial situations of many of the elderly.

The work ethic was an attempt to provide a security that the human situation does not permit. Its consequences are evident in our culture. The work ethic is a historical aberration that has had its four-hundred-year reign. Social pressures and human wisdom are pushing us to return to the main ethical tradition of the Western world, which is an ethic of faith, hope, community, justice, and love. Work has a place in this ethic, particularly because love requires that everyone contribute responsibly to the welfare of the community according to ability. A return to the more classical ethic of the Western world will provide us with an *ethic including work* that allows us to honor all persons, not only the most active producers, in their respective positions in life. Robert Wuthnow's empirical study *God and Mammon in America*[34] demonstrates the great ambivalence in American society about the relationship of the pursuit of money to spirituality. His edited collection of essays *Rethinking Materialism: Perspectives on the Spiritual Dimension of Economic Behavior*[35] is intended to stimulate a debate about American materialism. The purpose of this book is, of course, to explicate fundamental Christian norms. The internalization of these norms would in itself counter materialism. Here the attack is indirect: follow the Christian norms and you will not suffer from materialism. However, because the Protestant work ethic could be, and was, misperceived, as a Christian norm it required direct critique. So the issue is not the defense of an outdated, sometimes cruel work ethic, but the articulation of a new ethic including work within the framework of a broader, richer Christian ethic.

The Fourth Commandment is the final commandment of the theological principles. It moves toward the more humanitarian grounds of the final six principles. It is a transition principle because it protects the need for rest, and particularly for servants' rest, while grounding these protections in respect for God. In Exodus 31, the Sabbath is described as a sign between God and God's people through all generations. In itself it reunites love of God and love of humanity, or, as it is traditionally classified, it is the last of the first tablet of commandments, but it is also a bridge to the second tablet. As the rainbow was perceived as the sign of the covenant with Noah for the sake of the created world, the Sabbath was the sign for Israel of its covenant with God. Thus, for Christians, freed from the death penalties associated with violation of the Sabbath in Exodus 31, the day of Jesus' resurrection becomes a day that is observed "throughout their generations, as a perpetual covenant" (Exod. 31:16). Clearly, prophets and priests saw the seriousness of this commandment. In Numbers, the penalty for violating it was stoning outside the camp. Amos, Isaiah, and Jeremiah all regard Sabbath observance as "central and critical for the survival of community."[36] Twentieth-century Christians can regard these Hebrew judgments only as revealing the importance of a day of rest with God. In a culture with too little rest and too little worship, the importance of a day of rest with God takes on a critical importance.

# Concern for the Other

T he first four commandments are directed toward God. The Fifth Commandment makes a complex transition of application of the principles toward the other.

## THE FIFTH COMMANDMENT

The "other" of the Fifth Commandment is the closest other. Without the parents, the self would not exist. The mother and father are of course referred to as parents, as God is a parent. The movement from honoring God to honoring human parents is a shift, albeit the smallest shift possible, between the Divine and the human.

Assuming that the primary recipients of the Fifth Commandments are adults, the commandment refers to caring for adult parents. If its meaning is in how we honor them when they are dependent on us, it echoes the reference to the Sabbath in the Fourth Commandment. In their years beyond economic productivity or the biological protection of their children, parents are to be honored.

Walter Harrelson and some other interpreters argue for a negative short form of the Fifth Commandment: "Thou shalt not curse thy father or thy mother."[1] But the positive rendition of honor in our final text continues the positive presentation of the Sabbath principle and does not need to be set aside. "Honor your father and your mother, so that your days may be long in the land that the Lord your God is giving you" (Exod. 20:12).

The blessing of long days in the land is not so promising to urban dwellers disconnected from the land and anticipating their last years in facilities for the aging. Yet even if this is a later addition to give added reinforcement to the principle, it contains profound truth. Human beings live by generations, and the patterns of the parents form the children. Children who witness their parents caring for grandparents grow up to care for their parents also. Unless children can experience the honoring of the aged, they will in all probability not convey honor either. If one wants to be cared for and honored, one must also deliver such care. Life will be cut off to the extent that one does not honor the aging parent.

The parent is often the closest neighbor and one whom, in many cases, we need to be reminded to honor. The emotional tangle among children and parents may make it something of a task to honor them. The imperative understood as a morally binding principle furnishes a motivation to do that which we would do anyway if our relationships were completely healthy. The conflicts between the generations reveal why this is an imperative. It is vital to human life, and humans need a prod. Intergenerational cooperation and the treating of the elderly with dignity solidify the family and contribute to social health.

Both Luther and Calvin grounded the need to submit to hierarchical authority in the Fifth Commandment. Luther thought that all authority had its foundation in parental authority. This seems to be an unnatural extension of the imperative beyond the text. It may also provide a defense for governments and other hierarchies that, in our modern world, they do not need. There is in North American society so little compassion and care for the aging parent that the principle has all it can do when understood in the narrow and literal sense examined here.

Church experience with the aging process has taught that the process of retiring from one's paid vocation should be, as the Faith Presbyterian Church in Sun City's program Aging Creatively Together puts it, "a retiring to something." Retirement to a task or to a cause evokes its own honor. All need honor, and inasmuch as honor resides partially in relationships and work, they should be found even in retirement. Recent shifts in wealth, pensions, and governmental payments and services have left many of the elderly in strong financial positions, and honoring them may mean enlisting their assistance in helping others. Both John Wesley and John Calvin taught that the Christian life is neither in having too much nor in having too little. Our private charities and social policies should realize a middle economic position for as many of our society's parents as possible. Neither we nor our parents should have too much or too little. The honor due parents is not different from what love requires—it is only a further specification of love.

The modern notion of aging as an extended vacation must be rejected. Well-being in aging is secured by the continuation or deepening of intellectual and spiritual life. Powers may begin to slip even in early aging (sixty-five to seventy-five years of age) and certainly do so in middle old age (seventy-five to eighty-five), but the powers that remain must still be used in love of God and the neighbor. The old have resources in wisdom, experience, time, and financial resources to strengthen their progeny. As the aging have received from their predecessors, so they are obligated to provide for their inheritors. It is a time for acceptance of one's own life cycle, but to the extent that generativity is permitted it is to be sought. Daniel Callahan follows Simone de Beauvoir, Cicero, and William F. May in recommending activist virtues for the aging. He urges them to continue to exert themselves with spiritual vigor.[2] The Fifth Commandment encourages their continued vigor in the service of love for their neighbor. We need to avoid sweeping generalizations here. Obviously, aging requires both disengagement and engagement with the responsibilities of society. The important point is to get over the earlier themes of total disengagement or enforced idleness at a certain age. We honor the aging by allowing them to find their own levels of activity, and in so doing we strengthen our society.[3]

As we honor the elderly by encouraging their contributions to society, we dishonor them by encouraging them in idle or exaggerated consumption. Projections that the Social Security and medical costs for the elderly will force the government to abandon all other social welfare programs in the next century are a call to change social policy. We must not take everything we can get. Many of us, as we move into the aging process, will have to collect less than we regard as our due, either voluntarily or by a change in policy. The elderly will have great political power in the United States in the next century, and we will have to limit our use of that power for our own privilege. Much of the preponderance of wealth the aging will have in the next century needs to be transferred to the education of the young. We may hope for this to be accomplished socially through taxation on Social Security payments, pensions, and wealth. If it is not accomplished through taxation, educational institutions will have to teach and persuade the elderly with wealth to share it with society for educating the coming generations.

Erik Erikson regarded the possible fruits of the last stage of life to be integrity and wisdom. To reach such a stage and to have one's integrity and wisdom recognized would be a fulfillment of the honoring of parents. Such a development is a social project requiring many adjustments in our society and presupposing much discourse and not a few political changes. Old age must have meaning, and this meaning can be found in the maximization of the central values of this study: love, justice, and community. The sharing of one's self, time, and life in service, the nurturing of relationships, the struggle with the evils that thwart justice, and the giving of one's accrued resources contribute to meaning and are all characteristic of the possibilities of old age and of retirement.

Daniel Callahan's comments on the Fifth Commandment noted that it explained neither the meaning of "honor" nor the limits of filial obligation. Each generation that recognizes the special biological, emotional, and psychological bonds between parents and children wrestles with the resultant obligations.

The imperative is to honor; it does not require self-sacrifice of one's own life or opportunities. In many cases, honoring and caring for the parent require the support of other family members, friends, voluntary community agencies, private services, and governmental support.

Callahan seeks other support for the requirement to honor and to care for vulnerable parents. He remains unsatisfied with arguments from "equal mutual moral duties" or "voluntary affection."[4] Within the community of the church, it suffices to say that this obligation stems from this ancient commandment that the church affirms. The obligation is reinforced by demands of justice and community, and overwhelmingly by love. Our parents are among our closest neighbors, both biologically and psychologically, even if not geographically. Moreover, the obligation is prudent because, generally, as we care for our elders so we have a possibility of being cared for by children, friends, community institutions, and government.

The struggle to honor our parents is won by everything that increases dignity in aging in the context of the greater society's welfare. It means, as does every other virtue, the acceptance of limits. Human life is not without limits. We are mortal, and life is relatively short even now. Callahan wisely noted that societal goals include life well lived within a limited life span. Human life is not to be wasted in fighting against mortality by those who have completed a "natural" life span. American society will probably work out limits on its ability to continue the delaying of death through technical wizardry and huge expenditures. The solutions will come through ad hoc budgetary decisions in government, hospitals, health care agencies, and families. The Christian contribution is not to prescribe a solution but to insist on "honoring" within reason and limits, and to remind society that the necessary human deaths are not the end of God's mercy.

## THE SIXTH COMMANDMENT

The commandment not to murder another human being seems to be the simplest of the Ten Commandments. The difficulty resides in deciding what constitutes murder or the illegitimate taking of another life. Hebrew ethical teaching held this principle, "You shall not murder," while affirming killing of idolaters, murderers, adulterers, enemies in war, rebellious children, and homosexuals. Obviously, when we teach this commandment as a principle of morality to adolescents in our confirmation classes, we mean it in a much more restrictive sense than did the Hebrews. Current debates about the breadth of this principle concern how more restrictive twenty-first-century Christians are going to be than their Hebrew predecessors.

In Christian ethics, with the ultimate principle being love, tension resides over whether the love deepens or broadens the teaching. John Calvin deepened the commandment, insisting that Jesus taught that we must not be angry with others to the point of wishing them harm. "This law also forbids murder of the heart, and enjoins the inner intent to save a brother's life."[5] For Calvin, it instructs the Christian to observe the unity and solidarity of humanity and to refrain from the festering anger that promotes violence. The positive implication is that we are to seek the neighbor's safety.

Others, notably Walter Harrelson and Karl Barth, have generalized the Sixth Commandment. Harrelson points out that the teaching does not make distinctions and so he broadens it to include the proscription of capital punishment and abortion. Barth broadens it by interpreting it through a critical appropriation of Albert Schweitzer's "reverence for life." This allows Barth to stress that God forbids many kinds of killing that are not condemned in scripture. For him, the weight of God's command stands against abortion, suicide, and euthanasia. Barth's arguments are profound, but his reading of the commandment not to murder through the lens of "reverence for life" rather than the more absolute ethic of love binds him to an unnecessary legalism.

A reading of the Sixth Commandment as an important imperative through the Christian understanding of a love ethic frees us from making this commandment an unnatural burden. The commandment as principle is universal. All societies prohibit and punish the crime of murder. Beyond the universal is the recognition that different societies define different actions as murder and prescribe different penalties for them. Contemporary societies would regard some of the actions for which the Old Testament requires capital punishment as not deserving of explicit punishment by the legal system. American society is currently engaged in a struggle to determine whether abortion, euthanasia, and assisted suicide should be illegal or legal. The fact that the Bible does not prohibit these acts does not determine whether Christian ethics should proscribe them. Other trajectories of biblical interpretation might persuade the Christian community to act against forms of killing that were not explicitly proscribed by biblical commandments. Christians need to be very careful, however, that they are not just projecting their own legalisms and prejudices when they harshly condemn practices not proscribed in scripture. An example might be that it is easier to approve of a church calling for abstinence from tobacco than to approve of a church prohibiting wine. Tobacco was not known by the biblical writers, and they had no knowledge of its negative effects. Wine, on the other hand, was known by the biblical writers, and while drunkenness was condemned, the drinking of wine was not. In fact, it was regarded as a blessing and is associated with ceremonial use through Jesus' own actions. There are arguments against the use of wine, but it is more persuasive to argue against a practice unknown in scripture than against a practice known and not criticized.

The importance of this commandment as deepened by Jesus to forbid evil intentions through anger clearly proscribes murder and urges us, as Calvin saw, to provide for security and safety for all neighbors. Recognizing that the community of one's church shapes the interpretation of the teaching according to its understanding of justice, a study of ethics must still make its recommendations as to interpretation. Brief comments on individual killings, abortion, euthanasia, capital punishment, social neglect, and war, when considered as a whole, will reflect the meaning of this principle for today's Christian community.

## Murder

Martin Luther makes plain that in a world full of evil intentions that could lead to murder, God's commandment is a necessary wall of protection. All live within reach of injustice and violence, and we are not to murder or take human life unjustly. "This commandment is likewise a wall, a fortress of defense, about our neighbor to protect him in his liberty and to guard him from bodily harm and suffering."[6]

One individual is not justified in taking the life of another even if subjected to the worst provocation. Neither drunkenness nor deprivation is an acceptable excuse for the taking of another human life. The community must encourage the governing institutions to do their duty to provide protection against murder. Governing officials who cannot provide such protection must be dismissed and leaders chosen who can fulfill the first obligation of government, which is protection in an unjust, violent world.

A Christian may, in rare cases, take a life in self-protection when cornered, but of course the first responsibility is to flee the evil attacker and not needlessly take a human life. The obligations to defend the innocent are more demanding. We are duty bound out of love to defend the innocent against evil. We are not bound to defend ourselves unless there are no other options, but we must come to the defense of those innocent ones who cannot defend themselves. The defense of others is a more pressing duty than self-defense, but sometimes self-defense is also an imperative.

Christian ethics should not tolerate murder expressed as a response to provocation, social deprivation, family dysfunction, or similar excuses to which a sentimental society sometimes responds. The principle of no murder is meant for an unjust society of badly formed families; we have known no other. It must be regarded as an imperative for human life.

## Abortion as Birth Control

The controversies surrounding abortion intersect the struggle for political power in the American empire. The issues are debated within churches and in the political arena. In fact, the first bitter, personal exchanges between the presidential candidates in the 1996 presidential election were over the morality of the candidates and their perspectives on abortion.

On a Sunday morning as I walked toward the steps of my local Presbyterian church, I was confronted by Roman Catholic nuns and Pentecostal lay preachers. Armed with arguments from natural law and the Bible, they joined together to criticize my church for supporting the "right to choose" side of the abortion debate. Here three Christian communities disagreed. Not all within my own denomination supported its moral teaching, and not all within the other two agreed with theirs. The distance between Presbyterian and Roman Catholic forms of argument was easily made clear. The Catholics argued for the natural and necessary consequences of intercourse and the sinful nature of any interference. The Protestants, affirming sexuality, argued for the desirability of family planning, covenanting with anticipated children, etc., and no agreements were possible. The Pentecostals were unable to provide any specific biblical injunctions against abortion because there are none, but they were able to interpret "Do not kill" as an anti-abortion imperative. The Catholic sisters agreed with this interpretation but hung their argument on the naturalness of live birth following from intercourse. Obviously, there are three different communities of scriptural interpretation here. The Presbyterians translate the scripture "Do not murder" and do not regard the fetus in the first two trimesters as a human person who could be murdered. The Presbyterians tend to support the Supreme Court whereas the others fault the Court and support their communal interpretations. The Presbyterians further argue that neither birth control nor abortion is condemned in the Scriptures although moral misconduct is. There is no biblical prohibition of abortion.

Several factors have led Presbyterians and other mainline Christians toward the exclusion of abortion or birth control from the strictures against murder. First, the presence of women in the official deliberating processes of the church involves in the moral debate those Christian women who have in conscience elected abortion for themselves. Second, the pressures of population escalation on the earth's capacity to sustain the environment have inclined mainline Christians to support family planning, which often increases the need for abortion when other means of birth control fail. Third, the middle-class reality of mainline Christian families does not encourage them to lead lifestyles of single parenthood or huge families. Their choice of lifestyle inclines them to want the possibility of abortion in case of unwanted pregnancies.

More to the point, however, is that in the two decades of debate within the mainline denominations, opponents of the choice of abortion have been unable to produce biblical arguments or rational arguments sufficient to challenge the presumed right of the Christian woman herself to decide her intentionality regarding new life she finds within her.

Rather than wanting to increase radically the population of the earth, mainline Christians are tending toward urging the reduction of human births through birth control and planning. The emphasis for life here is on the careful nurturing of wanted children and the increase of justice on earth. Projected world populations approaching ten billion human beings would threaten both justice and community and are not to be encouraged. Most mainline Protestant denominations are supportive of the *Roe v. Wade* decision of 1973 and affirm that elective abortion should be available during the first two trimesters of pregnancy.[7] The decision to complete a pregnancy bears heavy responsibilities that should not be a matter of state coercion before the age of fetal viability.

In the absence of biblical prohibitions of abortion, state permission of abortion, and church communal decision making regarding the appropriateness of abortion in many cases, abortion cannot be regarded as prohibited by the Sixth Commandment. Paul Lehmann rejected the right-to-life movement as well as the woman's-right-to-abortion position. His major interlocutors on this question were Paul Ramsey and Dietrich Bonhoeffer;[8] probably his own ecclesiastical body with its many women present could have provided a better context for dialogue. After saying that there were three positions—no abortion, justifiable abortion, and the right to abortion on demand[9]—he rejected all three options. He stipulated instead that "abortion is not justifiable, but it is forgivable." He also vigorously defended the present freedom under the law of conscience as the basis for deciding the issue.[10] Rather, it would seem that this is an issue in which Christian freedom is provided and the debate and/or reasoning of the conscience is what is helpful.

In the United States, three-quarters of all legal abortions are secured by unmarried women. For more than half of those unmarried women, the abortion is in their first pregnancy. Clearly, in most of these cases legal abortion is the final means of birth control. Either their attempts at birth control failed, they neglected to use it, or they were denied the capacity to use it by their partners. About a third of all pregnancies in the United States are aborted, another 20–33 percent result in miscarriages (spontaneous abortions), and a third are completed.

The seeking of an abortion where birth control procedures were conscientiously undertaken, but failed, seems relatively straightforward. If sexuality was an act of responsible intimacy without intention of producing new life and means were used to prevent pregnancy, the technical termination of an unwanted pregnancy seems the logical solution.

Despite frequent church teachings that abortion is not to be used or regarded as a means of birth control, that is exactly what it is. Abortion is the means, the final means, of preventing live births. There are no biblical prohibitions of, or sanctions for, either birth control or abortion. The ethics of birth control and abortion are matters of church tradition, reason, and debate over the interpretation of experience. The Roman Catholic prohibitions of both birth control and abortion make a sort of sense. The church wants to encourage the growth of more human life and regards this as an imperative not subject to human control, or at least to effective control. Protestant churches, which are more subject to judgments of women than the male-dominated Catholic Church, have in the twentieth century affirmed birth control and some abortions. Even a Barthian ethicist like Jan Lockman, who strongly rejects abortion, would not make it part of the criminal code. In this debate, Protestants in the United States often defend the *Roe v. Wade* decision and, while holding various moral judgments, urge that abortion not be subject to legal prohibition until late in the pregnancy.

Starting from the imperative of love and the need of love for human selfhood, conception does not in itself produce the obligation of the development of a human person. In the absence of commitment to the full development of a human person, a woman is not obligated to bear a child any more than she is obligated to conceive because she has a sexual relationship.

Human sexuality has functions beyond the development of more human lives. Human nature under God produces spontaneous abortions or miscarriages by the millions. Human beings who do not intend to produce more human life are not obligated to produce it even if they have sexual relationships. Love accepts a great deal of human freedom, and to force a woman to carry an unwanted fetus is neither love nor justice.

The care of children requires vast commitments, and without those commitments the nurturing of a fetus to its birth as a child is not obligatory. The recognition of abortion as a means of birth control, of course, removes all doubt about the appropriateness of abortion in cases of incest and rape. Each state will, through legislative politics, decide at what point the state should exert its influence in protecting potential citizens. In the United States, the wisdom of locating this point near the beginning of the third trimester is moving in the direction of the point at which the fetus is viable to become a child without extraordinary means of care being taken.

Obviously, prevention of unwanted conception is more desirable than abortion, although technology may make this distinction less significant. The Christian community has responsibilities to prepare its people in knowledge of the better means of birth control, while providing the full interpretation of Christian responsibility in sexuality and family life.

## Euthanasia

Modern society forces the question of euthanasia, an "easy death," to the forefront of moral debate. At the time of the incorporation of the principle of "no murder" into the law, respirators, feeding tubes, antibiotics, and modern health care were unknown. Does the capacity to keep one alive require that one be kept alive? A consensus seems to be emerging in church teaching and the "living will" movement to allow people to die once they have been rigorously ascertained to be terminally ill. Roman Catholic freeing of medical personnel from the requirements of extraordinary treatment and Protestant recognition that the "cessation of life may be a relative good"[11] are moving toward a wide consensus of permission to die. In Christian thought, death does not have to be fought against heroically. If suffering is unbearable and an illness is irreversible, care, not efforts to cure, is the obligation of love. If the benefits of living are seen by a person to be outweighed by the burdens of continued suffering, society is not required to keep that person alive against her or his own wishes.

The practice of passive euthanasia obviously is easier to accept than active euthanasia. To let someone die by withholding aid that would prolong his or her life is different from participating in a practice that hastens death. The New York State Task Force on Life and the Law recommended against legalization of physician-assisted suicide in May of 1994. Somewhat more than two dozen states outlaw assisted suicide. In 1996, federal appeals courts struck down laws prohibiting physician-assisted suicide in Washington and New York States. Assisted suicide is often practiced even where it is illegal. One member of the New York panel thought that keeping physician-assisted suicide private was better than creating a broad policy legalizing the practice.[12] Although a legal line may persist between refusing medical services and all forms of assisted suicide, it is clear that in certain circumstances both may be Christian moral options. The need for relaxation of legal guidelines that keep functioning human bodies in a persistent vegetative state becomes more apparent with the realization that there are thirty-five thousand cases[13] in which the distinctively human functions have been lost. The lines between passive and active euthanasia are not always clear but often a clear distinction can be made. Treatment of a patient with a pain medication that speeds up death or at least risks shortening her or his life is acceptable if the patient is already recognizably dying. Some churches, such as the Christian Methodist Episcopal Church, are clearly opposed to active euthanasia, while others, such as the United Methodist Church, have considered the issue but have not taken an official stand.[14] The living will, which specifies that a person does not desire certain interventions at the time of dying, is recognized as helpful. The questions of active euthanasia and assisted suicide are hotly contested. It seems that rigidly protecting a dying person from death is not a Christian goal. Christians accept martyrdom and death in the service of others, and their fundamental salvation message focuses on one who overcame death by accepting it. The norms for Christian consideration in these debates are expressed in care, dignity, compassion, community, and justice. If health care is to avoid becoming the enemy, it must relax its tenacious hold on life per se and accept that death is not the enemy. In the debates over health care financing, reasonable limits on expenditures to prolong dying life must be evoked. This will mean that many of us will die sooner rather than later. The life-extending medical services purchased by those with greater wealth or insurance may often prove to be just another curse of having too much wealth. For the society as a whole, resources need to be invested in basic, preventive health care and the extension of life at the end reduced.

Francis D. Moore, M.D., now professor emeritus of surgery at Harvard University, insists that clinical as well as ethical judgment is required. One has to know that a disease or injury is terminal before hastening death. For Moore it is a practical decision: if one cannot heal, then relieve suffering. After more than half a century of practice, he shared his wisdom:

> Doctors of our generation are not newcomers to this question. Going back to my internship days, I can remember many patients in pain, sometimes in coma or delirious, with late, hopeless cancer. For many of them we wrote an order for heavy medication to be given regularly by the nurses. Morphine by the clock. We were assisting with a softer exit from this world. Nurses helped willingly. This was not talked about openly and little was written about it. It was essential, not controversial.[15]

This seems to be the trend. Prolonging suffering by moral principle seems macabre. To assist the nearly terminal patient or the "brain-dead" patient to continue to "live" on is not a worthy goal of treatment. The love of neighbor, in these cases, overrides the reluctance to allow human life to end.

Obviously, human rights groups, medical practitioners, courts, state legislators, and patients' families are all involved in the controversy over assisted death. The brief discussion of the principle of "no murder" here does not answer the question. It only suggests that the question cannot be resolved by appeals to this principle, and that it involves a social-legal decision as to how best to provide care in terminal and near-terminal cases.

Christian moral analysis of suicide, assisted suicide, and the withdrawal of extraordinary means of life support is different from the analysis of these issues by the medical profession or by legislative bodies. Christian ethics, given the injunctions not to murder and in all things to practice love, does not necessarily assume that ending a life violates an oath "to do no harm." Death is a necessary part of life, and it is surrounded ultimately by God's gracious care. Christian analysis does not have the commitment to prevent death that the medical industries have. Death is not an enemy. It is a natural part of the created order. We are finite, and no medical science can overcome finitude. Legislators worry about past horrors such as those practiced in Nazi Germany and about future precedents, as well as about voters and campaign contributions. Christian analysis is now concerned about fair laws. There have been abuses in the past and there will be more in the future, but the legislative task is to be as fair as possible now. Not many dying patients choose to hasten their death. When they do, death can be permitted and we can help. The state of Oregon, in which religious participation in the form of church attendance is relatively low, has provided for legal doctor-assisted suicide. As of the finishing of this book, only one patient has chosen to speed up death under the provisions of the law. Oregon is one of only a few places in the world where physician-assisted suicide is legal. Speculation about the nonuse of the legal procedures focuses on the nonspecificity of the legislation for doctors and nurses and on the possible reluctance of physicians or patients to expose themselves to the publicity that would attend the first use of those procedures. The provisions[16] requiring certification by two physicians that the suffering patient has six months or less to live provide a measure of security against abuse that encouraged Oregon legislators and voters to approve the law.

A recent study showed that one in five nurses of the sample had practiced euthanasia or assisted suicide. Both doctors and nurses challenged the study, which was published in the *New England Journal of Medicine* on May 23, 1996. Dr. John W. Hoyt thought the practices to be very rare, and nurse Judy Stupak thought the decision was God's. She reportedly said, "I think that's God's decision and if it's their time to go, he'll take them."[17] In this study by David A. Asch, 129 nurses reported assisting in deaths 553 times over their careers and 124 times in the last year. The requests for help in dying came from the patient 133 times, from a family member 264 times, from a nurse 60 times, from the attending physician 271 times, and from another physician 146 times.[18] In some cases the request for assistance in dying came from more than one source.

There will be abuses as we move away from considering assisted death of the terminally ill as murder to regarding it as "recognition of brain death," assisted death, or euthanasia. Certainly it would be a legalistic abuse to force the terminally ill to suffer because the medical technology for prolonging life is available. Knowledge and goodwill toward the patient are the crucial factors in preventing abuses in assisted death. God is present in life and death and in the power of being that sustains those who live or die or assist in life and death. The Christian view of death is to regard it as a necessary passage in the context of God's love. Christian concern for observation of moral principle in life cannot be permitted to override the imperative of love. The passage should be in the context of care and not prolonged in suffering.

## Capital Punishment

While there is no legislation in the Bible against suicide, biblical tradition permits capital punishment. Love does not prohibit all capital punishment. Love can produce judgments in some extreme situations that, for the good of the community, some must die. Biblical morality certainly recognizes many deaths as serving the good of the community.[19] The evaluation of specific Old Testament statutes requiring the death penalty, in light of the depths of love, modern tolerance, modern psychology, and specific teachings of Jesus, requires the abandonment of many of those statutes. The church will not ask for the death penalty in cases of adultery, homosexuality, stealing, violation of the Sabbath, crimes committed by those defeated in holy wars, or rebelliousness in children. There are many specific requirements for the death penalty in scripture and in past social practice that must be set aside. The question remains, however, whether the death penalty should be absolutely denied as a social sanction. It is very difficult, if not impossible, to apply the death penalty fairly in modern society. In American practice it is usually the poorly educated, the mentally handicapped, or those subject to racial discrimination who are executed. Most advanced industrial societies survive without the death penalty. The death penalty is irreversible for its victim, and the justice system is so unfair as to make such a punishment seem indefensible. However, public support of the enemies of society for the rest of their lives also seems unjust. Isn't there truth in the idea that one who kills with the sword shall also die by the sword? Sanctions of capital punishment for murder, armed rebellion, and treason have been levied throughout history. The reform of the criminal justice system is an ongoing process that requires more Christian energy and church resources than it receives. In death penalty cases, extreme care must be taken to protect prisoners' rights, and sufficient appeal processes must be made available to protect against errors in the system. Absolute certainty is not available to human beings in these matters, and so the standard of "beyond a reasonable doubt" must be sufficient. Christian ethics pushes for fairness in the leveling of the death penalty, but Christian ethics does not require the lifting of this sanction from every crime. Christian ethics is, of course, not the determiner of the criminal justice system; much more primitive forces—revenge, deterrence, social violation, and punishment—are at work here. But in their contribution to the debate, Christians may in good conscience hold on to the practice of exacting a life for a life in certain categories of crime, believing that sin has done so much destruction in some lives that it is no longer necessary to sustain those lives that have taken other lives or betrayed the life of the community through treason.

## Social Neglect

Both Martin Luther and John Calvin understood the Sixth Commandment to mean that we were obligated to rescue others from suffering and from threats of evil. We are, according to Luther, to learn from this commandment "that we show to everyone all kindness and love."[20] And Calvin tells us, "The Lord has bound humanity together by a certain unity; hence each one ought to concern oneself with the safety of all."[21]

Other commentators have asserted that this principle may be violated by Christians most of all through social neglect.[22] As we are implicated in racism, unjust welfare policies, and urban poverty, we are implicated in murder in our city streets. Starvation, when we have not acted to stave it off (and our national policies regarding food and aid have encouraged it), indicts us. Greed that leads to murder, like governmental policies that lead to cruel death, is in a broad reading of this commandment our responsibility. Our hands, as North Americans, are not free of innocent blood. Too much killing and too much starvation have resulted from our policies for us ever to be innocent. Prayers of confession and repentance must be radicalized in light of this commandment until our policies change.

To a degree, our national policies lead to poverty abroad. Revolts against poverty challenge the status quo. Because we were allied, for either cold war or economic reasons, with the indigenous defenders of the status quo, we protected them. Our defense of the status quo or domination of poor countries for the sake of those national elites leads to our killing of the rebels and to our training and paying for the killing of the rebels and their families. The injunction not to murder requires not only changes in military policies, but also changes in business practices. We must be certain we are doing no harm as we conduct business; otherwise, our practice may lead to murder.

The reality of social neglect and the ignoring of the harm that we do leads to the question of war. The letter of James taught us this connection nineteen centuries ago: "What causes wars, and what causes fightings among you? Is it not your passions that are at war in your members? You desire and do not have; so you kill. And you covet and cannot obtain; so you fight and wage war" (James 4:1–2 RSV).

All of the principles and consequences are interrelated. The elite in the United States increase their power and wealth to the disadvantage of the poor in countries from which we extract resources and food. The elite, acquiring resources and food cheaply from poor countries, maximize their domestic power. Consequently, the elite of the United States and the elite of the poor country can both maximize their power at the expense of their respective poor. The poor in both countries are unable to gain in relation to the elite.

The poor can and do, in many economic periods, lose even more power. In their powerlessness and squalor, they may in the presence of power and wealth become self-destructive. The neglectfulness that the Sixth Commandment rules out can inspire self-hatred or hatred of the elite. As reforms fail and hatred expressed toward the elite is repressed, self-hatred and warring on one's own poor community may result. Still, the commandment guards against murder. The only world we have is unjust, and in this world, murder is denied both to the socially aggrieved and the socially satiated.

## The Justifiable War Tradition

The commandment not to murder has been understood to prohibit war by only a small minority of Christians. Generally speaking, Christians have participated in the wars of their nation-states since the development of modern draft systems for raising large citizen armies. The feudal system enlisted Christians in the smaller armies of the premodern world. This system limited war somewhat by proclaiming times and places at which war was not to be conducted. At various times, monks and clergy were exempted from the obligation to serve in wars. On the other hand, the church encouraged crusades, the conquests of non-Christian peoples, and participated in the warring politics of feudal Europe. Both the Roman and Byzantine empires had their military policies blessed by the churches. The serious prohibition of Christians from military service was engaged in by the Christian pacifists and, in the first two centuries of the Christian era, by most of the church. The assumption of political responsibility by the church led to military participation. So the slaughter of Christians by other Christians became routine. Since Ambrose, parts of the church have tried to think about war rationally in terms of criteria for justification of war. The justifiable war as a tradition became the predominant way of critical Christian thought concerning war.

The perspective taken on the tradition of the justifiable war is crucial.[23] It is of central concern that this tradition be examined in light of an ethic of the just peace. For the Christian life, the ethic of the just peace ought to predominate. Consideration of questions regarding the justice of particular wars or justified participation in a particular war is a secondary part of any adequate Christian ethic. Even after all that it has been possible to do for peace has been undertaken, the morally sensitive Christian will be confronted by the question of whether a particular struggle involving armed forces should be entered. The justifiable war tradition itself has this requirement: for a war to be accepted, it must be a matter of last resort. We live in a world besieged by war and rumors of war, a world predisposed to war. The most peaceful nation will be confronted by the question of engaging or refusing to engage in wars in which issues vital to its well-being are involved. The Christian individual cannot escape reasoning about the morality of particular conflicts that threaten life, family, and community. Even if we were to achieve an international order that would reduce the current international anarchy, decisions about threats to that order would still have to use moral criteria about the just or unjust use of military force.

Those who are seeking the peace of God still live in a world in which war is to be expected. Some wars can be avoided, and international conflicts are often resolved without war. The twentieth century has been characterized by war, and even the most peaceful have to think about the reality of war. Those who try to achieve peace after the style of the Romans and who mix the use of force with diplomacy have to think about justifying war. Christians who want to be politically responsible, while seeking to make war less likely, must also be able to reason about each potential conflict while holding that reason within a Christian theological perspective.

The justifiable war tradition is not primarily an issue of biblical ethics. The wars of Israel are seen in the perspective of God controlling the affairs of humanity, and they seldom rise to the perception of human beings reasoning about the appropriateness of war. The hunger for peace is a major motif of biblical faith, but the role of humans acting as agents to achieve that peace or to prevent war is not often acknowledged. Jesus resisted the appeals to force and did not adopt the Zealot option of resisting Rome by force. His early followers sought to participate in God's peace, but they did not actively try to formulate state policy. Despite the blessing of the peacemakers, the avoidance of Zealotry, and the ethic of nonresistance, Jesus does not unequivocally provide advice about how his followers are to live regarding conflict between states. The historical probability is that he anticipated the end of history and God's complete victory as more imminent than the possibility of his followers succeeding to power in Rome. These earlier followers of Jesus addressed in the New Testament were a relatively separatist, sectarian movement without political power.

The first three centuries of the Christian era found Christians opposing war, although some soldiers were converted to Christianity. Disarmament was not a requirement of conversion. By the end of the second century, Christians were in the armies and many Christians were witnessing that the Christian way was that of nonviolence. From the end of the second century until the time of Constantine at the beginning of the fourth century, evidence of the Christian presence in the armies increased while the voices of the major theologians opposed Christians taking human life in war.

**Augustine of Hippo.** The situation changed with Constantine's victory over his foes. Constantine favored Christianity and used it as a civil religion to cement together the torn fabric of the empire. On his deathbed he was baptized, and in his life he turned the empire toward the faith he had adopted. Given its growing civil status, Christianity began to adjust to its imperial prerogatives. Ambrose, the spiritual father of Augustine, used the just-war teaching of Cicero to justify the Christian use of force in defensive wars. Augustine himself was to give to Christian thought the outlines of a position justifying the use of armed force. His reflections shaped Christian morals on the issue and laid the groundwork for both the Roman Catholic theory of Thomas Aquinas and in Protestantism the thought of John Calvin and Martin Luther.

Augustine (354–430) lived in an age of war and plunder, and none of his writing glorifies war. He had a great aversion to war and scorn for those who gloried in it. War originated in sin and was not to be praised. His major work, *The City of God*, elaborated the search for peace and the peace of God. Peace was the aim of all peoples, but few found it, and the peace achieved in the earthly realm was usually only an armed truce. The Roman empire's peace, even in its successful years of the past, had led to civil and social wars.

In a letter to Boniface, the Count of Africa, Augustine criticized the personal morals of Boniface and reminded him of his spiritual destiny. He instructed him to "Love the Lord thy God with all thy strength: and love thy neighbor as thyself." He reminded Boniface that in a personal conversation he had urged Boniface not to retire to a monastery, but to fulfill his earthly responsibilities. He praised his earlier work as a military commander when he had defended Africa against the invaders. He urged him, now, to secure the peace so that Africa could live in harmony. He urged on him the necessity of ordering his commanders so that the aggressors could be defeated and peace be secured. As he wrote elsewhere, he advised Boniface: "Therefore, even in waging war, cherish the spirit of a peacemaker, that, by conquering those whom you attack, you may lead them back to the advantage of peace; for our Lord says: 'Blessed are the peacemakers; for they shall be called the children of God.'"[24] The urgings of Augustine on his friend to stem the "African barbarians" did not bring an end to the wars, or peace to Africa. Shortly after Augustine's death, his own city of Hippo was devastated. His testimony to Boniface reflects the insight of Augustine that wars in defense of people and the order of the state could be morally defended.

The goal of any justifiable war is still peace. Peace is the great goal of humanity, and the inner desire to achieve peace must be the aim of any war. This is the appropriate presupposition for all Christian thinking about war. Peace, not just a Roman peace or a truce, reflecting the deep Old Testament longing for fullness of life and the New Testament sense of peace as a blessing, is the goal. Peace as harmony among people is the theme of Augustine's great philosophy of history in *The City of God*, and it points to a fullness of the meaning of peace similar to the definition of justice in Plato's *Republic*.

A war, to be rightly engaged in, must vindicate justice. This is not to imply perfection in history, but certainly it excludes wars of selfish conquest or illegal wars. In Augustine's thought, it is close to the first requirement that the intention be peace. It must accomplish peace or harmony among people rather than contribute to disharmony, discord, and further wars.

The disposition of those engaged in the war must be love. Augustine's Neoplatonism could permit him to devalue the body and be fairly casual about the possibility of loving the one whom one slays. Yet the requirement of love stands as a testimony against the hatred that usually accompanies war. It distinguishes justifiable wars from fanatical crusades in which love of the enemy is rejected. The love ethic that dominates Augustine's thought leads him in the direction of responsibility for those who cannot protect themselves. Boniface would have retired from public life, but in this world Christians are obligated to fulfill their roles as public citizens to protect order—even though disorder is contained within the public institutions. Love is also obligatory toward those one opposes in war.

It is this requirement to protect the innocent through the agencies of public order that underlies the further requirements of a justified war. Such a war must be carried out by those responsible for public order. Love is expressed through the ambiguous institutions of the state as they properly fulfill their responsibility to protect the citizens. Only much later in Christian history, after ideas of the sovereignty of the people had been accepted, could the idea of a justified war be transmuted into a justified revolution.

Roland H. Bainton, in drawing on the studies of Gustave Combes, understands Augustine to require also that the conduct of war be subject to moral rules.[25] The rules were drawn from classical sources and prohibited massacre, looting of temples, and atrocities, and required that dealing with the enemy be honest. Augustine saw the very barbarians who were invading Rome as demonstrating the influence of Christianity in their attempts to humanize war.

For Augustine, Christians would participate in war only in their official capacities in government or in the army. The private citizen had no right to take the sword even in self-defense. Clergy and monks, because of their religious vocations, were excluded from war. The monks were to seek perfection, and their obligations forbade participation in war as well as marriage and the owning of property.

Augustine's ethic clearly excluded most wars from the recognition of justified warfare. War was a horrible evil, and the Christian was more to be praised for avoiding war through negotiation than for engaging in a war—even if it *was* justifiable.[26] Basically, only wars of defense or wars waged to right objective wrongs could be justified. Even when war was justified, the Christian could engage in it only with a sorrowful mind.

Augustine's position, in summary, was that of an ethic of love applied to difficult choices in a sinful, warring world. He used insights from scripture, classical philosophy, and the history of the world, but he transformed these insights through the ethic of love in order to promote peace. The openness to some participation in war, combined, however, with political responsibility, could lead others less rigorous in their commitments to peace to rationalize the participation in wars that Augustine would have regarded as unjustified.

Augustine's influence continued in church circles, but the influence of his just-war tradition was minimal.[27] Popes used his political ideas in their own way, and Byzantium, the major center of Christian civilization, was relatively free of Augustine's influence. The church tried to restrain war through the truce of God and the peace of God. Gradually, some merging of the spirit of the conquerors and the teaching of the church emerged in the rules of chivalry. The wars of the Crusades were of a spirit quite contrary to the just-war tradition, and the crusading religious war emerged as a third option in the Christian ethic of war.

In the twelfth century, Roman law was revived by Gratian's canon law. Augustine was the major source on the ethics of war in Gratian's codification of law, the *Decretum*. James T. Johnson locates the origin of the medieval theory of just war with Gratian and his successors in canon law.[28]

**Thomas Aquinas.** Augustine had written at a time of the destruction of civilization. Thomas Aquinas (1225–1274) wrote at a time of the rebuilding of civilization. He is portrayed as calm, with a book in his hands. The Crusades were not yet finished; religious extremism, papal schism, and the Black Death were in the future. Political institutions, law, universities, cathedrals, and business were being developed. It was a mediating time, and the great work of Aquinas was to mediate the newly discovered Aristotelian philosophy into Augustinian theology.

Aquinas did not criticize the Crusades; in fact, inasmuch as they had been waged to defend the rights of Christians in pagan lands, he approved of them. His own noble family, the Aquino, suffered under war. He himself chose the contemplative life and did not become, in his writing, a party to the struggles of his day. He turned down the proffered archbishopric of Naples, which his family wanted for him, and continued his teaching and writing.

Aquinas's writing on war is brief. He draws on Augustine to support the conclusions about war drawn from natural law. The natural law is the inclination to good, which corresponds to human rational nature. His teaching on justifiable war is in his most sustained treatise on political philosophy within the *Summa Theologica*. The natural law participates in the eternal law of God's mind; it is the way rational creatures reflect God's law.

Thomas presupposed some unity in Western Europe, even though Christian Spain was fighting to drive out the Muslims, internal wars among Christian princes continued, and neither the emperor nor the pope could effectively govern. City-states were emerging, and in England and France the foundations of the nation-state were slowly taking shape. The empire was beginning to come undone, but still there was sufficient unity to articulate a universal ethic based on rational principles. Aquinas's thought still undergirds Roman Catholic thought on war and is foundational to the pastoral letter of the U.S. bishops. Protestant theologians used his thought to reinforce their rejection of American participation in the Vietnam War. Aquinas listed the principles in a systematic way, but such a listing cannot obscure his own sense of a universe full of people conjoined to both evil and good. Through the agency of ordered life, the good in humanity could order and contain the evil, thus expressing more fully God's intention. Part of the good ordering of the human community was the need to defend the common good against assaults by the enemy, even by resorting to war.

In the *Summa Theologica*, Thomas put his views succinctly:

1. The war must be declared by the competent ruler who has the duty to defend the state.
2. There must be a just cause for the war. (He quotes from Augustine to the point that the war is to correct a wrong.)
3. There must be "a right intention on the part of the belligerents." The desire to hurt, the thirst for power, the cruel vendetta are all condemned.[29]

This thought of Aquinas has been expanded in various ways by other moral theorists. Joseph C. McKenna has expounded Roman Catholic just-war thought in seven principles:

1. Legitimate authority declares and executes the war.
2. The injury that the war is intended to prevent must be a real injury (not a fiction).
3. The seriousness of the injury to be prevented must be proportionate to the destructiveness of the war.
4. There must be a reasonable hope of success. (McKenna: "Defensive war may be hopeless, but offensive war must contain elements of success.") Pope Pius XII ruled out offensive war as an instrument of policy. No movement across boundaries can be justified.
5. War must be engaged in only as a last resort.
6. The intention of entering into the war must be just.
7. The measures used in conducting war must be defensible. Preservation of noncombatants has always been a factor in the question of a just war.[30]

**John Calvin.** John Calvin (1509–1564) continued the Augustinian tradition. In his exposition of the Sixth Commandment, "You shall not kill," killing means murder. He deepens the commandment to exclude hatred. The neighbor is to be held sacred. "If you wish or plan anything contrary to the safety of a neighbor, you are considered guilty of murder." Intent to do harm is condemned—even murder of the heart is forbidden—for God looks on one's thoughts as well as one's actions. However, this strong teaching also encourages responsibility: "We are accordingly commanded, if we find anything of use to us in saving our neighbors' lives, faithfully to employ it; if there is anything that makes for their peace, to see to it; if anything harmful, to ward it off; if they are in any danger, to lend a helping hand."[31]

This responsibility to prevent harm means that the magistrates must defend their people. The responsibilities of the rulers to punish wrongdoers for the public's protection extended to the ruler's responsibility to protect their territory from invasion. Calvin's reference to the rule of natural justice is to defensive war *only*. He believed that the Old Testament declared such defensive wars to be lawful and that the New Testament contained no rules against the lawfulness of such wars for Christians. He urged all the rulers to be very cautious in regard to war. All other means should be tried first. Following Plato, he argued that the object of war must be peace.[32] On this right of defensive war followed the appropriateness of garrisons, alliances, and the possession of civil munitions—that is, the means to defend one's territory. The alliances he mentions as appropriate are also defensive in character. The needs of Geneva, a small city-state, were well served by the factors Calvin mentioned. His ministry would include the strengthening of the city's defenses and defensive alliances.

**Application to Our Time.** Obviously, the defense of the American empire is a long way from the defense of Geneva. The Presbyterian Church, however, as recently as 1969, advocated the just-war tradition as a way of thinking about issues of Christian participation in war. The tradition was affirmed as a way for individuals to think about war and to decide on their individual participation or refusal to participate. The General Assembly quoted from a Presbyterian ethicist's book, affirming six principles as representative criteria:

1. All other means to the morally just solution of a conflict must be exhausted before resort to arms can be regarded as legitimate.
2. War can be just only if employed to defend a stable order or morally preferable cause against threats of destruction or the rise of injustice.
3. Such a war must be carried out with the right attitudes.
4. A just war must be explicitly declared by a legitimate authority.
5. A just war may be conducted only by military means that promise a reasonable attainment of the moral and political objectives being sought.
6. The just-war theory has also entailed selective immunity for certain parts of the population, particularly for noncombatants.[33]

Such guidelines, whether regarded as rational reflection on the natural order as Augustine taught, or as principles of a natural law as Aquinas thought, or as a distillation of the moral tradition of the Western world, are to be used as we consider just war.

These guidelines do permit limited uses of military force in defensive wars. They clearly prohibit massive bombing of population centers as exercised in World War II and the Vietnam War. They rule out wars of aggression and wars to gain political influence over other countries or for political advantage. They can, if amended, be used to justify some wars of revolution against governments that oppress their people. For Christians who regard the defense of the innocent from loss of their lives or liberties as an action to be taken sorrowfully out of responsibility, they provide a means of moral reasoning.

These criteria clearly regard as illegitimate any wars that are conducted for selfish national interest calculations. Most wars that characterize our warring planet should be regarded as immoral by Christians, using these criteria. Weapons of mass destruction, whether biological, chemical, or nuclear, are clearly unable to be used under the absolute prohibition of protecting the lives of noncombatants. These weapons cannot be limited in their destruction to legitimate military targets except in a few highly unlikely scenarios. The targeting of these weapons on available military installations, at the present time, involves the intention to murder millions of citizens—including millions of children and other noncombatants. Such weapons mean that the war cannot be a responsible act of self-protection. The available evidence regarding nuclear war points to unacceptable levels of ecological destruction and possibly the end of human history.

Ethics based on Christian realism permits limited use of deadly force by police officers defending themselves and others in society. It does not permit police officers to destroy an apartment house full of people to stop the illegal activity of a criminal. The analogy applies to war: some use of deadly force by the appropriate officers of a state is permitted, but Christian ethics does not permit the destruction of an enemy nation's people, even in the defense of others.

The Christian ethic is not only an ethic of means and ends, it is also an ethic of intention. Jesus was concerned about the immortality of the person's mind, as well as the immorality of the person's actions. It is immoral to intend to do evil. Therefore, we cannot intend to destroy a nation's children, even if that nation attacks ours. We cannot morally tolerate a policy that threatens the children of a rival power. Deterrence fails not because it may not work, but because it is itself an evil intention. Thus, under the conditions of some modern wars, Christians arguing over the ethics of responsible love in just-war reasoning will be led to nuclear pacifism. When they focus on the intention of deterrent policy, which will under certain conditions destroy the other nation's people, they will reject it. To reject the deterrence of nuclear holocaust is not the same as rejecting deterrence by means of legitimate deployment of armed forces. The churches need to make their moral judgments clear.

**The Catholic Bishops.** The pastoral letter of the U.S. bishops on war and peace, "The Challenge of Peace: God's Promise and Our Response," which used just-war criteria, arrived at a slightly different position. The bishops were led to "a strictly conditional moral acceptance of nuclear deterrence" and stated that they could not "consider it adequate as a long term basis for peace." They then offered several suggestions for moving beyond deterrence. They also said that they could not approve of every weapons system or policy designed to strengthen deterrence. The bishops would not reconcile just-war criteria with approval of the present system of deterrence or with the plans for installing the Strategic Defense Initiative system to defend land-based missiles. The same moral arguments render morally unacceptable the development of Russian, Chinese, French, and British arsenals of mass destruction. The intention of nuclear war is wrong—even if it is a response to the failure of deterrence. The bishops' willingness to reconsider their position points toward the weakness of their moral acceptance of nuclear deterrence.

The French bishops' meeting at Lourdes on November 8, 1983, issued a statement titled "Winning Peace." It is a rigorous, imaginative statement by the bishops of a country with its own nuclear deterrent. The bishops admit that their deterrent, wherein the strong are deterred by the weak, is an anti-city strategy. Still, they insist that the threat of using nuclear weapons must not be treated morally the same as the actual use of such weapons. "Threat is not use." With the German bishops, they argue that "charity cannot replace right." They recognize two evils: capitulation and counterthreat. They think that counterthreat is morally acceptable only if it is to deter a potential aggressor and not for strategic advantage. Furthermore it must meet certain conditions:

- Overarmament is avoided: deterrence is attained the moment the formulated threat renders aggression by a third party senseless.
- Every precaution is taken to avoid "an error" or the intervention of a demented person, a terrorist, etc.
- The nation taking the risk of nuclear deterrence adheres to a constructive policy in favor of peace.[34]

The French bishops' statement failed logically because they saw but two options: capitulation and counterthreat. They were led by the position of their church and government to lend grudging support to counterthreat and to distinguish threat from use. The willingness to use force, however, is necessary to any threat, and one cannot intend to do evil. There were other options: diplomacy, negotiation, and the building of mutual interdependence between Russia and Europe were the most obvious examples. The bishops wanted diplomacy and negotiation; firm church opposition to the intent to use these weapons would encourage the nations to act reasonably.

**The United Methodist Bishops, 1986.** The Council of Bishops of the United Methodist Church in 1986 affirmed the continuing relevance of both the pacifist and just-war traditions. They were careful to set their study of the just-war tradition within the confines of recommended principles for a just peace. They respectfully noted that the Catholic bishops' pastoral letter of 1983 and the General Convention of the Episcopal Church of 1982 had both affirmed a policy of nuclear deterrence with qualifications. Their own finding was that nuclear deterrence as well as any use of nuclear weapons was morally untenable. Their analysis led them to affirm the just-war tradition and to state, "A clear and unconditioned *No*, to nuclear war and to any use of nuclear weapons."[35] Within the spectrum developed in the paper of possible positions on the morality of war, the bishops affirmed a nuclear pacifist position of no nuclear deterrence or use. This action by the leadership of the second-largest Protestant denomination was significant. It encouraged other denominations to push the increasing moral rejection of nuclear weapons. At a time when government policy was moving toward preparation to fight a nuclear war and justifying this preparation as strengthening a deterrent, church thinking, represented by the United Methodist bishops, rejected nuclear deterrence itself.

The just-war criteria, which are ways of thinking about permissible Christian use of violence for defense, are helpful guidelines for many of the conflicts that take place in the modern world. Counterterrorist policies, for example, need to be regulated by the just-war tradition's insistence on both just cause and just means. The modern weapons of mass destruction fall outside the permissible use of violence by Christians. Biological and chemical weapons carry inherently within themselves grave risks to noncombatant populations, which just-war thinking protects. Nuclear weapons have taken on the characteristics of suicide for the human race. Jonathan Schell's *The Fate of the Earth* summarizes and synthesizes the scientific evidence that nuclear exchanges among the nuclear powers could destroy all human life. The research reported by Carl Sagan asserted the high probability that even a controlled nuclear war of five hundred to two thousand explosions of strategic warheads would create a catastrophe threatening to destroy humanity.[36] Sagan referred to his group's findings by way of the science fiction terminology of the doomsday machine. We have created, unrestrained by just-war criteria, means of war that, if used, would threaten to kill us all. Some of the authors of the 1983 study made popular by Sagan moderated their claims in 1986 on the basis of new calculations. In particular, they tended to project a smaller temperature change resulting from a limited nuclear exchange, but the stressed dangers to biological systems remained as great as ever.[37]

Obviously, we know it is wrong to intend actions that threaten all of humanity. This conclusion can be reached without the just-war tradition. No Christian ethics can rightly argue for nuclear war. Christian ethics must also consider the intent of our planning. We must cherish the neighbor as made in the image of God and in our own flesh. As Calvin said, "He who has merely refrained from shedding blood has not therefore avoided the crime of murder. If you perpetrate anything by deed, if you plot anything by attempt, if you wish or plan anything contrary to the safety of a neighbor, you are considered guilty of murder."[38]

The United Church of Christ went further in opposing nuclear war than the other denominations in the 1980s. It had not been a pacifist denomination. Much of its theological view had been associated with the Christian realism of Reinhold Niebuhr and John C. Bennett. But gradually, as just-war criteria were either criticized or used in a way that showed deterrence by weapons of mass destruction to be immoral, the need for a change in church teaching was discerned. The change was announced by the General Synod XV in 1986. The United Church of Christ dedicated itself "in opposition to the institution of war." Its self-affirmation as a just-peace church in recognizing "the interrelation of friendship, justice, and common security from violence"[39] required it to make broad commitments. Support was pledged for resistance to militarism, peace education, peace centers, political action, and spiritual development. A new theology of just peace was put in place.[40] These developments of the 1980s were a foreshadowing of the ecumenical developments of the 1990s described in the concluding chapter.

Christian ethics, when it permits the killing of another human being, does so only under highly restricted conditions. Wars of defense and wars of revolution may occasionally meet these restrictions; nuclear war cannot. We have the just-war tradition and its insight in terms of what we are sometimes permitted to do to protect our neighbor. This tradition regarding weapons of mass destruction is clear: they are morally intolerable. If a government over a long period of time is threatening the survival of humanity on the planet, it begins to lose its legitimacy. Governments are constituted to restrain sin, to promote order, and to secure life and liberty for their people. In promoting the conditions of order and tolerable life, the quest for peace becomes a goal. The safety and welfare of all require an ethic of just peacemaking beyond that of the justifiable war.

## THE SEVENTH COMMANDMENT

The commandment "You shall not commit adultery" is placed exactly between "You shall not murder" and "You shall not steal." It protects the blood line of the man from being adulterated by prohibiting another's intercourse with the wife or the betrothed. Its relevance today in a culture of birth control and the nonpossession of women by men is debatable. Once mutual happiness as a goal and nonprocreative sexual intercourse are accepted, the foundations of the Seventh Commandment are weakened or at least shifted. Honesty requires that it be recognized that the original context of this moral prohibition has been altered. If the principle is to be defended, it will need to be defended on grounds other than male possession of women and danger to the inheritance line.

It is necessary to note the seriousness of the violation of the Seventh Commandment. In the Old Testament, adultery was punishable by death by stoning for both the violating man and the violating woman. In the early church, many theologians and communities of faith regarded adultery as one of three unforgivable sins, along with murder and idolatry. In its violation of covenant between two members of the Christian community or the Hebrew community, adultery challenged covenant or the legitimation of community itself and was treated as a serious threat. Recent commentators[41] on the Seventh Commandment have regarded it as a principle protecting marriage and family. Although adultery and divorce are not synonymous, those reflecting on the commandment often treat these issues together. This is a reasonable conflation of issues, because adultery is certainly related to divorce and to the resultant poverty of the less fortunate spouse and suffering of the children. Hebrew society, like all other societies, developed its own sexual regulations and related its religious sanctions to its taboos. Hebrew society, especially as reflected in the later writings in Deuteronomy and Leviticus, tightened up the prohibitions of this commandment considerably beyond its simple stark prohibition in the decalogue. The Christian church in its ascetic Hellenization took the ethic even further to where marriage itself was relegated to a status beneath celibacy.

Jesus' own teaching on adultery seems to represent a rigorous balance between ancient Hebrew harshness and Christian-Greek asceticism. No one should seriously argue that Jesus regarded adultery as an unforgivable sin, but neither should we argue that he took it lightly. When confronted by the woman caught in adultery, he protected her and reminded her accusers of their own failings. He named her "indiscretion" sin and ordered her to do it no more.

At another level, Jesus reminded us that our lustful intentions lead to wrong acts and that adultery has its origins in ourselves before it is expressed in violation of marriage covenants. Certainly he was right; all of us are guilty in our hearts, and in our generation, the majority of us are guilty in our actions. Our culture, in its advertising, literature, films, plays, and music, encourages us to commit adultery first in our imagination and then with the spouses of others. Our lack of modesty in clothing, beachwear, athletic wear, and advertising encourages a self-indulgent culture tempted to find expression overriding simple moral guidelines rooted in the ambiguous heritage of past guidelines regarding adultery. The origins of the cultural shift toward promiscuity are rooted in the decisions of Hollywood over a generation that, under the protection of the First Amendment, glorified promiscuous sexuality and neglected its consequences. The poor whose children cannot afford divorce or even the price of a movie have been taught to idolize and follow the promiscuous lives of the stars. The culture is so dominant, from the magazines displaying pornography at the checkout counters in grocery stores to the sexual content in many television programs, that personal moral resistance to such a culture is unlikely. It seems to me that this culture's breakdown of the taboos against adultery began in the films and spread to the rest of the culture. Adulterous presidents and religious leaders have also contributed to breaking down the moral bulwarks against violation of family standards.

Adultery is the enemy of "permanence, commitment, and fidelity," which Paulist Father Michael Hunt, Catholic chaplain at Tufts University, reports are the qualities people want.[42] Adultery, based in part in covetousness, leads to lying to hide the violation and participates in stealing from the violated families. The grounds for the principle of rejecting adultery are not what they were in Sinai, and obviously neither are the penalties, but the health of relationships, families, and society is still sufficient reason for rejecting adultery. Its rejection by the church in North American society, however, is a countercultural move. The culture is proadultery, and the church's ethic is counter to that cultural pressure. The church has its own sexual ethical problems. Many Catholics feel that their church has been too lenient with sexual offenders among the priesthood, and two-thirds of all Catholics reject their church's denunciation of birth control.[43] The scandals among TV evangelists have shown their moral zealousness to be hypocritical. Violations of the norm against adultery have hurt the legacies of major Protestant theologians. Despite all of this and more, there are sufficient grounds for reinforcing this principle of traditional Christian morality.

The strong affirmation of one principle is not a full sexual ethic. The principle of no adultery has implications and consequences for other norms and for society, but it does not answer the questions. However, it is sufficient to affirm a moral line in this discussion. Proponents of sexual ethics based on theories of human relationships may regard such a principled ethic as too rigid. The British Council of Churches Working Group report, *God's Yes to Sexuality*,[44] cannot affirm the principle as it deals with many relativities in different forms of relationships. Although the report emphasizes the strains on modern marriages, its refusal to state principles leaves the emphasis on moral relativity and personal choice. It seems wiser to affirm the rejection of adultery than to affirm the report's ambiguity as in its statement: "Ideas of fidelity in marriage built around sexual faithfulness alone seem too narrow a concept, particularly for our time."[45]

Situation ethics has a reputation for emphasizing the ethic of love and de-emphasizing other ethical principles. The ethics of this book is love with the recognition that love needs expression in principles. It does not disagree with the situationalist emphasis on context, although it affirms two contexts: (1) the context of the Christian church, which formulates moral principles, forms character, teaches the tradition, and models Christian life in the world; and (2) the context of the Christian in the world remaining loyal to God's will for the world. The context of the Christian in the world is not separate from the context of the church in the world. So the ethic of Joseph Fletcher's *Situation Ethics*[46] seems thin and often weak in its discussion of context. Neither the situation nor the Christian ethic seems to be understood.

Fletcher presents four cases to test his ethical method in *Situation Ethics*. The one in which he was most personally involved is very telling. He met a Christian woman on an airplane who was considering cooperating with a defense intelligence agency by luring a married Soviet spy into a sexual liaison so that the married man could be blackmailed. She had resisted the intelligence agency's pushing, but the agency had appealed to her patriotism. Fletcher said that he discussed the issue with her as one of "patriotic prostitution and personal integrity."[47] Fletcher does not resolve this case, but suggests that it is to be tested by love and knowledge of the situation. The ethic of the ultimate imperative sees this case differently. The recruiter for the agency, shrouded in secrecy, is an accomplished liar whom the woman cannot trust. He is requesting that she endanger herself by lying and committing adultery for an undesignated goal of the agent, for his sector of the agency, or for a perceived national interest based on either a wise or an unwise decision by a group of male decision makers. Fletcher perceives an ethical dilemma here that is to be resolved by love. On the other hand, as a Christian, this woman already has an ethics that prohibits lying and adultery. To lay aside these principles for an opportunity handed her by spies is potentially to deny who she is. There really is no moral dilemma here, given an adequate Christian ethics. Furthermore, the extent to which an intelligence agency is founded in deception and secrecy, and in this case was recommending adultery, reveals quickly that its interests should not be served. This case is too thin in its treatment of the reality of defense intelligence agencies. The three other cases Fletcher presents also have to do with people involved in systems of evil.[48] In all cases, ethics cannot be derived from evil situations, and the situations require much more analysis. A later section of this chapter shows the consequences of this ultimate imperative expressed in principles for the operation of one defense intelligence agency, the Central Intelligence Agency.

Marriage vows are not quaint, although they are violated more often than not. The affirmation of the principle of no adultery in a modern meaning of faithful sexual mutuality can undergird marriage in a stressful age.

## THE EIGHTH COMMANDMENT

The simple Eighth Commandment has been subject to extreme scrutiny over the object of "You shall not steal." Is all stealing prohibited, or is the object, as A. Alt suggested in 1949, a person? Does this commandment cover only kidnapping, or all theft? Alt and many who followed him argued that since many other forms of stealing are covered by the prohibition of coveting in the final commandment, this prohibition is the protection of the Hebrew man.

Those following Alt would see the selling of Joseph into slavery as the crime here prohibited. David Noel Freedman[49] thinks the archetypical violation of this commandment is Achan's appropriation of sacred booty in the book of Joshua. Childs[50] views the interpretations as possibly revealing a development from an original prohibition of kidnapping to a later, more general prohibition of stealing in our canon. Yet he recognizes that such a development is not yet proven. Harrelson,[51] regarding the narrowing of the original meaning to kidnapping as "unlikely," sees the Eighth Commandment "as a direct and general prohibition of theft."

Despite Lochman's beautiful argument that commandments six through ten guard (6) life, (7) marriage, (8) freedom, (9) honor, and (10) property, it still seems best to stay with the traditional interpretation that the prohibition of stealing protects all that one rightfully has from the ravages of others, including, of course, protection of oneself from robbery or kidnapping. Even Lochman, while holding to Alt's thesis, could not help but expand his chapter to protect possessions beyond the freedom of the self.

This traditional reading does not exclude kidnapping or enslavement from our contemporary reading of the commandment as a principle of love. Too few of our Hebrew or Christian predecessors have been able to protect humanity from being stolen and denied selfhood. While not explicitly naming this commandment, John Wesley used it. In his famous tract against the slave trade, he included all who benefited from it as guilty of "manstealing." For him, liberty was God-given and all who denied it violated the revealed law of God.[52] His arguments against slavery were thorough, utilizing human rights language as well as the biblical injunctions against murder and 1 Timothy 1:10 against kidnappers. He plainly stated that slaveholding was from greed and that condemnation awaited all who participated in slaveholding and its economy. His bold speech and writings condemning slavery revealed the social dimensions of his ethic and its grounding in his own evangelical relations with black slaves. Beyond the single cause, he saw the economic dislocation of ending slavery and advocated that fundamental societal reform. Throughout church history, though, Christians who said "You shall not steal" as prohibiting the evil of slavery were few. Lochman also saw the prohibition against stealing people as a denial of terrorist kidnapping. But in its broader meaning, the principle of not taking what is not one's own has thorough consequences. The reformers John Calvin and Martin Luther both used the Eighth Commandment forcefully. For Luther, stealing was rampant. He wrote: "In short, thievery is a universal art, the largest guild on earth. Viewing the world in all its vocations, it is a universal den of thieves."[53]

In Luther we find the principle that in business the Christian should not do harm to others. Taking unfair advantage through the misuse of power for one's own gain was considered stealing and was prohibited. John Calvin stressed the good that could be advanced by business and financial dealings more than Luther, but he regarded business that took goods by force or deceit as stealing. Flatterers may be guilty of stealing through their persuasive powers. Snatching the goods of others, even by "seemingly legal means," is stealing. Both the servant and the master are subject to trying to steal from the other. The fulfillment of the commandment meant to Calvin respecting the rights, goods, and needs of others and fulfilling the many social obligations we have to others. He concluded his comment: "Moreover, our mind must always have regard for the Lawgiver, that we may know that this rule was established for our hearts as well as for our hands, in order that men may strive to protect and promote the well-being and interests of others."[54]

Following Luther's sense of the widespread violation of this principle and Calvin's awareness that it was for our hearts to express God's compassion for the world, we can express it as a principle of Christian ethics to forbid stealing. Such an expression includes Coffin's judgment that "wealth and poverty are, to be sure, relative terms, and there will always be richer and poorer people; but no Christian can assent to the notion that earth is so constituted that many must necessarily be nearly starving."[55]

So where wealth was accrued through violence and exploitation, as in the great wealth piled up through exploited labor, it was stealing and was prohibited by God. This was true of most of the great family fortunes built on the suffering of slaves, free labor, and the exploitation of populations in colonized nations. Of course, those exploited also stole, but those with power enforced the system. The guilt associated with stealing is more than a nagging feeling. Those who benefit more from misappropriation of the property and lives of others are more guilty and have more to repatriate than those who steal a little. Morally speaking, the taking of surplus food for the purpose of feeding the hungry is not stealing. Rather, it is an imperative that love demands. The law may exact punishment, but morally one is obligated to feed and care for those in one's responsibility and for others as one is able. Much of the taking of food by the world's hungry is justified, as is their taking of land and shelter from those who have a surplus. But those who hoard the surplus are guilty, and often massively guilty, of protecting by violence that for which they have no real need. It may be that even the poor accrue some guilt when they take what they need, but if this is so it is a very small sin. The use of violence and deceit by the wealthy to obtain and keep much more than they need is one of the world's great and most grievous sins.

Christian faith does not insist that all people are equal in ability or that all need exactly the same resources to fulfill themselves before God. However, it does not say that before God people are radically unequal and that the rewards of one's work should be disproportionate to the needs of others. No one needs what the American wealthy have or what the elites of other nationalities control. No one should have as little as the failures of American society receive or the hungry of the world obtain. The Eighth Commandment certainly contains the message that the sixteenth-century reformers found there—that Christians are not to exploit others by their business practices or the economic system.

No matter how scrupulous one is, if a corporate structure or a governmental policy assists some employees of a firm in becoming rich while others are kept poor, stealing has occurred. A system can steal systemically even while one operates according to the rules. This happened, for example, for a hundred years in Pittsburgh until the steel industry collapsed under the weight of generations of industrial acrimony. Of course, it happened in the steel industries and other industries in alternative economic systems as well.

There is also the stealing of natural resources from a country. Extractive industries often condone the taking of resources from a country cheaply while impoverishing the exploited region. Rain forest depletion around the world is a prime example of natural resources being cheaply extracted while the indigenous population is exploited, as in the Amazon region or the U.S. Pacific Northwest,[56] and the practice of stealing natural resources with the cooperation of governmental agencies is widely practiced. As in the case of the exploitation of labor, the exploitation of resources has produced huge family fortunes and the resultant corrupting political influence. In this perspective, the provision of adequate living through the development of resources so that the maximum number of efficient jobs are developed is a good, but the maximizing of a few huge incomes to the neglect of the population through the use of natural resources is stealing from public wealth. The ambitions inspired by laissez-faire must be curtailed by the provision for the common good and the limiting of stealing.

Wealth may be misappropriated through the taking of land, as well as the organization of labor or control of natural resources. Most borders in the world have been established through the use of force or the threat of force. The earth is full of the bones of predecessor peoples who were vanquished in the struggle for this land. In areas like New Guinea and Brazil, civilized forces are now taking the land from the native populations. In the United States, the process was completed almost one hundred years ago. In Asia, Africa, and Europe, one population continues to displace and destroy others. Human history is so bloody that moral judgments on this most important issue are difficult.

In my own experience, a Dakota Sioux once asked me where I grew up. When I responded that my childhood home was in Dakota City, Iowa, he commented that "it was a beautiful country." Of course, the Sac and Fox tribes had been there as well. A massacre of Sioux by a settler had left the perpetrator fleeing the country, and my family eventually appropriated his log house fifteen miles from where I was born four generations later. Was the land ours? We paid for it and claimed it as land granted by the president for service in the War of 1812. We farmed it. But native Americans had lived from it for generations. They had fought each other for it. Because of economic and agricultural changes, with my mother's death there was no one in the county with our name, though five generations of Stones are buried in the soil.

The struggle for land goes on. Ultimately, right titles to land were decided by the most recent victors. Often those decisions were grounded in sin. Probably the best we can do regarding land is to be sure our own acquisition of it was fair, support reparations to displaced peoples, honor recent boundaries, limit our own acquisition of land, support redistribution of the world's land to the poor who will farm it, and struggle against those who would replace the few tribal peoples who still lay claim to the land they have inhabited for significant periods of time. If land acquisition is supported by deception, murder, and cheating, it is wrong and the land is stolen. Such practices are characteristic of land acquisition and the displacement of peoples throughout the world. Most of the violence and repression of indigenous peoples is rooted in the seizing of their land.[57] The recognition that such land acquisition is stealing and morally wrong would be the beginning of wisdom.

Terry Anderson concludes his profound work on Christian ethics by referring to the difficult way we walk between pride, which pretends to know all moral truth, and sloth, which has abandoned the search for righteous living.[58] Life in the church, surrounded by grace, community, guidance, and dialogue about moral issues, provides an alternative. Because the world political economy is founded on conquest that is stealing and violence, we walk humbly as we seek to avoid stealing. Finally, we live by forgiveness, the forgiveness of God and our forgiveness of those who have stolen from us.

## THE NINTH COMMANDMENT

The Ninth Commandment is a principle within the legal language. It is a principle against giving false witness in court. The commandments themselves do not pronounce a prohibition against lying. Most of the expert Old

Testament commentators[59] recognize in "You shall not bear false witness against your neighbor" a limited injunction applying to legal proceedings. Other commentators, particularly in popular books, expand this commandment to include a general discussion of lying. Calvin and Luther both extend it to include the telling of any lie. Their interpretation has had wide influence in Protestantism. There is respect for truth in the Old Testament, but the most severe denunciations for not telling the truth are associated with the courts. It is a little surprising how many of the texts seized on by commentators to stress truth-telling relate explicitly to courts. Even Zechariah, which endorses truth, is related to the courts: "Speak the truth to one another, render in your gates judgments that are true and make for peace, do not devise evil in your hearts against one another, and love no false oath; for all these are things that I hate, says the Lord" (Zech. 8:16–17).

Too many discussions of the Ninth Commandment have obscured its public function and its reinforcements of justice in the courts. Lying, as such, seems not to have been universally condemned in the Hebrew Scriptures, as shown by the examples of Shiprah and Puah, the Hebrew midwives, deceiving Pharaoh, or Laban deceiving Jacob, or Jacob deceiving Esau, or Rahab deceiving the authorities.

The widespread practice of lying in the courts is repeatedly denounced and here brought within the central norms of Israel. Immanuel Kant's unwillingness to sanction a lie even to protect the innocent from unjust authorities was not the Old Testament morality, as the story of Rahab sheltering the spies witnesses to the opposite conclusion.

The wisdom in the commentators' extension of the principle to exclude false testimony against anyone in the public arena is closely related to the specific norm. False public denunciation can destroy accused parties before they receive a trial, or it can, by ruining their reputation, destroy them without a trial. It is still necessary to regard one crime as perjury and the other as libel.

The courts need to be reinforced by morality, which will reduce the lying and the perjury. Rules of evidence and proper procedure must be so guarded because misrepresentation is so widespread. The guilty plead not guilty and devise cases to cover their lies until overwhelming argument or a negotiated deal finally reveals their guilt. The determined holding on to a lie can often lead to a reduced sentence by virtue of a plea bargain to a less serious offense. At the same time, police are sometimes guilty of shaping their testimony to produce convictions even when they have to bear false witness.

At the conviction of Officer John Rossi in New York City for perjury in falsifying the arrest record, a comment was made that such practices are widespread. "According to officials with the Legal Aid Society, it is a practice that goes on frequently and mostly without sanction in the city's criminal justice system. . . . The police regularly invent witnesses, tailor their testimony to meet constitutional objections, and alter arrest records."[60] False testimony by both defense and prosecution tears at the court system, and as crime and corruption mount, the system becomes overwhelmed.

To be sure, this simple proscription, addressed to those who administer as well as those who are clients of the court system, cannot cure the courts' woes. But it does show the importance of faithfulness in the courts, as in marriage. These institutions are fundamental to society and must be protected from the rot that undermines them.

False witness and corrupt court proceedings are the normal reality of much of the world. Totalitarian societies conduct farcical trials to silence all dissent or to serve their rulers' delusions. Poor people, in most societies, have little protection from the courts, which systematically serve the interests of the elites. Generally speaking, the fate of indigenous populations at the hands of their conquerors' courts is to lose. So this principle of fair courts is a divine imperative and only infrequently a human reality. It is very important that, at least in the courts, truth be practiced. This repeated imperative in the Old Testament is both a divine imperative and a profound public ethic. To the extent that the Hebrews were able to achieve truth in their courts, they distinguished themselves from the world. The same is true for Americans or for Christians who serve in American courts. To the extent that the judiciary honors truth and the people in the court system honor truth, God is served and the courts are freed from the falsehood that characterizes the practice of law. This can be achieved only to the extent that Americans and Christian Americans are taught to be moral and have the character to live morally. The courts can, to a degree, maintain the morality of society, but to a greater degree they depend on the morality of the people.

The moral trajectory of the principle not to bear false witness against a neighbor is clear. One is not to maliciously destroy the reputation of another through polemic, gossip, writing, broadcasting, or false charges. The destruction of reputation runs rampant through our time, injuring many and detracting from the public needs that deserve to be met. Libel may lead to court also, but before it does, public morality should censure it. Reading this principle through the perspective of the ultimate imperative of love requires thoroughgoing change in the practices of negative trashing of character and the negative politics of the United States. Other trajectories correcting the false witness of movies and of much public programming on TV are suggested, but they require extension of the principle. Employees of public agencies with governmental functions are obligated under this imperative not to bear false witness in the courts. Special scrutiny must be observed by all those with public or governmental powers.

Despite the widespread lying in U.S. courts in cases involving sexuality, President Bill Clinton's false witness to protect himself before a grand jury in 1998 led to impeachment proceedings in the House of Representatives. This was compounded by his lying to advisors, cabinet members, and the American public. The political opposition to his administration could focus on weaknesses in personal morality and then trap him into untruthfulness in a case arising before his presidency. The trap was carefully set by attorneys of Paula Jones and Special Prosecutor Kenneth Starr's office, and it was sprung by Clinton's own false testimony.

Though his sexual conduct was inappropriate, it was the lying to the court and to government officials that provoked the ire of the American people. Lying about legal matters by the highest official in the government was regarded as a serious offense even by those who regarded the four-year investigation of the president as misguided and politically inspired. Moreover, political opinion before the 1998 elections showed that the public blamed the office of the special prosecutor and the Republican leadership of the House of Representatives for the manner of the investigation, the entrapment, and the release of sexually explicit details as much as they faulted the president for his failures.

The agency that has been particularly subject to criticism for lying in public or bearing false witness has been the Central Intelligence Agency. Its recent disclosures about lying to cover up the involvement of its clients in the murder of U.S. citizens in Guatemala have followed close on the heels of proof of its lying to Congress. Because of its role in national security and the cold war, its actions present a special case and deserve realistic moral analysis. Can the CIA be subject to the imperative not to bear false witness? Or, if bearing false witness is of the essence of spying, what can those committed to Christian ethics do in, with, or about the CIA?

## Truth and the CIA

In the late twentieth century, the life of the Christian is involved with institutions. For many in the United States, one of these institutions has been the Central Intelligence Agency. The criticism of Joseph Fletcher's discussion of "patriotic prostitution"[61] indicated the need for more moral analysis of the CIA. The Christian entering the realm of the CIA is still a Christian, even though normally subject to the interests and demands of the state as well as to the imperative of love and its implications for the meaning of justice and the moral tradition of the Ten Commandments.

The folly of Joseph Fletcher's goal-oriented ethic is illustrated by the news that the CIA itself had been betrayed by Aldrich Ames. So, to continue Fletcher's example, if the Christian woman had committed adultery to seduce a Soviet spy, Ames would have used the information for Soviet interests. Moral principles cannot be easily set aside for illusive goals and particularly for ends that are not under one's own control anyway. Moral rules safeguard one from the exploitation of others.

However, two great nations have been locked in conflict, which ended only when the Soviet Union collapsed and a new regime emerged. The conflict was one of the defining issues of the last four decades, and the need to collect, analyze, and use intelligence about the intentions and capabilities of one's enemy was real. The CIA and its morality are shrouded in ambiguity, and reflections on them should be stated carefully, if forcefully. The imperative of love and the Ten Commandments need to be contextualized. Part of that context was the cold war. Part of that context for Christian thought was (and is) also the biblical insights regarding spying.

## Biblical Faith and Spies

Our times are characterized by the importance of great spy institutions. Recent premiers of the former Soviet Union and presidents of the United States owed part of their power and their development to the KGB and the CIA, respectively. The KGB recently failed to overthrow the constitutional power of the second most powerful empire, and the CIA's secret wars, arms deals, and policies have shaken recent U.S. governments. Buried in deep secrecy, both the KGB and CIA have carried out functions of secret inside powers comparable to the governmental powers of smaller states.

The issues surrounding these secret agencies can be viewed through the lens of our biblical faith. The Bible impacts these issues in four ways. The first is in the provision of the basic theological worldview. What do we think of history, and of human freedom to change history? What is the meaning of good, of evil, and of the destruction of peoples, cities, and nations?

The Bible teaches explicit moral standards that the contemporary church affirms as normative. This study has summarized these standards as love expressed in justice, community, and the Ten Commandments. This second use of the Bible is the shaping of our moral principles.

The third is the shaping of ourselves. Our character, or the outlines of our self, or who we are, is shaped by biblical faith. Through biblically guided ways of living, through hymns grounded in scripture, through prayers derived from the Bible, through the teaching of moral rules, stories, and paradigms, the shape of the character of the self is formed. In the first three instances, the Bible comes to the issue. Its influence is there before we define the issue. In the fourth case, we take the issue to the Bible and learn what the Bible says about spying, covert actions, and intelligence gathering.

In Genesis, Joseph as economic overlord of Egypt accuses his visiting brothers, who don't recognize him, of being spies. Their response is: "We are honest men, your servants have never been spies." Spying is seen in contrast to honesty. The Bible implies that honest people do not spy.

In the course of conquering the Holy Land, Israel regularly used spies; the more interesting accounts of Hebrew spies are in the books of Numbers and Joshua. In Numbers 13, Moses chose a leader from each of the twelve tribes and sent them north to spy out the land. The instructions given were to spy out the land of Canaan, and to determine whether the people were strong or weak, and to estimate the population, the condition of the land, and the strength of urban fortifications.

After forty days, they returned with a report that the land was plentiful, the people were strong, the cities were fortified, and some of the inhabitants seemed like giants. In the midst of the people's crying and murmuring against Moses, Joshua and Caleb brought a minority report that the land was conquerable. This minority report was not accepted, although its bearers would become the leaders after Moses. Only Caleb and Joshua, of all the elders in the wilderness, would live to cross the Jordan. Majority and minority reports on gathered intelligence conflicted; enemies were perceived as giants, there were disagreements about military vulnerability, and spies chosen for their ability became future national leaders.

The Joshua who was seen as a spy in Numbers is not only spymaster but commander-in-chief by the time of the battle of Jericho. He sends two spies to Jericho. They take cover in the house of the prostitute Rahab, who thereby becomes a figure of some significance for the New Testament. Rahab protects them and lies to protect their cover. She becomes a heroine of Hebrew folk-lore. The spies, with her assistance, escape, and she and her family are spared the Jericho holocaust. She becomes the mother of Boaz and thereby enters into the eventual royal line of David's house, and ultimately appears in the genealogy of Jesus Christ. John Calvin's commentary does not excuse her lying. He sees it as a small evil act for the sake of the great good of delivering Canaan to Israel's conquest. John Calvin had no particular moral objections to spying, but he did not want to call the lying good. In the Bible, spying is generally associated with lying.

The writers of the New Testament agreed that Rahab was justified. But the letter to the Hebrews disagreed with the letter of James as to the reason. For Hebrews she was justified by faith; James, of course, regarded her as justified by her action. Here we have spying to gather military intelligence, a safe house, lying, and salvation.

At the heart of the secret intelligence industry, the moral dilemma is the question of truth. Interesting human intelligence data is gathered surrepti-tiously, and the acquiring of it requires secrecy, deception, and lying. Intelligence data, to be useful, must be true, but the collecting agencies are committed to lies. In the credo that William Casey formulated for the CIA, there was a reference to the CIA motto that is displayed in the lobby of head-quarters, "And ye shall know the truth and the truth shall make ye free." These words of Jesus are so far from the information-gathering techniques of spies that they appear ironic to Christian readers.

Clair E. George, who has been central to the CIA procedures, was indicted for lying to Congress. On August 5, 1987, Senator Sam Nunn asked George whether "lies were necessary in the conduct of clandestine intelli-gence operations."[62] Mr. George's reply is fascinating, given the indictment: "To think that because we deal in lies and overseas we may lie and we may do other such things, that, therefore, gives you some permission, some right, or some particular reason to operate that way with your fellow employees, I would not only disagree with, I would say it would be the destruction of a secret service in a democracy."[63]

Morally we distinguish between expectations for the conduct of church business and for contests with Hitler's Gestapo, or with Khrushchev. With Calvin, we can regard some lies as little sins serving large goods when they are exceptional. But a willingness to lie built into the foundations of an institu-tion is a serious fault. It promises trouble, and in democracy it is a harbinger of corruption and a threat to government by the people.

The New Testament is more unequivocally opposed to spies than the Old Testament. In Luke 20:20, the establishment sent "spies who pretended to be honest men" to find a pretext for turning Jesus over to the authorities. They tried to trick him with the question about paying tribute to Caesar. His escape from the agent provocateur has rung through history: "Give to Caesar what is Caesar's, but to God what is God's."

Paul has nothing but rejection for those "spies" who disturbed the Galatian church's peace, "who slipped in to spy on the freedom we have in Christ" (Gal. 2:4).

Judas, who betrayed Jesus for a mixture of reasons perhaps more ideological than monetary, forever bears the name of betrayer. He pretended to love Jesus and betrayed him to the greatest empire of the day. "Iscariot" may itself refer to a secret gang of political assassins. Judas's name lives in infamy. Throughout the history of the church, there have been those who, for money, through ideological blindness, or for power, would betray Christians to the empires. These New Testament examples sensitize Christians to expect imperial powers to use secret agents to penetrate religious organizations when they criticize governments. In our own day, we know of persecution of the church by the secret police of Eastern Europe and the Soviet Union. In El Salvador, we have the murder of nuns, priests, and an archbishop by forces allied with our agents and dependent on our financing. Imperial powers are ready to murder religious leaders whom they regard as threatening. Recently, the FBI sent agent provocateurs to pray in churches trying to shelter refugees from the practices of the Immigration and Naturalization Service, continuing the tradition. Spies are associated with untruth and treachery, and yet spying is not excluded. There are particular causes which justify spying, and spies may become honored, as were Joshua and Rahab.

The new Calvinist bishop of Hungary, Dr. Lorant Hegedus, who saw many Christian betrayals in four decades of communist rule, distinguishes sharply between government actions to infiltrate churches and actions of clergy themselves who serve as spies for the government. Those in the latter category have betrayed Christ; the former activity is simply what communist states do to attack Christians. It is evil, but it is not as heinous as the betrayal of brothers and sisters by Christians.

The imperative of justice gives guidance as to what types of spying might be acceptable. The need to maintain the integrity of the church and the commandments prohibiting the bearing of false witness, adultery, murder, kidnapping, stealing, and covetousness limit severely the opportunities for Christian participation in spying. Further moral reflection is needed to provide guidance for attitudes and actions regarding our current relationship, as a church and as a nation, with the Central Intelligence Agency.

## Morality and the CIA

The end of the cold war prompted a far-ranging debate about the CIA. The Soviet Union's demise left the United States without the originating cause of the CIA. The KGB's reduction and the change of its name to the Russian Central Intelligence Agency flatter its former enemy the Central Intelligence Agency, but these actions also leave all parties involved questioning the purpose of the American intelligence apparatus with its $30 billion budget. Most of the intelligence budget is, of course, hidden in the military budget, and the Pentagon controls the lion's share of the intelligence community. The military-run National Security Agency is the largest of the intelligence agency communities. Still, the CIA director has the coordinating and control functions of secret intelligence, and so the debate has focused on the future of the CIA.

The moral questions concerning the CIA are important, but they probably will not be decisive in deciding the future of the agency. The institutional purposes of a bureaucracy to survive and flourish are normally of more political relevance than any moral issues. Many careers and billions of dollars are at stake when the need for secret intelligence is under debate. However, the questions of worldview, goals of the agency, appropriate methods of the agency, its role in character formation of its personnel, and its fit in a democratic, liberal, capitalistic society are all issues of morality.

After World War II, Harry Truman terminated the CIA's predecessor, the Office of Strategic Services, because he knew that there were actions appropriate in wartime that ought not be continued in peacetime. The opening of the cold war resulted in his encouraging the National Security Act and the rebirth of the OSS as the Central Intelligence Agency in 1947. Later, in 1963, freed of the responsibilities of office, he recorded his reservations about the CIA becoming an operational and sometimes policy-forming part of the government. With the end of the cold war, the question comes up again: What ought we to do about secret intelligence and operations?

Thinking about morality and the CIA is similar to thinking about morality and Machiavelli. The subject concerns both morality and open immorality. Machiavelli, like the CIA, wanted to appear good. He, like most members of the CIA, was a Christian. He, like the CIA, was involved deeply in church politics. He wanted the good of his country, as does the CIA. He wanted to do well himself, as do most CIA personnel. He was willing to recommend killing, assassination, murder, and lying, as has the CIA in its practice. His politics were a mixture of republicanism and totalitarian practices, as have been those of the CIA. Reading about CIA atrocities and trying to think morally is reminiscent of the title of the recent study *Machiavelli in Hell*.

## Christian Realism in Cold War

Recognizing that idealistic moral theories would reject most of the premises of a secret organization, we need to turn toward realistic analyses to get within range of our subject. We are beyond the innocent morality of Secretary of State Stimson, who in 1929, regarding a proposal to set up a State Department intelligence service, said, "Gentlemen do not read other people's mail."

But where are we in moral discourse? Reviewing the differing positions of two Christian realists during the cold war may advance the discussion.

Christian social ethicists have not written a great deal about internal surveillance in the United States, or about the secret wars that the U.S. government has encouraged. The church generally has not known what was going on, and it has, in large part, acquiesced to government secrecy and even to government harassment and exploitation of the church by both the KGB and the CIA.

Reinhold Niebuhr responded to the *New York Times* investigation of the CIA in 1966 by writing a short critique of the agency. He echoed the fears that it "has indeed become an 'invisible government.'"[64] Its budget was beyond adequate review, and it subsidized universities, sponsored publications, supported organizations, and, most worrisome, affected national policy. Its agents often were more influential than ambassadors abroad, and its weight influenced policy. Niebuhr praised it for its role in the Cuban missile crisis and criticized its role in the Bay of Pigs fiasco. Plots to spoil Cuban sugar, to displace Prince Souvanna Phouma, and to support Ngo Dinh Nhu's secret police were criticized. Niebuhr, deploring the CIA's role in policy making, called for more adequate congressional oversight in 1966 to ensure democratic control over "these cloak and dagger men." Some of this control was achieved in the 1970s after the Senate and House investigations of CIA abuses. But in the 1980s, these controls were found to be inadequate as the intelligence agencies lied to congressional oversight committees. Secrecy and lying are close to the essence of the operations of these agencies, and this spills over into broader relationships. The secrecy, defended by lies to the supposed overseers, allowed people like William Casey, Robert Gates, and Oliver North to conduct their own anticommunist wars.

Within the Christian community of moral discourse, Ernest W. Lefever has made a moral argument for CIA policies. He drew on Paul Ramsey and Robert Tucker's studies on the just-war tradition. He assumed that the work of the CIA was a wartime, albeit a cold war, operation, and he reduced the criteria to three: (1) Is the object of the action just? (2) Are the means employed both just and appropriate? (3) Will the chances for justice be enhanced if the action succeeds?[65] Ramsey, of course, did not agree with Tucker, and his presentation of just-war theory was much richer and more fully developed than Lefever's.

The just-war tradition has been much broader than Lefever made it out to be. It is exactly the first principle of Thomas Aquinas, not mentioned by Lefever, that U.S. intelligence agencies have repeatedly violated in making attacks on other nations. Presupposing the necessity of declaring war, Aquinas wrote, "For the war to be just, three conditions are necessary. First, the authority of the ruler within whose competence it lies to declare war."[66] The other two principles Aquinas lists are just cause and right intention. Recent moral discussions have included criteria of last resort—i.e., all other means of resolving conflicts have been attempted, there is a reasonable chance of success, and there will be immunity from injury for noncombatants. The activities of secret agents in assassinating political leaders, fomenting revolutions in countries with which one is not at war, and launching undeclared secret wars clearly fall outside of the permissible in the moral theory of the just war. The KGB had no moral right to attack the government of Afghanistan, nor the CIA to attack the government of Nicaragua. Robert Gates's memo about bombing Nicaragua and Bill Casey's mining of Nicaraguan harbors were an immoral intention and an immoral action of war ruled nonpermissible by just-war theory. Many actions of covert policy of the CIA and KGB cannot be justified under just-war theory. This moral impropriety of many agency actions has led representatives of the CIA to repeatedly lie to Congress, the public, and their political superiors. This public, official form of lying is what is condemned by the principle "Do not bear false witness."

Beyond the cold war debates, Christian ethics is continuing to think in terms of just-war criteria. Ecumenical Christianity is also evolving teachings of peacemaking and just-peace considerations. The just-peace norms that are developing toward consensus[67] include policies that promote human rights, international organization, sustainable development, sufficient economies, and participation in decision making. Christian pressures drawn from the Old Testament covenants, prophetic teachings, and New Testament ethics are expressed in rational, generalizable norms curtailing lying, murder, and destruction. The gathering of secret intelligence itself has ample precedent in the Bible, and it has often been honored. The killing of internationals with whom the nation as a whole is not at war falls outside of the biblical and Christian ethical tolerance of ambiguity. The secret operations work of the CIA ought not to have its evil[68] obscured under the ambiguity surrounding the sometimes necessary clandestine gathering of information.

## Reshaping the CIA

Discussions by the chairman of the Senate Select Committee on Intelligence and the chairman of the Board of Visitors of the Defense Intelligence College recognize that the intelligence community needs reorganization.[69] The CIA director realized this need, but wanted to keep the reorganization and the downsizing to a minimum. A former director, Admiral Stansfield Turner, recognizing that the original cold war purpose of the CIA was gone, suggested new purposes in business, in developing countries, in ecology, and in drug and arms trafficking.

We can assume that intelligence budgets are to be reduced. Where should the cuts come? Turner reported that one-third of the intelligence budget is under Pentagon control, and another half is under joint military and CIA control. Turner called for the appointment of a director of national intelligence, which could reduce the military share of the budget because less military intelligence is required.[70] Turner also threw off as an aside that the CIA has not been very good at military intelligence anyway. If this judgment were combined with Senator Daniel Moynihan's comment that "for a quarter of a century, the CIA has been repeatedly wrong about the major political and economic questions entrusted to its analysis,"[71] we would have a bleak picture indeed of the CIA's capability.

Turner expected a downsizing of the effort spent on intelligence vis-à-vis the Soviet Union, which was the original purpose of the CIA. He saw new priorities for U.S. intelligence in the "new world order." He suggested the need for economic intelligence to increase national economic prospects. He expected the government intelligence resources to spy on economic competitors and to obtain the information necessary to strengthen U.S. corporations. He also wanted "more emphasis on political intelligence in Third World countries." He further recommended that these same forces work on ecological issues and drug trafficking. He did caution that "we will not want to be caught by friends in the act of spying."[72] He argued that all agencies of the U.S. government need to be instructed that spying is policy and that they are to be part of it. Such a vision of the future begs all of the questions. Why would any rational person expect spies to be good at ecology? The trial of General Manuel Noriega of Panama proved that secret agent networks are not the best way to stem drug traffic. Significant economic analysis will come from the universities and the business world, not the CIA. It makes no sense to witness the intelligence community's admitted failure to understand its big project, the Soviet Union, and then to conclude that it would be good at a whole set of other tasks. It is unlikely that the CIA's role in business would be useful—witness the CIA's inept role in the Bank of Credit and Commerce International (BCCI) The ethos of American business is difficult enough without welcoming governmental secret agencies into the picture. The CIA tried to disassociate itself from its first exposed major work in international business competition. Its contracts with the Rochester Institute produced a scandal exposing the president of Rochester's CIA role, and resulted in his resignation. The circulation of the report itself, *Japan 2000*, inflicted one more minor wound on tense Japanese–U.S. relations.

Neither the training and practice of spies nor the elements of character encouraged in covert or clandestine operations prepare intelligence agents for helpful cooperation in civilian business, and their role in arms sales is not above criticism. The biblical view is that no nation is in control of the world, the perspectives of all humans are limited, and God laughs at the pretensions of rulers, who in their pride, rebel against God. Spying is much more incidental than former spymasters can ever believe. Now is the time to think smaller, to reduce U.S. claims, and to find ways to play our appropriate role. We really do not need to pay for, or try to manage, the Shah of Iran's secret police, Noriega's drug trade, Somoza's secret police, or Marcos's budget. In all four cases U.S. funds promoted dictators who oppressed their people, with CIA complicity. Finally, all four dictators were overthrown.

## Personal and Public

Norman Mailer was applauded at the CIA for his book *Harlot's Ghost*. But certainly he was wrong when he recommended the continuation of secret operations, for such activities have been central to CIA involvement in the Bay of Pigs, the Contras, Watergate, Guatemala, and Iran. Under secrecy, with no adequate review, evil is unleashed. Mailer's book reveals the problems of character that evolve from unchecked secret power. In reforming the CIA, secret operations must be ended, and any future need for secret operations should be a direct presidential, military operation where accountability and discipline are possible. For too long, our own domestic politics have been polluted by character faults tolerated in secret wars and secret operations, and we must cut this evil off to prevent future Watergates and foolishness in the Caribbean.

Intelligence we need, but having a central location for intelligence gathering is presumptuous. Vastly reduced intelligence operations in the military, the National Security Agency, the FBI, the AEC, and the DEA, and increased reliance on universities, intellectuals, academic studies, think tanks, and public policy institutes, will provide what is needed.

So, on the personal level, the moral problem Fletcher provided us with is not a moral problem at all. The woman needed only to decline the immoral service for which the defense intelligence agency tried to recruit her. Even thinking pragmatically, it was the moral failure and the economic failure of communism that brought its empire to an end. The intelligence service had little to do with the outcome. The Aldrich Ames case is evidence that in the world of secret intelligence, the Soviets won.

But beyond our hypothetical case or the moral squalor reported by Norman Mailer, more Christians should have said no when covert intelligence agencies requested their services. There has been too much secrecy and too much lying within the agency for it to be trusted by people who want to live and act morally. William Sloane Coffin Jr. is an example of one who wrote about his time in the CIA. He enthusiastically entered the CIA, as a divinity student with skills in Russian, during the Korean War. In Europe, for three years, he trained Russian emigres to return to Russia to spy for the CIA. According to his account, they were to gather mainly nonmilitary but societal intelligence. Apparently, all of the agents were killed and the security of the entire operation was betrayed. Coffin was too young, too incompetent, for such work; perhaps he was simply too Christian for it. Most of those whom he trained were Orthodox Christians who were joining a betrayed cause out of their religious belief. Later he repented and came to see, in addition to the futility of most such operations, that we as a country had no business trying to overthrow other people's governments.[73] Usually we cannot succeed, and when we do there is still the probability of government by terror and tyranny, as in Guatemala.

The strength of the United States lies in its economy, in the intelligence, education, and morale of its people, in its regular armed forces, in its institutes, think tanks, and universities, in its republican form of government, and in its religious spirit. Cloak-and-dagger operations, bombs in the night, disinformation, and all the rest really have very little to do with U.S. strength. Mostly they are an embarrassment. The intelligence services did the country great disservice in overestimating the strength of the Russian adversary, in not foreseeing its imminent collapse, and in underestimating the significance of the changes in the Soviet Union as late as 1988. Private citizens using books and newspapers did better. My son's report on the Baltic states in 1989, which predicted that they were going to be independent or risk civil war, was more accurate than the CIA's analysis as publicly discussed. My own book *Christian Realism and Peacemaking* (Abingdon, 1988), written in 1987, compares very favorably to known CIA estimates of weakness in the Soviet Union. Those who went and saw for themselves knew better than a CIA blinded by cold war passions. Roy Godson's essay "Intelligence for the 1990's"[74] reported on a colloquium by the Consortium for the Study of Intelligence involving top intelligence analyses and experts. The meetings and Godson's later report still planned on a stronger strategic power in the Soviet Union in the 1990s. The continued presence of the Soviet bloc in Eastern Europe was counted on as one of five major conclusions. In 1963, Allen Dulles, CIA director from 1953 to 1961, told me at a luncheon at International House, New York City, that his chief problem was that people who were to receive CIA analyses on their desks when they came to work had already read the *New York Times* and as a result would not take the CIA information seriously enough. In fact, more accurate reports were available from the *New York Times* than from the CIA if the former were read without cold war glasses obscuring one's vision (this is my opinion, not that of Dulles).

In general, Christian morality as applied to international relations lies in the norms of the just-war tradition and in the seeking of a just peace through international order. The norms of sustainability, sufficiency, and participation of the World Council of Churches need to replace lying, secrecy, and clandestine operations. Intelligence must be gathered, prudence honored, and, in exceptional cases, spying undertaken. But Christian pressure must be in the direction of openness, truth-telling, non-killing, democracy, and reduction of the causes that give rise to secret agencies and secret police. On the international scene, this means that the expulsion of agents from the Eastern churches' offices and a purge of the Russian Orthodox church of all KGB influence are to be welcomed. We in the church, particularly in our mission efforts, need to be vigilant against agent penetration as well. Particularly, we need to be scrupulous in preventing Christian missions from being coopted or used by U.S. intelligence and covert operations.

In *The C.I.A. and the Cult of Intelligence,* Victor Marchetti and John D. Marks have summarized a major needed orientation.[75] The United States is strong enough to get out of the gutter and conduct an honorable foreign policy. To that end, we need to recommend to all our senators and representatives that they get some of the funds we need for public expenditures and welfare help from slashing the $30 billion cold war budget of secret intelligence. The covert wars and dirty tricks need to be stopped, or in the rare cases where they are necessary, moved to the Pentagon. Counterespionage also needs to be isolated from Central Intelligence information collecting and analysis. A much reduced information gathering and centralizing function is justified, but preferably in a new agency.

## THE TENTH COMMANDMENT

In the Tenth Commandment, the spirited nature of the law probes the secret envy and avarice of the human heart. The goodness of the law confronts the inner desires of human nature that lead to disaster. It was this principle, understood as God's law, that convicted Paul and drove him to reflect on the law as spiritual and on his nature as sinful. He could not escape the contradiction of this commandment in himself: "For I do not do what I want, but I do the very thing I hate" (Rom. 7:15). He said that he would not have known what it meant to covet if the law had not taught him. Then his sin used his knowledge of the law to produce covetousness. It was this law in which he particularly noted the futility of the law by itself.

Calvin[76] understood Augustine to have taught that perfect love would have driven out even covetousness. The presence of covetousness as a wanting of that which is not justly ours and an inclination to grasp it violates the love of the neighbor. It also violates the love of God. Colossians 3:5 describes "covetousness which is idolatry" (RSV).

This tenth prescription is not criminal law, but it is ethical principle. It is a principle of the ethics of the human spirit. It is true that one cannot love God and the neighbor with this unjust desire.

The order of the Deuteronomy final commandment sounds better to modern readers in that the wife is not so clearly indicated as part of the husband's possessions. "Neither shall you covet your neighbor's wife. Neither shall you desire your neighbor's house or field, or male or female slave, or ox, or donkey, or anything that belongs to your neighbor" (Deut. 5:21).

Luther wisely stresses that here the intentions of the righteous are confronted. We are not to want to take our neighbor's possessions even if we could take them legally or by manipulation of the system.

The debates over the meaning of the Hebrew verb hamad,[77] translated "covet" or "desire," reveal how this final principle unites character and action. We are forbidden certain desires, and if we were living in security and love, we would not want those things that were our neighbor's. This principle, like all of the other nine, is brought into the New Testament, showing the oneness in Christian morality between the Decalogue and the New Testament morality. But, as in all morality, the principles were reinterpreted in the teachings of Jesus and the letters of Paul, as they were later throughout church history.

Albrecht Alt had limited the Eighth Commandment to the stealing of persons or the kidnapping of a free Hebrew male person. The Tenth Commandment could be seen then as prohibiting the stealing of property. This allowed a relationship to be seen among the last five commandments as the protection of life, marriage, freedom, reputation, and property.[78] But, as the case against restricting the Eighth Commandment to kidnapping rather than stealing is not totally persuasive, "covet" in the Tenth Commandment can be read as referring to the motivation to take what is not one's own. The protection of the wife also repeats the prohibition against adultery, so the distinction restricting the lusting after, rather than the active stealing or adultery, holds up. Jesus' deepening interpretation censuring lust, as well as adultery, had its precedents here in Exodus and Deuteronomy.

This principle is a refutation of much of modern life, but it is not a refutation of legitimate commerce or appropriate social decisions for the good of the community. What is forbidden is that which violates the love of the neighbor and the justice of the community. One can admire the weedless lawn of a neighbor and pull the weeds from one's own yard, but one is not permitted to violate the neighbor's will and take the lawn one admires. Commerce is permitted—one can buy the neighbor's lawn—but the overpowering of the neighbor or the lust to overpower the neighbor to claim the neighbor's possessions for one's own is forbidden. Freedman saw the taking of Naboth's vineyard as reflecting Ahab and Jezebel's covetousness, just as David's taking of Bathsheba reflected covetousness. The Tenth Commandment is different from the other commandments in that it prohibits no punishable offense, but the desire that leads to the punishable offenses (in Hebrew society) of the other commandments.[79]

Covetousness, the lusting after that which we do not have, is the motivation of much of our lives. It needs to be distinguished from the enjoyment of the good in appropriate measure. To enjoy nature, for example, is a good and to want to do so is appropriate. But to exploit nature for one's profit in a way that destroys its beauty and sustainability is the fruit of covetousness.

"You shall not covet" may become one of the most important moral principles in the struggle to sustain nature and preserve the remaining wilderness. Human efforts to subdue must be limited. Morality is about limiting human powers to appropriate expression. Long before the last ancient tree is cut, humanity sins in organizing its life to covet the forest, its people, and its animals.

The organization of economic life or certain professions, such as law, so that there is no time for family, recreation, worship, and rest, is rooted in covetousness. People work in sweatshops because manufacturers covet the profits from their work. States and economies are organized to keep income for workers as low as possible because of covetousness. The ruling classes covet extraordinary amounts of products and opportunities, so they force suffering on the rest of the people. The taking and hoarding of riches by those who covet the most are extraordinarily hurtful to the society and are morally wrong by the standards of the Bible and Christian moral teaching.

In American society, the last two decades of the twentieth century have seen the maximization of the power of advertising and the reduction of opportunity to acquire the goods by the poor of the population. This combination of teasing and denial produces rage in the poor, which occasionally explodes in urban communities. At the same time, the power of the successful and covetous increases, and their relative success makes it less likely that the pain of the poor will be alleviated by helpful measures. American society is both cooperative and competitive. To the extent that it is competitive, the "war" against poverty was lost in the 1960s. The population that won the war has increased its resources, its social organization, and its wants since the "war" was fought. The reaching of the urban underclass becomes more and more difficult with the increased power of the winners. All of this is spiritually rooted in covetousness, or the lusting after that which we do not have and which, in justice, we do not have a right to take. Finally, the limiting of the self's desires and intentions is a protection of the other. "You shall not covet your neighbor's possessions" is another form of "Love your neighbor."

# Guided in the
## Spirit of Jesus

The Ten Commandments express in more detail the commandments of Jesus to love God totally and to love the neighbor as the self. An interpretation of Christian ethics must come to terms with the ethical teachings attributed to Jesus as the inspirer and founder of the church that nurtures and promotes these teachings today. The argument of this interpretation of Christian ethics developed so far is that the double love imperative is the foundation of Christian ethics. This foundation is explicated in the books of the Bible affirmed by the early community of Jesus' followers and is expressed socially in the ethics of justice. This community that evolves through history in its ethical interpretation displays continuity by its continued emphasis on the double love commandment and its expression in the two tablets of the Decalogue to love God and to love the neighbor. The Decalogue itself is interpreted by the double love commandment, which is a prerequisite for any scriptural interpretation.[1] Paul not only put love first in his hymn of love in 1 Corinthians 13, but he also reasoned explicitly that the commandments are all summarized in love in Romans 13. "The commandments, 'You shall not commit adultery; you shall not murder; you shall not steal; you shall not covet'; and any other commandment, are summed up in this word, 'Love your neighbor as yourself.' Love does no wrong to a neighbor; therefore love is the fulfilling of the Law" (Rom. 13:9–10).

Jesus himself was a teacher of moral wisdom,[2] and the first and predominant Gospel of Matthew has preserved this image and some of his teaching. The Gospel of Matthew preserves this teaching while providing a narrative based on Mark. The purpose is to provide the good news that God's activity has culminated in Jesus as the Christ, Messiah, or Anointed One, and that the reign of God is presently to be joined. This teacher of moral wisdom or prophetic philosopher[3] of Judaism is known only in these sources from his later community, which ascribe to him this central place in the plan of God. He has become already in Mark and the expanded Gospel of Matthew not only the teacher of wisdom but the wisdom of God. So the teacher became that which was taught. He was taught, in a language not his own—that of synagogue Greek—to a Gentile world beyond his own.

His own origins as a follower of the apocalyptic-political prophet John the Baptist, as well as the early development of the church in the climactic events destroying Jerusalem and Judaism in its temple form, obscure his own message, as does the focus on himself as the work of God. His ethics is set in a particular religious context by the writers and editors of the Gospels. The writers of the Gospels were themselves creative theologians out of a context different from both Jesus' context and our context. Moreover, Matthew particularly expressed the religious meaning of Jesus in the symbols of the Hebrew Bible in its Greek translation. The ethics of Jesus is not available to us outside of these religious contexts. Our task is to understand it for our religious context. The contemporary reader can proceed with the help of commentaries to interpret the ethics of Jesus. There is no possibility of an uninterpreted ethic from Jesus, because the very sources we have are interpretations, as Jesus was himself an interpreter within Judaism. Yet within that qualification, reliable knowledge of the outlines of Jesus' historical life and his ethic is attainable.[4]

Here, certain themes or trajectories are added to his message of the double love commandment, community, justice, and the Ten Commandments. These themes are rooted in two realities: the historical reality of Jesus, and the reality of today's church in contemporary society.

The first theme is the rule of God expressed in the New Testament as the reign of God or the reign of heaven. This is the will of God being expressed in mature human lives in community and in society to the degree possible under historical conditions. It was inevitable that this would revive apocalyptic connections, whether the apocalypse was the destruction of the temple or the call of John the Baptist for repentance as the reign of God begins. These apocalyptic elements are present in the New Testament, but it is inadequate to regard them as determinative of the ethics of Jesus. It was also almost a necessity that flawed human leaders of the church would eventually confuse the rule of God with life in the church. In any case, it happened. Today we know that neither the church nor apocalyptic judgment is the reign of God. The rule of God is realized in those who submit in trust to God and live in its fragmentary realization here and now. To accept God's reign is to live in trust, freedom, and love as these are historically known. The emphasis is not on rules, but on relationships with God and other human beings. These relationships, however, are summed up in ethical patterning called principles.

The second theme is loyalty to God. This repeats the first tablet of the Decalogue as well as the first of the double love commands. It is an expression of Jesus' radical monotheism. In the tradition of the great prophets, all other centers of loyalty are relativized. Only God is absolute. Also, all virtues other than love of God are relativized. As H. Richard Niebuhr put it, the human values that Jesus magnified, hope, love, faith, obedience, and trust, are all related to God.[5] Disaster soon follows if hope, faith, obedience, and trust are placed in anything other than God. In another study, he succinctly summarized the purpose of the church in terms of the double love commandment. He focused the purpose of the church radically into the purpose of all the law and the prophets. The church's purpose is to encourage and increase the love of God by humanity and the love of humanity by humanity.[6] This explanation gives a central meaning to the reality of the church. It recognizes the sociological reality of the church. It respects the human need for religious community. Yet it keeps the reminder of the commandments before the church. The church serves the reign of God under its twofold imperative. Because Jesus is so close to God, his ethical teachings have the combination of radical imperative and ultimate graciousness. As Matthew ended his writing of the Sermon on the Mount, "for he taught them as one having authority, and not as their scribes" (Matt. 7:28).

A third theme is that Jesus was a healer. All the sources describe his compassionate application of healing power. Health accompanied him, and he provided healing. The healings, whether of blindness, fever, hemorrhaging, leprosy, paralysis, or mental illness, are seen in terms of Hebrew Bible prophecies (Matt. 8:17), extraordinary powers, and conflicts with the authorities. Christian ethics receives a trajectory of compassion translated into practical action here. Often the practical actions of compassion lead to tension with the establishment. In Matthew, the healings follow immediately after the teaching in the Sermon on the Mount. Matthew has the pattern of teach how to act, act oneself, and then conflict follows. Matthew presents a very practical Jesus who actually does the work of healing. Christians who have caught the imperative to bring healing with all their power to those who suffer disease and illness are standing squarely within the Jesus tradition. The healing of the wounded traveler by the Samaritan was in terms of practical care; it expressed love. According to the Gospels and Acts, Jesus' followers and disciples also participated in healing events. These healings were both signs of a new reality and the practical application of the ethic of love.

It could be noted here how closely the love ethic approximates the Golden Rule. Matthew presents both. The Golden Rule in one form or another appears in many religious traditions. Here it has the summary authority of the law and the prophets in the love commandments. Its placement near the end of the Sermon on the Mount reveals the healing to be the actual practice of the ethic. The Golden Rule, like the double love commandment, needs no eschatological context. It approximates natural law and it expresses the foundation of justice. "In everything do to others as you would have them do to you; for this is the law and the prophets" (Matt. 7:12).

Both the double love commandment and the Golden Rule express an activist stance. They do not accept suffering fatalistically or promote the religious transcendence of pain. Especially when seen in connection with Jesus' constant, challenging mission of healing, there is a commitment to praxis here. The healing ministry is the major rival to the vocation of Jesus as teacher. Together they dominate his ministry as portrayed in the Gospels. Jesus cannot be plausibly presented as one who tries to influence imperial social policy. Nor can he credibly be regarded as a political revolutionary. Of course, once healing is organized by politics in imperial policies, this constant ethic of healing has consequences for those policies, as does his teaching, but this is not to regard him as a policy advocate or expert. Our policy advocacy can be and for Christians must be illuminated by his actions and teachings, but the relationship is an indirect one.

It seems to this reader that Jesus did not advocate hedonism or egoism. He presupposed, I believe, that his moral teachings would fall on various souls, some mature and some immature. The presupposition was that hearers were capable of following him and of joining in the reign of God. I do not think he commanded people to love themselves. He must have presupposed the humanity of those he taught. If they had been so broken, crushed, or lost that they despised themselves, the Golden Rule and double love commandment would not have been adequate guidance. The normal self-acceptance that Jesus' moral teaching presupposes is grounded in the trust that one is created and loved by God. Some self-acceptance and societal acceptance are needed if Jesus' moral teaching is to be heard. The fact that some oppressed people grow up without consciences and that some oppressors have destroyed their consciences is recognized. Not everyone can or will join the rule of God. Obviously, many have not, some cannot, but Jesus' moral teaching is directed to those who can. Some, such as the rich young ruler, will still reject the rule and leave Jesus sorrowfully.

The ethic of Jesus is that of the religious prophet. This fourth characteristic of his ethic derives from contemporary understandings of prophetic ethics as well as from the Gospel sources. Luke is the most explicit in identifying him as a prophet. The people of the synagogue of Nazareth reject his announcement of his call in the prophecy of Isaiah. Then he says: "Truly I tell you, no prophet is accepted in the prophet's hometown" (Luke 4:24). Moreover, Jesus' baptism in the Jordan by John is presented in an interpretation of John carrying out Isaiah's prophecy and preaching a prophetic-critical message of the political order and urging repentance, sharing of property, and righteous living. The Gospel of Mark has Jesus compared to Elijah at the transfiguration and at Peter's confession of his messiahship. Others are reported to think of him as one of the prophets in Mark 28:8. Someone in the crowd says, in John 7:40, "This is really the prophet." However, the Gospels clearly present him as the Christ or the Anointed One in a manner that eclipses the prophetic title. He is a prophet, and the interpretation or transformation of the messianic role by the motifs of Isaiah's suffering servant figure deepens the very Christology of the Gospels. Although it is inevitable that Christianity's devotion to the risen Lord will eclipse the prophetic aspect of Jesus, for his ethic and our ethic, the prophetic ethic must be honored. The church is encouraged in this honoring by Judaism's willingness to recognize the prophet in him. Even more so, Islam's high celebration of Jesus as a prophet is a welcome addition to an interpretation of his ethics. The prophetic story is one of the central stories of Hebrew faith, and it has shaped not only Jesus and his contemporaries, but also those who wrote the New Testament about Jesus.

What is this prophetic ethic that it deserves to be seen as a characteristic of Jesus' ethic and of our ethic? The prophetic ethic is centered on monotheism and ethical rigor. It holds that God has standards and that the violation of these norms corrupts and destroys a society. Within these corrupt societies, which oppress the weak and pollute the courts and government, are spokespeople for God who speak for righteous conduct and redress for the oppressed. The prophetic ethic is a critical ethic that faults religious, social, and political leadership for the suffering of the people. The prophets, to the extent that they are able to read the signs of the times, describe often in poetic or religious language how social disaster will strike the corrupt societies. Almost universally the prophets also hold out hope. The hope may be for restoration or a new future after destruction. However, sometimes the hope is for salvation from destruction if a society repents. The short books of Amos and Jonah are almost ideal types of prophetic ethics. Jonah's Nineveh repented and was saved. Amos's Israel rejected his teaching at the hands of religious and political leadership. Rejection of critical prophets is the more normal response of religious-political leadership, as it was for John the Baptist, Jesus Christ, and his followers.

Jesus' attacks on the religious-political leaders of his day—symbolic actions, cleansing the temple, ethical rigor, special relationship with God, care and ministry for the oppressed, and criticism of riches—are all characteristic of prophetic ethics. His prophetic ethic took him into harm's way at the hands of political powers, but he himself did not exercise political power in the way of the world. His way was the prophetic way. Religious needs for affirmation always threaten the prophetic critic. In a world besieged by problems, threats, and oppression, the church today needs to nurture the prophetic spirit much more consistently than it has. In concluding this brief description of Jesus' ethic as that of a religious prophet, it completes the circle to note that the Gospels represent the love commandments as the summary of the law and the prophets.

A characteristic of Jesus' ethic is that it was an ethic for a community he founded. He gathered followers, bound them to himself in loyalty, and generated the religious power that they would recognize as resurrection after his crucifixion. The community nature of Christian ethics is so centered that it was noted after the love commandment as the second theme of contemporary Christian ethics.[7] The theme should be clearly highlighted: Jesus himself founded a movement that proclaimed him Christ and initiated the Christian church. His intention to live in the reign of God could not be contained within the Judaism of his day. Consequently, even though he may at first have been a reformer, opposition to him and his movement separated him from Judaism. Luther as a Catholic monk reformer founded Protestantism. John Wesley as an Anglican priest–reformer founded Methodism. Jesus as a Jew founded Christianity. The New Testament is full of the pain of the conflicts and separation struggles that characterized the Jesus movement. The Gospels are written out of the *Sitz im Leben* of separating or recent separation from the synagogue, and these conflicts color the presentation of the Jew Jesus who founded the church.

Characteristics of the ethic of Jesus can be seen in the shaping of the early movement. It is an inclusive community with significant roles for women as leaders, supporters, and first witnesses to the resurrection. It includes early Gentiles as racial-religious barriers are overcome. It is so free of class distinctions that the whole issue of Jesus' own class origins remains unresolved. Should he be called a peasant? What class is a carpenter? Do the references to him as rabbi imply formal education, or is this title only honorific? It seems unlikely to me that the religious leaders, lawyers, and scholars would have taken him as seriously as the Gospels indicate if he had been an uneducated peasant, as John Dominic Crossan would have his readers believe. This inclusive movement is characterized also by nonchalance regarding the family structures of the patriarchal traditional of Judaism. Jesus is casual about his own family, recognizing in his movement the central community. The church would, of course, divide families as loyalties to church superseded those to traditional families (Luke 12:52–53). Even so, today's church differences and church commitments can divide and tear apart families as well as reinforce family values. Another characteristic of Jesus' followers is that, although they ask Jesus for special and hierarchical considerations, they do not receive them. They are a community without hierarchy except for the focus on Jesus and his leadership. The concepts of bishops, patriarchs, and archbishops are so far removed from Jesus as to be laughable. Most religious hierarchs he encountered treated him as an enemy. The community around Jesus does not try to overthrow the world's hierarchies, patriarchal families, or gender and racial discrimination; rather, in its own living of the reign of God, it moves toward a fellowship of love wherein all those distinctions fade.

In the violent twentieth century, activists have discovered a principle of Jesus that has been obscured for centuries. Mohandas K. Gandhi and Martin Luther King Jr. discovered in Jesus a suffering-transforming love and based their movements against imperialism and racism on it. Glen Stassen has interpreted much of Jesus' teaching as transforming initiatives. He sees Jesus laying down a way of meeting conflict that can lead to just peacemaking. In these views, Jesus acts with power to change the situation. In all cases, the actors themselves have to be changed. One does not become a *satyagraha* actor for Gandhi simply by volunteering, and King's civil rights movement trained and prepared its workers spiritually when it was at its best. For Stassen, the Christian becomes an activist, but nonviolently to change the definition of the context of action. He argues persuasively that Matthew's Sermon on the Mount and Luke's Sermon on the Plain teach reconciling, risky acts. Again and again, the teachings in Matthew 5 follow a threefold pattern: "You have heard it said . . . , but I say to you . . . : do this," and the conclusion urges reconciling acts. Through these constructed sermons of Matthew and Luke, the advice to actively move forward is given. One corrects the situation by correcting oneself and by acting. His teaching had authority, and his advice near the end of the sermon was "In everything do to others as you would have them do to you; for this is the law and the prophets" (Matt. 7:12). The hyperbole in these writings needs to be finessed, not exaggerated, but the sayings are not impossible for one in a Christian community or religious ashram. Gandhi and King read Jesus imaginatively and correctly, as Stassen has done. The advice is direct: Don't judge, for you will be judged, correct yourself, then you can help your brother better. This does not condemn us to any inevitable judging; it leads us away from judging toward self-correction. The truth is not only in the contrast between judging and being judged but primarily in self-correction and helpfulness to the other. I do not read Jesus as requiring all of his followers for all time to become absolute pacifists, but I believe he puts the emphasis on transforming initiatives toward just peacemaking. Jesus did not advise public officials on policy, but his way of being toward the other for the other's good is fundamental to his ethic. The striving with the other can lead to fundamental conflicts, and Jesus knew that these sharply expressed conflicts might lead to death—but the reign of God was worth many conflicts, and he provided guidance for his followers who would suffer them.

These few principles of Jesus do not replace the thousands of books on Jesus and his teachings. Their summary here is intended to illustrate how the love imperatives in community, seeking justice, interpret the Ten Commandments and then enrich that understanding of love with guidance from Jesus and the contemporary church interpreting him. To sum up, the additional principles here are: (1) seek the rule of God, (2) place ultimate loyalty in  God, (3) heal the sick, (4) honor the prophetic spirit of the Bible, (5) locate oneself in a community nurturing the spirit of Jesus, and (6) discover and practice transforming initiatives of just peacemaking.

The principles stated here are those of Christian ethics. They cannot be lived without conflict. The story of some of the theories of these conflicts needs to be reviewed before proceeding with recommendations for some problems of Christian living in the twenty-first century.

# Part
## Three
# Public Life

# Personal and Public Morality

hristian ethics as summarized in the double love commandment seeks community and justice. The most important principles of this ethic have been expressed in a rigorous application of the Ten Commandments. Are these commandments for our public lives? Are they intended only for our personal lives? How sharply should we distinguish between Christian personal ethics and public ethics?

Christian ethicists often draw the distinction between personal and social ethics. Peter Paris of Princeton Theological Seminary shared reflections on his 1988 experience in South Africa with a small group of ethicists over lunch. He described the horrendous reality of the black population living under apartheid. The political-economic system forced millions to live in situations of degradation. His descriptions of the hostels in which black workers lived were particularly poignant. The social conditions under which the workers lived corrupted their personal existence. Paris, on the one hand, is inclined to argue that a person cannot be more moral than the political system permits without undertaking risks of persecution or death. On the other hand, he met many people living among the oppressing groups who seemed to be moral in their personal lives, but who blinded themselves to the social oppression under which millions lived.

Images from the films about Adolf Eichmann swarmed into my mind as I listened to Peter Paris. I remembered the pictures of the Eichmann family decorating a Christmas tree while the Jewish population was riding the rails to the concentration camps. Extreme conditions of oppression call to mind situations in which social degradation has inclined both oppressors and oppressed toward immorality, and yet others may somehow remain unmindful of the suffering, strive against the oppression, or achieve moments of moral dignity amid the worst social situations. Social immorality in an organized political-economic system drives the people in the system toward immorality. Still, there is a transcendence of immorality in its organized form that permits lives of moral dignity and even moral heroism.

A sensitive moral critique of the United States would reveal a society in which the dominant class benefits at the cost of the lower classes. The cost of racial discrimination still denies the proportional benefits of the society to groups outside of the establishment groups. The society is protected and projects its power and influence by threatening the destruction of perceived enemies. The constructs of our minds and our society tend still to reinforce lesser achievement and fulfillment by women than by men. Politics is corrupted by the influence of financial power, and the economic system is morally very ambiguous. Is it possible to live morally in such a system?

Christian theology provides various answers. A major answer is, of course, that the world is corrupt and Christians live more by forgiveness than by moral achievement. Still, Christians strive to be moral and to live responsible lives without inflicting harm. Christians are under obligation to love the neighbor and to seek justice. In the society, action often involves the utilization of the clumsy social institutions of politics, government, police, and economics. All of these institutions are deeply compromised by the use of violent force, presuppositions of greed, and a history of organized sin or evil. In the United States, these institutions all presuppose competitive capitalism and racism. Can we use them morally?

Stephen Mott has faced this issue. He believes that individuals may not avenge themselves according to Romans 12:19 while the ruler is "the servant of God to execute wrath on the wrongdoer" (Rom. 13:4). He does not believe that Christians are free to use force even to protect themselves or their property, although the state may. Still, he does not want to divide Christian ethics. "We are not faced with a dualistic ethic: there is not one ethical standard for private and intimate life and a different one for commercial and political life."[1]

Mott thinks that the same criteria apply to personal and to state decisions, but that state decisions are more complex. His understanding of love provides sanctions for the use of jails, fines, force in protecting others, police forces, and just revolutions. He is one who, with a deep sense of the evil of the world, leads Christians to engage in creative reform through politics. Of course, to use politics morally and creatively, politics itself must be reformed. Has Mott, in his optimism about reform through politics, neglected the moral ambiguity of American politics itself? Politics is both the self-interested pursuit of power by individuals and groups and the ordering of our society for social good. We must not neglect the corruption of the political process while urging that love use politics to reform the society. Christian ethics cannot assume a classical Greek or civics textbook perspective on politics. Love could, perhaps, be applied directly, as Mott applies it, to a good political order, but we do not have a good political order. His argument that love uses the sanctions of jails, fines, and violent revolutions neglects the realities of these processes. Daniel Berrigan, who is acquainted with the realities of fines, jails, the power of the state, and militarism, perhaps sees more deeply on this point than Mott. He describes the corruption of his own beloved order as he reflects on Jesuit colleges.

Jesuit campuses, peopled by apolitical refugees from the heat of the times, Jesuits and others, are a seedbed of reaction and militarization. There the ROTC marches, government research is lusted after; and theology bows in shame. Thus, in the phrase of Niebuhr, and according to a process he scarcely understood, do moral men clot and form an immoral society; even one named so nobly, Jesuit.[2]

Berrigan refers to moral people whose community within the church is corrupted by the governing arm of the society, the government. If we bracket his assumption of moral people, we still have a corrupt community and an immoral government. His perspective and his life are witnesses to a moral challenge addressed to community and society.

What can be said about the quandary introduced here? The perspectives of Augustine, Luther, and Calvin may provide us with enough background to understand what Christian realism was attempting to accomplish with its sharp distinction between Christian personal and social ethics.

## ASCETIC CHRISTIAN COMMUNITIES AND THE PUBLIC ROLE OF CHRISTIANS

This short discussion of Augustine does not imply that Augustine proposed a distinction between personal and public morality. His distinction is more obviously located between the requirements of ascetic Christian communities and the public role of Christians. He can be seen as the major voice in articulating early Christian realism, but probably not as one who radically separated personal and public morality for Christians.

For Augustine, the Christian ethic is for those who would love rightly and not for those committed to the dying world. The goal of the Christian life is to participate in God through knowledge of God and to participate in the divine love, thereby finding eternal happiness. Faith, hope, and love are the summary virtues of Christian faith that are expressed in the classical virtues of courage, wisdom, temperance, and prudence, making these virtues expressions of love. "His distinction between the two cities is a distinction between archetypes. The one consists of those who wish to live after the flesh, the other of those who wish to live after the spirit; and when they severally achieve what they wish, they live in peace, each after their kind."[3]

The City of God is the city of those who seek the peace of God according to God's way; the city of earth is the city of those who seek the peace of the world in the world's way. A Protestant reading of Augustine stresses that the cities are not exactly historical institutions but that the City of God and the city of earth are reflected in the institutions of the church and the state. The Christian—Count Boniface, for example—is criticized for not fulfilling Christian sexual morality, but is enjoined to protect the peace of earth through the use of the sword and state power.

Augustine has political ideas, but not a political theory. His eye is on the City of God. In society, human beings, not structures, are the focus. The state originates in sin, and the history of human beings in the state is bloody. The governor of the state should serve as a Christian in two ways that are denied to private citizens: the ruler must govern for protection and the mutual welfare of the citizens and must use force to punish evil and maintain the earthly peace.

The Christian lives in the City of God, which is in pilgrimage through the city of earth. In this pilgrimage, the goals of the economy can be accepted. The aims of the two cities are different. The City of God is more focused on an otherworldly thrust, with little emphasis on working for the earthly peace about which Augustine is pessimistic. The church is not against society, but it has a different aim. Augustine is something of a cultural relativist sensing that people are governed by a diversity of laws and institutions, and he has few moral absolutes for human society. He does not expect much improvement in society. Society could be improved if all were Christian, but because this will not happen, there is not much emphasis on social reform.

Still, in a remarkable section of *The City of God* (V:24) Augustine writes in the familiar "Mirror of Princes" genre of the happy Christian emperor. The Christian emperor can in this life be happy in hope and govern with justice, benevolence, minimum force, mercy, pardon, and the restraint of personal drives toward luxury. Such a leader is to rule by fearing, loving, and worshiping God, and with concern that the true worship of God be extended. Constantine is seen as the model of the Christian emperor (in V:25). The fates of his immediate successors, even though they were Christian, were less happy.

Augustine blurred the distinctions between church and government as he gradually moved from a position of freedom of religion to a position of government suppression of heresy. He finally used Old Testament texts and the New Testament reference to compelling people to join the feast of God to reinforce his own observations about the benefits of successful persecutions of the Donatists. His earlier insights in *De Vera Religionis* that Christ did nothing by force seems, of course, from our perspective, superior to his later hardening.

Many of his references to government are overly pessimistic for the formation of Christian social theory. Perhaps he was misled by his Stoic myth of a Golden Age. The insight that "righteous men of previous times were made shepherds rather than kings" blurs some distinctions between animals and human subjects. He needed more insight on limiting rulers and a more fully developed sense of justice. There are resources in the Bible, including justice and shalom, that he needed to develop. A social hermeneutic of the New Testament could have led him to find resources that he did not utilize. Our social ethics might better turn to the "Mirror of Princes" insight than to the dualism of the two cities or to Augustine's views on persecution of heretics. Reinhold Niebuhr, who drew so much from Augustine, came in his later writing to regard Augustine's social pessimism as overdrawn for democratic political ethics.

## TWO KINGDOMS

The contemporary distinction between personal and public morality owes something to Martin Luther. Luther himself did not make the distinction between the personal and the public, but rather between two kingdoms. His ethics flow from his understanding of radical faith responding to unmerited grace. This, and the sad state of the Roman Catholic penitential system joined to the sale of indulgences, led him to overthrow several characteristics of the ethical system of his day. There were to be:

1. No double standard of ethics for the laity and the monks
2. No system of accruing merit through good works
3. No winning of justification through works or indulgences
4. No hierarchy of ethical merit

Ethics is absorbed by theology. Humanity cannot fulfill the law; even the Ten Commandments cannot be obeyed. The attempt to obey the law or ethical principles makes the law and God into enemies. Even if one did fulfill the commandments out of fear, it would be wrong. All acts not fulfilled by joyful, loving response to God's grace are violations of God's will. The motives for Christian ethics are gratitude and love. The Christian remains a forgiven sinner and acts on the basis of faith. Works are the fruits of Christian life, but are not the roots of Christian life.

For Luther, then, much of Christian life is undefined by law. What is important is the grace of God. The commandments provide a structure, but one cannot fulfill them. The commandments make sense only when the *creed* is inwardly appropriated and we can pray the Lord's Prayer. To Luther, the importance of memorizing the commandments, the creed, and the Lord's Prayer is clear. He says the commandments are a summary of Christian life, but later he says that without grace, no one can fulfill them.

An ethics of radical faith and love responds to God in faith and in acts of love. Karl Holl wrote in *The Cultural Significance of the Reformation* that proper moral acts could, through grace, be decided and chosen by the Christian believer. Paul Lehmann argued in *Ethics in a Christian Context* that without principles, the Christian could stand and obey God. This is true for a Martin Luther, doctor of scripture, subject of monastic discipline, and student of Christian morality. Most of us can find the moral way, but only adequately if we are in a Christian community of discourse with the knowledge of the community's history of moral principles presupposed.

Luther did not distinguish between the commands of Jesus and the counsels of Jesus as medieval morality had done. The asceticism of the monastery was rejected. Humanity serves God radically, absolutely, in all of life. The *vocation* is not just a religious vocation but is any worthy vocation. There we are to serve God. One ought not to aspire to the vocation of another, but serve where one is called. We are not responsible for all of the world, God is responsible; we are responsible for our vocation.

Persons are responsible for their own lives and before God for their salvation. There is no goal of individual autonomy. The introspection and pursuit of inner religious life received emphasis here. Luther is mystic and finds God in the personal will. The Protestant individualism of disconnected individuals comes later. James Nichols says that the "mutual ministry of all Christians" is better than the "priesthood of all believers." We are to be priests to our neighbors. The prescribed channels of the church are not necessary. One can be Christ to one's neighbor.

I have often, following my teachers, described Luther's ethic from the perspective of a personal and a public ethic. The personal ethic stresses the spontaneous response of the Christian as well as the commandments. Luther is against both papal authority and antinomian extremes. As a pastor, he is on the side of authority against chaos, yet he believes that if we had enough spirit we could write our own commandments. He is freer from the Bible than is Calvin; the authority of the *Word of God* is sometimes scripture, but more typically it is Christ.

The social ethic is distinguished as being of an ad hoc character, without a system. Luther gives advice in a revolutionary situation. He expresses his concerns for the poor, arguing against unfair prices, gouging, etc. He is against crusades and wars of conquest. He is pushing the society to reform itself so that the freedom of God's Word is ensured. The state should protect the church. In society, we can follow natural law and reason guided by biblical understanding. In earthly societies, we are expected to obey the law, and expect to suffer under dumb, if not malevolent, rulers. Luther describes himself as having written so often on the two kingdoms that he is surprised there is anyone who doesn't know it. Its extreme presentation is in "An Open Letter Concerning the Hard Book against the Peasants."[4] Grace and mercy are present in God's kingdom. Love, service, and joy all belong to God's kingdom. In the kingdom of the world there is punishment and wrath. The evils are suppressed for the protection of the good. The Christian is not to slay or take revenge on anyone. All suffering is to be endured. But in the world's kingdom, there is strict punishment or God's wrath for the wicked for the end of protecting the righteous. Having rebelled, the peasants have no claim on mercy; they are to be punished as is appropriate for rebels in the world's kingdom. The distinction defends Luther's harshness against the peasants, but it does not make very good sense.

On the one hand, he argues, Christians are to endure robbery, arson, murder, and so forth. On the other hand, Christians in office are to punish these very evils without mercy. It is the two kingdoms that are confusing; a simple distinction between actions appropriate to the roles of citizens as distinct from those of public officials would have sufficed. The lines between the two kingdoms cannot be drawn precisely enough to confine mercy to one realm and the sword to the other. The dualism of the two kingdoms may free society for critical examination by secular means of study, but it also frees society from prophetic critique and from the continuing leavening pressure of

Christian witness. It tends to confine love and mercy to the more immediate areas of life, freeing most of life from heightened ethical responsibility.

## SPIRITUAL AND POLITICAL GOVERNMENTS

It should not surprise us that Calvin's distinctions come closer to our modern view of personal and public ethics. His influence in American Protestant ethics and American constitutional arrangements is immense. Calvin's distinction is between two governments. The first is spiritual and the second is political. The former "pertains to the life of the soul while the latter has to do with the concerns of the present life"—i.e., food, clothing, and social laws. "For the former resides in the inner mind while the latter regulates only outward behavior." He also calls one the "spiritual kingdom" and the other the "political kingdom." They are to be distinguished and related. He wants to avoid applying the radical freedom of the inner Christian conscience to the outer realm of the public arena. The laws of conscience apply to the inner person and the other to civil justice.[5]

According to Calvin, the dangers to be avoided in public policy are the dangers of chaos founded in antinomianism and the dangers of tyranny founded in elevation of political rulers to contend with the rule of God. Government is necessary and provided by God for the welfare of humanity. Christians serve in it under the orders appropriate to human government. Natural law, reason, and social customs all influence the shape of government, which is subject to criteria of equity and love. The *Institutes*, beginning with an address to Francis I and concluding with political theory, does not leave the political realm to its own devices, but neither does it attempt to subject the state to the internal guidance of Christian conscience. Calvin's teaching and practice is to guide the state toward equity and liberty under law while respecting state dynamics. Society may be immoral, but it is to be reformed. People may be immoral, but Christians are justified and they are to be sanctified. H. Richard Niebuhr saw Calvin correctly when he portrayed him as a transformer of culture in both theory and practice.

In a pluralistic culture like the United States, we may be less sanguine than Calvin about legislating to protect proper worship and doctrine. However, legislating to protect freedom of worship and state actions to preserve freedom of religious conscience are appropriate. Calvin's worst crises came in using city power to suppress heresy. We do not have either the need or the appropriate social context for such oppression. History, since Calvin, has permitted the church to return to its earlier and better ideas of restricting the state from legislating in matters of faith. His insight, however, that ethical guidance for the inner Christian life is different from laws for the state, is wise. Particularly where ethical guidance for inner Christian life varies among religious groups, it is helpful to remember that social legislation and government are distinguishable from our finest personal ethical insights. This brief survey may provide enough background to consider the problem of personal and public morality in a twentieth-century thinker.

## INDIVIDUAL AND GROUP MORALITIES

Reinhold Niebuhr's goal in distinguishing between personal and public morality was to contribute to the struggle for greater justice.[6] He wanted people of great ethical sensitivities to participate in the necessarily ambiguous struggles for social justice. He knew that perfectionists could, by their sensitivities, exclude themselves from the political process. He wanted to avoid that exclusion. He thought people who were striving to be good should participate in the social struggle even though aspects of it would offend their sensibilities. Moral judgments of the personal lives, as well as the public lives, of political leaders were still valid, however. He, too, would reject as political leaders persons who exhibited known character flaws. The distinction was not drawn to excuse immorality in personal life, but to encourage people who would be moral to engage in public life, where morality was necessarily so imperfect.

In personal life, Niebuhr's morality was severe. It was a conventional Protestant morality inspired both by duty and by unselfishness. The ideal was unselfish care for the other. It was usually expressed in a deontological reading of the Protestant tradition inspired by the self-giving love of Jesus. In conversation after conversation with him, I came to know him as forgiving, but holding the highest standards for moral achievement of those whose lives he touched.

The concluding chapter of *Moral Man and Immoral Society* is Niebuhr's most developed reflection on the subject. His analysis of society leads him to find an "irreconcilable conflict between the needs of society and the imperatives of a sensitive conscience. . . . One focus is in the inner life of the individual, and the other in the necessities of man's social life. . . . These two moral perspectives are not mutually exclusive and the contradiction between them is not absolute."[7] This does not mean that political wisdom is to be freed from the pressure of moral critique. Moral goodwill is a necessary ingredient of the political process. He does not intend to free the "children of darkness" from the "children of light," but he wants the children of light to know that in politics their absolute insights are subject to compromise.

Perhaps my experience as a father with children in the public schools will illustrate Niebuhr's point. My children attended the tough urban school across the street. I did not want them to be protected by private schools. As a social moralist, I wanted them to know the society while transcending it and becoming equipped to reform it.

Every day we discussed school before praying over our evening meal. My children were raised to pursue truth with full seriousness, but they also had to meet a school schedule that interrupted this pursuit. They had to be protected by police, many of whom were racists. The funds had to be raised by a taxation system that was far from just. My children defied some absurdities (one defied for four years the required pledge of allegiance; we took his defiance to the Board of Public Education and won his rights). Other absurdities they compromised with daily. The facts of crowd control violated their sensibilities.

As a parent, I campaigned for school board candidates who would integrate the schools. As parents with a concern for academic achievement, we accepted the academic tracking that partially segregated them in the high school. I organized Christians to paint over racial slurs in public places in the neighborhood directed at school integration. In practice, we discussed realistically the racial tensions in the school. Black children came to our home and we visited occasionally in their homes. American society forced us to be pragmatists with ideals where urban society interacted with our children. Personally they overcame racism in their hearts, while remaining realistic about the public schools. Such is the fate, I believe, of a sensitive conscience in society. Our children will live, I pray, with a vision of the disinterestedness of a "Tolstoy, a St. Francis, a crucified Christ," to take Niebuhr's examples, but with an eye on the social reality of public education, which is a political process involving interested groups depending on public tax money. To return to Niebuhr, politics is not just self-interested group egoism:

> A wise statesman is hardly justified in insisting on the interests of his group when they are obviously in unjust relation to the total interests of the community of mankind. Nor is he wrong in sacrificing immediate advantages for the sake of higher mutual advantages. His unwillingness to do this is precisely what makes nations so imprudent in holding to immediate advantages and losing ultimate values of mutuality. Nevertheless it is obvious that fewer risks can be taken with community interests than with individual interests.[8]

His argument moves back and forth, wanting as much social reform in society as possible but wary of claiming impossible goals for social reform. He knows that ideas and reform movements can change society, but he also knows about the forces of group egoism that prevent the growth of greater justice.

Finally, Niebuhr's answers are more in his discussion than in any neat formulation of a position, but he does say: "It would therefore seem better to accept a frank dualism in morals than to attempt a harmony between the two methods which threatens the effectiveness of both. Such a dualism would have two aspects. It would make a distinction between the moral judgments applied to the self and to others; and it would distinguish between what we expect of individuals and of groups."[9]

He summarizes:

> To some degree the conflict between the purest individual morality and an adequate political policy must therefore remain. The needs of an adequate political strategy do not obviate the necessity of cultivating the strictest individual moral discipline and the most uncompromising idealism. Individuals, even when involved in their communities, will always have the opportunity of loyalty to the highest canons of personal morality.[10]

The social context of *Moral Man and Immoral Society* was the Great Depression. Questions of whether workers engaged in industrial sit-downs were morally required to remain nonviolent divided the Fellowship of Reconciliation (FOR). Niebuhr, who was in the minority and would accept a violent response by workers to violence inflicted on them by the owners, resigned as president of the FOR. His pacifism was waning, and his book represents that struggle. He gave up his pacifism, first for the domestic struggle, and later for the principle of economic sanctions to stop Italy's invasion of Abyssinia. Pacifism would remain, for him, an expression of an absolute ideal. Nonviolent strategies for social change were often adopted by him, but the world, as he saw it, did not consider nonviolent strategies to be the only moral options within society. Gradually, he became known as a critic of Christian pacifism, although he welcomed it as a witness and welcomed nonviolent protest as a sometimes preferred social strategy, as in the case of Martin Luther King Jr. His social morality became utilitarian or, in contemporary terms, consequentialist within the contexts of Christian anthropology and the theology of history.

His later chapter[11] on collective egoism develops and expands the insight that collectivities lack the capacities of the individual to hear moral critique, to repent, and to engage in self-sacrificing love for the other. Group pride leads to idolatry: "The nation pretends to be God."[12] Some of his finest writing is on the expressions of sin as pride in the collected egoism of the nation. Nations or minorities within nations can hear prophetic critique, but functions of the nation at all analogous to a self with moral capacity are very weak. The collective life is always connected with the sin of pride in Niebuhr's analysis.[13] Still, relative moral judgments must be made, and to be moral they must be in the direction of justice.

In his final revision of his political philosophy, Niebuhr affirmed the distinction between the egoism of individuals and the "self-regard of class, race, and nation," although here he referred to a discussion in one of his later seminars and to a suggestion that John Raines had made. "A young friend of mine recently observed that, in the light of all the facts and my more consistent 'realism' in regard to both individual and collective behavior, a better title might have been *The Not So Moral Man in His Less Moral Communities*."[14]

I find the distinction useful for the theological students I teach. It helps inform them of why group strategies are necessary to overcome institutional racism. It makes sense of Niebuhr's writing on racism and the need for a multifaceted strategy using institutions of church, voluntary association, and state to work at overcoming it. The Protestant theological students I teach need to overcome illusions that individual good can overcome racism. Their hearts need to be convicted and freed of white pride, but then they need to accept rough tactics of working in society to attempt to overcome the institutionalized effects of racism. Affirmative action programs at home and sanctions against South Africa were supported by Protestant activists who came to see the need for strategies of rough justice to break down the institutions of racism. Niebuhr's own social ethics and practical theology included over the years several tactics that idealistic Protestants would have found hard to support.

In the 1920s, in Detroit, these tactics included plans to enforce fair realty practices, abolish separate schools, integrate police and fire departments, and launch various programs for education and self-improvement of blacks. In the 1930s, they involved founding and supporting an interracial cooperative farm in the Mississippi Delta and articulating strategies of nonviolent protest, economic boycott, and tactics of a Gandhian sort. In the 1940s, they involved counseling of black students in New York as they worked in their churches to break down segregation and to empower their people. In the 1950s, Union Seminary became an organizing center for the struggle to attack segregation. Arriving in 1960, we were immediately enlisted in nonviolent campaigns at civil and economic sites. Also, in the 1950s and 1960s, the seminary, allied with Martin Luther King Jr., continued to send volunteers throughout the South and into the northern struggle at the local Woolworth stores, banks, and the South African embassy. The work for equality in politics was carried on by the Americans for Democratic Action, the Liberal Party, and the Democratic Party and through personal persuasion and written argument, but the tactics for change in church and society were much broader and deeper than was known by many who have commented on Christian realism.

I am now less critical of Niebuhr's distinction between personal and social ethics than I was in my 1972 book,[15] but this distinction is subject to misuse. In Niebuhr's writing the distinction was used to encourage moral people to practice moral politics in an immoral society. It was not intended to shield immoral politicians from moral censure. It has become an apology in some for a realistic politics divorced from morality. The role of the church as a mediating community, shaping persons and influencing society, could have received more emphasis than it did in Niebuhr's writing. The personal and the social, of course, are mutually interdependent, but there is a potential for ethical achievement and transcendence of egoism in the personal life that is lost in social life. My appreciation for his way of putting the distinction has increased in part because I have become a little less of a child of light as I've matured, but more because I understand better the complex practical theology he was teaching and living out as a professor of social ethics at a seminary. His claims for the church as an ethical agent were appropriately modest, but his influence on the church through the seminary, his students, and his writings was immense.

Niebuhr's distinction between personal and social morality was more like that of Calvin, who also knew that humanity was a social being, than like Augustine's or Luther's. I do not think the distinction is particularly biblical; rather, it is an insight drawn from observing human morality. It could be used as a hermeneutical device for examining biblical moral teachings, but I suspect that it would reveal only the obvious—that the Bible is full of social morality, personal morality, and morality for particular communities.

A distinction between private and public morality could be used to reinforce gender oppression. All of the theologians noted here were male, and the distinction is not utilized by the more relational ethics of women authors.[16] If one is to use it, one needs to be realistic and accept that the realm of the family is a complicated political reality and not an ideal realm of innocent love. One has to be clear that women are not relegated to the ethics of the private realm. The 1930s, when Niebuhr, wrestling with his social idealism, evolved the distinction, was also a time of greater idealism about the family than is possible in the 1990s.

The Supreme Court has recognized a right of privacy in its decisions about *Roe v. Wade*. It has effectively ruled that state interest does not override the privacy of the female person during the first six months of pregnancy. The personal ethical decision of the woman regarding a fetus overrides whatever public interest there is in the decision regarding abortion. With these repeated decisions, the Court has overturned other legislative bodies' actions that insisted that the public welfare extended further into the woman's private decision making. Similarly, more sexual practices are being regarded as private and beyond the reach of state regulation. These issues are not the same as those discussed by theologians seeking a personal-social ethical distinction, but they point, even in law, to a private realm beyond legal reach.

It is a distinction between the most sensitive personal morality and public morality that is appropriate. A distinction is not a division or a wall. The person lives and acts in society. The society forms the person, but the person is more than the society. The distinction is best used by morally sensitive persons who must compromise and form coalitions to secure social reform in society. Its worst use is by realists or cynics who would use it to shield institutions, social policies, or politics from moral judgments. The gain in understanding a distinction between personal and social morality attributed to Niebuhr is available without the customary confusion. Calvin's distinction between the spiritual and the political will suffice. The distinctiveness Niebuhr found in the personal is all spiritual. The human self in touch with God and to some degree transcendent of self-interest can imagine and sometimes accomplish nobility scarcely available in politics. The call of the church to live by a high morality derives from its partially spiritual nature, not from personal or individual morality. The church, in fact, molds and challenges the personal morality of its members, lifting them to a greater morality partially through its communal nature. The wisest approach is to accept the distinction between personal and social morality for its appropriate applicability, but to insist that the more important distinction rests between humanity's spiritual functions and its political functions. Even here, Christian morality insists on only a mild dualism, knowing that there are spiritual dimensions of political life as well.

# Economic Disparities

Two visual images initiate these reflections on economic disparities. The first is the sight of an elderly man outside a Pittsburgh grocery store dressed in rags and searching in a dumpster for something to eat. The second is an Indian woman with her child strapped on her back emptying a street wastebasket in Guadalajara seeking a morsel for her baby. What are the interconnections beyond these visual impressions? Is the malnutrition of poverty in Mexico related to the same degradation in Pittsburgh? Are my office window in Pittsburgh, the hotel balcony in Guadalajara, and the airplane ticket connecting them related to this grinding down of the poor? To the extent that economics studies the use of scarce resources,[1] as Paul Samuelson's famous introductory text suggests, the scarcity of resources for the poor is of the first order for economics.

The major input of Christian ethics to the discussion of economic disparities is of course the double love commandment. Christian ethics helps economics most by insisting that it be autonomous neither in theory nor in practice. Economics takes place in God's world, and the first requirement of all thinking about economics is a focus on the ultimate source of all value, God. Economics has to be relativized and humbled before it can be made truly useful to the poor. The place of economics is within the ethical framework of passionate devotion to God and service to the neighbor. Christian theological ethics needs to keep economics within its framework and not permit it practically or conceptually to stand alone as if its purpose were to rationally plan the marketplace for those with financial power.

The double love commandment is absolutely binding, and it provides the framework for economic discussion. The founder of modern economics, Adam Smith, knew this well. As an Enlightenment Christian, his moral philosophy may have been less orthodox than contemporary theologians would urge, but he had his priorities straight for his ethics published in 1759: "All affections for particular objects, ought to be extinguished in our breast, and one great affection take the place of all others, the love of the Deity. . . . The sole principle and motive of our conduct in the performance of all those different duties, ought to be a sense that God has commanded us to perform them."[2] The context of this passage was his stress on how religion motivated human conduct, and that one did not rely on a sense of duty alone. His development of the argument also expressed his reliance on the imperative to love our neighbor and how we loved ourselves not out of imperative but for our own sakes.

The rich sense of how economics was part of the subject matter taught by Christian moral philosophy has of course faded. We are also neglecting the sense that economics was to reflect on how we could increase the production and the welfare of the poor. Without ethics, economics is a dismal body of reflection on human making and getting. Christian economists have argued that its lack of theological and ethical rigor has contributed to an economy in which the numbers of desperately poor increase, worldwide unemployment grows, and economic growth fuels ecological degradation.[3]

The anthology *On Moral Business*, edited by three ethicists and an economist, includes Max Stackhouse's short interpretation of the Ten Commandments. He notes that these ten prescriptions of covenant ethics are not just an old document, but that they are moral guidelines for our day.[4] "Not with our fathers did the Lord make this covenant, but with us, who are all of us here alive today" (Deut. 5:3).

His relating of the commandments to their economic implications generally concurs with the scriptural study in chapters 4 and 5 of this volume. Repetition of three emphases and the urging of them with passion are part of the ongoing tasking of Christian communities seeking justice.

1. The requirement of sabbatical rest on the seventh day also commands work and implies woe to a society that denies its people work.

2. The commandment against stealing prohibits fraud, exploitation, and the taking of what the poor must have to survive.

3. The final commandment reaches to motives and denies covetousness of the other's property. This cuts directly against the lust for disproportionate shares of wealth. One should not scheme to get more for oneself at the expense of the community. All of the other commandments also have deep economic consequences, but these three especially point toward some of the structural issues that need reform in our emerging world economy.

It seems clear from economic reality, economic theory, and my perspective that the world's economy will not be the laissez-faire economy dreamed of by French Enlightenment philosophers or the communally planned economy of their German-Russian revolutionary heirs. Rather, history has conspired to defeat capitalism and socialism. Capitalism was abandoned in the Great Depression of the 1930s, and socialism in the revolts of the late 1980s. Christian ethicists, long beholden to socialist paradigms, should have known we were neither good enough nor smart enough to totally plan our economy. Similarly, the tradition of restraint, law, and resistance to egoism should have kept Christian ethics from endorsing laissez-faire, especially in its limited social Darwinist expressions. It is platitudinous to endorse mixed economic models today, but such is our reality. God has graciously allowed the extremes of capitalism and socialism to fail and humanity to grope pragmatically toward mixed economies. When, in the context of Indian socialism under Rajiv Gandhi, I argued for mixed economic strategies, Indian socialist Christian friends accused me of advocating only "mixed up" economics. But this is reality. Personally, in the years when my children were in college, our ample family income came from ecclesiastical sources, mostly from endowments invested in stocks, bonds, and other investments. About 40 percent of this went to taxes, another 12 percent to pay tuitions at private and public universities, about 6 percent to the church and to charity, and the rest to the market. An economy in which 42 percent of income goes to the market does not deserve the name of a market economy. Others' taxes and tuitions may be higher or lower, but nationally about 35 percent of the gross national product (a terribly unreliable guide) goes to taxes. The economy of the United States is a mixture, and so are the economies of the rest of the world. Taxes are higher in other industrialized countries, and are very difficult to collect in most of the world, but in the world system, governments play a major role along with corporate powers, independent smaller entrepreneurs, and organizations. Yet, given this reality, Christian ethics must not think from the standpoint of mixed economy; it must proceed from its normative traditions, which in the end will urge policies of change for this mixed economy and for all others.

There is a trajectory of economic ethics, which I regard as my own, that runs from John Calvin to the present. John Calvin was present as the world shifted from the Catholic great chain of being of social organization dominated by the church to a much more chaotic jumble of competing powers including semiautonomous economic organizations. Other Christian voices—Adam Smith, Emil Brunner, and John Bennett—will be noted for particular accents before mainline Protestant church studies of economics are analyzed and complemented by a few reflections from Catholic teaching in order to present an agenda for Christian moral pressures on our American mixed economy.

## MIDDLE-CLASS VIRTUES

John Calvin gave a distinctive shape to a branch of the Reformation called Reformed Christians. These Christians are distinguished by emphases on the sovereignty of God, commitment to a piety of religious experience, and personal and social life regulated by Christian ethics grounded in the will of God.[5] Economics refers to investigations of systems of political-economic decisions that shape the production and distribution of a society's goods and services. In the case of John Calvin, economics refers to teaching about money, interest, welfare practices, and practical political-business decisions made in Geneva from 1541 to 1564.

Calvin did not develop a philosophical moral theory. Rather, he taught moral obedience to the will of the sovereign God. This will was found particularly in the Ten Commandments. The remainder of scripture's moral teaching could be related to the Decalogue. Jesus did not really add any new moral teaching, but purified the morality and returned it to its true meaning in the Decalogue. The Reformation ethics is not a new ethics, but a return to Mosaic ethics in light of the new situation. Of course, scripture had to be interpreted, and this gave the interpreter of scripture, particularly Calvin himself, a high role in teaching the meaning of God's law. Natural law corresponds to God's law, but in Geneva or wherever Reformed ethics was taught, the exposition of the Decalogue was the chief guide to morality. The law, properly taught, convicted human beings of their sins, constrained the wicked by the fear of public penalties and the fear of hell, and counseled the faithful in reforming instruction on how they should live. Calvin's faith is in a message of grace, but instruction in the things needful to do is required. However, the instruction could serve as grounds for legalistic requirements, as it did in Geneva and elsewhere.

In Geneva and generally in Reformed circles, the Decalogue was expounded to people participating in the growth of urban and citizen power as the feudal system was being displaced. The practitioners of Calvin's ethics were becoming middle-class people and participants in ownership of European urban civilization. They were originally middle class in economic position, although many Protestant refugees flocking to Geneva were in fact poor. They were also middle class in outlook, preferring citizen control to oligarchical or monarchical political control and a mixture of lay-clerical control of the church to a clerical-hierarchical control of the church.

There is a moral seriousness to the ethics of Calvin. God is a judge, the law is known, and it is interpreted by a lawyer-theologian in its clear sense with full, moral rigor. If the world does not correspond to the ethics, then, ordinarily, so much the worse for the world, which must be changed. There is not much in Calvin about a duty to work hard. He rather assumes hard work, but he wants it to be clearly understood that hard labor does not provide wealth. Only God provides wealth. No one is advanced unless God advances them. Idleness is criticized, humanity since the Fall has been intended to labor, but the words of Calvin do not incite people to extreme labor. His attitude toward work is revealed in his commentary on the story of Jesus with Mary and Martha. Martha is rebuked only for her frenzied efforts. Her efforts on Jesus' behalf, according to Calvin, were appreciated. Mary's willingness to sit with him and be instructed was carefully guarded from encouraging indolence. Calvin went on in his commentary to say, "We know that people were created for the express purpose of being employed in labor of various kinds, and that no sacrifice is more pleasing to God, than when everyone applies diligently to one's own calling, and endeavors to live in such a manner as to contribute to the general advantage."[6] For Calvin there is a time to hear and a time to act. Calvin even concluded from the Mary and Martha story that Christ "would rather have chosen to be entertained in a frugal manner, and at moderate expense, than that the holy woman should have submitted to so much toil."[7]

Calvin's example, of course, was of a great activist in constant practical and academic labor. Few have equaled his literary outpouring, but we do not find in Calvin's teaching the advocacy of driving, anxious labor that a simple reading of Max Weber might lead the student to expect. Nor do we find the popular notion that Calvin related salvation to hard labor.[8]

In Calvin's hands, *honesty* became the honesty of spirit as well as of the strict word. Business trickery or chicanery was condemned as dishonest and also as stealing. The structures against false witness were broadly applied. The Ten Commandments were interpreted vigorously to reinforce a strict commercial ethos. The common meaning of "business is business" received no toleration from John Calvin. Even legal practices that deprived people of their property were regarded as stealing. Exploitation by the rich and powerful of their material edge to increase the poverty of the poor was equivalent to brigandage.

So sobriety, frugality, family discipline, and honesty all reinforced middle-class lives and often contributed to their business success, but the strict enforcement of the morality of the Ten Commandments, with an eye open to the needful protection of the poor, separated those who internalized Calvin's moral teaching from cruel business or legal practices. The least received special protection from the Christians and from the government. But there is a special reason why God declares that he takes the foreign-born, the widows, and the orphans as his wards. Where evil is more flagrant, there is more need of potent remedy.[9]

The virtues of Calvin lead to practical policies assisting the poor, but neither to a special blessed place for the poor nor to a proletariat as a special class.

In Calvin's view, money and goods ought to circulate in human society for the welfare of all. Humanity in solidarity one with another would participate in contributing according to each person's vocation to the good of all. However, selfishness has led to the theft and hoarding of society's goods by a few. Mammon has come to dominate and to ruin the common life. The natural, relative economic equality and mutual service have been violated. God is using both the church and the state to restore the original intentions. The church teaches and acts to promote equality and restore human solidarity. Calvin said that God wills there to be proportion and equality among us— that is, each one is to provide for the needy according to the extent of one's means, so that no one has too much and no one has too little.[10]

The church helps people put their property to the use of all. "The crying differences between rich and poor thus disappear."[11] In the church, the charity one owes to the neighbor is assisted. The church, through the restored service of the diaconate, reaffirms human solidarity through concrete service. It also, through preaching, teaching, and lobbying, insists that the public organs of society meet the needs of the people. The restoration of the dignity of people beginning in Christ is alive in the church and moves into state policies. Jesus himself gave up power and riches to enter into the condition of the poor, and his struggle with the evil of poverty is the proper work of the church and the state. Calvin and his pastors lived in conditions close to poverty, raising funds for the needy and lobbying the state to act for the poor. The goal is a society of neither poor nor rich, but of a working, contributing class with sufficiency for life at a modest level.

## USURY

Under Calvin's influence, restrictions against lending of money for economic production were put aside. His exegesis of Deuteronomy 23:20 became the rallying cry for the expanding middle class to overthrow the remnants of the legislation of the Middle Ages that had hemmed in the lending of money.

Since the time of Jerome (340–420 c.e.) and Ambrose (340–397 c.e.), Western exegetes, church councils, and jurists had wrestled with the Deuteronomic prohibition against interest taking.

"On loans to a foreigner you may charge interest, but on loans to another Israelite you may not charge interest, so that the Lord your God may bless you in all your undertakings in the land that you are about to enter and possess" (Deut. 23:20).

All Christians were included as *brothers*; the lending to foreigners was seen by Ambrose as lending to *enemies* at interest. The trend of medieval writers was to rule out all loans at interest. Various escape clauses were worked out, including sometimes the toleration of Jewish lenders to Christians. Casuistry proliferated to make loans possible, and before the Reformation, many ways around the prohibition were established.

Martin Luther dealt differently with usury at various historical crises in his career and was unable to resolve the issue clearly. In the end, he surrendered regulation of interest to the princes and authorities. He would regard as usurious only an excessive rate of interest.

Calvin taught that Deuteronomy 23:19 refers specifically to the Hebrews; it does not bind Christians who are bound by rules of charity and justice: "There is a difference in the political union, for the situation in which God placed the Jews and many other circumstances permitted them to trade conveniently among themselves without usuries. Our union is entirely different."[12]

Usury is not universally permitted and needs regulation, but its general prohibition was smashed by Calvin. "Usury is permitted if it is not injurious to one's brother." Calvin is not, of course, renouncing the call to Christian community. Whereas the Hebrew and medieval communities had prohibited the taking of interest within the community, the new community permitted it. Such a shift in interest taking has caused Benjamin Nelson to suggest that the meaning of "brotherhood" in community was diluted to the point of "Universal Otherhood."[13]

Calvin's exegesis and writings reveal a healthy respect for the special structures of Hebrew society and Genevan society. The Hebrew neighbor needed to be helped; God, in charity, required that the help be given without charging interest. In general, interest was permitted. Since Genevan development required interest-bearing loans, they were to be regulated by standards of justice by the government, because otherwise, powerful people would exploit the poor. Calvin rejected the age-old theory of Aristotle and Thomas Aquinas that money could not produce money, and he recognized the right to receive money for the use of one's money. In summary, he recognized God's ordering sovereignty, the need for capital to produce capital, the need for regulation of capital, the need for new practices to meet new situations, and the special needs of the poor.

## APPLIED THEOLOGY

Calvin's real world involved shopkeepers, traders, and craftsmen as well as clerics and academics. He was relatively free of the medieval distaste for commerce and of Luther's preference for the pastoral life. His world was that of urban commerce, and he affirmed it. The exchange of money and goods was affirmed. The institution of money itself was not suspect; God had provided it for the good of humanity.

For Calvin, money is a test for humanity. It tests one's humility, and it is to be used charitably. On the one hand, the money one receives is a divine favor, totally undeserved, and on the other hand, Calvin actively struggles for just wages for clergy, for himself, and for other workers.

Evil is found in the use of money since the Fall. Although money is a good, its use historically leads to distortion, oppression, and economic chaos. People come to follow the human god of mammon, and mammon rules over much of humanity by the corruption of the human heart. This takeover of the human heart is a hidden victory. Mammon then works against God by trying to confine God's rule to the things spiritual while allowing mammon to rule in the economic realm.

The Reformation in Geneva threw both the ministry and the social welfare organizations of the church into confusion. Calvin's recruitment into the Reformation of Geneva left him with responsibilities to try to reorganize both. The traditions of social welfare of Geneva influenced his work as he influenced the traditions of Geneva. The civil government had taken over all of the church revenues and attempted to reorganize the welfare system. During his temporary exile in Strasbourg, Calvin came under the influence of Martin Bucer, who used the churches to supplement the municipal welfare system. Calvin later adopted Bucer's ideas of the order of the diaconate for ministry to the poor, and through a process of adjustment and change, applied them to Geneva on his return to leadership in that city. For Calvin, the deacons were not to be subsumed as apprentice priests or priests' assistants, but to fulfill a more biblical role of primarily ministering to the poor.[14]

Calvin and the pastors supervised and intervened in the affairs of the hospital-general, which was supported by the city government. The hospital-general provided housing and food, as well as medical services, for orphans, the aged, and the needy. It also provided out-client welfare services, and its organization included services in times of plague. The hospital-general was clearly an institution where the religious and secular understandings and institutions met in the administration of social welfare.

Other aspects of applied theology led Calvin and William Farel to institute the first free public education for both sexes and to found the university. Beyond the welfare system and education, the work of Calvin and the pastors reached out to suggestions for railings to protect children on stairs and balconies. Fires and chimneys were regulated, and efforts were made to clean the town and to repair the streets. Of current interest, also, was Calvin's demand for the securing of strict legislation prohibiting the recruitment of mercenaries from Geneva.[15]

Regulation of prices for the necessities of life was an accepted principle of the early Reformation in Geneva. It followed that business practices of artificially raising prices received Calvin's criticism: "Today when everything has such a high price," Calvin says, "we see men who keep their granaries closed; this is as if they cut the throat of a poor people, when they thus reduce them to extreme hunger."[16]

The state had the responsibility of regulating business both for its own efficiency and for just management, as in the cases of the medium of exchanges, weights, measures, coins, and contracts,[17] and for the protection of the population. The major example of regulation of an industry from Calvin's time is that of printing. Printing represented the new technology. The industry had been slipping somewhat in Geneva before the Reformation. As an intellectual center of the religious revolution, Geneva had a great need of printing. The religious needs intersected with issues of wages, hours, collective bargaining, and relationships among masters, journeymen, and apprentices. The industry in France was subject to conflicts and strikes, and the government took the side of the owners. In Geneva, with the intervention of the pastors and the leadership of Calvin, a paternalistic council prohibited collusion by both owners and workers. After the demands of two pastors were presented to the council, the whole industry was regulated following the presentations by the interested parties.[18] Regulation of the printing industry for quality was undertaken by the council, and when it concerned church publications, the weight of clerical intervention was felt. The ordinances passed at Calvin's insistence lasted until the time of Napoleon.

Geneva's regulation of industry, of course, was not innovative. This regulation preceded laissez-faire economics. It was standard, but it was different from regulation in France in that it favored the workers as well as the owners. The regulation was, of course, reinforced by the high view of government help by Reformed theology in general and Calvin in particular. The governing authorities were the agents of God for the welfare of the people. In the face of that practical power and its theological justification, owners and workers had to adjust.

Calvin recognized this high doctrine of government in several of his writings. One interesting formulation of this high calling of the civic official is found in his "Instruction of Faith," a compendium of the Institutes that he prepared: "The Lord has not only testified that the status of magistrate or civic officer was approved by him and was pleasing to him, but also he has moreover greatly recommended it to us, having honored its dignity with very honorable titles."[19] Here is Calvin's enthusiastic "yes" to government. However, even in the next sentence the possibility of a "no" to an unjust government is heard. Justice and judgment are required of these lieutenants of God. The text of Jeremiah in which Calvin grounds the requirements of justice and judgment requires one to do justice, to protect the weak, and to spare the innocent. Jeremiah thunders on that if the people obey, right government will prevail; and if not, there will be destruction. Rule, then, is subject to justice and judgment. Within two paragraphs, Calvin states plainly that any orders by governors contrary to God's will are to be disregarded. Peter is turned to with his witness that we must obey God and not human authorities (Acts 4:19).

The welfare of the people, then, is a clear responsibility of the government as Calvin understood it. The tendency toward governmental control of business is clear in Calvin's writings and actions. Tendencies of later-day Calvinists toward affirmations of laissez-faire economics and social Darwinism do not seem to have a grounding in Calvin. The cruelty of unregulated social Darwinism certainly is not compatible with Calvin's teaching. At one level, an affinity with laissez-faire economics seems possible. If it were more efficient, if it produced more goods for people in need, would Calvin have not accepted it? He was able to adjust Christian ethics to changing times, but laissez-faire economics is beyond the level to which he could have adjusted. He was a person of the sixteenth century with a sense that theonomous society was possible. An autonomous society of all competing according to their own passions and desires was unthinkable. To many, Geneva with Calvin probably seemed heteronomous, but to Calvin it was moving into theonomy in the free acceptance of God's law. The heteronomy of medieval Europe and the autonomy of modern capitalism were both foreign to Calvin; in fact, he was closer to medieval Europe.

All of his economic ethics is secondary to serving the Kingdom of Christ. After affirming the priority of the divine blessing, "We must prize the blessing of God as more valuable than the entire world," he could turn to economic ethics as a secondary matter. In this second rank came the need to "honestly work for a living," the requirement to live moderately, and the duty to "employ the power which riches give in aiding neighbors and relieving them from suffering." "Riches are a means to help the needy. That is the way to proceed and to keep a happy medium."[20]

## THE HARMONIOUS SOCIETY OF ADAM SMITH

Adam Smith's moral theory presupposed that people were primarily self-interested but also possessed virtues of sympathy for other creatures inasmuch as they were like themselves. From this mixture of self-interest and sympathy, the use of reason could derive morality. Economics was understood as part of the moral philosophy that Smith taught at the University of Glasgow (1751–1764). The moral philosophy also encompassed the philosophy of religion. Smith's religion, like his life, lacked the passion of a John Calvin, but it sufficed for his membership in the Church of Scotland, an heir of Calvin. As with Calvin, love of God and love of neighbor were central pillars for Smith, but the details of his morality on worldly matters rested on appropriate behavior as appreciated by the reason of an eighteenth-century gentleman-scholar.

Smith as a person was a somewhat distracted, eccentric scholar of immense knowledge, which he organized systematically and rationally.[21] First as a teacher of logic, then as a writer on astronomy, he was impressed with the regularity and harmonious nature of life. These harmonies were grounded in the nature of the heavenly bodies of astronomy or the human nature expressed in the social studies he undertook. All were grounded in God, but God did not interfere often with the regularities of the created order.

So as Smith describes how the self-interested person gathers wealth, he notes how this maximizing of wealth by each individual contributes to the total accumulated wealth of the society. The individual who by nature accumulates, barters, and trades does not necessarily intend the good of society, but as long as one promotes the purpose of self-accumulation rationally and appropriately, the entire wealth of the community is increased. "One is in this, as in many other cases, led by an invisible hand to promote an end which was no part of one's intention."[22] The assumption is that one trades or sells one's labor at the highest possible rate of return in a competitive society according to the principle of marginal utility. As long as people so engage to mix their labor with the available capital and resources of a society, the wealth of the society will grow. Smith had used the phrase "invisible hand" earlier in his moral philosophy to mean not the maximization of wealth, but the distribution of the necessities of life by the wealthy through their employment of others. The phrase seems to be used more naively in the moral theory to assert that all have roughly equal access to equal peace of mind if not to all the necessities of life. "The beggar who suns himself by the side of the highway possesses that security which kings are fighting for."[23] In its usage in the moral philosophy, "the invisible hand" is used in parallel construction with the divine providence, which, dividing the world unequally, still also provided for the happiness of the poor. The blithe assumption that people are treated roughly equally needed to be tested by more empirical observations of the squalor of eighteenth-century England and the cruelty of its developing mines and factories. In his earliest reference to the invisible hand in his writings on astronomy, it had been to the noninterference of the invisible hand of Jupiter in the regularities of nature. The other use of the term in *The Wealth of Nations* is similar to the assertion of rough human equality in *The Theory of Moral Sentiments*. It is only in the use of the invisible hand to mean the results of the maximization of marginal utility that the term has cogent meaning for economic ethics.

Smith's revolutionary goal in his *Wealth of Nations* was to show that the natural laws of human nature would, if allowed to flourish, meet utilitarian goals of greater happiness for more people. The principles of the division of labor joined with the increasing productivity of machines would increase the wealth of a society. The market worked better than planning for the maximization of the wealth of a nation. The market's natural functioning to increase wealth would be undone if the government, serving business interests, tried to direct the market or to prevent international trade by restrictive practices. Generally speaking, the people—that is, the consumers—would be best served by less government interference for particular business interests. Similar to the possibility of government corruption of a market was monopolistic corruption of a market. Both had to be exposed as irrational impediments to the good of the consumer and the growth of wealth.

There are great moral blinders on Smith. If he is compared with his contemporary John Wesley, also educated at Oxford, the contrast is very sharp. Wesley pleaded for and organized the poor, fought to abolish slavery, and worked to reform the prisons. Smith failed to support these reforms and was rather naive about the corruptions of the human spirit. Nevertheless, he optimistically projected human economic development and increasing human happiness through rational choice in economic matters.

There is some harmony in human affairs, and a dynamic society requires less control than characterized Smith's forebear John Calvin. The England of 1776 corresponded in many features to what Smith saw, but there was much unrelieved misery that he did not comprehend. He was correct that rational, economic competition implies cooperation, which can increase the wealth of all. He, of course, had little sense of the limits of nature, but at least he did not ascribe all value to labor and capital; he recognized natural resources as contributing to wealth. Our contemporary world economy reflects his analysis and confronts his thought with issues of which he was little cognizant. His analyses of the division of labor, industrial development adding to labor, unplanned cooperation as the function of a market, the need for world trade for wealth development, and the dangers of particular interests dominating government or business and corrupting the market are all fruitful contributions to ongoing agonizing over economic injustice. Smith's enlightenment optimism regarding harmony stemming from pure competition seems quaint to a generation raised on Karl Marx, Charles Darwin, and Sigmund Freud. It appears as an assertion close to economic autonomy without the disordering reality of sin and the orienting reality of the Kingdom of God.

## EVANGELICAL ECONOMICS

John Wesley's passion rings through his writing on economics. Whether he is describing the inexcusable suffering of Africans forced into slavery by Europeans or the vile conditions of the English poor imposed by government and establishment, he is never temperate. His language, syntax, and argument call for fundamental economic changes. Some of his writing is descriptive, but with his eye on the Kingdom of God, he is able to see clearly and to describe the squalor of human life. Africans are thrown off slave ships to the depths of the Atlantic and English are forced to find their food among dung heaps because of sin expressed in greed.

Wesley (1703–1791), a contemporary of Adam Smith, knows of the harmonious aspect of society as Smith knows of the conflictive nature of society. Both thirst for order and for sufficiency for the people of eighteenth-century England. But Wesley, with a longing for perfection and a deep awareness of sin, hopes for more transformation of people and society than does Smith. He seems also to see the need for transformation more clearly than Smith. Smith's human nature is inclined toward morality because of natural human sympathy for other beings like oneself. Wesley's human nature is driven toward morality because of evangelical confrontation and divine imperatives.

Wesley's demands for mercy and justice in the economic world follow from his observations, study, and work with the despised of the world. There is an immediacy to his pleas for justice that in the contemporary world has resonated in the theologies of liberation. Yet most of his pleas are for reform. He does not expect the king and parliament to be overthrown; in fact, he dreads revolution, whether in America or France. His specific recommendations are for reform, but in most cases they could be achieved without revolution. Historically, most of them have been approximated, even if not sustained, without revolution.

His advocacy of the abolition of slavery was the most far-reaching of his reforms, as some of the prosperity of England depended on the wretched practice of the triangular trade. Whether wealth would be served or not, slavery was wrong and all were admonished to end it. Europeans were guilty of worse practices than any of the pagan empires Wesley knew about, and economic necessity was not a valid argument for maintaining slavery. The fact that it was supported by human law was irrelevant in the confrontation with God's law. As with Bartholomé de las Casas and Pope Paul III in the sixteenth century, he argued that those subject to slavery were potentially subject to Christ and they had to be freed for their evangelization. For Wesley and the best of sixteenth-century Spanish Catholicism, humanity was to be free by nature and sought out of the evangelical thrust of the gospel. The arguments of the establishment for keeping slaves were couched in terms of economic necessity; in fact, slavery stemmed from greed, not need.

Monopolies in agriculture and the consumption of grain by horses desired by the wealthy as a sign of luxury drove food prices for the poor to formidable heights in Wesley's analysis. The monopolies in agriculture needed to be broken up and the luxurious keeping of horses ended by legislation to restore small agriculture and fair food prices.

In Wesley's eyes, unnecessary military expenses, especially unneeded fortifications, had pushed up the national debt, thus raising interest rates. The wasteful military expenditures needed to be curtailed and the national debt retired.

He recommended changes in employment policies. His particular passion was to reduce the price of food, which used up nearly everything the poor could earn. Burdensome taxes, and the high prices of land, food, and other goods, he attributed to governmental expenses and resultant government debt accrued in military expenditures.

Wesley wrote that thousands were starving in England, and that their starvation was rooted in unemployment. Without funds for anything but food, the poor could not buy the goods that the unemployed might have produced. Because he regarded all property as subject to the will of God for its wise stewardship, the luxuries of the rich were regarded both as unnecessary and as a drag on the economy. He advocated steep taxation of luxuries. Believing in the wisdom of the day regarding supply and demand, he advocated getting resources into the hands of those whose demand would create more products. Thwarting the needs of the poor were the establishment's passion to live in luxury and the use of the government toward that end. He knew that certain practices, such as the use of grain in the overconsumption of alcohol, needed to be stopped, and that other privileges of the rich, such as luxuries, large estates, and consumption of grain by horses, needed to be limited to achieve a healthy economy. He was skeptical of the Christian establishment's will to change. So he advocated for his own religious compatriots lives of economic discipline and effort with the goals of earning all one could without harming self or others, saving all one could without depriving one's family, and giving away through the church and then to the broader population all one could after family needs had been modestly met.

Wesley did not make contributions to economic theory. He did not, at length, present a systematic perspective on economics. But he had no reservations about relating faith and its consequences directly to contemporary economic practice. His calls for economic change toward justice and for the poor were very bold. He knew that Christian economics was about getting scarce resources in an abundant land to those without economic power. Furthermore, on each page of his economic writing one feels the dialectic between self-help by the poor and criticism of the powerful establishment to practice just stewardship.

In fact, the Wesleyan-organized cell movements provided the discipline, hope, organization, learning, and networks that lifted many of the early Methodists out of poverty. Religiously inspired communities of economic ethical orientation may still be one of the greatest antidotes to poverty for many societies.

## LIMITS OF ECONOMIC ETHICS

Emil Brunner, also standing in a Calvinist tradition, challenged the economic equanimity of optimistic Christian economics in 1932, on the eve of the National Socialist revolution of Adolf Hitler. For Brunner the whole spirit of modern capitalism was a celebration of a rationalized, technocratic individualism that denied Christian faith. The Christian faith stressed communal responsibility for and dependence on other beings, whereas capitalism stressed human autonomy. The imperative of the values of capitalism to honor the bottom line compromised the absolute loyalty owed to God and regularly violated mutual support for other human beings. Capitalism as organized selfishness upset ethics of service, humility, and sharing. Brunner's understanding of Christian ethics required involvement in the economic order. The order provided for humanity and was God's gift to humanity. Economic life was also radically fallen and in rebellion against God. One could not participate in economic life without sin. His words regarding Christian ethics and economics are very forceful:

> The Bible places the economic problem in the very center of its thinking; the prophets, as well as Jesus and the Apostles, explain the law of love mainly by using illustrations drawn from the economic order, and their imperatives deal mainly with the ethical aspect of economic life. In any case, an ethic which ignores economic problems has no right to call itself either a Christian or a Scriptural ethic.[24]

Brunner put the emphasis on the disorder of the economic order. The arrangements for providing humanity with sustenance dominate everyone like a fate. Most efforts to change economics fail because the forces are too great to be significantly altered. Theologically, the economic system reflects the truth of the doctrine of original sin; it is here before there is any conscious participation in it or choosing of it. The temptation is to accept service of mammon in whatever system one encounters it. This temptation has to be resisted because of the obligation to fight idolatries, the imperatives of serving the neighbor, and the need of the Christian person to resist evil in the self.

Brunner is antiutopian. General schemes of new orders hold very little interest for him. They are not the call to Christians, which is service, resistance, love, and work within the concrete order in which one is called to live a vocation.

Yet he expects Christians to resist the evil in capitalism and to look for and, to the greatest extent possible, struggle for a new order in one of the actual movements for a new order. Of course, political and economic actions are for him relative goods. But they are important. The movements for new order must not be absolutized.

Brunner's recognition of the hold of the sin of selfishness on economics inclines him to be forcefully critical of the order of capitalist economics. The recognition of the complexity of the economic forces and the reality of human finitude keeps his recommendations for planned social policy modest. Interestingly, in his *The Divine Imperative*, he urges Christian critique and resistance, but he argues that the church should not advocate social policy. He does not think it is the church's business to enter into the relativities of social policy. *Agape* for him is better preserved in its absoluteness, in its witness, and in its concrete spontaneous service to the neighbor in need. In his abandonment of social policy by the church, he moves away from the Calvinist understanding of church.

## THOROUGH REFORM

John C. Bennett used to assign Brunner's *The Divine Imperative* to beginning theological students at Union Theological Seminary, where he served as professor and president. Previous to World War II, he found socialistic tendencies in Christianity and affirmed Brunner's critique that capitalism was "irresponsibility developed into a system."[25] With other Christian ethicists, he moved from socialism to advocating mixed economic solutions and systems during the late 1930s. Bennett did not share Brunner's cautions about direct church involvement in the moral dimensions of social policy. His activism and social advocacy stemmed from his history in the Presbyterian Church and from his later ordination in the Congregational Church. After a lifetime of writing on Christian ethics and economics, he summarized his mature views in several recommendations. In 1975, he advocated:

1. Medical insurance for all
2. Guaranteed minimum income maintenance
3. Efficient, highly progressive income taxes
4. Guaranteed employment, with government as the employer of last resort

At a more fundamental and difficult level of achievement, he also advocated:

1. Establishment of public control of private economic empires. Without a socialist panacea, the mixed economy must be made to work free of monopoly powers and private undue influence on government.
2. Protection of the most vulnerable in economic decision making
3. Increasing public participation in economic decisions
4. Reducing the military's share of the national budget
5. Reducing U.S. consumption of the world's resources
6. Energizing the U.S. contribution to reducing world malnutrition[26]

When Bennett died in 1995, all of his 1975 agenda remained to be accomplished. His recommendations seem to represent Christian pressures for humane economic policies that are appropriate to this mixed economic system in the opening years of the twenty-first century. His voice had responded to the pressures from the world's poor and theologies of liberation, and two new dimensions were added: the recognition of ecological limits and the realization that economics mattered to women as well as to men.

## FEMINIST PERSPECTIVES

The irruption of women into the debates over economic ethics is modifying the discussion. Rosemary Radford Ruether's *The Radical Kingdom* broke new ground in Christian ethics by its favoring of the voices of the oppressed in 1972. In the next few years, women's work in ethics developed, reaching a high point in China in 1995 at the United Nations Conference on Women. In this short period, it became recognized that one cannot think about ethics without listening to women. Despite solid work by Beverly Harrison, Karen Lebacqz, and Carol Robb, most of the contributions to religious economic ethics listed in the resources prepared by Barbara Andolsen and Mary Hunt[27] are of essay length, and the major books by feminist Christian ethicists in economics are still to be published. Much of the work of women scholars has related economic issues to ecology and to family issues. The type of more abstract economic analysis condemned by John Cobb and Herman E. Daly seems to be only minimally present in these newly emerging women writers. These connections of religious ethics to ecology and family economics are promising. They may reveal strengths central to women's religious ethics that are deficient in male ethics. There is enough insistence in women's writings on relationality, solidarity, and bondedness to anticipate a shaping of the field in these directions. They are present in male authors too, of course, but the emphasis in women's ethics on ecology and family incorporates these values of ethics of relationships, solidarity in community and nature, and bondedness to people and actual life. It could be furthermore expected that the issues of poverty will be kept in the forefront of ethics by pressures from women. Some choices of women's ethics in the directions of Marxist analysis or cooperative societies will marginalize their work in the emerging worldwide market economy, but even then these models can engender resistance to the prevailing economy and preserve some valuable insights.[28]

Karen Lebacqz's *Justice in an Unjust World* and Bebb Wheeler Stone's "Celebrating Embodied Care: Women and Economic Justice"[29] express several values that may become constitutive of women's Christian economic ethics. They both are very biblically grounded, and the Scriptures are exegeted rigorously. They both are dependent on sources from developing countries. They both draw on personal experiences and embody their reflections in themselves. Lebacqz puts better than any other ethicist how she has been both oppressor and oppressed. She walks through the dialectic and refuses to fall prey to dualisms. Stone learned in India that the really interesting struggles for women involve not formal rights but substantive justice, to use Beverly Harrison's category. Justice is bread, water, and health care. At the root of justice, economic ethics, and feminism is the struggle for life. Stone affirms a strong bonding of women and their children and therefore a priority in the struggle to preserve that life. In this essay, she affirms feminism, Christian realism, women's embodied care and social change, a global perspective, and traditions of justice. The method was to relate stories of women's empowerment in the poor, contemporary world to biblical stories to encourage women's empowerment. She seemed to unconsciously anticipate Rebekah Miles's suggestion that Niebuhr's Christian realism needed to make more of freedom in women's bonding with children.[30] All three of these feminists find power in these connections to biological life that men neglect at their peril. The theme of "embodied care" seems very close to the early Greek meaning of economics as care of the household.

The critique of economic development plans has turned lending agencies' attention toward women's perspectives in development projects. We may hope that the presence of women in economic ethics will help keep the focus on real people in need.

## TOWARD A MODERN REFORMED ECONOMIC ETHICS

Reformed Christians in the United States are more than 450 years removed from John Calvin, and they are even more than two hundred years removed from Adam Smith. Neither the tight control of the economy by the city council guided by Reformed biblical teaching nor the eighteenth-century free market economy moderated by human sympathy will serve as an adequate ethical guide for our contemporary situation. Each group needs to develop its own ethic in light of its traditions and its analysis of the situation. Reformed Christian ethics applies scriptural themes interpreted theologically and correlated with an analysis of the situation to suggest guidance for the doing of justice in the contemporary situation. Churches in the United States have since the 1930s been articulating ways of understanding the economic order in relationship to ultimate theological themes. The 1980s saw a flourish of reflection on these issues. The Presbyterian Church (U.S.A.) has been engaged for two decades in the process of preparing its own policies on economic justice. A particularly useful summary of theology and economics and an ethic of justice was prepared by the Council on Theology and Culture of the Presbyterian Church (U.S.A.) and published by the Presbyterian Church (U.S.A.) as a study paper in 1984. The paper recognizes that all of scripture is relevant to the discussion of economic justice, but it highlights several themes as being of particular importance to those claiming the Calvinist or Reformed tradition.[31]

## CHRISTIAN FAITH AND ECONOMIC JUSTICE

The first claim of the study paper is that God alone is sovereign. This claim is grounded in two covenant statements. From Exodus 20:2–3: "I am the Lord your God who brought you out of the land of Egypt, out of the house of bondage. You shall have no other gods before me." In Deuteronomy 6:4–5 the commandment is: "Hear, O Israel: The Lord our God is one Lord: and you shall love the Lord your God with all your heart, and with all your soul, and with all your might." This expression of radical monotheism, which is the distinctive contribution of Israel's religion to the world, relativizes the claims of other realities. Money or profits are not to be central as the idol of mammon is not to be worshiped. Military might ought not to dominate or consume a nation's life, because the idol of Mars has no claim to be an authentic god. With radical monotheism providing a unitary focus for the world's loyalty beyond the phenomena of the world, a sense of trustworthy order can arise. The world is not chaos haunted by competing deities, but one world of ordering purpose. Success and efficiency in economics can be respected and honored but not worshiped, for the world is finite, human life is mortal, and God ultimately rules. With the sense of rule comes the possibility of justice. All earthly standards of justice are reinforced by the awareness of a God whose nature is to be just and to require justice. The earthly or human standards of justice are also seen not to be ultimate justice, but human relative approaches to justice.

A second confessional claim is that the world is God's creation. The first verse of the Bible is a poem of creation perhaps taken from liturgical materials. "In the beginning God created the heavens and the earth." The religious meaning of this verse is not in speculative cosmology or scientific speculation, but in the sense that the world depends on God. The world is from the one who seeks justice in the world now. Human beings can live with awe depending on the goodness of the Creator. They can seek out their role in life to love the Creator and to care for the creation in a sense of being supported by the very forces that formed the universe. In such a vision, it is a persuasive argument that the true purpose of humanity is to return humanly conscious, free love to God. The affirmation of God as shaper of the world evokes the claims that the world is good, is for all to enjoy, and is not ours, but God's world. Human beings are caretakers, stewards, or economists caring for the world, but are not its owners. John Calvin insisted that we were free to make frugal and moderate use of the world's bounty while taking care of the land and its possessions for others to use and enjoy. All of humanity reflects the creative work and may respond to the one whose image they share.

The third major definition of God is that God's nature is that of love. The Bible is full of the analogies of God as lover, mother, father, husband, and wife. God actively seeks out the response of human beings to be joined together in community or covenant relations with the Divine. All humanity is of one family and is to be bound in covenant love. This love is constitutive of the true nature of the human situation and is a corrective love that exerts special efforts to restore the lost. So, in Matthew 25, the ultimate nature of love is seen as the sick, the hungry, and the imprisoned are served. Family or covenant love, with its depths in the divine nature, pursues the suffering to restore them to wholeness. Where one in a family suffers, preferential action is taken to restore the basic community of the family. In economic ethics, this means that the poor must be restored to a rough equality in the system. Preferential treatment of the poor is necessary for equality or fair treatment in the society.

A final characteristic of God leads directly to the requirements of economic justice, for it is God's nature to be just. "The Lord is just in all ways and kind in all God's doings" (Ps. 145:17). The covenant of Deuteronomy expresses it, in Deuteronomy 10:18, "God executes justice for the fatherless and the widow and loves the sojourner, giving one food and clothing." To love God is to seek justice, for God's will is justice. Christian reflection on justice highlights the importance of equality to the meaning of justice. In the 1980s and 1990s, inequality in the United States and particularly in urban areas increased. The study paper placed equality as its first principle of justice. The study paper found in both the Old Testament and the U.S. Declaration of Independence a commitment to equality. Our ongoing history has shown the need to broaden the concept to include, as God intended, the equal rights of women and the descendants of former slaves. The paper's assertion of the place for equality contradicts current American practice, trends, and even the avowed positions of many Christians. Agreeing on the meaning of justice is not the important thing, no matter how important some consensus is for Christian social strategy. Reinhold Niebuhr's counsel is well taken:

> The positive Christian contribution to standards of justice in economic life must not be found primarily in a precise formulation of those standards. It must be found rather in strengthening both the inclination to seek the neighbor's good, and in the contrite awareness that we are not inclined to do this.[32]

A fifth theological assertion that reflects the Reformed tradition's relationship with the economic world is that all people are involved in sin. Sin is the refusal to live in a trustful, loving relationship with God. Such a refusal violates the purpose of the universe and breaks the possibilities of free, fulfilled, trusting human existence. Each human repeats the failure of the species and both the person and the species are living at cross-purposes with the spirit and purpose of the world in which they exist. So the products of the species, whether spiritual or material, are flawed, and humanity exists in institutions both physical and mental that partially fulfill and partially negate the meaning of humanity. Everywhere humanity turns to organize its existence, the inherited institutions serve God's purposes only ambivalently, although sometimes they become so flawed as to stand directly against the divine will. The economic institutions of the city are a prime example, producing a mixture of life-giving and death-dealing products. Civilization, the life of the city, is itself deeply flawed, founded in murderous conquest as well as life-giving movements. The reality of sin forces those who trust God to be consistently engaged in reform movements for life. They must in loving trust of God engage the negativity of their own lives as well as the negativity of society. None of the economic institutions can be separated from the need for renewal and reform. The reformers themselves carry the negativity of the flaw of sin in themselves, and so they must also continually reform their efforts at reform.

There are moments of free, trusting, loving action, and many movements are characterized by an abundance of reform and trusting action. But corruption of the good is never far away from humanity, and social strategies can be creatively engaged in only when the presence of the distortion of the human species is accepted.

The recognition of sin leads to the final theme to be asserted here in Reformed theological ethics of economic life. There is hope. The daily recitation by Christians of the prayer of Jesus, "Thy kingdom come on earth as it is in heaven," expresses this hope. It recognizes the ultimate sovereignty of God and the presence of God's victories of love in the economic world in which we live. Between cynicism and utopianism lies the realm for hopeful reforming action. It is possible for a rough justice to be done. Poverty has been and can be overcome. Reform of our economic structures is possible. The blight of cruel nineteenth-century capitalism has been moderated for most of the population in the United States. The deadening despair of the economic dislocation of the early 1980s is being transformed for thousands. None of the threats of overpopulation, poverty, limited resources, growing pollution, or technological destruction through war is a final threat. There are moments and movements of new life that are visible in the urban setting. The churches are communities with the responsibility for modeling, demonstrating, interpreting, and sometimes instigating these movements and moments of new life. The Christian hope is a hope for the present and for the ultimate victory, as the last book of the Bible proclaims a new city. Christians who really hope for the final victory of God portrayed in Revelation as the New Jerusalem are also engaged in the penultimate struggles within their cities.

## JUST POLITICAL ECONOMY

The church went ahead with its economic conversations and in June of 1985 encouraged the use of a study paper titled *Toward a Just, Caring, and Dynamic Political Economy*.[33] As this book was being completed, the Presbyterian Church had not yet been able to adopt a contemporary, comprehensive policy for the church on economic justice. The study paper reflects a teleconference finding and several years of committee investigation and debate, but it was turned aside from becoming policy for various reasons. The deepest reasons were that the proposed policies were inadequate for either theological understanding or an adequate comprehension of world economics. The study paper stresses the importance of economic justice, the illusive character of economic justice, and the Calvinist sense that human activity can contribute to making a society more just. It rejects "rugged individualism" as appropriate to Christian character. In agreement with John Calvin, the social nature of humanity is assumed and the test of all economic action is seen in the welfare of the community. Government has legitimate and necessary roles in making choices and in ordering economic life. The study paper sets itself against the mound of negativity that attacks government in itself.

There are elements of a just political economy that are beyond government or economic institutions—particularly voluntary associations and families. The committee chose to emphasize economic choices while recognizing that international forces, noneconomic choices, finite limits, and a large government role were all givens. The paper sought to develop a Christian-Reformed approach to economic ethics.

The largest section of the paper discusses the specific groups that compose the bulk of the people suffering from poverty in the United States. While Presbyterians have traditionally done well, the economy from which they have benefited has not done well in providing for minority racial groups, undocumented persons, American Indians, women, people with disabilities, and poor children (one out of five in the United States). The paper makes specific policy recommendations for reducing the suffering in these groups.

The paper finds great dangers in both the debts of developing nations and the debt of the United States. The document is pro-growth for the developing world and finds such growth to be imperative. On U.S. debt, the document favors increased and fairer taxes, reduced military spending, and greater social spending. Although the paper does not state it this way, the position assumed for the sake of greater equity is of reducing the burden of being poor and decreasing the benefits of being rich. Almost every proposal is in the direction of reducing the present extreme inequalities in the United States. Generally, the policies recommended would reduce the economically privileged positions of many Presbyterians.

The tax policies of the early 1980s are seen as favoring the wealthy and penalizing the poor. The paper calls for several changes in tax law; perhaps the most radical suggestion is the shaping of tax policies so that great wealth could not be inherited. Inheritance taxes are regarded as too low. The power of the wealthiest four hundred controlling 40 percent of the economy of the United States is regarded as a danger to democracy. Lester Thurow's analysis of the wealthiest four hundred is presented in the document.[34] The paper does not follow Andrew Carnegie's view that inheritance weakens character and it recognizes the need for encouraging some inheritance, but it stands squarely against inheritance of massive wealth. Several aspects of tax policy are discussed; the committee recommended the creation of a special church study on taxation to pursue the issues.

On military spending, the study paper recommends immediate reduction to the level of the early Carter years accompanied by a negotiated freeze on nuclear weapons development, the return of some of the engineering talent to the domestic economy, planning for economic conversion to peaceful economic pursuits, and education on the folly of selling arms to the world.

Several of the concerns raised in the study paper had by 1998 already become national policy—e.g., notification procedures for plant closings, lowering the value of the dollar, and attempted moves in the direction of simplifying tax policy. Other concerns, including moves toward planned industrial policy, remain in the shadows of public debate. Some issues, such as increased social protection for the poor, increased inheritance taxes, moves toward conversion to a peacetime economy, and development of significant policies to overcome world hunger, are still very much the positions of small minorities. The most important aspect of the acceptance of the study paper by the church was the paper's conclusion that "we need to make conscious effort to ensure that Christian values shape our own choices and activity in the area of political economy, as individual Christians and as corporate Christian bodies."[35] This affirmation itself is central to the economic ethic that this book espouses. It sets aside the myth of unregulated capitalism informed by Adam Smith, social Darwinism, and the notion of extreme individualism producing a fair economy.

Evidence that the Presbyterian Church is carrying on the work of attempting to define policy for a just political economy is seen in three consultations among theologians, economists, and activists held at Ghost Ranch, in Abiquiu, New Mexico, in the summers of 1985–1987.[36]

In the 1990s, the Presbyterian Church (U.S.A.) expanded its emphasis on economic justice in several directions. Its policies on work and vocation stressed that vocation is from God and is a lifetime combination of paid and unpaid work. Spiritual growth is almost part of vocational development. Work is in need of continual reforming so that it can be a joyous response to God and the transformative work of Jesus. The report, in the best of the theology of John Calvin's spirit, urged policies of fairness, greater equality, and service to the common good. It urged an active role for government in providing work where the profit sector could not. The policies of "God's Work in Our Hands: Employment, Community, and Christian Vocation" could be called "structuralist" by the church's critics. This church, with a majority membership of Republicans and Independents, reinforced the activist role more closely associated with New Deal policies than with the New Democratic principles of President Clinton. It did not need to emphasize discipline, work ethic, and the pursuit of success, because Presbyterians tended to have more of these valuable emphases than they needed. The same 1995 assembly that passed the paper calling for full and fair employment specifically supported in other actions the Equal Credit Opportunity Act, the Community Reinvestment Act, and the Fair Housing Act. The 1995 assembly was Calvinist in its theology of vocation, activism, and support of government. It did not share in national trends of negativism toward government and emphasis on individual achievement.[37]

The new emphasis in work emerged most forcefully in *All the Live Long Day: Women and Work*, a paper adopted three years later by the assembly. This paper worked specifically from biblical traditions and stated that: "The economy is the divine plan that enables people to live together in just relationships in the whole inhabited earth."[38] This theocentric paper then marched through the inequities in employment in church and society regarding women and proposed reforms. This report demanding economic justice for women was buttressed by the new Christian-feminist scholarship that developed the underlying biblical and historical authority for the recommendations for change. The theology could be said to be fulfilling a characteristic urging of liberation theology that theology be critical reflection on the reality of church life. Women of the church are now in paid employment; the task is to humanize that employment and make it more fair.

During the same period that policy justice for women regarding work was ending, the economic dimensions of ecology were being addressed in the church. *Keeping and Healing the Creation*[39] was published in 1989 as part of the policy process producing new policy in 1990 by the General Assembly. Further resources were proposed in "Restoring Creation for Ecology and Justice," which appeared in 1996.[40] Again, these policies and resources represented the interpretation of church language, policies, and practices with the ecological movement already well developed. The "greening" of church policy was accomplished under the leadership of Dieter T. Hessel. The work was also heavily influenced by William E. Gibson, Holmes Rolston III, and Robert L. Stivers. The extent to which the mind and life of the church were changed depends on the implementation of the policy in accordance with the priorities of the church.

Finally, the adoption of "Hope for a Global Future: Toward Just and Sustainable Human Development" completed the international dimensions of economic ethics that the church had lacked.[41] The policies here developed balance the needs for human development and ecological protection while calling for significant alterations in economic practice. The guidelines urged in the policy are grouped under: (1) Sufficient Production and Consumption, (2) Full Respect for All Human Rights, (3) Just and Effective Governance, (4) Universal and Adequate Education, (5) Population Stability, (6) Environmental Sustainability and Food Sufficiency, (7) Ethical Universality with Cultural and Religious Diversity, (8) Dismantling Warfare and Building Peace, (9) Equitable Debt Relief, (10) Just and Sustainable International Trade, and (11) More and Better Development Assistance. The policies guide most aspects of the church's international ministry and provide pages of recommendations for voluntary associations, governments, and international organizations. The four-year process of study provided a relatively complete paper that took account in its final stages of the issues of human sustainable development, women's rights, and the ecological justice movement. The earlier lacunae of the 1980 economic studies seem now to have been rectified. The theological ethical work has been done for each emphasis in different styles, which complement each other. A relatively complete economic ethic is discernable in the church, and it could be integrated into one coherent document now.

## LEARNING FROM CATHOLIC ETHICS

In today's ecumenical Christian cooperation, sources other than a particular denomination's traditions must be consulted for ethical wisdom. The Roman Catholic bishops' pastoral letter on economic justice has become an important source for all American Christians to read and reflect on.[42] The bishops' pastoral is directed first to the membership of the Catholic Church and then to all who will consider its moral arguments. It is a mainstream American document introducing its readers to the American economic life with its successes and failures. The bishops' pastoral regards its most authoritative contribution to be "The Christian Vision of Economic Life." This section on biblical perspectives and ethical norms is very similar to Protestant writings on the subject. An ecumenical consensus is appearing. The themes of creation in God's image, people of the covenant, the reign of God's justice, discipleship, poverty and riches, and the community of hope are all familiar to Protestant ethics. Protestant ethics will tend to regard the brief section on living traditions of economic practice as being a little selective in its history, and overly congratulatory of the church's role in economic practice and ethics. However, this does not override the general appreciation for the biblical perspectives presented before the examination of the traditions. The vision of the bishops' pastoral is one of human solidarity for the welfare of all people guided by norms of love, solidarity, justice, and participation. The ethics of solidarity requires that work contribute to the good of all and that special effort and consideration be given to those who have suffered, most particularly the 33 million poor in the United States and those near poverty who suffer deprivation. The bishops' pastoral keeps in view the 800 million in absolute poverty and the 450 million malnourished beyond the United States while focusing on domestic injustice.

The bishops' pastoral also recognizes the importance of the ecumenical contributions to current thought about economic justice and especially mentions that Catholics can learn from the strong Protestant emphasis on the vocation of the laity.

Among the issues selected for policy discussion, the most emphasized is the need for full employment policies, and the second most emphasized is the struggle against poverty. The inequities in income and wealth in the United States are recorded. In 1983 it was found that 86 percent of all financial assets were held by 10 percent of American families. In terms of income distribution, the United States was found to be more unequal than most industrial nations. These inequalities were regarded as unacceptable by the bishops. Several policies were discussed as possible ways of combating poverty and unemployment.

The insistence of the bishops' pastoral letter on policies reflecting solidarity, special consideration for the poor, economic participation, and sharing of power is transformative of the American economy in its implications. Conservative and neoconservative critics have caught these emphases and are threatened by the long-range implications of the largest church in the country pushing for the necessary changes.

Carol Johnston found the bishops' pastoral letter to be particularly helpful in its emphasis on grace and its avoidance of Protestant moralizing and imputation of guilt in matters of economic justice. The emphasis in the pastoral is on the grace of God permitting human economic life and leading to transformation toward an economic working for all. She became quite eloquent in praising the bishops for avoiding works righteousness as they chose instead to work for empowerment by sharing a rich Catholic, American vision. They addressed their constituency and did not contribute to a division between the "poor" and the middle class of which most Catholic readers of the document would be members. Her major criticism[43] is that the paper lacked a fuller discussion of sin and the need to counter power with power. From a Protestant perspective, vision is tempered with the reality of sin, and policy recommendations must guard against the accumulation of inordinate amounts of power in any hands, state or private. Beyond this criticism, however, she affirms that Reformed Christians can learn economic ethics from the pastoral letter.

Obviously, the present situation in religious economic ethics reveals convergence between Catholic ethics and Reformed ethics. This has not always been the case. Calvin's Geneva revealed dependence on Catholic economic ethics and practice but broke with the Catholic ethos on interest payments and vocation. Modern Catholic ethics agrees with Calvin on the necessity of interest payments, and the bishops' pastoral suggested that Catholic ethics should learn from Protestants about vocation. A contemporary social scientist who grew up in Pittsburgh has suggested the existence of a distinct Catholic attitude toward welfare and charity that is quite different from the Protestant ethic of Max Weber and the social Darwinism that characterized late-nineteenth and early-twentieth-century Pittsburgh. John E. Tropman[44] argues that Catholic ethics generally has (1) ambivalence concerning wealth, (2) an instrumental attitude about wealth, (3) strong support for family, (4) a high tradition of charity, (5) respect for bureaucracy, and (6) a nonpunitive attitude toward economic failure. In combination, he suggests, these values made Catholic ethics more supportive of welfare policies than the classical, ascetic Protestant ethic. Tropman's work includes a request that more work be done to investigate the existence and social importance of a Catholic ethic in America. On the face of it, the massive presence of Catholic Welfare Services, the efforts of Catholic schools to educate the urban poor, and the larger percentages of Catholics supporting the welfare-oriented policies of the Democratic Party provide evidence for his thesis. R. H. Tawney's[45] research showing that the rise of the ascetic Protestant ethic in England correlated with the decline of the willingness of that society to protect the poor would also support Tropman's thesis. The work of Harold Wilensky[46] also provides evidence that Catholicism has contributed to the forces encouraging the development of state welfare systems. Tropman has an important thesis. But it does not explain the convergence of Reformed economic ethics and Catholic ethics discussed in this chapter. Both Catholic ethics and Reformed ethics have been shaped by the agencies of developing industrialism and by the egalitarian pressures from leftist political parties and egalitarian and justice-oriented political philosophies. A further Protestant contribution not sufficiently addressed by the Weber thesis was the proliferation of Protestant welfare societies and voluntary associations that have characterized Anglo-Saxon expressions of Protestant ethics. The richer classical Protestant ethics of a John Calvin, or contemporary Reformed economic ethics, is not well represented by the Weber model of a secularized Protestant ethic joined with social Darwinism. Tropman[47] wisely notes the importance of the founding ethical moments of a culture, which shape succeeding generations. I think he is correct in regarding these founding moments of the American urban scene as being distinctively of a Protestant ascetic ethic variety. So the ambivalent nature of Protestant ethics is exposed both in urban practice and in contrast to the beginning research on Catholic ethics. This ambivalence is also noted by the bishops' pastoral letter, which affirmed the need for emphasis on the vocation of the laity and its own high regard for the meaning of work contributing to the total personality. The ascetic Protestant ethic described by Weber was better at unleashing energy to produce results than it was in distributing the wealth. Tropman's reference to Spanish culture in the New World is also ambivalent. Quoting Octavio Paz, he says, "For the society of New Spain, work did not redeem and had no value in itself."[48] This lack of something like a work ethic in the Spanish culture of the New World will have to be seen as one, even if only one, of the variables that have left the society of New Spain so poverty-stricken. The task remains in economic ethics to value work highly while not idolizing it.

Events of the late 1980s and 1990s widened the gap between the social teachings of the Catholic Church and its membership. The hierarchy insisted on absolute prohibitions of birth control and abortion, and Catholics practiced both. Much of the population also moved out of the Roosevelt New Deal coalition to support Republican politicians. This led, in a practical sense, to numbers of Catholics supporting reduction of the welfare system even though their churches supported it and utilized its resources for support of the poor. The Catholic hierarchy could support the Republican Party for its intolerance regarding abortion, and Catholics, particularly males, rejected the more liberal politics of the Democratic Party. Hostility against the extremism of groups associated with the civil rights movement and the anti–Vietnam War movement brewing for a generation were given expression in the election of a Republican congressional majority in 1994, according to Samuel G. Freedman.[49] The new middle-class, highly educated, suburbanite, male Roman Catholic was likely to express this class position by voting Republican. The female Roman Catholic, while enjoying the same status, was more likely to support the Democrats because of gender-related issues more recognized by the Democratic Party and its more generous view of the need for welfare support. So, by the late 1990s, gender was as important a variable as religion in affecting voting behavior. Roman Catholic women would translate their values into political expression that would correlate more closely with Presbyterian social teaching than would the political expression of Presbyterian men. Presbyterian men would in their votes tend to support Roman Catholic views on abortion by voting Republican, as would large numbers of Roman Catholic men, although neither group would actually agree with the hierarchists' teaching on sexuality and abortion. In 1996, Bill Clinton depended on the votes of Roman Catholics to retain the presidency. The Protestant vote by itself would have elected Bob Dole. Support of the welfare aspects of mixed-economy capitalism seems to depend on women more than on men. From the Christian community, only the Protestants can express this politically while remaining consistent with their churches' teachings.

The imperative of love of neighbor requires that the consequences of the current economic reality in light of Christian faith be related to the unresolved sin of the American republic, racism.

# Racism

Our children experience the rage produced by racism. My daughter's friend from her creative writing class killed a teenaged girl with a sword, and my stepson's friend, a champion quarterback, was slain in a late-night ambush at Wendy's. The children of racism, reflecting self-hatred and meaninglessness, destroy each other in our American cities. That a mother dependent on welfare feels she must spend eighty dollars a month to buy "burial insurance" for her children is certainly not an adequate answer.

Can the majority of Americans who are neither oppressed nor confined to poor urban ghettos find an answer? After forty years of struggling against white American racism, I must admit to having experienced some weariness in the struggle. The racism of our empire still has echoes in my own soul, I know, and temporary weariness is partially an excuse for the racism I have not yet escaped. But in a day when neither the Christian church nor either political party effectively addresses the racial disease of America, the imperative to do so remains. The answer to weariness or defeatism concerning the struggle against racism is more rigorous exercise in the cause. The Christian ethic is clear and unambiguous and there are practical steps to be taken. One may slow down to fill one's lungs, but the race still lies ahead and the course is to be finished. Writing as one of the privileged majority, I take as my inspiration in the Christian ethics of race my elder brother Martin Luther King Jr., with whom I ran until racism martyred him. Cornel West is my guide in contemporary interpretations. William Julius Wilson provides a vision of the necessary social program. Ronald Peters and James Cone both provide the corrective of the priority of the church community for Christian antiracist actions. Peter Paris reminds me that both African American and European American churches will need to become more politically relevant before this race can be finished. The dependence on all these African American writers reflects the intention of this piece to address white racism against African Americans rather than other expressions of white-supremacist racism in the United States.

There have been gains since Martin was murdered, but there have also been losses by the African American community. The gains have moved perhaps 25 percent of the African American population into the middle class. This economic fruit, prompted by the civil rights struggle, affirmative action, political gains, and cultural and athletic achievements, has produced real qualitative changes of existence for many. The end of legal segregation likewise has made life much more tolerable for African Americans. However, the forces of displacement of African American agricultural laborers in the South and urban deindustrialization in the North have left the urban African Americans without sufficient employment opportunities. Without work or wealth, the urban population is beset on every side by social ills. Meaning in America is tied to enjoyment of the material blessings of someone's work, and without that connection, meaning is threatened if not overthrown. The American dream encouraged by all avenues of communication becomes a constant, threatening nightmare when all hope of it is denied. A society that promises economic success, including property ownership and an automobile or two, weakens its meaning-making institutions of school, church, and voluntary association when it does not deliver. The weakening of these meaning-making institutions abandons the delivery of meaning to television and Hollywood, which serve the corporate-financial interests that subject the poor to the nightmare of the materialist American dream.

Before turning to the ethic, I will permit myself a summary in stark terms. Urban America has seen the flight of white leadership and black middle-class leadership. The neglect by traditional leadership classes has been accompanied as never before by the inflammation of materialistic aspirations of instant gratification, the toleration and encouragement of drug abuse beyond humanity's ability to tolerate it, and the retail delivery of massive numbers of weapons into the inner cities. The withdrawal of work opportunities from the inner cities has left this deadly brew that leads to early death and social malaise.

## THE IMPERATIVE AGAINST RACISM

There are forms of emphasis in Christian ethics other than the double love commandment, but this book contends that it is the original, most enduring, and most appropriate way of expressing Christian ethics. It assumes rather than demands the context of Christian faith. The Christian knows that one is loved and treasured by the creative power of the universe, God. One is then directed to respond with total allegiance, in "heart, mind, and soul," to that God. Out of one's sense of affirmation, one is further commanded to love the other as one's self. That is, one is to passionately seek the welfare of the other. Obviously, this commits the Christian to oppose racism, which degrades the very being of both the racist and the oppressed. Fundamental to this ethic is the denial of ultimate loyalty to race, clan, or nation; only God is ultimate.
One may not be valued above another because of race; each one counts as one whether Samaritan, Jew, Pharisee, or priest. Racism directly contradicts the

double love commandment in its simplest and most sophisticated expressions. The New Testament author who wrote, "If you claim to love God but do not love your brother, you are a liar," put it as plainly as it can be said. There is no salvation for racists.

The double love imperative drives directly to community and justice. Community reflects love, and justice institutionalizes it, protects it, and makes it applicable. Community and justice are also the answers to the questions implied in liberal and conservative quests to overcome racism. The double love commandment also means that, beyond community and justice, life must be recognized as being grounded in God.

For me personally, all this has meant that I have been unable since becoming an adult to bind myself to the Christian community of any church that was not racially integrated. One does not insist on this as the only meaning of Christian ethics for all Christians; sometimes it is demographically impossible. But if one is a Christian leader in a time of a degenerate racist crisis, one certainly must exert leadership to ensure that Christians experience integration before God in some of their worship and some of their activities. Before implications of Christian ethics for opposition to racism are discussed, a review of the origins of modern racism is order.

## MODERN ORIGINS OF RACISM

Racism in the Christian, Western world is a modern form of human ethnocentrism. It expresses the power-driven impulses to seek security and advantage in dominating another group identified by supposed racial characteristics. It arises from the human tendency to dominate those defined as the other. It is an expression of sin—a rebellion against the source of life that tries to find security in domination over others.

Ethnocentrism, the attaching of superior value to people in one's own group, has ancient roots, but racism in its Western expression is modern. The caste system of India, founded in color, expressing the domination of the light-colored Aryans over the darker native peoples of the Indian subcontinent, could be regarded as an ancient form of racism continuing into the modern world. The modern racism of the Christian West seems to lack such ancient roots.

George D. Kelsey, a teacher of Martin Luther King Jr., began his study of racism by writing, "Racism is a modern phenomenon. It is a product of modern world conditions."[1] He found its origins in the European justification of domination over colored races that came about after the religious sanctions for that domination had become less persuasive to the modern world. The white conquest and exploitation of colored peoples led to the need to legitimize that dominance. The ideology of that legitimization became part of Christian Western civilization. Sin, one could say, became structured into the characteristics of the Western mind and is still being passed on from generation to generation as explanation and justification for the continued dominance of white peoples over colored peoples. So the false consciousness or ideology that white people are superior, which was derived from their original conquests, continues to exert its power. Racist presuppositions explain and seem to justify black poverty, illiteracy, and social problems encountered in the modern world. So the justifications for that cruel system of slavery foundational to the colonization of the Western world continue to corrupt the Western soul and to distort American life.

Kelsey's work of the 1960s has been reinforced by the findings of Frank Snowden in *Blacks in Antiquity* (1970) and *Before Color Prejudice* (1983), which provide detailed evidence that skin color was not used by ancient peoples to oppress others. Professor Nicholas F. Gier argued in 1988:

> The ancient Mediterranean civilization constituted genuine multiracial societies. Snowden shows that black Africans were respected as soldiers, craftsmen, writers, priests, and musicians. In fact, no occupation was denied to them and both blacks and whites worshipped together at the same temples. There were also no laws against intermarriage and mixed couples were common.[2]

Early Christianity made no distinctions based on color. Racial ideology is a modern phenomenon (except, perhaps, in India), drawing on the phenomena of white conquest of colored populations, slavery, and the failures of Western philosophy and science. Racism among Christians is a historical aberration that, although rooted in the potential weaknesses in human nature, is not a necessary expression of humans.

The racism that characterizes the white population of modern metropolitan life is an organized system of prejudice, domination, and oppression based on racial identity. Racism may or may not be intended, but it is the system that has perpetuated white privilege and the white control of the dominant institutions in the society in a manner prejudicial to the development of colored human potentiality. This meaning of racism as organized sin requires both individual and institutional change. The World Council of Churches report on racism announces:

> It is institutional racism which is causing the greatest suffering to the greatest number of people today, and it is the collective power of the churches and other groups which is required to combat institutional racism.[3]

In North American cities, it is this ideological, institutional inheritance from slavery that expresses itself in the poverty and violence of inner-city ghettos. The poverty and violence breed resentment and alienation, which, with the frustration of the civil rights movement of the 1960s, exploded in mass riots. After the repression of the riots, hostility degenerated into alienation of the blacks and apathetic response by the dominant white rulers.[4]

## CHRISTIAN FAILURE IN RACE RELATIONS

The church's failure to free its people from racism is among the greatest of its modern moral debacles. The Christian failure to prevent the Nazi Holocaust and the church's complicity with imperial rapacity over other peoples may be even more significant failures. Hopefully, such heresies have been vanquished, but the heresy of racism continues.

According to Cornel West, 69 percent of Louisiana born-again Christians voted for racist David Duke.[5] These Christians teach racial superiority to their children, and they prefer to continue worshiping at segregated churches. The civil rights movement was at its center a movement of Christian social action, but with its success, martyrdom, and decline, the churches have retreated from the struggle. The churches still keep eleven o'clock on Sunday morning the most racially segregated hour of the day. Very few churches are integrated, and black Christians maintain their churches as the major African American–controlled institutions. Separate worship legitimizes racial separation and instinctive feelings of superiority or oppression. Major, mostly white denominations have been able to elect African American leadership, but the practices of white churches hinder most African American Christians from feeling comfortable in the predominantly white institutions. African American church life is necessary for the protection of black religious culture and for the identity of African American Christians in an unequal and unjust society.[6] In these African American religious communities, the potential for self-affirmation as a loved child of God supported by an antiracist community exists, if the church leadership will direct that community's original antiracism. African American Christians in predominantly European American churches continually struggle to maintain their identity and dignity while affirming the struggle for inclusive churches.[7] White churches fund programs to empower African American churches to serve their communities, but paternalism and harassment of black initiatives remain as constants. Racism is so much a part of the Christian church that the church cannot form itself into a swift sword for racial justice at the end of the twentieth century.

It is not enough to contrast the Christian ethic of love with Christian practice or racism. This is in part the inevitable distance between the ideal and the real, or between philosophy and politics, or between theory and practice. These dualisms are real and are overcome more in imagination than in reality. It is true that racism will finally disappear when the material domination of colored peoples by Europeans is undone, but before this can happen, those who live an ethic of love have a lot of work to accomplish in understanding and dismantling the ideological supports of racism, many of which are grounded in church life.

There are four major reasons for the current church's laissez-faire attitude toward racism. First, there was a failure of nerve; empirical evidence shows that Christians have become weary, apathetic, and frustrated in the battle to secure racial justice. Second, church members in the majority community never really overcame their ignorance of the complexity of racism. Third, efforts to establish racial justice were perceived as threats to the unity of local congregations and denominational structures. Faced with the conflict, the church blinked and largely conceded the struggle. This avoidance of conflict for unity also had economic overtones: few were willing to risk the wealth of the church for racial justice. Finally, deflection of ethical consciousness into educational programs relieved the ethical tension. Activists became lecturers and teachers, and few church policies were changed. Even when internal church life was changed, very little Christian social action for the broader common good outlived Martin Luther King Jr.[8]

However, there remain great resources for racial justice within the Christian church. The African American churches are a great reservoir of those who suffer from racism and who remember that there was once a time when their churches led the struggle. The clergy of these African American churches cope daily with the fallout from racism, and thousands of them are potential leaders of a new struggle. The European American churches also have thousands of well-educated, articulate leaders, many of whom have access to the halls or at least the ears of the socially, economically, and politically powerful. This white Christian leadership may be even more vulnerable than the African American Christian leadership to social and economic sanctions. But the church is very malleable when the moral issue is starkly clear. The ultimate imperative is very demanding on this issue and is clearly the dominant way of expressing it in the African American church community in the trajectory from Martin Luther King Jr. through Peter Paris and Cornel West. This issue may become more pointed when it is focused on one American city.

## CHURCH, RACE, AND PITTSBURGH

Before his death in 1968, Martin Luther King Jr. had directed his thoughts to economic discrimination, lack of opportunity, and poverty in the black community. He had started preparations for the March on Washington to protest the lack of resources allocated to the black community. The war in Vietnam denied the war on poverty the funding it needed. King had joined his economic critique with the critique of the war. Resources sent to enable black soldiers to kill Vietnamese denied black families in the city centers the resources they needed. King's protests cost him his life. On the death of King, Pittsburgh, like most other major urban centers in the United States, was subject to rioting and arson. King had rejected black violence as an option for fighting white oppression for both moral and pragmatic reasons. Violence was immoral because it violated the humanity or the image of God in the other human being. It was pragmatically wrong because black violence would lead to white military repression.[9]

Now the plain, inexorable fact is that any attempt of the American Negro to overthrow his oppressor with violence will not work. We do not need

President Johnson to tell us this by reminding Negro rioters that they are outnumbered ten to one. The courageous efforts of our own insurrectionist brothers, such as Denmark Vesey and Nat Turner, should be eternal reminders to us that violent rebellion is doomed from the start.[10]

King did all he could to stave off violent black rebellion. He taught that the Watts riots of 1965 had been futile. He saw in violent black rebellion a pursuit of defeat and self-destruction. Power was to win by the vote, organization, argument, moral pressure, and economic development, not by losing a violent struggle.

In the anger and rage over his assassination, his words were forgotten. Four hours after his assassination, the rioting started with a firebomb attack on Bedford Avenue in the Hill district (one of three major black ghetto areas in Pittsburgh). The majority of those who joined in the rioting were black youth. Businesses, both black- and white-owned, were burned and looted, while some businesses were protected. Even as recently as 1998, many of the business places were still boarded up and abandoned. On the Hill and in Homewood-Brushton, the shopping areas never recovered. In studying the riots, the Mayor's Special Task Force[11] noted the persistence of discontent in ghetto areas arising from years of poverty, discrimination, and neighborhood deterioration. The task force did not find governmental or social resources seriously directed toward alleviating the conditions that had produced anger and despair. Very few resources for building pride, identity, or self-determination were to be found within the black economic resources. The assets of the twenty largest black-owned businesses would not begin to approach the resources, for example, of one of the better-endowed white churches. The Task Force recommended the restoration of order, the upgrading of the ghettos through massive development programs, and the reordering of city priorities to meet the needs of the rioting areas. In fact, order was restored to repress the rioting, and the other two aspects of the report were neglected.

The outcome of the riots repeated Pittsburgh's history of failed outbreaks of violence. Originally, the native Americans were of too meager numbers to resist the immigrants. Even when adjoining areas were reserved for the American Indians, the immigrants from Europe flowed in with numbers that were impossible to resist. The Indian allies of the French might behead their victims and place the heads on stakes decorated with the kilts of the Scots, but still the Europeans came on. The county seat of Hanna's Town in Westmoreland County, which included Pittsburgh, was burned by Indians, but the immigration was too strong to resist successfully. Pontiac's war of 1763 lay siege to Fort Pitt, but Pontiac's confederacy was defeated at Bushy Run. Grotesquely interesting was the introduction of bacteriological warfare from Fort Pitt, as Indian emissaries were given blankets and linens from a smallpox hospital. In 1794, the Whisky Rebellion asserted frontier resistance to Alexander Hamilton's tax on spirits. Houses were burned, people were shot, and Pittsburgh was threatened with destruction. Local forces broke the rebellion before Washington's militia arrived. The independence of the frontier was surrendered to the newly independent union of colonies. Churches that had supported the popular War of Independence refused to legitimize this local rebellion. Attempts by labor to organize for their welfare produced social struggle and armed conflict in the Railroad Riot of 1877 (sometimes celebrated by the radical left as the first Pittsburgh Commune) and the Homestead Strike of 1892. Local dissidents have been able to destroy property and take a few lives in the struggle, but they have never been strong enough to defeat the national or state-supported armed forces.

After the fires of the 1968 riots were put out, tactics returned to the nonviolent social struggle against racism. The campaign to secure places for blacks in the craft unions took to the streets in the fall of 1969, producing major demonstrations and securing pledges of some minority employment. An interracial, ecumenical church was founded in the Oakland area (the university medical center complex of Pittsburgh). The church, now named the Community of Reconciliation, still flourishes in 1999 and is an expression of Christians overcoming the racism that divides their society. The indefatigable efforts of the National Association for the Advancement of Colored People and the Urban League keep the issues of racial justice before the consciousness of those who will listen. The picture is not all negative. Gains in black employment have been recorded, some improved housing for the poor has been built, and the schools are less racially segregated than they were in 1968. Blacks have realized some power in the school system through their presence on the school board and in the classroom. Public employment is decidedly more integrated than it was in 1968. Still, the countertrends of increased drug abuse, more single-parent families, inadequate achievement in school, disproportionate unemployment, and economic decline of once-thriving black shopping districts leave a picture of blacks worse off in the city of Pittsburgh in 1999 than they were in 1968. Middle-class black out-migration from the city denies the black community many of its potential leaders in a manner similar to white flight depriving the urban white society of leadership.

The two leading black writers who write about Pittsburgh have left Pittsburgh and flourished in other cities. John Wideman's novels capture the rhythms of Homewood, and people who grew up with him identify with his books and with his tragic life. August Wilson, the playwright who releases the spirit of the Hill in his plays, remembers a particularly poignant symbol of religious turning away from the reality of black poverty. The Church of St. Benedict the Moor, a Roman Catholic church, was spared the urban removal that devastated or ended the black community of the lower Hill. The homes of about 1500 families were replaced by parking lots and the Civic Arena, but the church remained. The church is often the site of black organizing and the originating point for black protest marches into the city center. Wilson recalled that in the 1960s the church decided to put a statue on top of its steeple: "And when the statue was unveiled, . . . Saint Benedict was opening his arms to the skyscrapers and department stores and turning his back on the Hill."[12] So it always is.

Racism understood in Pittsburgh as the white majority's disposition and practice of sanctioning the oppression of the black minority is involved in almost every urban issue. Walter Lippmann pointed out, before the 1968 riots, that gains for black Americans required gains for the American cities. Without prosperity in the cities, the prosperity of blacks as an urban people is doomed. Failures of city schools, city housing programs, city prisons, and city employment all involve racism. Every black American I have talked to for a significant period of time has been abused because of his or her race. Racism translates into discrimination and abuse, and it scars the humanity of both the abuser and the victim. The plans to improve the cities through the Great Society and the War on Poverty were burned in the Vietnam War, and they have not been redeveloped as the country has suffered under anti-urban administrations. The cities were ineffective in delivering votes in crucial states that require large urban pluralities to elect pro-urban administrations. However, urban or anti-urban policies never make it to the forefront of the campaigns. The political calculations to reduce Jesse Jackson's power in the Democratic Party, based on the desire to attract independent voters and to regain Reagan Democrats, thwarted effective campaigning among black urban populations. Alliances within the Democratic Party will be hard to maintain. White blue-collar workers and the unemployed in Pittsburgh did not vote for Jackson, and black enthusiasm for the ticket that snubbed him was minimal. So little federal help for the cities and for reversing racist patterns in the city can be expected. To fight racism is to fight minority poverty, for the two major aspects of overcoming racism are redistribution of economic power and redistribution of political power.

The reduction of the manufacturing base of the city's economy impacts the black community, where unemployment is usually twice as high as in the white community. The good jobs in the service sector of the community require technical skills and education. The options for blacks are successful, job-oriented education, the military, or the streets. The inner city allows participation in the underground economy, which can sustain survival but very little advancement. The perceptions and realities of racial discrimination impact on blacks and discourage them at a time when success requires high motivation. Joblessness resulting from inadequate education and discrimination reinforces a negative cycle that spills into other social evils. A young black man named Aaron Hill, describing his inability to find an adequate paying job, talked about the lure of the illegal drug trade:

> I get mad that I can't find a job with better pay. I could sell drugs and make $1500 a day. I've been asked to sell drugs because I'd be reliable—I don't use them.
>
> But I don't want to do it—don't want to put that kind of shame on my family. My grandmother's a churchwoman and if she heard I was dealing drugs, she would have a heart attack and die right there.

It's not just my family. It's wrong to sell drugs—you're just out there killing people. But if I didn't have a family, I might take a chance. The money's tempting, but right now it's not tempting enough.[13]

The lack of jobs reinforces dependence on welfare, life in the underground economy, the selling of drugs, participation in theft and robbery, and even the weakening of the black family. Unemployed males are not good candidates for marriage. Births out of wedlock, single-parent families, the resultant cycle of welfare dependence, and poor education are all partially attributable to unemployment.

Senator Daniel Patrick Moynihan has suggested the revival of afternoon mail delivery as a means of combating minority unemployment. The Postal Service has been a major provider of good jobs for minorities in Pittsburgh. Leon Haley, the late executive director of the Urban League, said that what is needed most is ten thousand good jobs paying ten dollars per hour with benefits for people with basic skills.[14] Employment is a key to overcoming racism, and employment is mutually related to education.

No one issue will be the key to reducing racism understood as systematic oppression. The problems are as broad as the finances of the black family, the housing of the poor, educational achievement, employment possibilities, and the total human situation. The welfare of the minority population of Pittsburgh depends on the welfare of the entire city.

Jovelino Ramos, who directs Presbyterian work to combat racism at the General Assembly level, regards the development of a comprehensive strategy to fight institutional racism as the current task of the church.[15] The published strategy *Racial Justice in the 1980s* was limited to a general but holistic description of plans for the church. It appears that the churches, after the confrontations in the 1960s and 1970s with African American church leaders demanding reparations for slavery and racism, are now trying to find church strategies for fighting racism within the church. The social currents seem to be running against a real church struggle against racism. Only churches that act to combat racism can expect to overcome racially intolerant and repressive attitudes. White churches must be active against racism for the health of their own souls. The issue is really quite stark. The New Testament witness was, you cannot claim to love God and hate your brother or sister. You cannot even claim to be a follower of Jesus unless you are actively engaged in overcoming the evil that oppresses your sister or brother.

From our course in church and local society, students have gone out to work on educational issues, food programs, prison ministries, halfway house ministries, health services, housing ministries, political campaigns, city management, and urban ministries. All of these activities are part of the antiracism agenda, but Pittsburgh lacks a comprehensive strategy with significant action components to combat racism. There is very little theological education on racism and even less dialogue among black and white ministers on the theological issues of racism. Black churches understand better than white churches the relationship of urban church to urban society. White churches understand better than black churches how to get money and education in this society. Black churches know the pain of urban life in ways that some white churches need to learn about. Both black and white churches have a lot of street wisdom, survival skills, and knowledge of how to accomplish desired goals. Their respective bodies of knowledge, both appropriate for different aspects of the urban environment, may be enriched by being shared. Alliances for theological discussion for social change are needed in a period in which the popular social culture is running in another direction. The city cannot be made better without black gains, and significant black gains are not to be won by polarization of the races. Alliances will need mutual empowering for the common goal, which requires a new place of significance for black participation.

In the midst of the emergence of the black power movements in American society, Professor Joseph C. Hough Jr. wrote about strategies for white churches.[16] He categorized white churches as liberal, apolitical, and white supremacist. The white supremacist churches were to be regarded as part of the problem. Hough cautioned about the need to remember that we are all sinners, but white supremacism needs prophetic criticism to be exposed as sinful. Even from white supremacist churches, the gospel can empower individuals to become transformed. Racism can be overcome. It must be challenged. Hough regarded the apolitical congregation as the majority type of congregation. Here, individuals can be recruited for work on race relations, and funds for fighting racism can be raised. It is also important to continue to focus church education on racism for the sake of the individuals reached and also so that active church programs for combating racism are not opposed. The apolitical churches tend to be threatened by movements they regard as extreme, so as pressure for racial justice develops, it is important that the apolitical churches remain apolitical. Hough wrote also about churches of a "distinctively liberal type." Such a church is a representative of the few predominantly white churches in which a majority become politically involved in an issue of racial justice. This type of congregation might initiate projects or ally with other agencies for action. Hough's suggestion that a majority of members would become involved in political action to empower blacks is probably too high a criterion for any white church in Pittsburgh to meet. Still, there are those white congregations that will take public stands against racism and allocate funds to the struggle for racial justice. Although Hough's typology of three types of white churches—liberal, apolitical, and white supremacist—may be too simplistic, it points to the need for prudent, multipronged strategies for attacking racism.

The day of white ministry in the urban black ghetto is over, but as white churches again learn to address issues of racial justice, the need for channeling of resources through black-controlled urban-action projects will become evident. At this level, the need for regional, denominational, and ecumenical agencies to develop means of supporting black projects, actions, and agencies becomes clear. Out of these shared programs, the shape of the political agenda to be developed by the churches will be defined more clearly, for although the rhetoric of "black power" is passé, the need for empowerment of black people is more urgent than ever. The church as a constituency of conscience has an important role to play in developing a shared political agenda with the poor minorities.

## THE AGENDA FOR THE NEW CENTURY

After the 1992 political eclipse of Jesse Jackson, neither major political party was willing to seriously promote the agenda of either the city or the African American poor population. Statistics showed that the poor were not voting, anyway, but even more ominous was the withdrawal of the urban young from the African American churches. Without developed, organized religious hopes for those living in a political vacuum, even the school could be perceived as the enemy. The school's promises to lead students to economic opportunity were not believed by kids who left their unemployed fathers, mothers, uncles, and aunts to attend schools usually staffed by white teachers and administrators, too many of whom lived in white suburbs. In the late 1980s, I heard of a macabre suggestion by a Michigan executive regarding Detroit. He was reported to have said, "Build a wall around Detroit and send in all the drugs and guns they will use." In the 1990s, it was done. The walls were social racism, and the guns and drugs were provided. The kids, in ritualistic rage, killed their own kind.

Cornel West has described the problems of the urban poor as too little love and too little money.[17] These problems are interrelated: the lack of theological conviction that one is loved by God, reinforced by community, denies the resources needed to overcome enforced poverty. West sees that the liberal structuralism, which could be associated with the history of the Democratic Party that rejects the city to win the suburbs, still affirms part of the New Deal and the Great Society. Liberal structuralists affirm government solutions: full employment, health care, improved education, child care programs, and the sustaining of affirmative action.[18] These liberals hope for justice, defend democracy, call for political participation, and generally avoid radical analysis or policies. On the other side of the issue, when it is joined, are the conservative behaviorists who resist government initiatives for the poor and "promote self-help programs, back business expansion and non-preferential job practices." They urge African Americans to live the Protestant work ethic, to fit white stereotypes for success, and to assimilate.[19] According to West, both misconstrue the problem, because values and structures are interrelated at every level. The problem is nihilism and despair reinforced by the socioeconomic, political struggles.

If West is correct about the debate, his recommended solutions point in a helpful direction. He criticizes African American leadership and urges a religiously based prophetic politics grounded in the ethic of love that pushes for a more radical redistribution of property and power than either party to the debate recognizes. Between Jesse Jackson and Toni Morrison's *Beloved*, William Julius Wilson finds the resources for self-affirmation in spite of oppression and the project of prophetic-conversionist politics. Those poles give the general outlines needed to achieve that stance of: "Yes, I am oppressed but I will do well, by God, while doing good for my neighbors." Such a stance is ultimately victorious and finally undefeatable. The conservatives are right that African American despair must be overcome, and the liberals are right that the structures must be righted, but neither party is capable of addressing the interrelatedness of the problem. As a white author-activist, it seems to me that the racism in both parties to the debate must be noted. The liberal, structuralist elite will sacrifice racial justice for power, as will the conservative elite. Both of their programs are distorted by racist protection of power. The liberal, structuralist programs of hope can be developed only with significant African American input sufficient to forge the compromises to ensure gains for urban poor while protesting liberal structural power. The conservative side offers nothing much of political value to poor African Americans. But the agenda of an engaged African American church might continue to move right socially while moving powerfully left in politics. In any case, without both psychical renewal and political participation, the urban poor have no chance. Meanwhile, the majority churches need both the rule-based ethic of the Ten Commandments and commitments out of reinforcing community to a politics of justice beyond self-interest. Given dramatic improvement in leadership, this combination could move beyond black nationalism and white racism for a season to alter the structural realities of America. Given the athletic and cultural heroism of African American leadership, the recovery of love, the change in the material opportunities of the culture, and a commitment on the part of white leadership to force a change, greater justice could be won.

William Julius Wilson's program for work in the ghetto offers a set of structural remedies that could provide policies for the religiously based struggle that is needed to move toward justice. Wilson notes the conservative concern about culture and character and nods to racism as an explanation for violence, degradation, and dysfunctional families in the urban centers, but he focuses on joblessness. When work is not available, the rewards of work in structure, discipline, and financial opportunity disappear, producing social failure. Wisely, he does not want to apportion blame, but to find solutions. He is wise to attack social inequality in general without a focus on race and to support social solutions that will raise the life of all of the poor. In my view, the social programs that will succeed and be sustained will not be race-specific. The improvement of the whole common good will do more to eradicate racism than race-specific programs that are too vulnerable to racial backlash.

Most of Wilson's proposals focus on enriching opportunity for the entire society so that children, including the deprived of the ghetto, can see hope and seek work that will be available. (1) Education must be improved, with required performance standards and the overcoming of the gap in achievement between inner-city and other schools. (2) French welfare policies for children include three levels—"child care, income support, and medical care"—and equivalent provision is needed in the United States, particularly for the poor. (3) Many forms of traditional and/or metropolitan partnership for the inner city, providing resources that are lacking, need to be reinvigorated. (4) In regard to employment, Wilson focuses on "for profit" placement centers in the inner city and a reintroduction of the Works Project Administration to help move people from welfare to public work and eventually to the private-profit sector of the economy. Some victims of ghetto deprivation will probably never be rehabilitated, but the greatest beneficiaries from the inner city will be the children who would be given opportunities and resources to approach "the American way of life."[20]

Wilson's policies of the liberal structuralist type are wise. He needs to include the demolition, rehabilitation, and restoration of the housing stock of the inner city, particularly the failed projects type of housing. Such a widespread initiative, coupled with paid labor based on Habitat for Humanity's skills training and enthusiastic organization of people, could provide many of the jobs needed. Further opportunities are in child care, postal delivery, the rebuilding of public facilities, and serious recruitment for antidrug policy enforcement. The building and staffing of schools for the children of the baby boomers provides another opportunity for massive employment even before the opportunities of high-technology employment are calculated. Wilson talks about a twelve-billion-dollar cost to train and employ one million workers who are now on welfare.

Cornel West has called for radical policies of redistribution. He is correct that the struggle for much greater social equality needs to be reinvigorated. Wilson's policies are ameliorative. Massive redistribution of income or land in the United States is not on the agenda for the foreseeable future. Still, greater equality is an ethical imperative based in the whole Christian ethic of this study. Wilson's general policies, funded by even a 50 percent reduction in military spending and the funding for the various cold war–related intelligence agencies, would move programmatically, prudently, and cautiously in the needed directions. Eventually, taxes provided by the newly employed would pay for the investment. Maintenance, health, and education for a child for twenty-one years provides a worker for another four decades.

The pragmatic meliorism of policies like Wilson's deserves the support of vision from religious communities. Religious ethics in the United States, predominantly Christian, can provide the fire and the passion to win these minimal achievements of justice. All of the mainline denominations know that such policies are appropriate. African American churches understand these needs out of their pain.

The defeat of health care provision for the whole citizenry and the reduction of welfare without the provision of jobs are symptoms of the moral vacuity of American Christendom. The naive rush of conservative Christians into the political arena occurred too quickly for them to bring their biblical, social ethics with them. They were organized by political conservatives around moral slogans governing deep areas of moral concern. But the need for social analysis to be conjoined with gracious understandings of transforming or creative justice was overlooked. When the new religious right recovers its biblical roots and American public responsibility, it will be a force to be reckoned with in overcoming the structural racism that reinforces poverty. Until that time, African American religious leaders and ecumenical Christian leaders will have to lead in articulating Christian public ethics. As they do, the sociologists and policy advocates will recognize that the churches must be taken more seriously in the social agenda than Wilson's essay suggested. The major lesson for African American church leaders from the religious right is the need to organize and vote. Without voting by the African American population, the power relations that reinforce racism will not be overcome. The major lesson for mainline Christians regarding their loss of control of the Republican Party and the weakening of the moral concerns of Democrats in the public arena since FDR is the need for coalition building. Racism will not be overcome without the alliances of whites and blacks that gave rise to the policies of the Great Society, which actually for a few years reduced the income gap between the poor and the wealthy, eased racial tensions, and freed considerable numbers of African Americans to gain middle-class opportunities. As hard as it is for whites to understand black nationalism and Afrocentric emphases, and to endure the rage of the dispossessed, they must reach out and support African American progressive leadership. Cornel West and William Julius Wilson show the way to white Christians who are serious about their Christian ethics.

# Political
# Apathy

**M**any Americans do not recognize the importance of American politics.[1] With only 30 to 40 percent of eligible citizens even voting while a small elite of political participants are left to make the decisions, representative democracy is being squandered. Political participation and voting rise with income. This correlation is mutual, because participation in the political process assists in raising one's standard of living, and participation in the higher standard of living encourages one to defend it politically. Those who participate politically tend to prosper, and those who do not decline.

Obviously, justice will not make gains in a time of increasing political alienation, but it is never really in the self-interest of those who rule to help increase political participation from below. Certain parties or candidates may need votes from the lower class, but no great efforts have been made to involve lower-class people in the political process since the Great Society's attempts at community organization and Jesse Jackson's early voter registration campaigns.

This alienation and voter apathy contradict the importance of controlling an influential government. Not only are the economics and politics crucial for the peace and human development of the world, but on the domestic scene, one-third of the economy is derived from the spending of tax monies. There is no area of American life that is free from political decisions. Neither the spiritual life of the churches nor the life of the wild beast in the deepest forest is totally free from the reach of the American political process. As the importance of American politics grows more and more, citizens are defaulting from it.

The decline is attributable to many factors, an analysis of which requires more work, but several factors are obvious. The tendencies toward mass, bureaucratic, technological societies reduce the sense of the relevance of individual participation. Skepticism about one's voice, vote, money, or work having an influence or even counting has increased. The professionalism of politics and the massive expense of supporting that professionalism disempowers the citizen. The reduction of the citizen's role in voluntary associations also disempowers the potential activist voter. Television isolates people from their communal life, and suburban voters are isolated from the urban life they pass by in their automobiles.

In addition to the alienating isolation of the contemporary citizen's life, political scandals have deepened political cynicism in the public. In politics, skepticism is a virtue and realism is a necessity, but cynicism, which cuts the participatory nerve, is deadly. The cynicism is deep and needs to be countered by information and hope. It is not only scandals that have contributed to cynicism; failed dreams have also embittered many. Disllusionment associated with the civil rights movement and the peace movement has left nothing but cynicism for those overly dependent on dreams.

Added to apathy born of alienation and political cynicism is ignorance. American education at the public school and university levels does not educate young people to understand or participate in politics. Participation on an admissions committee in a university religious studies department and at a seminary reveals that most college students applying for graduate study in religion do not even study politics. The American public is ignorant of the issues and the importance of American politics. The 1996 conventions of the two major political parties seldom raised the level of discourse to a serious conceptual level. Political rallies in American cities could be distinguished from rallies for football games, but the differences between the slogans producing cheers for the two types of teams were disturbingly slight.

If the critique of the American citizenry as apathetic, cynical, and ignorant is correct, how can this be impacted by the theme of the ultimate imperative? What is the role of Christian ethics in revitalizing the American republic and its politics? The exploration leads through many issues, but in the end it asserts that there is *meaning* and that this meaning is grasped by the imperatives of a Christian way of life.

## GOD AND CAESAR

The question of the relationship of God and Caesar is not a new issue, yet it arises today with a fresh urgency. All human communities have had to resolve the problem of the relationship between their deepest religious loyalties and their practical decisions about government. The solution of one society has never prevailed over all of humanity. In our day, the crisis between religion and government has disturbed regimes in Central America, Iran, Afghanistan, and Poland. Recent politics in the United States has been energized and disturbed by new forms of Christian political activism. Religious divisions have contributed to recent political conflicts and wars in the Sudan, India and Pakistan, the Middle East, Northern Ireland, and elsewhere. Currently, political leaders and scientists are taking serious account of religious forces. As religious leaders and students of religion have learned, their religious practices have political implications that they cannot ignore.

Members of the church know that the sovereignty of God and service of God are of utmost importance in their lives. Some also know that the practical exercise of politics—the process governing human life—interpenetrates most areas of our lives. Questions of life and death, whether considered on the global scale of peace and war or the personal scale of human rights in abortion, have both theological and political dimensions. Both God and Caesar are involved. There will be no peace without politics. There will be no answer to the vexing questions about abortion without politics. Human history, through which God works to realize divine purposes, is subject also to the politics of human beings. These humans act out of a mixture of religious judgments and political judgments.

So we are inevitably political and religious. The God-Caesar question will not let us go. The question flows through the Scriptures. We are confronted with a variety of solutions. God moves Joseph into a position of authority in Egypt, and then Egypt oppresses Israel. God leads Moses out of Egypt, and the confrontation between Yahweh, the God of Moses, and the god-king Pharaoh disrupts Egypt. The tribes of Israel are joined in a religious confederacy to resist the Baalistic city-states of Canaan. Kingship is granted Israel only reluctantly by Samuel, for he sees the rejection of God in the institution of kingship. Prophets and priests struggle to work out a solution to the problem of religious loyalty and political loyalty. In Amos the struggle is between the prophet of God and the priest of the court serving the king. Through periods of political success and political failure, from David to the Exile, the question is not absent. The struggle of the Jews for pure religion breaks out into political conflict with their Greek and then their Roman masters.

Jesus himself, from his birth to his death and resurrection, was involved in the political-religious controversy. The stories about his birth involve promises of the overthrow of the established order in Mary's Magnificat and Herod's perceived threat to his rule by the birth at nearby Bethlehem. His death was an act of political execution and his resurrection a surprising victory over the political order that had attempted to silence him.

Luke described the charges brought against Jesus by the elders as "perverting the nation," "forbidding tribute to Caesar," and proclaiming himself "Christ, a King" (Luke 23:2 RSV). The three Synoptic Gospels related Jesus' own avoidance of the trap about paying taxes. Confronted by the disciples of the Pharisees and the Herodians, he avoided affronting either Rome or Judaism by saying, "Then render to Caesar the things that are Caesar's and to God the things that are God's" (Luke 20:25 RSV).

Political thinkers have had to deal with the meaning of this aphorism in varied historical situations since that day. What is appropriately owed to Caesar, and what is reserved to God? Different political orders work out this issue differently. Jesus himself only avoided the verbal trap of his enemies. Soon he was to surrender his life to the representatives of Caesar. Could there be anything on earth more completely God's than the life of Jesus? Yet it was laid down before Caesar. The Gospel of John makes it clear that Pilate, the representative of Caesar, was acting under God's authority. Pilate, overwhelmed by the issues of the crowd's religious-political convictions, finally acquiesced to the crucifixion. The saying of Jesus on rendering to Caesar and to God points toward the need for a distinction, but it fails to draw the line for Christians or for Jesus himself.

Religious faith and politics are not the same reality, but they cannot be totally separated. On biblical grounds they cannot be separated, although distinctions can be found. Empirically they cannot be separated, for many of the political conflicts of our day involve dimensions of faith.

Political authority, like water, is ultimately from God. Neither water nor political authority is a god, although in certain cultures both have been worshiped. Governments, like irrigation canals, must be organized by people; the breaking of either can create chaotic conditions. Often both canals and governments must be changed. Paul was confronted with Christian extremists in Rome who were tempted, in the name of Christian freedom, to be careless of political authority. His response in Romans 13 has protected political authority with religious legitimacy to both the health and the detriment of the people.

> Every person must submit to the supreme authorities. There is no authority but by act of God, and the existing authorities are instituted by him; consequently anyone who rebels against authority is resisting a divine institution, and those who so resist have themselves to thank for the punishment they will receive. For government, a terror to crime, has no terrors for good behavior. (Rom. 13:1–3 NEB)

These words seem hard to those of us who are conscious of our own religious liberty, which comes out of a history of revolution. The Calvinist revolutionary John Knox understood the sentence "For government, a terror to crime, has no terrors for good behavior" to be foundational to the argument. Therefore, when a group of people were a terror to good people, regardless of their claim, they were not God's government and they were to be replaced. Usually, however, the text has buttressed authority and recognized the high place that governing authorities have in God's work. Too seldom has attention been given to the last sentence of Romans 12: "Do not let evil conquer you, but use good to defeat evil" (Rom. 12:21). The last sentence in the section on government is also relevant: "Love cannot wrong a neighbor, therefore the whole law is summed up in love" (Rom. 13:10). Paul, expecting the end of history, had a problem with Christian extremists and ordered caution about challenging government. He, himself, of course, challenged it unto death. His advice to the Romans was meant for their time, but it has relevance to our time as well. He urges us to regard proper governmental authority as serving God and to see government in the context of good defeating evil. The summary of law, rightly conceived, is love.

The early hearers of the Gospel according to John anticipated martyrdom as Jesus and his disciples were martyred. The background of the New Testament is religious and religious-political conflict. The New Testament concludes with the oppression of the saints by Rome and the overcoming of

Rome in an apocalyptic vision. Thus, the Scriptures provide a plurality of answers to the question of the relationship of faith to politics.

Church history shows that the church has attempted many solutions to the God-Caesar problem. The early church defied the state's idolatry, and it was persecuted. Often it still is persecuted. Ascetics withdrew from the state. In small communities, the church still withdraws. The Roman Catholic medieval church attempted to run the state for Christian purposes, and Christians who would run the state are still active. Martin Luther tried to keep the church distinct from the social realm, recognizing that God governs both realms. In practice, often the church became subservient to the political needs of the rulers. John Calvin tried to reform the state while recognizing that the state is not and cannot be the Kingdom of God. The church in Reformed lands was tempted to establish a theocracy where it had the power.

John Calvin taught, and political history affirms, that no one form of the state will serve different peoples. Each government must correspond to the limits and possibilities of the population it governs. Social science confronts us with a variety of models of solutions to the God-Caesar issue. Beyond recognizing and describing the plurality, social science can help only a little in our search for the answer to the perplexities of the God-Caesar relationship.

Consequently, the search for wisdom regarding the religious-political question begins in a recognition of: (1) the inevitability of the issue, (2) the importance of the issue, and (3) a variety of answers to the issue found in the study of the Bible, church history, and social science. All three sources provide wisdom. The Bible in particular provides controls on the options that are open to contemporary Christians in their resolution of the problem. From our history we learn of a particular Reformed way of perceiving these scriptural controls as well as a style of political action. Social science also helps us understand the contemporary problems surrounding the issue and describes alternative consequences of certain choices.

The crisis of the relationship between faith and politics involves not only religious issues but also the changing political scene. The American political system is troubled. The national leadership has been highly unstable. Presidents have been assassinated, have retired under criticism and intraparty conflicts, have been forced to resign under clouds of political scandal, and have been defeated at the polls.[2] The media, the reform of the primary system, the computer, the political action committees, and the new religious-political groups—all have had an impact on a system characterized by political apathy toward and suspicion of the political process. The American political system is an old system that has evolved greatly and that is undergoing intense strains. Can the ecological issues be handled by the system given its strong commitments to individualism and laissez-faire? Is the system adequate to meet the needs of the urban population of the country? Can a just migration policy be developed with all the pressure groups and fears that surround the issue? Finally, and most important, can a just peace be secured on this side of the cold war? All of these four issues, addressed theologically and ethically by the church, will require political leadership, which is not visible on the horizon. Fundamental questions are on the national agenda, but most political leaders seem to be ducking, refraining from leading, settling for oversimplified media answers, serving special interests, and concentrating on getting reelected.

## THE AMBIGUITY

The complexity of the relationship between faith and politics is inherent to the nature of politics as well as in the demands of faith. The classical political philosophy articulated in the fourth century B.C.E. regarded politics as the governing for the good of the people of the city. Politics was a branch of ethics. Thomas More in the sixteenth century continued this theme in his writing of *Utopia*, as he portrayed an ideal society. Caught up in the religious-political controversies of his day, More the author was martyred. Socrates and More both presented a view of politics as ethics, and both made the ultimate sacrifice. An alternative view is perhaps best represented by Niccolò Machiavelli, a relatively religiously indifferent thinker of the sixteenth century, in *The Prince*, in which politics is characterized as basically the search for and maintenance of power. This view, too, had its forerunners in the writings of the Greek political thinkers, particularly the cynics. In this view, politics is a relatively amoral skill of ruling the people. Neither view in its pure form is sufficient. Ethics and politics are not united, but neither are they completely separate.

Politics on every level is obviously self-interested people pursuing their own advantage through the use of government. However, politics, particularly where it is exercised through democratic procedures, also requires a vision of the public good to be served. Politicians must represent themselves as expressing the best interests of those they represent. Too narrow a pursuit of self-interest exposes the politician to criticism and the profession to a reputation that cheapens the meaning of politics. Even self-interest must be disguised under promises to work for the civic good. Politics is a mixture of serving self and serving the public. People try to be ethical as well as political, although they are not perfect in either attempt. In politics and ethics, the search for both the public good and self-interest leads to uneasy compromises.

Christians understand this political ambiguity as rooted in our human nature. We are inevitably sinful in our political actions. All of our political actions reflect our own self-interest or our own perspective. The best hopes for our political life reside in knowing our sins as well as the sins of others and acting accordingly to minimize the effects of sin. We may still be called to martyrdom. The willingness to accept martyrdom is essential to Christian political action. Not only Jesus and the apostles but also countless Christians have taken this route. The refusal to compromise on ultimate issues is a mark of Christian participation in politics. Recognition of our own sins, however, guards us against a willingness to force others into martyrdom and points toward the need for compromise and prudence in political action. Sin in politics, both as a distortion of our created goodness and as the refusal to live in love, is not to be celebrated but to be recognized as the context for repentance, change, and transformation. Knowing that we exist in a violent world, we try to be peacemakers striving to realize God's peace or shalom. Our tools for achieving peace are awkward; still, as Augustine, bishop of Hippo in North Africa, taught at the beginning of the fifth century, we must use these imperfect tools. Faith gives a context for knowing that God wills people to live together in trusting, wholesome relationships. Hope provides a motivation for engaging in a politics of expectation that life can be more just. Love requires us to respond to the love God has shown by providing loving service to our neighbor. These central Christian virtues transform but do not annul the way Christians in society try to order society through moderation, courage, wisdom, and justice.

## RESERVATION AND COMMITMENT

Until the founding in the twentieth century of frankly secular states, most earthly rulers in Christian civilization were Christians. Maybe they were not thoroughly Christian, but they were baptized and most confessed themselves to be Christian. Christianity, since the overthrow of official idolatry, has been quite political. The Christian hopes and values of their populations nurtured the politics of these societies. The societies were not secular; they were religious in Christian terms. Still, the Christian faith could not be reduced to politics. Memories of prophetic distance between religion and politics were never completely eclipsed. Monastic groups withdrew from the politics of the state, although in both Eastern and Western Christendom they would return to reform politics. Clergy would demand and receive some exemptions from political responsibility. Religious visionaries would reawaken again and again the hope for a reign of God that was different from political kingdoms. A faith with even a somewhat dim memory of Jesus could not equate Roman rule or its motley heirs with the reign that Jesus announced.

Christianity, along with Judaism and Islam, is among the most worldly of the world's religions. Yet, there was a reservation about political involvement that remained. The human spirit could not be satisfied with the peace of the city of the earth; it sought the peace of the City of God. A person caught up in the love of God knows that earthly justice is usually only rough justice. It is not enough. We pray for the coming of the reign of God daily in the Lord's Prayer, recognizing that these earthly kingdoms or people's republics are not God's fulfillment of human community.

Western Christianity in its Catholic and Reformed traditions is committed to political action, but it also has a reservation about political action. Not all of life is politics. There is a freedom in the human spirit that is too great for any of our political organizations. The neglect of this religious reservation about politics has led and can lead to a religious fanaticism in politics. The human spirit, the imaging of God in humanity, is too free to be satisfied by any political settlement. Knowledge of the greatness of the human spirit as well as knowledge of human sin must help Christians affirm a religious reservation about politics as well as a commitment to politics.

## TWO ROOTS OF POLITICAL THINKING

In the closing days of the Weimar Republic, in 1932, Paul Tillich reflected on the relationship between faith and politics. The new pagan, political cult of Nazism threatened to overturn the weakened republic, which was also under attack by communism and by a collection of conservative political interests. Tillich's essay "Two Roots of Political Thinking"[3] made a contribution that is still relevant. He argued that traditional regimes often were founded on the sacralization of political systems in root myths of the society. Ancient Egypt and Babylon were characterized by myths that supported divine kingship and religious hierarchy and wove into the myths of creation the divinely ordered present government. Religion and politics were one, with politics favoring a particular religion and religion legitimizing a particular political order.

In Israel, prophets arose and criticized the political order in terms of their understanding of God's covenant with Israel. Amos, for example, witnessed to God judging all nations by justice. Also, he held out the possibility of repentance or change for the political order. The present rulers were not merely to be legitimized but were to be judged by justice, and there was a sense of historical movement or expectation. By hearing judgment now, better order could be established.

Consequently, one root of political thinking was the myth of origin involving worship of the motherland or fatherland, the sacralization of kingship, and the blessing of customary rule. The second root of political thinking had a sense of historical movement and evaluated rule by a standard of God's justice; it was the prophetic critique of a sacral politics.

Despite a tendency in the Middle Ages to sacralize the papal-Caesar settlement, the Western world kept alive the second root of political thinking until it broke forth again, borne by the movements of the Renaissance, Reformation, and Enlightenment. Democratic politics, capitalism, and socialism all contained this movement of historical expectation and the centrality of justice or political ethics.

The Weimar Republic was an expression of this second root of political thinking. However, it was not strong enough, given economic depression, to withstand movements based on the myths of origin. The monarchists expressed the myth of origin, but they were enfeebled by the lack of a sense of historical expectation; they were simply trying to return to the past. The forces supporting the Weimar settlement seemed to lack sufficient respect for the truth of the myth of origin. They were critics of the past without deep roots. The Nazis expressed a romantic myth of origin with a sense of future transformation in the dream of a Third Reich. They had the power of a myth of the past and a myth for the future, but they had no sense of justice or any critical understanding of human reality.

Democracy depended on critical reason, but in a period of worldwide depression it was a weak opponent to romantic, pagan myths of ancient Germany united with a promise of a political messiah and a transformed future. The churches, both Protestant and Catholic, were politically inept. The universities, the press, and other moral-cultural institutions were in disarray and were unwilling to fight for the weakened liberal culture. The fury of romantic myths and fighting cadres of Nazis overwhelmed them.

Protestants were too willing to abandon the political realm, and Catholics were too willing to compromise with an evil regime to maintain their prerogatives. The democratic, mixed economy of the Weimar Republic could possibly have defeated the Nazis with more sophisticated understanding of the need to maintain a promise of a better order with justice and a willingness to fight the rising tide of barbarism. The churches, however, could not understand this and would not fight.

From Tillich's essay, we can conclude that the liberal republics of the Western world are weakened if they do not understand the need for maintaining a sense of the myths of origin. Myths of origin in our day are expressed in terms of civil religion. But civil religion is not strong enough in periods of stress, unless it maintains a sense of expectation or future promise combined with a strong commitment to social justice. Justice cannot be only the agreement of a society to order its life in a certain way; it must also be grounded in the conviction of the reality of a sovereign God, who requires justice in periods of stress as well as in times of affluence.

In our society, the civil rights movement, particularly as it was led by Martin Luther King Jr., combined the affirmation of the American myths of origin in the Declaration of Independence, the Constitution, and the American dream with the demands of justice for the oppressed and the poor. The movement combined a willingness to fight, albeit nonviolently, for justice, with a grounding of the fight in the democratic ideals of the country. The sense of expectation that the country would change in the direction of fairness toward its oppressed was vital to the success of the movement. When this expectation was lost with King's assassination, and as the movement surrendered the nonviolent strategy, it clouded its ideals to the point that its achievements were limited. Myth, critique of myth in terms of justice, and sense of expectation are vital to the expansion of further democratization in the liberally oriented republics of the Western world.

## THEOLOGY OF LIBERATION

An exciting recent movement toward the relation of politics to faith is the theology of liberation. Theologies of liberation have been grounded in various social movements. Commentators distinguish among women's theology of liberation; black theology of liberation in its various forms of Caribbean, North American, and African theologies; and Latin American liberation theology. All these forms of liberation theology identify with the social-political

causes of their respective movements and engage in theology as critical reflection for and on these historical movements.

The victory of the Sandinista revolution in Nicaragua and the role of theologians in that revolutionary movement produced an urgency for the
examination of liberation theology in Latin America. The Latin American
form of liberation theology had arisen from theological reflection on new
forms of Christian community. Several thousand (perhaps a hundred thousand) grassroots Christian communities, known as base communities, sprang
up the 1970s and 1980s. These communities united for worship, Bible study,
social analysis, and mutual support. A fascinating example of their dialogic
work together is recorded in the four volumes of Ernesto Cardenal's *The
Gospel in Solentiname*,[4] in which one can learn how peasants, artisans, poets,
and priests studied and lived together. The reality of suffering under the
Somoza regime is dramatized through the voices of peasants and accounts of
martyrdom. The process of a developing Christian political consciousness is
revealed. Eventually, the Bible study, social analysis, worship, and mutual
support led some to participation in armed revolution. Two priests in the
dialogue—the author and his brother, Fernando Cardenal—were members
of the revolutionary government. The United States undermined the
Sandinista government, fearing Marxism and greater unrest in Central
America. The long history of U.S. resistance to revolutionary movements in
Central America dominated U.S. policy in the region. The Somoza family,
whom the Sandinistas overthrew, had been U.S. clients. The director of the
CIA, William Casey, made the defeat of liberation theology and of the
government in Managua his own personal crusade. With the support of
President Reagan and the CIA-backed Contras, he succeeded.

The battle at the foreign policy level was also an intrachurch battle. Pope
John Paul II feared and criticized the development of a popular or people's
church. His own politics and theology inclined him to distrust Christian,
common fronts with Marxists. He warned against ideological distortions within
the popular church, meaning the Christian base communities. He appealed for
the recognition of the authority of bishops in the church. The continuing
struggle in Latin America is not only one of popular Christianity versus hierarchical Catholicism. The struggle goes on within the hierarchy as well, as the
results of the Bishops' Councils of Medellín and Puebla reveal. The Protestant
churches of Latin America split, also, on the issue of political involvement to
change the present system. Thus, Christianity in Latin America, which has
been supportive of the present social situation of terrible poverty, extraordinary
wealth, and military repression, was thrown into confusion.

The social reality out of which Latin American liberation theology has come
is one of degrading poverty and military oppression. The liberation theologians
have abandoned all hope of assistance with development from the developed
countries under the present structures. They see the relationship between
the developed countries and the poor countries as one of the rich exploiting
the poor and enforcing that exploitation with whatever means necessary.

Five central themes of liberation theology are: (1) God is on the side of the oppressed; (2) in Latin America, oppression is systemic; (3) participation in liberation is a work of salvation; (4) the church must become the church of the poor; and (5) theology is critical reflection on the project of social liberation.[5] The origins of liberation theology were rooted also in the experiences of Gustavo Gutiérrez with the reforming-socialist military government of Peru. Its failures, along with the later defeat of democratic-socialist forces in Peru, led to the abandonment of the early revolutionary hopes. In my opinion, as the world changed, the radical-revolutionary hopes and program as seen in Gutiérrez's 1968 *Theology of Liberation*[6] gave way to the more traditional strategies of Christian social theology. In 1999, liberation theologians, while active in the causes of the poor, are still seeking a contemporary agenda.

An engagement with the movement articulated by liberation theology can help Reformed Christians to: (1) rediscover their own history of political involvement with the poor; (2) rediscover the political dimensions of neglected portions of the Bible; (3) reexamine the connections between Calvinism and capitalism; and (4) remember that Calvinist Christians are committed to social reform.[7]

Comparative reflection on the Calvinist heritage and the emerging work of liberation theology, then, helps us to rediscover our own social ethic and to challenge our complicity with suffering and murder in Latin America. Calvinism has some cautions to offer the liberation theologians. Theology is about God and strives for universality. The doctrine of sin is central to any theology and particularly to theologies of politics. In Reformed theology, scripture is primary; it informs experience.[8] We can say in liberation theology that theology must include critical reflection on the liberation of the poor, but we must say it in light of the whole of scripture.

Reformed theology in dialogue with liberation theology is helped to hear afresh its commitment to transform the world. Reformed theology will still insist that the reign of God is always relevant to political change, but not the same as political change. It cannot give up its insight that politics is ambiguous while calling for a theology of politics to serve the poor. Reformed theology insists on a religious reservation about politics that disinclines it from affirming utopian politics while affirming a politics for change inspired by the reign of God.

## THE NEW RELIGIOUS RIGHT

Religion thrust its way into the American politics of the 1980s with surprising vigor. Religious rhetoric had usually been a part of political campaigning. In some regions of the country it was politically important to be religiously correct. Most successful politicians learned early that even if they were not religious, it was smart to appear religious near election time. In the election of 1980, however, conservative, particularly fundamentalist, religious leaders organized voter registration drives, television political campaigning, political rallies, and direct-mail campaigning that startled the nation. The conservative religious leaders utilized all the tactics that the moderate-to-liberal religious leadership had exercised over the years and added an increased capacity to raise funds, a more sophisticated utilization of television, and computerized lists for frequent political and religious mailings that outshone the tactics of their opponents. Liberal senators and representatives were defeated, and the new Christian right appeared as a political force to be reckoned with.

There are two perspectives for understanding the fundamentalist contribution to the politics of the new right. The first perspective sees fundamentalism as a militant demand for a respected place in society by those whose values and views had been dismissed by the secularizing society. Fundamentalism was an almost irrational project of those whose America had changed in undesirable ways. The second approach views fundamentalism as an ideology with deep roots in the mainstream of Protestant evangelical theology. George Marsden suggests a synthesis of the two views.[9] Yes, the fundamentalists who are now political activists are bitter that their country has become pluralistic, secularized, and, in their perspective, internationally weaker and sexually depraved. However, fundamentalism is also a complex belief system, as coherent as many others, with its own distinctive traditions and deep roots.

In the current scene, political fundamentalism is affirming the political activist side of the evangelical tradition, which is a modification of the Puritan perspective by the experience of the nineteenth and twentieth centuries. This perspective sees an America turning away from its foundations of Christian principles. God's blessing on America varies with the degree to which America obeys God's laws. Of particular concern to the religious right are laws protecting the nuclear family. Abortion, pornography, and homosexuality are evidences of the flouting of God's laws, and America is receiving God's anger in its decline. The Equal Rights Amendment was seen as an assault on God's law of how the family should be structured.

The demands for countering the teaching of evolution and for prayer in the public schools are both seen as restoring America to its more Christian roots. The practice of the new religious right is part of the democratic process, but its program is a return to a perception of a prior order. The myth of a righteous-Christian America is used to change governmental policy in a time when the pluralistic-critical-liberal myth seems to be tottering.

Other elements of the purer America myth are a strong national defense and laissez-faire economics. More investment in defense is assumed to produce greater wealth. The myth, then, is of a religious America that will not demand sacrifice or tough decisions from anyone. Prosperity and security will flow with an opposition to the deviant sexual practices of others, the renewal of prayer in schools, the defense of creationism, and general moral revival.

This myth is not very strong, but in periods of great stress, revolutionary myths may not need to be particularly credible to exert influence. Particularly if the public is willing to accept slogans as guides to politics, oversimplified television messages and mailings can undercut the information and debate needed to make a republican form of government function.

## THE MORAL MAJORITY OF JERRY FALWELL

As the Carter administration fell apart under the pressures of a declining economy and the hostage crisis in Iran, lower-middle-class white Christians found a new standard-bearer in Jerry Falwell. Evangelicals and fundamentalists who had supported the Christian candidacy of Carter, the born-again Niebuhrian, turned now to a conservative candidate under the bombardment of the new Christian right. The techniques of the electronic church and the computerized direct-mail techniques came of age in a new Christian coalition focusing on an aging movie actor, Ronald Reagan, who demonstrated a flair for the politics of projecting an image of political strength.

Jerry Falwell, the pastor of the then fifteen-thousand-member Thomas Road Baptist Church of Lynchburg, Virginia, was chosen by the leadership of the National Conservative Political Action Committee and the Committee for the Survival of a Free Congress to set up the Moral Majority to target the evangelicals and the fundamentalists. Falwell's "Old Time Gospel Hour" established him as a leading voice of the fundamentalists, and under his organization the Moral Majority became the most important of the religious coalitions to support political conservatives in the 1980 elections.

Falwell interpreted the appointment as a divine mandate to take action to save America. The Moral Majority was divided into a political action committee organized for direct-mail lobbying, the Moral Majority Foundation for coordinating voter registration, and the Moral Majority Legal Defense Fund. Falwell was elevated to national prominence, appearing on the cover of *Newsweek* on September 15, 1980, and becoming a household name. His conservative politics merged nicely with Governor Reagan's views and the platform of the Republican Party, which Falwell called a "dream platform." He described Moral Majority, Inc., as a morally oriented, special-interest, political organization without a theological line but dedicated to conservative concerns.

The target-list strategy for defeating certain candidates has precedents in special-interest politics in the United States. So does the evaluation of candidates by selected issues in their voting records. It was the cooperation between Protestant ministers and TV preachers, combined with direct-mail campaigns, that was new. Some claimed that 72,000 clergy utilized their churches for fund-raising, voter registration, and political organization.

Falwell did not support all the activities of the new Christian right. He neglected the Washington for Jesus rally, but helped organize the Dallas assembly in which Governor Reagan endorsed the new Christian right while President Carter and Congressman Anderson stayed away. Falwell's power mounted during the campaign as he met with William Brock, chairman of the Republican Party, visited Reagan's suite in Detroit, and campaigned for conservative candidates. The senatorial candidates supported by the Moral

Majority all won (except Paul Gann in California), helping to move the Republican Party from a 41–59 minority in the Senate to a 53–47 majority. The leadership of the coalition rejoiced after the election, celebrating the establishment in power of conservative politics.

Influence is difficult to estimate. Interpretations of the contribution of the Moral Majority to the Republican victory vary. Its contribution was not repudiated by the voters; its candidates won. Liberals without a candidate of their own to head a ticket were in disarray. Although they leveled various attacks on the Moral Majority, they were not able to find effective means of dividing the Moral Majority and its presumed constituency of conservatives. Evangelical Christians still voted for Jimmy Carter, but the new Christian right cut into that support. The shape of the economy, the Iranian crisis, and the religious right all helped to defeat Carter. At least two of the three primary causes were the results of peculiar combinations of religion and politics.

Falwell's influence in national politics seems to have peaked in the 1980 election. He was less influential in 1984. By 1988, Pat Robertson was carrying the torch for the religious right. Falwell had overextended himself in attempting to clean up the finances of Jim Bakker's entertainment, broadcasting, and religious businesses. Falwell returned to the more traditional roles of broadcasting, administering, and ministering. He preached conservative politics on television, but his political organizing was drastically reduced. George Bush's rise to prominence in the Republican Party began to return the party machinery to the more traditional moderates who had come to dominate the party in the post–Iran-Contra years of the Reagan administration. The sex scandal involving Jim Bakker revealed the vulnerability of TV preacher-politicians to issues of sexuality and for a while diminished their public moral influence. The sexual issue also upset the Democratic front runner and revealed that as recently as 1988, the American electorate was not accepting any sharp distinctions between politicians' private lives and their political policies. In August of 1989, Falwell quietly closed the Moral Majority organization and rededicated his energies to TV evangelism, Thomas Road Baptist Church, and Liberty University, which had grown from a small college into a university with eight thousand students.

As a self-styled fundamentalist, Falwell believes in the inerrancy of scripture in matters of faith and practice as well as history, geography, and science. He believes that the Bible tells him that humanity is living in the last days. The Christian church, after a life of two thousand years, has almost used up its time. Before Christ returns there will be a seven-year struggle characterized by the persecution of Christians and a Russian invasion of Israel. At Armageddon, Satan will be defeated by Christ, who will reign bodily for a thousand years preceding the final judgment. Other leading TV preachers hold about the same position of premillennialism. The present is characterized by movements toward Christian unity, falling away from Christian faith, lack of public leadership, immorality, wars, and materialism, all of which point toward the approach of the last days.

Falwell sees himself as helping to prepare America for the last days. His version of civil religion is a Christian-American religion replete with the symbols of flag, public monuments, American success, the promise of redemption, middle-class moralism, and democratic politics conservatively oriented. His road show of Liberty Bible College students was interestingly titled "I Love America."

The concern about sexuality is foremost in Falwell's *An Agenda for the Eighties*. Secular humanism and liberalism in both politics and religion must be combated, but the primary interest in the document is sexual. The vital issues of the Moral Majority included a pro-life, antiabortion stance, a pro–traditional family position, opposition to pornography, and an anti-ERA platform. Among the ten most important issues are separation of church and state, opposition to illegal drugs, support for Israel, strong national defense, equal rights for women through state legislative action, and the autonomy of state Moral Majority organizations. Four of the ten issues deal with sexual-political issues. Heterosexual promiscuity and homosexuality are also strongly condemned.

The most developed argument in Falwell's book is the attack on current abortion policy in the United States. He merges the testimony of scientists and doctors with biblical proscriptions against killing to defend "the unborn child" as a person. No exceptions permitting abortion are mentioned, and the fear that approval of abortion will lead to widespread euthanasia is argued.

Many of the concerns about humanism in the public schools are rooted in a fear of sexual permissiveness. Several pages of *An Agenda for the Eighties* focus on homosexuality, family, artificial insemination, selective breeding, and genetic engineering, recommending certain legislative acts and opposing others. As is common in the TV medium, sexual fears are played on; nothing remains private. TV advertising uses sex to sell toothpaste and automobiles; in Falwell's case, sexual fears are used to sell conservative religion and conservative politics.

Falwell's book treats racial justice and world hunger with less significance than it treats pornography. National defense is given less coverage than homosexuality. If this book had been confined to sexuality and religion, its coverage might be noted without comment, but given its claim to represent the significant issues of the 1980s, its public focus on these sexual issues, its recommended legislation, and its passion must be highlighted.

Falwell's stance on sexuality and politics has been characteristically one of human life regulated by moral law; certain choices are either right or wrong. It reveals no awareness of the tendencies in mainline Protestant churches to speak of sexuality in terms of appropriate human behavior or of the open Catholic teaching in *Human Sexuality*. This view also is characteristic of Falwell's writing on international politics. The world is divided into the children of light, or the United States and its allies, and the children of darkness, or the communists and their allies. Communists are described as godless liars and cheaters. Falwell's simple moralism is buttressed by quotes from the cold warrior General Lewis Walt. The need for a renewed effort to strengthen U.S. national defense is buttressed with a reference of Jesus' refusal to honor the devil by jumping from the pinnacle to tempt God. The "free world" includes South Africa, Taiwan, South Korea, and U.S. allies in Europe, and it must be defended. Detente is attacked, and further arming of the United States is encouraged.

Falwell believes that God curses those who curse Israel and blesses those who bless Israel. "To stand against Israel is to stand against God." Among his own priorities is the protection of the Jewish people. He takes the promise to Abraham in Genesis 15 to mean that modern-day Israel shall rule from the Nile to the Euphrates. "We believe that Genesis 15 sets the boundaries of Israel and supports its claim to the land." This view lacks all appreciation that the Davidic kingdom once approximately fulfilled those boundaries and that the Old Testament attributes its demise to God's dealing through human agents to change the boundaries. It takes no note of the point that Muslims also claim descent through Abraham. He claims it to be a literal understanding, whereas in reality it is only a fanatical claim.

Falwell closes his *Agenda* with an appeal for fundamentalists and evangelicals to unite to create a great revival in the United States. Throughout the book, he is sensitive to certain criticisms directed at the Moral Majority, and he makes it clear that he does not want a religious dictatorship to be established, nor does he want to violate the separation of church and state. He claims that the Moral Majority wants to protect the "total freedom" of all Americans. His claim that the organization would not endorse specific candidates can be taken lightly given his own campaigning for Senator Grassley and for the program of the Moral Majority. Like his misrepresentation in Alaska of an interview with President Carter, his political rhetoric led to a faulty memory. He participated deeply in the conservative shift of the North American ethos during the Reagan years. The mixed results of the Reagan legacy and the move back toward the center under Bush and Clinton may incline fundamentalists toward less moralism in politics.

The mantle of deeply conservative religious-political leadership was passed in the 1990s from the rather crude Falwell to the much more politically sophisticated Pat Robertson. Robertson's run for the presidency was turned back by moderate Republicans. The success of the Christian Coalition was sufficient to help elect local and state candidates in the 1990s. Their alliance with Newt Gingrich in 1994 produced a Republican manifesto and Republican energy that were stalled by President Clinton in 1996. Although the coalition could force an antiabortion plank at the convention, the more moderate candidates Dole and Kemp ignored the extreme right-wing aspects of this platform. At the time of the convention, candidate Dole would even say that he had not read the platform. In late 1998, the conservative Christians had a very strong position in the Republican Party, and the campaign for control was not over.

The commitment to political activism on the part of religious conservatives is to be welcomed. They certainly are correct that their faith impels them to participate in moral reform of the United States. Criticism that the new Christian right oversimplifies political issues must also be directed at many if not most of the politicians in the United States. The very reliance on television for political information oversimplifies the choice before the body politic. The organizations of the Moral Majority, the National Christian Action Coalition, the Christian Voice Moral Government Fund, Religious Roundtable, and others are designed to avoid improper intrusion of the church into government.[10] They are skillfully using voluntary association models of organization to impact public policy and politics. The most compelling critique of their politics is that it is unbiblical and immoral to support policies that hurt the poor. We violate shalom and Jesus' call for us to be peacemakers when we support the increased buildup of nuclear weapons. Policies and programs that encourage moral and political absolutes are inherently detrimental to a political system that requires compromise. Religious conservatives' preferences for laissez-faire economics, Victorian images of the family, and absolute support for Taiwan and South Korea are not biblical imperatives. Prescriptions for and predictions of the future of the world are not available in Revelation, which was written in and for the Roman empire. Genesis does not teach a scientific theory of geology or the historical origins of humanity.

Voters will support right-wing religious leaders naively. Many have also supported progressive religious leaders and their candidates naively. Both forms of political naivete are to be deplored. But the challenge to a more serious religious-political engagement should be welcomed.

## THE CHURCH AND THE STATE

The history of the church's engagement with the state shows that no one pattern of church-state relationships is absolute. Our American pattern of maximum freedom for the church to worship, teach, proselytize, and act in society is still not the predominant pattern among most of the world's population. The combination of the freedom of religion clause and the no establishment clause in our Bill of Rights was a bold act at the time of its promulgation. It defied the commonly accepted patterns of Europe. Gradually, freedom of religion has become an increasingly accepted norm of humanity, but in practice it is severely curtailed throughout much of the world.

The history of the relationship between church and state in the United States, even with the constitutional basis, has been an evolving process that has still not reached a final form. The churches in America have learned to be thankful for their freedom from the state. This freedom has encouraged the health and vitality of the churches themselves, prevented discrimination against particular expressions of religious conscience by other religious groups, and left religious groups free to witness to society in terms of their religious convictions.

The people of the United States are a very religious people, as studies from de Tocqueville to the latest Gallup poll have shown. It is inevitable that a civil religious spirit arises, and within limits it is appropriate for this common religious sense to be evoked at national ceremonies and in times of stress. The danger of civil religion lies in its tendency toward national idolatry. This danger is best avoided by the various faiths criticizing civil religion if it becomes too nationalistic or too sentimental. Abraham Lincoln's skillful use of biblical faith is a good example of the biblical teachings of God's transcendence and justice correcting civil religion's tendency to become too provincial or partisan. The vitality of the churches' own teachings is the best protection against the dangers inherent in civil religion.

The Supreme Court has opened the door, if only a crack, to government support for parochial education. The argument of supporters of parochial education that, in the name of fairness, their schools deserve more public moneys has some merit. However, the explosion of parochial education that could accompany any widespread system of financial support of any schools parents might choose would vitiate the public education system. The religious education children need can be provided through church educational programs without government support. Both on constitutional grounds and for reasons of the public good, continued reluctance to provide public moneys for church education seems a wise policy. The Supreme Court's rigidity on nonsupport for parochial education may have saved the country from a deeper crisis in light of the current explosion of religious schools.

The abortion issue has traditionally raised questions about the relationship between church and state. The power of the Roman Catholic Church to exercise political clout on this issue has been deeply resented by Protestants and secularists alike. It has seemed as if one church's theology has been overriding the theological positions of other churches. The emergence of this issue as the banner issue by the new religious right complicates the picture even more. After surveying the many denominations that oppose legislation outlawing all abortion, John Bennett warned: "An absolutistic law against abortion would force many people in these religious traditions to act against their consciences, but the absence of such a law does not force anyone to go against his or her conscience."[11] Still, because some regard abortion as murder, the struggle will go on. The struggle over a constitutional amendment will be a political fight reflecting deeply held religious beliefs. Christians who may generally deplore most abortions will not want to see overly restrictive laws infringe on conscience. They have recognized that in some situations abortion can be responsibly chosen. To justify the demand for antiabortion legislation or the withholding of public funds for abortions for the poor, the argument will have to be established that such acts will produce less social harm than the present national policy respecting the privacy of the woman's conscience.

Roman Catholics and Reformed Christians discussed the abortion issue during 1976–1979 in Round III of the Roman Catholic/Presbyterian-Reformed Consultation. The Reformed commentary on the joint statement on abortion is here affirmed:

The separation of church and state in the United States should not be so interpreted as to preclude the right of the church to influence civil policy. However, the very separation of church and state places certain limits upon the manner of the influence which the church exerts. No limit is placed upon the church's right to influence civil policy by educational methods.

Nor would we seek legislation which curtails the freedom of religious expression for others. Accordingly, no legislation should require abortion where forbidden for religious reasons, nor preclude abortion where it is desired for religious reasons. Thus attempts to influence policy in the United States should focus on the secular aims of the legislation rather than the religious beliefs of those who promote or those who oppose it.

Moreover, single-issue advocacy is of exceedingly high risk for Christian activists, both to the state and to the church. It harms the credibility of the church as a trans-political institution when the church appears to be no more than one more political pressure group, and it threatens the integrity of the state by weakening the broad base of political leadership.[12]

Voluntary prayer is now an option in the public school system. The issue is whether schools can recognize and encourage a form of prayer that does not move toward establishing a religion or that does not violate someone's freedom of religion. It is hard to conceive how a prayer can be addressed to God in particular words without choosing a particular form of prayer. If the Virgin Mary is addressed, or if the prayer is in the name of Jesus, it advocates a certain religious interpretation. A period of silence might be constitutionally acceptable, but then only minimal gains will have been made for anyone's religious sensitivity. It is better for the sake of our pluralism and our freedom of religion not to coerce any youngster religiously in the schools. Parents and churches can present teaching in prayer and the child will pray and be reverent in all of life as it is appropriate in our culture. The types of prayers that might be adopted by our school boards or our teachers are bound to be offensive to some and in many cases not very religiously profound. Prayer may be left to the individual, the home, and the church and left out of the public schools in any formal sense.

Prayer in the public schools, like required teaching of creationism, is an important symbolic issue for the new religious right in its campaign for American nostalgia. The establishment of either would not add to the education or piety of our children.

The New Testament teaching about church and state can be summarized as: "Civil authority is part of God's plan and ruling, but it is not in itself divine. Only God is Lord, never Caesar!"[13] Peter put it for himself and the apostles: "We must obey God rather than men" (Acts 5:29). The church as God's gathered people listens to its own sources of truth and goes its own way. This will inevitably, from time to time, bring the church into conflict with the state.

1 Samuel 8, in which Samuel agrees reluctantly to end the period of charismatic-religious leadership in Israel and to give Israel a king, underlies much

of the political theology of this chapter. 1 Samuel 8 testifies that even king-ship is given by God to humanity. Charismatic-religious leadership was preferable, but it failed in Samuel's sons, who took bribes and perverted justice. Kingship became necessary, but 1 Samuel 8 details the burdens of taxation, the taking of children for the military, the seizing of the land, and the pretensions of government. Religious leadership concedes reluctantly to government, because government is awkward, expensive, and usually unjust. Yet government is necessary; even God wills it. 1 Samuel 8 captures the sense of the ambiguity surrounding politics that this chapter affirms. It recognizes the religiously sanctioned need for government. It points to the need for continued critique and participation in the government as Samuel himself represented it. Historically, we can see that here in scripture religious-political leadership is succeeded in history by a more secular-political leader-ship that is still under God. There is not only a provisional separation of religion and politics in Israel but also a continuous engagement best repre-sented in prophetic religion.

## CHRISTIAN POLITICAL ETHICS

A central question of political ethics is: "Why ought one to obey the state?" A Christian political ethic poses a different question: "How can we love God in serving our neighbors through politics?" The purpose of humanity is to love God and to help our neighbor know the love of God. Therefore, Christian political ethics cannot be autonomous; that is, Christians cannot think of the state as an order independent of God that they are free either to remold or to rebel against apart from God. Christian political ethics is not heteronomous; that is, the laws of the state are not obligatory on Christians apart from God. Christian political ethics is theonomous; it is the ordering of government for the purposes of God.

There is, of course, much human wisdom about political order founded in either autonomy or heteronomy or even in non-Christian religious traditions. But the Christian political ethic is seeking to understand the political dimen-sions in light of God's purposes for humanity. Human wisdom will be utilized, but it is to be evaluated in terms of the insights of Christian faith grounded in the revelation of God's nature in Jesus as the Christ.

For Christian political ethics, all human wisdom about political order must be regarded from the perspective of how it serves the concrete good of our neighbor. God wills the freedom and peace of the world's people. The Bible provides us with testimony to the occasion of God's struggle to realize shalom and freedom for the people of Israel and the church. This testimony of God's love being expressed in rulers, in legislation, and in movements of liberation, both spiritual and political, is the guide for contemporary formulation of Christian political ethics.

John Calvin's *Institutes of the Christian Religion* distinguishes between the spiritual realm and the political realm. They are distinguished but related.

Calvin writes more about the ordering of the spiritual realm, but the ordering of the political realm is a clear responsibility for the Christian. In fact, no earthly vocation is of a higher calling than that to political responsibility. The ordering of the political realm is carried out by reference to the natural law. The natural law expresses the law of God in terms of justice, which is the purpose and norm of all human laws. If laws express justice, it is not necessary in Calvin's political theory that they correspond to the particulars of biblical law. Biblical legislation was detailed for its day; in our day the standard of justice will inform us as to the detailed laws for our time.

In Reformed thought, liberty can be obtained in the spiritual realm without being realized in the political realm. Given the tyrannies most people have lived under, we are thankful that spiritual freedom can exist without social liberation. Freedom in the political realm cannot exist without freedom in the spiritual realm. Freedom, particularly Christian freedom, in the spiritual realm drives for expression in political freedom. It is a great thing to know both spiritual and political freedom; God wills it.

To quote Max Weber: "Politics is a strong and slow boring of hard boards."[14] To be Christian, a political ethic takes cognizance of the human refusal to love and fear God and of the inhumanity neighbors render to neighbors. It acknowledges that people will misuse political power when they achieve it. In short, it takes account of sin. Sin basically is the refusal to trust and love God and the resultant disarray in human relations. Racism, sexism, militarism, and economic exploitation all have their roots in the human refusal to trust God. Humans violate the freedom of other humans and organize their political world in rebellion against God. Still, God works through the political world to protect humanity and to counter the results of human sin. Therefore, politics remains ambiguous. It is both God's working to liberate humanity from human evil and an expression of human evil. The reduction of the human evil to manageable proportions is the never-ending task of anyone who, inspired by God's love, takes up the task of political responsibility.

The biblical term for the goal of the political life is "justice" (Amos 5:21–24; Mic. 6:8; Jer. 22:15–16; Isa. 1:14–17; Deut. 16:18–20; Ps. 33:5; Prov. 21:3; Rom. 14:17). A just order presupposes the denial of oppression and liberation from the oppressor. It involves the overthrowing of human evil. It is fair distribution of the earth's resources so that all have the opportunity to flourish. It is the recognition of each person's right to be a free human being. Justice is the expression under conditions of human sin of the imperative of God to love one another. The Christian sense of justice is more than Aristotle's "To each his due"; it is to each his or her due as a loved child of God.

Many institutions of life contribute toward justice. The political order, however, as the central coordinating order of society, has particularly awesome responsibilities in securing a reasonable approximation of justice. Pure justice either in its philosophical expression or in terms of total equity is unattainable in history. God's love, however, requires the constant struggle for justice and the removal of those who in their roles as public servants impede justice. John Calvin wrote of God's overthrow of intolerable governments and said: "Let the princes hear and be afraid."[15]

The history of Western society since the Reformation has been a long, bloody struggle to achieve a tolerably just order. Christian political thought, while seeking to realize justice as the social realization of love, has learned from this history. The Reformed churches were not, in their origins, tolerant; revolutionary movements never are. The failure of any one form of Reformed thought to carry the day within the sectarian controversies led it finally, in John Locke, John Milton, and others, to recognize that toleration was a principle of justice. God tolerates many errors, and political society can tolerate error, encourage pluralism, and survive when people covenant together to respect diversity. The U.S. Constitution, in forbidding the establishment of religion and encouraging freedom of speech, assembly, and press, recognized the need for toleration. The Constitution also recognized that legislation had to be adequate to the social dynamics of a society. So while ignoring Thomas Jefferson's recommendation of frequent revolutions, it provided for the reform of constitutional order. The Reformed concern for proper polity and democratic procedures in church government reinforced the movement of government of the society according to democratic and predictable rules of behavior. The distribution of the powers of government among different centers both protected liberty from tyrannical usurpation and forced governmental decisions to be acceptable to major interests within the society. It also slowed down the process of governmental decision making and allowed considerations of prudence to exert weight on decisions. Although the distribution of powers was probably instituted to avoid the perceived dangers of either mob rule or tyranny, it also reflected Madison's realism about the human beings who would actually administer the government.

The movement of large segments of the population into the political process of the country has increased the pressures for equality and liberty. Equality means the elimination of arbitrary distinctions in society. The basic recognition that people are equal in their rights and that all people are to be treated equally pushes the reforming agenda in society. The present degree to which one's opportunities are determined by the social stratum into which one is born is revolting, even if less obnoxious than at some previous periods. Given the recognition of equality in the 1776 Declaration of Independence, the 1789 Declaration of the Rights of Man, and the 1948 Universal Declaration of Human Rights, the continued existence of oligarchic privileges on the basis of birth in Western society is a measure of the gap between ideals and reality. The resistance to the straightforward Equal Rights Amendment also bears stark evidence of the ancient and persistent privileges claimed by men over women.

Martin Luther King Jr.'s use of the text from Amos 5:24, "Let justice roll down like waters," was an appeal to liberty as well as to equality. Liberation from the oppressive terror of the white population was the goal, as well as social and economic equality. Wherever oppression exists, liberty is to be struggled for, and God, according to the Bible, does not use only the means of the ballot box or nonviolent resistance to change the mind of the oppressor. In the United States, the ballot box and nonviolent tactics of coercion may be the best tools, and God may move people to their use, but they are not the tools of God for many other situations. Liberation, like equalization, is a principle of justice, but it is not a self-sufficient definition of the goals of political thought. Political ethics is complex, requiring the ongoing struggle for justice as an expression of God's love. In the Western world, equality and liberty are mediating principles of justice. They are guided by actions that will order a society toward justice through toleration, predictable rules, prudence, and personality.

To recognize personality as part of the meaning of justice is to honor the wisdom in all of the declarations of the rights of humanity and to resist tendencies to reduce personality to a thing. Basic to the meaning of justice is personhood, and any movement that reduces people to less than persons is to be resisted. There is a spiritual freedom of the person even in situations of oppression, but that freedom is not justice. It is unjust to treat people with less respect than they have as images of God on which their personhood depends.

The goal is the maximum human liberty tolerable without harm to others. Calvin argued for liberty without licentiousness. Law is a bulwark against disorder. However, as law relies on sanctions, it can become oppressive. As the state legislates morality for the common good, it must exercise caution that protects liberty while legislating against truly harmful acts.[16] Arguments for particular legislation must be grounded in the moral consensus of the nation and must correspond to standards of natural law summarized as justice.

So Christians are called, out of a love for God, to be politically active. They are expected to recognize the political order as an ambiguous arena in which they work with God. Freedom in Christ is not dependent on political freedom, but it contributes to political freedom. Longing for the coming of God's reign, the Christian does not expect worldly utopias but knows that God seeks just order for the children of God. A just order will practice toleration, government by rules, prudent politics, and the protection of personality. Liberty and equality are expressions of love to be striven for in societies, which will realize them according to their own history. God will, in God's own way, beyond our knowing, bring fulfillment in the community of God.

Although the politics of liberation theology and of North American fundamentalism have both contributed to the vocabulary of religious politics, neither is adequate for our political life. Religious faith has been too closely tied to political practice, and neither social revolution in Latin America nor the Contract for America from the religious right has served either religion or politics well. The more complex task of energizing the religious people of the United States to apply moral energy and passion to the moral ambiguities of American political practice has not been fulfilled. Jesse Jackson's speech at the 1996 Democratic Convention represented the moral passion of a Christian activist, but there are not enough voters who will follow a Democratic liberal or an African American preacher to enact much of

Jackson's vision. The relevant political choices are nearer to the center of the American population. The center is likely to prevail politically. If it will accept the reality of the religious aspirations of the American people and pursue equality in freedom, ecological responsibility, integrity in government, and peace wherever it is possible, it will provide moral leadership also. If it can work toward all of this while maintaining a dynamic and more just economy, it will achieve human political work reflecting God's work.

The aspects of personal life that are relevant to this political renewal are not the focuses on "feelings" and sexuality that characterize the mass media. The personal aspect that is needed is the connectedness of people to the political process. Not only must the people vote, but they must also talk politics in private and public, relying on both their knowledge of public philosophy and their religious hopes. Without their generous financial contributions undergirding the reform of political financing, they will be kept irrelevant. So all citizens must put money where their talk leads. Finally, all citizens, especially associations of citizens, and particularly churches, must stay in contact with elected officials and the nonelected bureaucrats. Public participation is a necessary requirement of a better political order. Knowledgeable parents will not entrust their children to the public schools without visitation, contact, conversation, and involvement, and responsible citizens will not allow others to govern their lives without their participation. Widespread voting, funding, and contact inspired by religious moral concern will reform our political life.

# Ecological Corruption

The planet earth is groaning under the burden that humans place on the ecological system. From the garbage and oil that pollute the ocean to pesticides that cause leukemia and attack the human neurological system, life is under assault. The earth, which supports humanity, is beautiful, but it suffers under human carelessness and malignancy. As I look at my old ecological essay of a quarter of a century ago,[1] the threat to nature has increased and the trends are more foreboding. A friend has put it, "If present trends continue, we don't."[2]

The threat is to the narrow band of ecological support for human life. If humanity attacks this system too much it will weaken itself and perhaps in large part collapse. The radical reduction of human life on the planet would permit the recovery of the planet and other patterns of life to resume the story of natural life on earth. Yet, neither humanity nor God wills humanity's destruction. The human story is not over. The promises of good human life with God on earth are still seeking fulfillment. Yet present trajectories are dangerous and provide part of the context for any investigation of ecoethics.

The groaning of the earth, while it awaits redemption, expresses Christian theology's major model of history. Good and evil grow together until the end.[3] History does not redeem nature, but historical forces of good and evil contend in ambiguity for our human response. The issues become more complex as the powers of humanity for increased evil and good expand.

Ian Barbour spells out this ambiguity in *Ethics in an Age of Technology*. Technology has provided growing food production, better health care, increasing living standards, and a communication revolution.[4] However, disasters from Three Mile Island in Pennsylvania to the *Exxon Valdez* oil spill in Alaska show the weaknesses of humanly managed technology. Pollution increases because of technology, and the needs of a growing population cannot be met by foreseeable developments. A quarter of a million children die each week from malnutrition and preventable diseases. Resources are given over to the development of weapons and the affluence of military machines. The threat of massive destruction looms over modern and less developed societies alike. Barbour sees the conflict over values as the deciding variable in the development of technology and the future of humanity on earth. Beyond the debates over values loom the political struggles. Science promises no solutions without ethics and politics. Reinhold Niebuhr addressed this issue in 1937: "science can sharpen the fangs of ferocity as much as it can alleviate human pain," for "intelligence merely raises all the potencies of life, both good and evil." Science, by increasing our power, inclines humanity to forget its finitude, which "offends not only against God, who is the center and source of our existence, but against other life which has a rightful place in the harmony of the whole."[5]

The human response to the threat to the environment is under way. Although the scientific community is still in disagreement, ecologically concerned people have pushed through treaties to slow the emission of carbon dioxide. Carbon dioxide, which is essential to life, is added to the atmosphere in excessive amounts by burning of fossil fuels. As carbon dioxide absorbs infrared energy from the sun, it gradually threatens to warm the earth. If the atmosphere retains more heat, the earth's temperature may rise.[6] Scientists suspect that continuation of current rates of emission would raise the earth's average temperature, causing icecaps to melt and other climatic changes to occur. Barbour fears that the sea would rise "between eight inches and five feet . . . by 2030."[7] Perhaps 20 percent of the earth's human population would be displaced. In response to the perceived threat, the United States has recently accepted the Earth Summit's climate change treaty, has begun developing non-gasoline-burning automobile engines, and has promised to enforce antipollution legislation. Whether moves by Germany, Japan, the United States, and other industrialized nations to reduce the emission of carbon dioxide can offset pressures to increase it is still a controversial question. Because the industrialized Northern Hemisphere is the major culprit, the major changes and leadership in reduction will need to begin here. The World Council of Churches convocation asked for a 3 percent reduction per year by the industrialized countries toward a world goal of 2 percent reduction per year.

Similarly, companies are phasing out the use of chlorofluorocarbons (CFCs), which drift into the stratosphere and destroy the protective ozone layer. The ozone layer has been damaged, though the extent of that damage is debated.[8]

Likewise, the destruction of water, plants, and structures by acid rain is inspiring demands for limits on the combustion of fossil fuels. New technologies, citizen action, and new legislation are being used to combat this danger.

There is evidence of significant response to the overpopulation of the earth. Some authorities argue that birth control awareness and technology have reduced family size in poor nations. Contraception has been shown to be effective. Recent figures estimate that 51 percent of women in the poor nations now utilize family planning. Thailand's fertility, for example, dropped 50 percent "between the 1970s and the 1980s."[9] Such radical declines in

fertility require funding and public support. Survey results indicate that millions more would use contraceptives if they had them. Attitudes toward
family planning have been shown to be more open than many had feared, and
further expenditures on population control would help deflect the population
bomb. With the information about birth control being widely disseminated,
religious resistance to birth control is becoming less effective. The Roman
Catholic Church, the largest and most powerful religious institution, is unable
to maintain the loyalty of its own membership on this moral issue. It has the
power, however, to intervene in international meetings, such as the 1994
Population Meeting in Cairo, and to slow down international movement
toward reducing population growth. The contradiction of an institution run
by celibate priests insisting that married women be denied resources for family
planning is striking. No religious institution with significant participation by
women would tolerate the absurdity of denying parents the capacity to join in
determining their responsibilities to and the sizes of their families. Still, even
with progress being made in reducing fertility, the threat to the environment
posed by overpopulation is felt in every area of ecology.

*Agenda 21*, the report of the United Nations' Rio Conference on the environment, was less helpful on the issues of the world's rain forests than it was on
proposals for reducing carbon dioxide emissions. The concern over carbon
dioxide emissions leads to the question of the fate of the world's rain forests.
The clearing and burning of the rain forests contributes to the buildup
of carbon dioxide in the atmosphere. It is this buildup that led the U.S.
Environmental Protection Agency to issue warnings about the "greenhouse
effect" in 1983. The clearing may also contribute to a general drying out of the
area, because trees release moisture into the air. Some witnesses comment on
the drying out of Manaus at the center of the Amazon rain forest. Scientists
disagree about the various climatic effects of destroying the rain forest. Some
think deforestation of the Amazon basin and other rain forests contributes
to flooding. The fear of depletion of oxygen from the atmosphere has been
abandoned as photosynthesis is countered by oxidation within the forest.[10]

The clear link between the destruction of species, known and unnown, and
deforestation is beyond dispute, as is the destruction of the indigenous population of the Amazon basin. The reduction of the tribal population in the
region from six million to two hundred thousand is a reasonable estimate of
the cost of the extraction of wealth from the rain forest since it was opened
up to the powers of civilization. The reflections here are confined to the
Amazon area, because it represents at least half of the remaining area of trop-
ical rain forest in the world. It is less attractive to loggers and developers than
the world's other rain forests, and so the probability is that it will be destroyed
last. The issue is whether humanity is fated to destroy this ancient forest and
the species that inhabit it. When contemplating how little is known of the
great wealth of species in the forest, Roger D. Stone joins with those who
plead for its preservation in moral terms: "How can man justify the willful and
near-instant destruction of our greatest cathedral, a monumental work whose

contribution, by millions of different forms of life, required millions of painstaking years?"[11]

My own travels from the confluence of the Negro and Solimões Rivers to form the Amazon introduced me to a region described as "paradise" by my guides. Much of the Igapo (flooded black-water rain forest) is best described as Edenic. True, certain species have been depleted, there is evidence of gold mining, and signs of the intrusions of civilization are occasionally visible. However, one can sail for hours without seeing another human being. The vast parade of forest birds is only occasionally broken by the sounds of one's own boat engines or by passing traffic. For a thousand miles across country, if it were passable on foot, only the occasional trail would be crossed. To swim among the dolphins in the Rio Negro at flood tide is to encounter "almost Eden."

The reports from the surrounding Brazilian states of Pará and Rondônia are bleak, however. Flying out of Manaus, the capital and heart of the state of Amazonas, one passes over the developing highways and the burnings that signal the death of the forest. If an area the size of France has already been cleared, and each year sees the destruction of an area comparable to that of Belgium, this last great forest of the tropics is seriously threatened.

Here, sustainable development translates into harvesting the forests. The needs of the people, national sovereignty, and "forests as resources" are the dominant points of view. We are now at the crisis point where all the rain forests of the world are at risk. All of the world's significant ancient forests are threatened. Human numbers, technology, and needs could soon eliminate almost all of the original rain forests. About a third of the old forests remain, with the Amazon basin being the most defensible, but even the future of the Amazon is bleak. The past encroachments of civilization for slaves, minerals, cotton, rubber, fish, animals, and converts has reduced the population of the Amazon. The forest is being reduced from the south, the east, and the west. The military roads and government policies of peasant settlement have both contributed to the reduction of the fragile environment. It seems that once the rain forests of Africa, Indonesia, and Southeast Asia are consumed, the exploiters will also come to harvest the Amazon. The Amazon has foiled the development schemes of previous adventurers, but the cutting of the forest could be the end. The nutrient-poor soils in most of the Amazon basin will not support an agricultural population of any density, so the future is bleak. There are international movements afoot to rescue the Amazon from development, but the roads and the exploding metropolitan center of Manaus are foreboding. Still, huge reserves like Jau National Park are possible, and reserves for indigenous peoples may be successfully protected. Funds for protection of reserves and for scientific research can be supported. Symbolic boycotts of rain forest wood and animal products may, when coupled with education, help stop the premature destruction of the rain forest.

The concept of partially saving the Amazonas forests by establishing parks and reserves requires some critique. The reserves for people can only isolate the indigenous population from the real world. The Brazilian government does not provide sufficient resources to protect parks and reserves, and so they may become exploited. The development of reserves for populations or extraction of resources indicates they will be managed by elites.[12] Natural areas with sparse population appeal to tourists and the industries they support. Nature reserves appeal to scientists for research. Extractive reserves are for those who can exert the political-economic clout to do the extraction. The Amazon and its people cannot be saved by international organizations and lines drawn on maps by planners. The rights of the forest peoples can be protected only through their own efforts, with support from Brazil and abroad. The issues are fair prices for their products, indigenous participation in decision making, and discouragement of immigration into the forest. Hecht and Cockburn have summarized the struggle as follows: "If there is one word that is the keystone to their demands and hopes for the future, it is the single word on which all hopes for the Amazon rest: justice."[13] Although the extent of the danger to the environment will remain incalculable for the foreseeable future, the case for the serious threat to the human support system is potentially too great to be neglected. Jared Diamond, professor of physiology at UCLA Medical School, writes:

> Now that the risk of nuclear apocalypse appears to have receded, the chief risk to the world in which my sons will reach maturity has become the risk of an ecological holocaust. Nor is that risk hypothetical: the world's biological resources are already being destroyed at an unprecedented rate, and at present rates the destruction will come to a climax in the next century.[14]

In terms of the ethic articulated in this study, the prohibitions of covetousness and stealing are part of the provision of justice or a fairer order in which nature and people can flourish. The perspective of God's rest and the need for humanity to rest from work is also the key to the holistic perspective that could aid us in preserving God's earth.[15]

## CHRISTIAN ETHICS

The gradual awakening of humanity to its perilous treatment of its ecology is part of our contemporary religious situation. As with Rachel Carson's warning of the threat to songbirds posed by the use of DDT, we respond with corrective measures. Our consciousness of the ecological crisis forces us to discover processes for correction. A change in the way humanity organizes its social-economic life requires a moral change. In Christian ethics, this moral change requires us to turn toward sources of appreciation of nature in the tradition we have been neglecting, and to remind Christians of the self-limiting tendencies of their normative tradition.

The commandment to love God and the neighbor may not directly include the flora and the fauna, but in its implications it cannot be separated from them. God creates and loves the world, and rejecting this attitude is an act of human pride and ingratitude. If we are to love our human neighbors, we need to respect and care for our natural environment. To say that we love a neighbor while neglecting or threatening the material world of that neighbor is to live in an impossible ideal world in which nature does not count.

To have no other gods than God, the creator and liberator God, is to refuse to worship any cause, idol, economic system, or ideology that would use human energy to destroy the ecological context of human life. To worship the source of life is to become respectful of all life and to refuse to treat it lightly.

In our Sabbath traditions we are ordered to rest. The land is to be allowed to rest. The workers are to be allowed to rest. In learning to rest and in being instructed to rest, even when we want to work at projects, there is a graciousness that overcomes human anxiety to produce. The one day in seven is not as relevant legally as in the recent past, but the value of stopping and releasing everyone from labor is of great importance to nature.

The commandments not to covet and not to steal would prevent the covetous stealing of the land that supports indigenous populations. The ecological issue is for both people and land and for their harmonious coexistence. If we would not steal the rain forest from its inhabitants, it would not be threatened. These moral traditions seem foundational, but in the conquest of the world by the Europeans they are the traditions that have been repeatedly set aside in the pursuit of wealth. The moral sympathy that Adam Smith saw as the foundation of moral principles is overridden by the need to have more. If the moral sympathy for one's human neighbor is not enough to stop the killing of the native population, aesthetic appreciation or a sympathetic reaction to nature will be insufficient also. The Christian interpretation of stealing has also included acquiring by fraud and the legal deprivation of the weak of what they need. While new sensibilities regarding nature need to be cultivated, the observance of our basic moral codes would prevent much of the worst of the despoliation.

## CURRENT NORMS

In addition to the basic norms of the Christian tradition, there are current norms. These norms are congruent with and traceable to Christian norms, but they are expressed more generally. They are norms for a universal form of discourse beyond the community specifically associated with Christian norms. At the end of the twentieth century, these norms are all candidates for acceptability in general moral discourse: sustainable development, sustainable society, integrity of creation, ecojustice, just peace, and a global ethic.

The term "sustainable development" has been growing in usage among environmentalists and ethicists. "Development" took a lot of criticism during the days of the dominance of the liberation theologies that were coming out of emerging countries. The need for "liberation" from structures of sin and fate pushed the more northern urgings of "development" out of the socially sensitive forum of debate for a few years. It has returned in a new form now coupled with "sustainable." This term "sustainable development" was popularized by the 1987 Bruntland Commission publication *Our Common Future*. It received a further boost by the publication of *Agenda 21*, the report of the United Nations' Rio Conference on economics and the environment. The worldwide acceptance of and rush toward "market economies" have also contributed to the popularization of "sustainable development." Sustainable development is a teleological goal or a utopia. It mixes ecological concerns under "sustainable" with economic growth concerns under "development." J. Ronald Engel points out that in this paradoxical joining, it reflects American convictions about sustainable forestry developed by Theodore Roosevelt and Gifford Pinchot.[16]

Engel's beautifully written essay notes that there are those who use the term "sustainable development" and modify it, and those who abandon it as an oxymoron within the "alternative development" movement.[17] He argues for retaining the term but protecting it from its traditional economic growth origins. He thinks it can become a basis for further discussion of global values. The Presbyterian Church (U.S.A.) modified the term in the development of its policy in "Hope for a Global Future: Toward Just and Sustainable Human Development."[18] The task force working on the policy recognized the ambiguity in the term and the dangers of simply adding ecological legitimacy to Western patterns of economic growth. The group listened to, and included in its report, voices from developing countries that were critical of the term, but then modified the term.

John Cobb, on the other hand, regards the costs of further industrialization and urbanization as intolerable and argues for a return to an emphasis on sustainable community. Community development means that community values prevail. He echoes Gandhian arguments for the preservation of village life and the return to less industrialized models for society. He forthrightly rejects the Bruntland recommendations for growth as absurd and asserts that "sustainable growth is an oxymoron."[19] Sustainable development has some good features as it tends to treat economics and ecology together. It is an integrative concept. However, the tension between sustainability and development is too great to hold the terms together happily. The thrust and power of the developmentalists will tend to override the ecological concerns, as they did in the Rio Conference's *Agenda 21*. The attempts to define sustainable development to the point of acceptability push it in the direction of utopia, and it is a utopia subject to easy misuse. The need for limiting human avarice and growth is better protected by focusing on traditional Christian norms and on the need to limit human growth and consumption. Leonardo Boff fears that sustainable development favors maintenance of the present unjust order. Different societies have different values and structures, and Boff proposes "a society with an ecologically sustainable development, in which that which is sustainable should be the ecology and not development."[20]

Earlier discussion at the World Council of Churches had called for a "sustainable society" in 1974. This concept evolved under the pressures of the "limits to growth" debate. Robert L. Stivers argued for a worldwide economy in equilibrium where the necessary production of industrialization was diversified in *The Sustainable Society: Ethics and Economic Growth.*[21] Not economic development, but policies to keep population and capital plant investment stable were advanced. The development of worldwide authorities to protect the sustainability of human society was accepted. The religious legitimization of economic growth or development was rejected. Such a goal required, Stivers suggested, new appreciations of nature, reforms in religious life, changes in consumption patterns, and new solutions to problems hidden by the pervasiveness of growth. So the projected changes were immense. At present, while the "limits to growth" conclusions are not accepted totally, the general concept of a sustainable society is probably more helpful than sustainable development.

Recently, Stivers has been articulating an ethic of integrity. He expounds it in three dimensions. Personal integrity is the harmonization of intention and action. Social integrity includes justice, equality, freedom, participation, liberation, and sufficiency. The relationship among all of these factors requires more discussion, but Stivers's presentation is compatible with the discussion of love and justice in the third chapter of this volume. The final meaning of integrity is in the sustainability of nature. Environments evolve, and humanity is part of those environments. The "integrity of nature" norm has its relevance in the insistence on the protection of the variety of "systems and species." The integrity of nature means that nature is good in itself in its growth, dynamism, evolution, and change. The violation of its integrity is labeled "sin" by Stivers.[22] The "integrity of creation" norm adds the ontological dimension to our consideration of ecoethics. Beyond the norms that guide our decisions as to what is right, the basic goodnesses of personhood, society, and nature need to be recognized. This affirmation echoes God's affirmation in the Hebrew traditions of creation and provides a norm against human violation of nature.

The concept of ecojustice appeared in church social teaching in the early 1970s. It combined three concepts: the need for "economic justice for persons within the limits imposed by the need for a sustainable environment"; the valuation of living things, including people, above property rights; and the need for technology to remain the servant of human needs.[23] As it was developed, it clarified the norms of sufficiency and sustainability. Ecojustice remains as an appropriate, logical, and necessary extension of the concept of justice with advantages over "sustainable development."[24] It also seems unlikely that "sustainable society" will rally a movement. However, ecojustice inclusive of sustainability, sufficiency, society, and integrity, including justice, participation, and liberation, seems adequate to inspire and also to suggest limits. It has also been expressed as ecological integrity with social justice. For Christian ethics, it echoes shalom as comprehensive well-being in human society at home in the natural world.

Both integrity and ecojustice remain as norms. These norms shape the practices of those who honor them, but they are more neglected than honored. The struggle for recognition of these concepts as important norms is still under way. A survey of theological education in the United States in 1993 showed that most theological seminaries still do not integrate these concepts into their curricula.[25] Similarly, the inspiring work of the Parliament of the World's Religions neglected ecojustice concerns in its final statement. It focused on global order, human rights, nonviolence, economic justice, truthtelling and gender equality. The section on nonviolence contains a statement on the need for harmony among people, the cosmos, and nature. Responsibility is assumed for protection of nature. Destruction of the biosphere is condemned.[26] But neither the relationship with nature nor a strong ecoethical emphasis was part of the declaration. Hans Küng, the signatories, and the lack of development of this theme in the world's religions all bear part of the responsibility for this relative neglect.

In the Christian tradition, the trend is toward inclusion of ecological themes in theological and ethical work. The works of Ian Barbour, John Cobb, Dieter Hessel, Sallie McFague, Jürgen Moltmann, Larry Rasmussen, Rosemary Ruether, Roger L. Shinn, and Robert Stivers are representative of this trend. The World Council of Churches has focused much of its reflection on ecoethical themes.[27] The prognosis for a church that teaches seriously the need for personal, social, and natural healing is improving. In social ethics, the growing ecumenical and denominational effort to articulate principles of just peace bodes well for ecological thought. Just-war thinking has not been conceived for the protection of nature, whereas it appears that just-peace thinking will be more inclusive.

Despite the havoc wrought on nature by Christians, I would not advise them to overthrow or radically change their traditions. It is hard enough to persuade people to protect the common good and act morally for the interests of others without proposing also that they reform their deepest beliefs. The major stream of Western thought relevant to the ecological crisis has been theocentric ethics connected to the covenant tradition. For better or worse, Western Christian society will sink or rise with this tradition. Nature mysticism, social Darwinism, and naturalism are all too implicated in the demonic failure of Nazism to be credible alternatives for the West. The ethical imperatives of the theocentric ethic need emphasis; the theocentrism does not need deemphasis. Neither nature on earth nor humanity in nature on earth is central. God is real and central, as God will be after both humanity and earth's nature have vanished. Both humanity and nature are properly decentralized in Christian theocentric ethics.

Dieter Hessel's wise essay[28] on the competition between naturalistic cosmology and covenantal ethics sees a complementary relationship between them whereby covenantal ethics is renewed by naturalistic interpretations. I doubt that naturalism can add much on the appreciation of nature that is not already in Genesis, Isaiah, Job, and the teaching of Jesus. Hessel wants to correct James Gustafson's theocentric ethic[29] with more of an emphasis on incarnation and the cosmological Christ. I cannot see that the cosmological Christ, a minor theme in Protestant thought, will add much to a theological ethic that a robust theocentric ethic lacks. Incarnation, like naturalism, is itself without an ethic until it is supplied, and in scripture the ethic is supplied by the covenanting God. The specificity that a theocentric ethic needs is supplied by relating it to the need for human advocacy to interrupt the despoliation of the earth. Furthermore, the earth is so divided and populated now that the enforcements against covetousness, stealing, and murder would preserve the wilderness that remains. If we do not permit the stealing of resources from public lands and if we stop the murder of the native populations of the wilderness, the corporate plunder of the world's wilderness will end. Ecology, of course, is broader than the protection of public resources and the world's poor in their traditional home-lands, but the further central points of theocentric ethics to love the neighbor, to treat one as one would be treated, and to promote justice as peace, equality, and freedom give us with minimal interpretation the required ethical founda-tions. The Ten Commandments start with the glory of God and end with the anathema against covetousness. Ethical rigor is needed rather than alternative theologies to the just God of the covenants.

Daniel Maguire also senses the weakness of Western religion in addressing the ecological crisis. It has been too patriarchal, too controlling, too separated from nature, and too critical of other religious traditions.[30] Maguire appears to want religion without theism, or at least without monotheism. The Buddhism and Hinduism of the East are not criticized in their variety of theistic, non-theistic, and polytheistic expressions. Maguire's critique of the failure to care for nature is confined to the Abrahamic-based religions. His essay, which begins with a critique of the population explosion and the need for state lim-itation of population growth, gives its second half over to questioning and challenging the cognitive status of God. Maguire remains very affirmative of ethics and, in general, of the social power of religion, but he questions the heart of Western religion in its monotheistic forms of Judaism and Islam or its trinitarian monotheism and Christology of the West, and then ends the essay with Robin Morgan's poem about peonies.

It is very doubtful that Maguire's attack on monotheism will contribute much to the ecological consciousness of Christianity. He pleads for the fol-lowers of Abrahamic religions to be accepting and tolerant, but such pleas from critical debunkers from inside probably are not as helpful as the same requests from Christian theists like Hans Küng. Christian ethics as discussed in this book does not work without theism. Those who attack theism will have a hard time formulating an ethic for Christians without God. It is far wiser to permit all religions to treasure their central symbols and to make their own contributions toward a global ethic sufficient to guide decisions for ecojustice fueled by the passions of the respective religions. God may be a problem for Daniel Maguire and for others, but this does not mean theism is a problem for most of its devotees. With Daniel Maguire, we want to say "Wow"[31] as we experience the beauty of the earth, but we do not want to deny ourselves or others the right to thank God for the beauty of the earth.

Finally, Christian theology's sophisticated system of symbols and logic, as well as its religious passions, produced the ethics that has given us both modern science/technology and the medical possibilities for the population explosion. To scrap such a system now for religious feeling and poetry[32] would be to cut the Western world's ethics adrift from its science/technology, which will be part of the solution to human hopes for ecojustice.

The ethic here corresponds partially to the ethic of Ian Barbour in *Ethics in an Age of Technology*.[33] It is a mixed strategy in that it qualifies consequentialist calculations of outcomes of social policies with both values and rules. Barbour's theory places more weight on values, partially because the stress on rules or principles has a tendency toward absolutism that he wants to avoid. Also, the stress on values such as sustainability, equality, and participation is translatable into reform of social policies. He recognizes, however, that principles can be applied flexibly. He may not sense how much value-laden work goes into the interpretation of principles, even principles as honored by antiquity and religious community as our Ten Commandments. Confronted by the pressures to push for maximum profits and growth in the economy, the easily communicable power of principles and their very sharpness are particularly useful in helping people understand their limits. It also affirms with Barbour the reluctance to rest our efforts for ecojustice in either naturalism or Eastern religious tendencies.

The Ten Commandments' injunctions against murder, stealing, and covetousness are basic. The developing norms listed by Larry Rasmussen[34] as participation, sufficiency, accountability, material simplicity and spiritual richness, and responsibility on a human scale reflect the norms of ecojustice and integrity of creation. Norms and values intersect, and of course, the interest is in their application, as Rasmussen suggests that God is in the details.[35] In the details, the moral principles get expressed in legislation as to which trees can be cut, which waters can be dammed, which pesticides are permitted, and the details of immigration rules, rules for procreation, and norms for population limitation.

Years ago during the cold war, I traveled by train from Moscow to Irkutsk on Lake Baikal in Siberia. On the train, a mathematician from Kazakhstan leaned with me against the window of the slow-moving train, misnamed the *Siberian Express*. As he watched a train laden with timber pass by us on the other track, he said, "Development is exploitation." This is often true. Rasmussen has reminded us to listen to the revolt against development in Chiapas, Mexico. The people there have protested in the name of human dignity against the development they have seen.

The goal must be sufficiency for all God's children and not development for the further enrichment of the rich. Tendencies toward exploitation of creation that enlarge the gap between the rich and the hungry are to be ended. Policies of greater equality in the industrialized countries that reduce the power and wealth of the elite are part of the struggle for ecojustice as much as are policies that decrease the gap between rich and poor nations. Recognizing with Maguire[36] that China needs population-limiting policies implies that the United States needs income-limiting policies. Greed, as well as population, must be capped to sustain the earth and to move toward justice and the integrity of human dignity.

An ecoethic is in formation. Ecojustice may prove to be a more powerful concept than sustainable development. The foundational commandments of love and their expression in justice will be central in this discussion. The penultimate principles found in the commandments are important contributions, as are the more contemporary formulations of norms. It is a rich discussion calling forth much energy in the Christian community. Meanwhile, many of the indices of destruction of nature are growing, and the issue needs to be won in the church for the sake of the world struggle.

# Peacemaking

Aristotle criticized Plato's vision in *The Republic* for ignoring inter-state relations. It was a fair criticism then and still is now. Today, any ethic that is silent on international relations is deficient. Social orders reflecting particular ethics are partially integrated into a world system. Ethical recommendations for a particular society that cause it to self-destruct in its encounters with international reality are truly naive. The prescriptive ethic of this argument originated in a particular community as the expression of God's will. It was that community's grasp of ultimate wisdom and imperative. Through Jesus, that imperative was broadened to universal dimensions, although still reflecting its particular communal roots and the new community recognizing Jesus as ultimate.

Through the prophetic traditions, the imperatives summarized in Jesus' imperative were broadened and specifically applied to the nations. Matthew judges the nations by their actions of provision for and visitation of Jesus' little disciples. This reinforces Amos's standards of justice by which he portrays God judging the nations and Isaiah's regarding the council of nations as the context for the revelation of the servant who suffers to bear the light to the nations.

This ethic of double love, community, justice, the Ten Commandments, and contemporary principles is applied through church, society, and nation to the arena of international politics. However, it also reaches out directly in its power to shape the global ethic of the growing ecumenical movement and in forming the United Nations, associated bodies, and declarations and policies of human rights to further influence the nations' role in international politics.

The discernment of the Christian tradition recognizes the difficulty of applying love and justice to the politics of nations. Nations are not governed by the stringent norms of personal religious faith but as conglomerates of interests in a relatively anarchic world. The norms for international behavior are formulated as appropriate for nations given the Christian tradition. Norms are not derived from the practices of nations, but from a perspective on inter-national relations reflecting deep moral traditions. The source of the norms mentioned above is biblical faith interpreted in terms of a philosophy of prophetic realism. The explanation of that philosophy in terms of the Morgenthau-Niebuhr school of thought prepares the intellectual context for expressing principles for the post–cold war world.

## THE MORGENTHAU-NIEBUHR SCHOOL OF THOUGHT

The perspectives of Reinhold Niebuhr and Hans J. Morgenthau were developed in the conflicts of democracy with Nazism and communism. While acknowledging their contextual limitations, what can we learn from these perspectives for the peacemaking tasks ahead? This chapter will synthesize their philosophies and present that synthesis as a recognizable school of thought. The argument assumes that, although the twentieth-century needs of American foreign policy shaped their thought, at its deepest roots were images of prophetic realism from the Bible. Between the Bible and foreign policy, both of them explored many sources of thought, both Western and Eastern. Rather than dividing them into Jewish realism and Christian realism, this study joins them as prophetic realism.

The Morgenthau-Niebuhr perspective on international affairs has been important in the preparation of policy papers for several of our mainline church denominations. It has not been the only school of thought, and it is probably less influential in denominational and ecumenical councils than it once was. Liberation theologies and feminist perspectives have eroded the Christian realist paradigms while both the National Council of Churches and the World Council of Churches have reduced their staffs and their influence in international affairs.

Because Christianity was originally pacifist and relatively nonpolitical, it is always tempted to return to its first-century origins and forget its Hebrew foundations. The churches are also tempted to become utopian because of utopianism's affinity with some strands of eschatology. Because some of the churches—Catholic, Calvinist (including the United Church of Christ), Lutheran, and Methodist, among others—are organized transnationally, they tend to tilt toward international organization that may obscure national power centers.

The Morgenthau-Niebuhr school, while clear about its peacemaking and justice commitments, has presented them in the context of power struggles among nations. This has been helpful in formulating church policy in seven ways:

1. The ethics of international affairs is not determined by the practice of international affairs but is found in philosophical and confessional sources of ethical wisdom.

2. The nations are important actors, but they are not gods, and the forms of governmental organizations vary widely, including clans, tribes, nations, empires, federations, alliances, and international organizations.

3. Although universal peace is not expected in history, many potential wars can be avoided; wars of mass human destruction, such as nuclear wars, must be avoided.

4. Political actors tend to corrupt political practice, but their roles are necessary and important, and the dangers of the corruption of power can be ameliorated.

5. The goals of foreign policies reflect the particular histories of the societies. In the case of the United States, the purposes of foreign policy include peace and justice as well as economic and strategic security. From the human rights wing of realism, particularly Jimmy Carter, Andrew Young, and John Bennett, the purposes also include the prudential promotion of human rights.

6. Nazism and communism required the responsible use of U.S. power, including force, and current crises still do, particularly for humanitarian rescue operations.

7. Finally, moving beyond Morgenthau and Niebuhr's context and time, the ethics of sustainable human development strategies and the ethics of just peacemaking can be articulated in realist terms congruent with Christian ethics.

Rather than repeating what I have written earlier on Hans Morgenthau and Reinhold Niebuhr, I have chosen to critique the work of Michael Doyle on realism. Michael W. Doyle's major book, *Ways of War and Peace*,[1] begins its close reading of theory with Thucydides. Doyle mentions that he begins his international relations class with the same author. Of the three major types of perspectives in his book—realism, liberalism, and socialism—the part on realism is by far the longest. The dominance of realist international relations theory is recognized, and Doyle defends it from many of the charges leveled at it. The concluding part of the book is entitled "Conscience and Power," a phrase quoted directly from Reinhold Niebuhr. The concerns for the roles of morality and religious movements in international relations are akin to Niebuhr's own probing of these issues. So what more could realists want? They would, I think, want to resist the too-tight, typological method of Doyle. Reinhold Niebuhr was scornful of his brother H. Richard Niebuhr's placement of himself in the "Christ and culture in paradox" motif in his definitive work *Christ and Culture*.[2] Similarly, I would protest against Doyle's labeling of Machiavelli and Morgenthau as fundamentalists. A sympathetic reading of either will not reduce it to Waltz's "Image 1,"[3] which attributes war to the defects of human nature. Machiavelli was very conscious both of the nature of the state and of international anarchy. Morgenthau's pithy, bold writing, like Machiavelli's, allows him to be misinterpreted as focusing primarily on the psychological dimensions of the elite. But his theory is too rich to be characterized as Waltz's Image 1. Doyle recognizes that Machiavelli and Morgenthau take aspects of Image 2, attributing war to defects in the state, and of Image 3, emphasizing international anarchy, as well. Such recognition is inadequate, however, because Doyle had before him the model of Thucydides' own "complex realism."[4] Why in an academic treatise would Doyle label as "fundamentalist" such a respected theorist as Morgenthau? The term "fundamentalism" arises from a protest of very conservative Presbyterians against the historical-critical method in scholarship and against modernism. This is a very strange term for scholars to apply to a Renaissance thinker such as Machiavelli or to an American-modernist, exiled Jew such as Morgenthau.

It would be foolish to deny the importance of religious anthropology to either Morgenthau or Niebuhr. They both regarded their anthropology as important to their political philosophy. It is equally important for clarity to note other important sources of their thought. There are unresolved tensions in both of their perspectives that would incline one to think of Doyle's concepts of complex realism or pluralist theory instead of fundamentalist-realist theory.

Before returning to the center of this thesis, permit me to digress further into a critique of the typological structure of Doyle's argument. If realism is one type and socialism is another, how are we to understand Reinhold Niebuhr, who first writes in a realist vein "The Morality of Nations"[5] while a socialist? No one can deny Niebuhr's recognition as a realist, but Norman Thomas also recognized "Niebuhr being considerably to the left of me" while Niebuhr served as vice-president of the American Socialist party. The realism itself continued into the 1950s, when Niebuhr and Arthur Schlesinger Jr. worked together drafting the foreign policy positions of the liberal Americans for Democratic Action. At least in the complexity of the biblically based realism of Niebuhr, the realist approach characterized both his socialism and his liberalism as these concepts were experienced in North American politics.

Morgenthau's five references to Machiavelli in *Politics among Nations*[6] include one that is affirmative of his insight, two that are negative, and two that are neutral. The chapter titled "Morality, Mores, and Law as Restraints of Power" stresses the reality of these restraints on power. It rejects the theories of Machiavelli and Hobbes and finds both biblical ethics and democratic constitutionalism to restrain power drives. The greater potencies of Locke and Augustine in comparison with the views of Machiavelli and Hobbes are affirmed. In *Truth and Power*,[7] an appreciation of Machiavelli's warnings to the weak of the dangers of depending on the powerful is balanced by two rejections of Machiavelli's morality and one neutral comment. The volume contains some of Morgenthau's strongest affirmations of Hebrew and Christian images of "wise and good rulers" as well as transcendent moral values. The case for Morgenthau's similarity to Machiavelli is defeated by Morgenthau's own meager references to him and rejection of his project at several points. On the other hand, all of the references to Thucydides in Morgenthau are positive. In Doyle's terms, Morgenthau belongs in the category of "complex realism," where Thucydides is the major example. The texts of both of our philosophers, Morgenthau and Niebuhr, reveal their essential agreement, some mutual dependence, and praise of each other's thought.

In a tribute to Niebuhr, Morgenthau spoke of Niebuhr's contribution to political thought in five ideas, all of which were near the center of Morgenthau's own thought. He then went on to say, "I have always considered Reinhold Niebuhr the greatest living political philosopher of America, perhaps the only creative political philosopher since Calhoun."[8] Eduard Heimann, who responded critically to Morgenthau's paper, also said, "I much admire the speech we have just heard by a man who has come to an alliance with Reinhold Niebuhr without being his pupil. Here are two movements, two ideas, moving closer and closer together until there is a kind of identification."[9] Niebuhr did not respond to the more detailed critique of his work by Heimann, saying only, "I am not certain that anything which I might do to amend or explain *the position which Morgenthau and I have in common* could quiet the criticism of my old friend Eduard Heimann."[10]

One of the more interesting conversations between Morgenthau and Niebuhr was in *War/Peace Report* in 1967. Here the two dialogued about morality and foreign policy, expressing their essential agreement. In response to the editors' attempt to propose a division between their thought, Niebuhr responded, "I wouldn't say that the views of Morgenthau and myself are 'somewhat different.' We basically have common ideas with certain peripheral differences."[11]

## PROPHETIC REALISM

So why denote Morgenthau and Niebuhr as prophetic realists? N. Benjamin Mollov's dissertation traces the documentation of the Jewish origins of some of Morgenthau's thought. He shows in Morgenthau's own writing his consciousness of himself as a persecuted Jew, as a Jewish refugee from Hitler, and as a supporter of Jewish causes, as well as his particular connections with the Lubavitch Hasidic community at the end of his life. Recognizing that Morgenthau did not have a prominent Jewish mentor in the study of politics, human nature, and international relations, Mollov's work credits Niebuhr as the source of Morgenthau's biblical, or what I call prophetic, realism. Mollov quotes Morgenthau from a lecture in political theory given to students at the University of Chicago: "A theologian like Reinhold Niebuhr has made the greatest contemporary contribution to the understanding of basic political problems rather than a professor of political theory."[12] Mollov refers repeatedly to Morgenthau's advice to politicians as prophetic speaking of truth to power and finds Morgenthau himself identifying with Isaiah "speaking in the wilderness."

Seeing Morgenthau and Niebuhr as prophetic realists echoes Paul Tillich's use of the "spirit of Judaism" and "prophetism" in his 1933 book *The Socialist Decision.*[13] Tillich could have used prophetic realism to describe the position that holds to the seriousness of divine judgment, the reality of moral principles, the contingency of history, the recognition of sin, historical catastrophes, human opportunity for avoiding political destruction, newness in history, and hope for humanity in the face of political failure and social collapse. Tillich described his own position challenging Hitler directly in the name of religion as religious realism. No one should claim the title of prophet for themselves. But there is a recognizable position here and enough continuity with Isaiah, Jeremiah, and Amos (Niebuhr's favorite prophet) to recognize the two German refugees, Tillich and Morgenthau, and their German American friend Niebuhr as prophetic realists. Furthermore, the term "prophetic realism" is applicable to their careers, whereas Doyle's categories of liberal and socialist theory are representative of only contingent aspects of the political thought of Niebuhr and Morgenthau. Jewish realism and Christian realism both grounded in the prophetic heritage are very similar. Niebuhr and Morgenthau are distinguished more by their spirituality than by the philosophic structure of their thought about international politics. The recent appearance of one of Niebuhr's prayers in a prayer book of Reformed Judaism reduces even this posited difference to a minor one.

Max Weber connects the term "prophet" in a sociological understanding with the rise of empires, with the proclamation of moral judgments, with the bearing of personal charisma, with the sense of a meaningful world, and particularly with international politics. "Their primary concern was with foreign politics, chiefly because it constituted the theater of their god's activity."[14] Later he wrote: "Hebrew prophecy was completely oriented to a relationship with the great political powers of the time, the great kings, who as the rods of God's wrath first destroy Israel and then, as a consequence of divine intervention, permit Israelites to return from the Exile to their own land."[15]

While it may be Niebuhr and Tillich who most closely resemble the prophetic type, I would include Morgenthau of the Vietnam War years as well. Further pushing of this theme of prophetic realism as understood by Max Weber would have to deal with the study of Weber and the appreciation of him by both Niebuhr and Morgenthau.

Another break of the prophetic realists with Machiavelli is that while they contended for their views, they did not pursue political power for themselves. George Liska finds Morgenthau's antithesis in Machiavelli. Morgenthau's liberal values meant that as a commentator he could not degenerate into *realpolitik*. He was interested in speaking truth and not fawning on the prince for power. He knew that the rulers would use power and he explained its intricacies, but its pursuit was not good in itself. Without mentioning it, Liska recognizes the tension in the title of Morgenthau's book of 1960–1970 essays, *Truth and Power*, and understands his distrust of power. "The distrust of power, fraught with the tendency to repudiate it under stress, comes through in Morgenthau's Niebuhrian (and Augustinian?) identification of the drive for power with sinful lust—with man's fall from grace into depravity."[16]

So in commenting on his own lack of academic ambition Morgenthau said, "And by no means am I sorry about this lack of political activity in my life. It has simply been a part of my whole personality to be theoretically interested in power but not personally so."[17]

## The Prophetic Realist Contribution

The contribution of prophetic realists has been to try to make the politics among nations work better. They have believed that such politics represents both struggle and cooperation. Both the struggle and the cooperation reflect the tendency among humans toward egoism and the preference for their own families and tribes. They have not written simply descriptively, they have written to persuade. They have wanted to persuade an empire tempted by swings toward isolationism, imperialism, moralism, Manichaeanism, and materialism to patiently conduct its affairs diplomatically and persistently in a manner of broadly conceived national interest and national restraint. In my reading, neither Morgenthau nor Niebuhr escapes from trying to reform U.S. policy; they provide a perspective on that policy. The perspective is in terms of a philosophy of history and a philosophy of humanity that can be regarded as a biblical and Augustinian expression of liberal ideals under conditions of international conflict.

Prophetic realism tends to be rather eclectic in its use of the history of ideas. While some of Niebuhr's ideas can be traced to Augustine, Kant, Marx, and Dewey, his synthesis is his own. One can find elements of Aristotle, Kant, Nietzsche, Niebuhr, and others in Morgenthau's thought. But Morgenthau's fashioning of all this into his own theory of international politics is, I think, a unique contribution. In *Politics among Nations*, in addition to dismissing Machiavelli, Morgenthau leveled a devastating blow at those who advocated the pursuit of power without regard to morality by grouping Nietzsche among the failures along with Mussolini and Hitler. There could have been no more damning of a philosopher in 1948 than the association with Mussolini and Hitler, as the United States had just fought them to the death. The recognition that international politics was not ethics preserved both fields and permitted a creative, dialectic relationship between the two.

Niebuhr expressed in his journal his sense of Morgenthau's accomplishment in his first book in English:

> The consequence of the element of contingency in the realm of history and of the relativity in the observers of history makes it impossible to reduce the stuff of history to pure rationality. For this reason history will remain a realm of contending social forces, and these forces will embody power and use power. Dr. Morgenthau shows very clearly why it is vain to hope for the gradual elimination of the moral ambiguity of politics through historic development. He contends that every moral action is more ambiguous than the abstract analysis of a moral action and that a political action is doubly ambiguous, for it involves the power impulses of a group. The general thesis is one which is not unfamiliar to readers of this journal. The book should have a wider acclaim than it will probably get.[18]

When Morgenthau listed Niebuhr's contribution, he summarized it as the rediscovery of the political person.[19] He meant that to a degree the political sphere was autonomous, that the lust for power characterized human political history and human nature, that the lust for power and Christian morality were not reconcilable, that ideology distorted political understanding, and that political history is not scientifically reducible to patterns because of its contingencies. His tribute to Niebuhr reflects Morgenthau's own understanding formulated in part 1 of *Politics among Nations*.[20]

Both Morgenthau and Niebuhr advised diplomatic adjustments, resistance to foes trying to dominate Europe, the encouragement of the United Nations, clarity in U.S. purposes, reluctance to use U.S. military force in Asia, and living with the insoluble problems of the cold war and nuclear weapons. Neither saw the imminent breakup of the Soviet Union or the rise of the ecological crisis. Neither was conscious of the recent thesis that liberal, mature democratic governments do not make war on each other. Nor did either contribute helpfully to the theory of economic development of the poor nations. They both criticized significant policy directions of the U.S. government, and both, as critics and as originators of concepts, served that government in its successful rise to world dominance.

## The Differences between Morgenthau and Niebuhr

The differences between Morgenthau and Niebuhr are relatively insignificant. They drew on each other's ideas. But Morgenthau, in at least two essays, expanded the gap between Christian ethics and politics more than Niebuhr would. For Morgenthau, the ethic of love was the polar opposite of the lust for power. For Niebuhr, love and power could be united; in fact, from one perspective, to say that love and power are ultimately united is to confess the reality of God, a good power. Niebuhr saw the seeking of power inordinately as the corruption of the love of serving community.[21] It was an inevitable fault but still parasitic on the good. This always led Niebuhr to see in a Calvinistic sense that politics was good. It was not only corrupt, it was fallen from the good. Calvinism, then, in Niebuhr or in Weber sees Christian ethics as committed to the good statesman. For Calvin, statesmanship was the most honored calling; this is not the case for Morgenthau. So Morgenthau's politics are rooted more in a sense of tragedy, while Niebuhr's politics from the New Deal forward stress irony more than tragedy. Niebuhr expected more in history than Morgenthau did, his shadows are less dark, and his premonitions of difficulty less apocalyptic.

Neither one of them anticipated a world government. Morgenthau used it as a utopian ideal to show that we had not arrived. For Niebuhr, world government was not on the horizon. His utopia was more eschatological: the Kingdom of God. Niebuhr used to tell a story that one afternoon the policy planning staff under George Kennan listened to the proposals of advocates of world government. Kennan is supposed to have said, nudging Niebuhr, that the difference between those of us on this side of the table

(the policy planning staff) and those on the other is that we believe in original sin and they don't.

## CRITICISM OF REALISM

The dominance of realism in the study of international relations and in the
study of Christian social ethics encourages much criticism. It is as if realism
must be criticized before new paradigms of understanding can be tested. My
own sympathetic reading of realism has not motivated me to set aside its general approach. To date, prophetic realism has demonstrated a more lasting
influence on Christian ethics than any of the Marxist-informed contributions
or the particularized contributions from special communities, or the optimism
associated with liberalism.

The realist philosophies of history and ethics derived from Christian and
Jewish faith communities and expressed in the philosophic language of the
Western world have provided intellectual resources for the guidance of policy
wiser than alternative philosophies. My own elaboration of Christian realism
has led me to want to make more explicit the relational quality of power
than some readings of Morgenthau have encouraged.[22] Also, I have wanted to
talk in terms of national purpose rather than national interest as the goal of
foreign policy. This renders more intelligible the value-laden quality of
the pursuit of foreign policy and also avoids possible reduction of national
interest to either security or economic concerns.[23] Sometimes, too, I have
appreciated the greater care with which my Oxford tutor, John Plamenatz,
analyzed concepts than did the realists with their rather equivocal terminology. However, these are all adjustments within realism that are easily reached
and not unwelcomed by the founders themselves. On the three issues with
which I sometimes had nuanced disagreements with Niebuhr, I suspect that
the disagreements were more a matter of style than of substance, though I
remained perhaps a little more of a child of light than his rather more somber
perspective showed him to be. During the 1960s I thought his polemics on the
evils of communism that Morgenthau shared were overdrawn. Now, on the
basis of Russian testimony, I think he was right. On revolution in developing
countries, I was more supportive than Niebuhr, but it did not come to much,
and he saw the cold war implications more realistically than I did. Although
both of us supported Labor government attempts to make peace with the
Palestinians, his was the less critical support of Israel. This is said from the
perspective of one who spoke for the campaign to free the Jews from the
Soviet Union and who also recognized the United States as the guarantor of
Israel's security. Niebuhr was simply polemical on this point beyond my com-
fort level. On nuclear deterrence, he accepted it as tragic necessity whereas I
criticized it as immoral.

While agreeing with Stanley Hoffmann that Morgenthau's central concepts need more rigorous analysis,[24] I believe that some of his other criticisms
seem overdrawn. The statement that "the realist . . . sees the world as a static

field in which power relations reproduce themselves in timeless monotony"[25] may be true of Machiavelli, but not of Morgenthau and Niebuhr. It is true that power is a central concept of psychological relations of control for Morgenthau, but one that is then elaborated and interpreted. The meanings are in the interpretations and context. It seems to me untrue to say that Morgenthau and Niebuhr analyze power "apart from the processes and pressures of domestic politics."[26] Nor is it true that the developed position of prophetic realism is "that the national interest carries its own morality."[27] Furthermore, Hoffmann's criticism that realism assumes a rational world of reality[28] is grounded in misunderstanding of the world of sin and modified chaos that realism describes with as rational a description as possible.[29]

Another of Hoffmann's critiques is that realism seems to be a philosophy designed for success.[30] I think he is correct. Raymond Aron's critique is similar—that, for a school of thought, realism goes too far in mixing theory and praxis. Both of these thinkers capture the pragmatic nature of realism and its consequentialist-oriented morality. The school is bound to the success of the United States, and the theory relates closely to foreign policy for a republic turned imperial in the twentieth century.[31] However, this may not be a weakness. Realist theory, whether that of Thucydides, Augustine, or Machiavelli, seems bound to certain historical periods, and this American form has not aspired to guidance beyond this particular nation. A world-based theory of international politics would be different and might be grounded in Immanuel Kant. It probably could offer as little concrete guidance as has the recent attempt at a global ethics.[32]

Continued focus on the criticism of realism would have to include reference to the ease with which cynics can hide among its teachings. Much of the criticism of the Morgenthau-Niebuhr school stems from the inability of critics to distinguish it from the Nixon-Kissinger policies,[33] but it has been the intent of both Morgenthau and Niebuhr to distinguish their thought from political cynicism. In fact, Niebuhr has kept the criticism of realism alive as well as the criticism of idealism. One can encourage cynicism and the other illusory moralism. Niebuhr's writing from 1932 almost sounds as if it could have been written in 1972 or 1984 or 1999:

> The last three decades of world history would seem to be a perfect and tragic symbol of the consequences of this kind of realism, with its abortive efforts to resolve conflict by conflict. The peace before the War was an armistice maintained by the balance of power. It was destroyed by the spontaneous combustion of the mutual fears and animosities which it created. . . .
>
> This unhappy consequence of a too consistent political realism would seem to justify the interposition of the counsels of the moralists. . . . Yet the moralist may be as dangerous a guide as the political realist. . . .
>
> An adequate political morality must do justice to the insights of both moralists and political realists.[34]

In the last major manuscript he completed, Niebuhr continued the same emphasis. The essay "A Critical Survey of Idealist and Realist Political Theories" criticized overly cynical tendencies in realism, repented of some of his overly strong polemics against the insights of idealism, and argued with the obfuscation of creative factors in human nature by his friend Morgenthau. While affirming a "moderate realism," he pointed out that the factors of values of cultures, prestige, power, and force in the behavior of nations were so complex in their interrelation that "both realistic and idealistic interpretations of national behavior" were refuted.[35]

The point of Niebuhr's critique of realists who would ignore values is to show that, despite their polemics against moralism, the prophetic realists at their best have consistently attacked cynics. Their other targets were those who would exploit the moral sensibilities of a people for their own purposes. This impatience with cynicism cloaked in piety is best expressed in "The King's Chapel and the King's Court."[36] With the fury of an Amos, Niebuhr criticized piety that, rooted in cynicism, did not produce justice. President Nixon proved his vulnerability to this charge by his thinly veiled reply to Niebuhr in his introduction to a book of sermons preached at the White House.[37] By the time the controversy broke into the open in 1969, John D. Ehrlichman, counsel to the president, was examining Niebuhr's FBI file.[38]

Both Niebuhr and Hoffmann[39] rejected the cynics and the idealists. Yet Hoffmann keeps up his criticism of realism, thinking that it is almost without a morality. I cannot find in his writings a close reading of Niebuhr. Such a reading might help him understand Morgenthau. But reading Morgenthau and Niebuhr can be frustrating to the unsympathetic. However, the realist is also frustrated in reading Hoffmann, who says in the same essay, "We are much less aware of it [moral awareness] in foreign policy making, partly because of the absence of a world community, partly because of the grip of the realist tradition,"[40] and in the following argument, "we are all realists now."[41]

In his conclusion, discussing the book he and Michael Smith are going to write, Hoffman says that he is a transformationist. The realists remain, I believe, incrementalist. Herein lies the difference: Hoffmann wants to synthesize idealism and realism into a transformist paradigm, whereas the prophetic realists think that they have already synthesized them in their incremental strategies for a tough world. The transformist paradigm is attractive, but it occasions too much backlash and it finally is too soft for the world, which will defeat it most of the time.

However, I believe that there are surprises that realism missed. First, although some predictions of the demise of communism can be found in realism, basically we were surprised. The strategy of containment, avoidance of major wars, aid to the underdeveloped world, economic strength at the centers, and ideological struggle was correct for the cold war. But realists, generally speaking, expected decades more of competition. Second, although Niebuhr's last published book[42] dealt with the theory of democracy, its world relevance, and its country-by-country prospects, we did not perceive that democracy in itself was a peacemaking force. We relied on diplomacy and neglected the power of democracy in itself for peace with other democracies. With President Clinton's 1994 State of the Union address, what had been the insight of political scientists moved into public politics: "democracies don't attack each other."[43] Liberal peace among democracies has become a useful principle and basis for various research programs in international relations. Without world governance or radical transformation, the expansion of the numbers of functional democracies with wise diplomacy may increase the zones of peace. Of course, the propensity of democracies to war on more authoritarian governments points to the need for liberal programs and analysis to remain realistic.

## DEVELOPMENT OF PEACEMAKING PRINCIPLES

As the nations closed out World War II, a group of Christians were formulating an ethic for international relations. They called it "just and durable peace." It did not last as a concept, but before it disappeared it helped the victorious allies see their way clear to found the United Nations and to impose peace settlements on the defeated nations that were less vindictive than the political slogan "unconditional surrender" threatened. In fact, the leading figure of the just and durable peace concept, John Foster Dulles, was the lead negotiator for the peace treaty with Japan. He was a remarkable person, and the Protestant peace movements have not seen his equal since his death as secretary of state under President Dwight Eisenhower.

In the 1930s, John Foster Dulles, grandson of Presbyterian missionaries and of a secretary of state, became enthusiastic about the ecumenical Christian contribution to peacemaking. The liberal-activist theology of his father, a theologian, merged with the worldly-wise ways of his mother's family to equip him to lead the international relations thinking of the Federal Council of Churches. His favorite uncle had been Woodrow Wilson's secretary of state, and when the uncle, the boy John Foster Dulles, and his grandfather, another former secretary of state, went sailing on Lake Erie, there were as many secretaries of state in one small boat as the country had ever seen. With his law firm severing its relations with Germany in the late 1930s, he wrote his first and best book on foreign policy, *War, Peace, and Change*. The influence of the French philosopher Henri Bergson was evident in the book in its emphasis on the dynamics of history. The vision of peace came from both his American context and the Christian faith. War was the imminent reality to be fended off with realism, change, and vision.

Dulles applied himself to the leadership of the Commission on a Just and Durable Peace of the Federal Council of Churches during the war. The commission set about defining the aims of war, as did many theologians and journals of Christian commentary. Here the lawyer pushed for simplicity and clarity and for organization under law. He dominated the commission, which was composed of rather formidable theologians. Paul Tillich attacked the legalism and the American imperialism implicit in the title "Just and Durable Peace." Reinhold Niebuhr decried the tendency toward moral simplicity in Dulles and always feared the appearance of self-righteousness as the fruit of simple moral judgments. Dulles pushed for results compatible with his theology and legal philosophy. Henry Pitney van Dusen referred to the work of the commission as a one-man show. When the results appeared, they were in the form of study books, principles of peace, applied political principles for international relations, church assemblies, an interview between Dulles and President Roosevelt, and a large-scale educational and lobbying effort on behalf of the evolving United Nations. Probably at no other time has the ecumenical church exerted as much influence on foreign policy. Following the war, Dulles would serve as a legal counsel to the U.S. delegation to the UN at San Francisco, and later as a UN delegate. He also undertook various negotiations for President Truman, including the role of the negotiator of the peace treaty with Japan. From the role of shadow secretary of state, he finally achieved, with Eisenhower's election, his goal of being secretary of state.

This chapter cannot survey the virtues and weaknesses of Dulles as secretary of state. Suffice it to say that as secretary of state he was concerned with safely grounding his political base with both the Republican right-wing-to-moderate power brokers and the president. He operated as a militant, obnoxious lawyer overstating his client's interests (the interests of the United States as perceived by the Republican, internationalist establishment) at every opportunity. Except for his brother's unfortunate intervention by the CIA in Guatemala, with its disastrous consequences, he kept the United States out of open warfare from 1952 until his death in 1959. Forgotten as a peacemaker, he was decried for brinkmanship; for him, as a lawyer and a partially secularized Calvinist, the two were not in opposition. Communism and the cold war changed him and the U.S. policy. Given the cold war, his earlier philosophy of peace had no space in which to grow. Perhaps now, with the cold war eclipsed, that philosophy should be revisited and examined for the concept of just peace that characterized his commission's work.

In 1942, the commission published a "Statement of Guiding Principles" in which the handiwork of Dulles was dominant. Beyond Dulles, however, these principles represented a typical, liberal, progressive Protestant perspective on just peace. First, they assumed a moral order and that the sickness of society was a violation of that order. Penitence is required. International anarchy, revenge, and retaliation must be replaced with international order through agencies. Economics must be reordered for the general interest of all nations. Military establishments, colonial relationships, and treaty arrangements all needed to be ordered by international organization. The human rights of work, worship, speech, assembly, etc., were demanded. The United States could not return to isolationism but must act responsibly for the general interest. The last three principles affirmed the special responsibilities of the church, active Christian citizenship to change the nation, and finally that the author of the moral law on which all depend was "God revealed in Christ."

Later these principles were translated into the more politically relevant "Six Pillars of Peace." More important here, the resolve to energize the U.S. commitment to a yet unknown international organization was found. The church authorities, speaking at the Delaware Conference in March of 1942, emphasized realism and hope. They knew of the need to weave international structure around nations. They also knew that the nations were not ready. So they forswore utopianism and worked doggedly for the best they could get in the United Nations organization.

In these thirteen principles of fifty years ago and in their translation through politics into the preamble and structure of the UN, we have already an incarnated theory of just peace. Corresponding commitments to work at foreign policy through the UN for the general interest of humanity might provide what we are looking for when we search for a theory of just peace.

The fury of the cold war hardened Christian judgment in the United States. Dulles is only one example. Just-war theory was elaborated by Paul Ramsey and many others while peace theory withered. The war, while encouraging many illusions and myths, was real. The United States and the Soviet Union contested their respective systems through surrogate wars in Europe, Asia, Africa, and Latin America. Only seldom did the United States and the Soviet Union come into direct conflict, but Greeks, Koreans, Vietnamese, Afghans, Iranians, Salvadorans, Nicaraguans, Indonesians, Guatemalans, Angolans, Ethiopians, Cubans, and countless others fought the war. The world paid the economic price. Only near the end of the war did the theory of just peace reemerge in a central way in Christian discourse.

Talk of just peacemaking emerged as Roman Catholics sought to deepen their theology of peace. In the United Methodist Church, criteria of a just peace were suggested in a policy on nuclear weapons, deterrence, and disarmament. In the United Church of Christ, just peacemaking insights were part of the recasting of the church as a just-peace church. Among Presbyterians, criteria of just peacemaking appeared as part of a study of the possibilities of Christian resistance to nuclear weapons and the militarism of the cold war.[44]

Christian ethicists commented on these converging trends in modern Christian thought. Glen Stassen, however, took the lead in theorizing about just peacemaking. He related just peacemaking to the Sermon on the Mount on the one hand and to practical politics of the nations on the other. His study *Just Peacemaking*[45] became a primer for many Christians who joined in the search for the development of the concept of just peacemaking. Furthermore, he took the lead in asking Christian ethicists to think together about just peace, first at a meeting of the Society of Christian Ethics and then at a working conference on the subject at the Abbey Center in Trappist, Kentucky, in 1994. Further work in 1995 led to the conference at the Carter Conference Center in Atlanta in 1996, which achieved a synthesis of scholarship and agreed on essays to further the results of the collaborative effort.[46] Although this new work is not a direct continuation of the pre–cold war peace efforts or the cold war debates, continuity across generations is represented in Stassen. His father, Harold Stassen, governor of Minnesota, candidate for president, and indefatigable worker for disarmament in President Eisenhower's cabinet, had as a younger man drafted the Preamble to the United Nations Charter. The elder Stassen argued for deepening the peacemaking work even at the time that Dulles as secretary of state was discouraging disarmament strategies with his cold war belligerency.

The post–cold war era presents a new situation. The debates about the morality of nuclear deterrence struggled to address a time of neither peace nor war but of great danger. So today, neither the category of pacifism nor of just war seems adequate, and we seek a moral paradigm to complement these age-old moral frameworks. Neither pacifism nor just-war theory is rejected. Pacifism is seen as a vocational decision for those who cannot morally support any armed conflict, even a humanitarian or peacekeeping intervention or a just defensive war. Just-war theory is a group of principles implied by the commandment not to murder, which distinguishes just wars from unjustifiable warfare or murder. The Christian ethical theory of this volume is particularly compatible with both justifiable war and just peacemaking theories. Pacifists, too, can affirm just peacemaking theory as a further explication of their position of refusing war. Just peacemaking is an approach to the creation of conditions under which the debates between pacifists and just war advocates would become fewer. Just-war theory recognizes that war is a last resort. In most of our interstate conflicts, just peacemaking work would precede and in many cases prevent states from ever reaching the last-resort situation.

As just-war theory is a set of principles for evaluating a proposed national policy of initiating war, so just peacemaking theory is a set of principles for evaluating a government's initiating of peacemaking practices. At the present stage of development, the principles are proposed as principled initiatives to be followed by Christians in developing state policies and hopefully to be adopted and advocated as a set of principles by the churches. The advocates of just-peace theory ground these principles differently. Some derive them from revelation in scripture. Others see them as a product of discernment of moral law in human history. Still others see them as the fruit of human moral discourse or the findings of social science. Most base them on some combination from different sources. This inquiry sees them as a development of moral reasoning grounded in the discourse of Christians in the twentieth century that reflects critical Christian thought about war and peace ultimately rooted in the justice and peacemaking imperatives of scripture. They are a contemporary elaboration of the commandment to "Love your neighbor as yourself." Finally, they are an affirmation by the human spirit of what we must do to resist the evil in our human nature that leads us to murder in war. Consistent with the blessing of Jesus for active peace work, "Blessed are the peacemakers; they shall be called the children of God," they are congruent with the Ten Commandments and the Sermon on the Mount.

This initiating quality of the just peacemaking principles is very important. The policy makers, organizations, and citizens need to act for peace rather than wait for war. In a state of modified human anarchy, such as our interstate-corporate world, initiatives must be taken to overcome the tendencies to wage warfare. War must be regarded as usually resting outside the moral limits of human action. The determination that war is morally repugnant is important, but working on the prerequisites for peace has priority here. The principles are not negative prohibitions, but expressions of moral imperatives formulated as action guidelines. They have the active formula of "Love your neighbor," rather than the negative prohibition of "Thou shall not murder."

The group of ethicists and political scientists referred to their initiatives alternatively as practice-norms or principles. "Principled initiatives" is the formulation of this author. Wide consensus was achieved around these ten initiatives, many of which contained many particular practices. The group knew its finitude and limits, as it was predominantly (75 percent), though not totally, white and male and North American. The group was uncertain as to how plainly to present the religious agreements and perceptions that supported the affirmations. It seemed best to this participant to present them as agreed-on practices or initiatives that the formulating group had conceived as helpful to the peace process. Particular theologies then can interpret them in their own way, because the principles of just war without specific theological context may be interpreted in several different theological contexts.

The theological context of this interpretation of the ultimate imperative regards the just-peace practices as useful initiatives to encourage. Christian realism assumes the ongoing season of wars and rumors of war while trying to avoid all wars that can be responsibly prevented. Many, probably most, of these wars will be civil wars, because the utility of international war in a market economy of trading states dominated by interacting democracies is very low. In this anarchic society, the intentional prizes are to be won by business and not by intentional war. Still, rational choice is only one of the modes of decision making exercised by nations, and racism, mental illness, paranoiac fears, fanaticism, greed, and false pride all have their roles in influencing and sometimes determining national policies in the international system. The great realist theorists Thucydides, Augustine, Machiavelli, Hobbes, and Morgenthau all lived in times of international terror. We, living in a less terrible time, may be able to stress the cooperative forces, and morally we must. However, the times of terror are here for vast populations and they may again be immediately upon us. Meanwhile, in the time given to us, out of the ultimate imperative, we for the welfare of the neighbor can use these just peacemaking initiatives. The ten principled initiatives that emerged from the Carter Center meeting are as follows.[47]

### 1. Recognize the emerging cooperative forces in the international system, and work with them.
Paul Schroeder found four current trends that moved him to emphasize the need for wisdom in cooperating with forces in the international system that promoted peace. In the late twentieth century, these factors were (1) the declining utility of warfare, (2)

the role of trade in the development of successful nation-states, (3) the increase of international communications, and (4) the increasing dominance of liberal representative democracy and market capitalism. His analysis, critical of neorealism while sympathetic to classical realism, affirmed the need to develop and cooperate with voluntary international organizations. Peace has only possibilities and no guarantees, but referring to Reinhold Niebuhr, Schroeder saw how institutions of international cooperation could be gradually developed. He took his stand with the problem solvers whom William Fox used to call the "pragmatic meliorists."

The danger in this principled initiative is that while these trends support the ideology and interests of the United States, they may oppose the self-understandings of some other nations. The world trends probably are running in the directions Schroeder avows, but resistance to them on the part of some countries may be fierce, particularly to the supremacy of democracy and market capitalism. This is a particularly apt principle for the United States and requires much more listening to the needs and aspirations of others in voluntary associations than U.S. diplomacy often grants. The United States needs to have its own aspirations remolded and limited somewhat by international associations rather than simply coopting all international organizations.

### 2. Strengthen the United Nations and international efforts for cooperation and human rights. Michael Joseph

Smith's paper argued that peacemaking requires armed intervention in conflicts to restore peace. National sovereignty may be abridged by multilateral intervention sanctioned by the United Nations for a variety of just causes. Like Schroeder's, his analysis of the international system revealed trends supporting some abridgment of sovereignty, peacemaking forces, and emerging possibilities for collective security. Some of Kant's prerequisites for peace are increasingly realized: the cost of war, the lure of commerce, and increased public participation in affairs of state. Human rights overrule nation-state sovereignty in legal precedent and moral weight according to Smith. He concludes by calling for a strengthened United Nations with a "standing volunteer military force" to enforce human rights and the capacity to promote peace.

This development is highly desirable in the post–cold war world with its diffused power. However, collective security and international organizations have been overrun in the twentieth century by fanatical nationalism and militarism. This, too, like Schroeder's recommendations, will be achieved incrementally, if at all. At the present time, the political will for such developments is lacking in the United States, Russia, China, Great Britain, France, and Germany. Some humanitarian interventions under UN authority will be possible, and if they are successful, they will contribute to the argument for the practicality of this initiative. At present, the record of the United Nations in the former Yugoslavia shows the moral ambiguity of the initiative.

### 3. Advance human rights, religious liberty, and democracy.

Buoyed by the advances of democracy and the mounting evidence that international relations between democracies are more peaceful than the relations between other nations, John Langan and Bruce Russett collaborated to argue for the peacemaking gains of advancing human rights and democracy. Protection of liberties of religious conscience and fundamental human rights is a requirement of democracies. To the extent that a democracy fails to provide such protection, it is regarded as immature (e.g., the United States before the achievement of universal suffrage). The struggle for religious liberty and rights promotes democracy, and the achievement of democracy ensures these rights. The absence of war among democratic states tends to confirm Kant's vision that democratic polity is a prerequisite of peace. With the achievement of democratic government by a slight majority of the world's states and the widespread appeal of democracy, a process toward just peacemaking may be evolving. These three values of human rights, religious liberty, and democracy are, of course, goods in their own right, but the evidence of peacemaking tendencies between democracies is a valuable insight for international relations. Unfortunately, powerful democracies have tendencies to wreak havoc on smaller, autocratic societies and to find themselves at war with totalitarian societies. The great democracies of France, Britain, United States, and India scarcely have histories free from war in the nineteenth and twentieth centuries. Struggles for religious liberty and human rights may encourage civil wars (such as in England in the seventeenth century and in the United States in the nineteenth century), and these struggles must be subject to political prudence, as must the campaigns for democracy. The literature of American foreign policy is filled with crusade mentality, and forces promotive of just peacemaking ought not to become teleological goals for self-righteous wars.

### 4. Foster just and sustainable economic development.

Degraded environments and declining economic opportunities lead to refugee problems, immigration problems, conflicts over resources, civil war, and international war. Rodger Payne, David Lumsdaine, and David Bronkema joined in advocating policies of sustainable economic development as part of just peacemaking. The economic development they advocated needed to be ecologically sustainable, to be focused on the poor, to be built around enduring relationships, and to account for human frailty, sin, and ignorance. The authors advocated a perspective that treated development as a holistic issue including political and spiritual as well as economic factors. Their explicit Christian advocacy on behalf of the poor reflected recent emphases in theological thinking. This advocacy was consistent with the discussion on ecoethics in chapter 11.

### 5. Reduce offensive weapons and weapons trade.

Barbara Green and Glen Stassen wrote about U.S. government and commercial policies to increase armaments in the world. The encouragement of massive arms trafficking by U.S. business and governmental policies is one of the most difficult hurdles for the realization of just peacemaking policies. The United States is usually the leader in selling and giving away arms while other countries, like Russia, China, France, Britain, Germany, Israel, Italy, and the Czech Republic, compete also for their share of this rich market. The fear of war drives nations to arm themselves, and the presence of arms encourages their use. Throughout the poor world, wars are fought with weapons sold or given to them by the rich nations. On this issue the democracies seem no better than the totalitarian states. In fact, it now appears that the democracies with market economies are the more able to subsidize the increase in arms trafficking.

Although many nations share guilt in the current arms races, the United States is the largest player in this dangerous game. U.S. arms subsidies fuel regional arms races, strengthen unjust dictatorial regimes, and arm potential enemies, such as Somalia, Iraq, and Iran. Armaments will remain part of human history, but a surfeit of arms is dangerous and economically counter-productive. The money spent for arms purchases denies the resources for needed human projects in food, education, housing, and health. Political decisions to deny resources to the poor in the United States are related to the arms manufacturers' contributions to U.S. political parties and massive subsidies to these companies and their stockholders. The fading of the recognition that arming evil rulers is itself an evil during the cold war was a moral loss. The resurgence of the moral recognition that arms buildups are usually an evil must be developed. The end of the worldwide cold war provides an opportunity to demand thorough decreases in these armament sales and profits.

**6. Support nonviolent direct action.** Susan Thistlethwaite, John Cartwright, and Gary Gunderson advocated the recognition that non-violent means of social change have a moral priority over violent means. Various nonviolent means were successful in the Gandhi and King campaigns. Recent successes in South Africa and Eastern Europe have demonstrated the practicality of nonviolent means of social change. I think the moral priority should be given to nonviolent means because they normally do less harm, but care must be taken with boycotts and embargoes, which often hurt the vulnerable segments of the population rather than the decision makers who exercise control. The authors of this initiative explained and evaluated the use of boycotts, marches, civil disobedience, public disclosure, accompaniment, safe spaces or sanctuary, and strikes. Moral philosophy must recognize the moral division between the use of violent and nonviolent means. This line should not be obscured in moral thinking. The criticisms of nonviolent means are usually based on their tendency to lead to their use of violence. The drawing of the line does not deny the possibility of justifying violent means under criteria of just-war considerations or appeals to self-defense or communal defense, but the recognition of the difference encourages the use of nonviolent means for the sake of justice and peacemaking before violent means are needed.

**7. Take independent initiatives to reduce hostility.** Glen Stassen provided the contemporary interpretation of independent initiatives that influenced the whole conception of just peacemaking. As both Gandhi and Martin Luther King Jr. recognized, the original source is Jesus, and Stassen's utilization of the Sermon on the Mount was discussed earlier.[48] The basic idea of the independent initiative is to take clearly interpreted peaceful action in a manner that encourages one's opponent to take a similar positive step. Such initiatives can reduce the perception of threat by visible action not dependent on negotiation. Negotiations must follow, but negotiation proceeds much better following progressive action. An initiative should be a series of acts that increase the security of the other while not weakening the initiator. Initiatives are best announced in advance and then carried out with clear explanations of the intent to decrease tension. Much of the disengagement of the cold war was achieved by independent initiatives by both the Soviet Union and the United States, and Stassen's book *Just Peacemaking* provides the story.

**8. Use cooperative conflict resolution and prevention processes.** Steven Brion-Meisels, David Steele, Gary Gunderson, and Edward L. Long Jr. formed a team to write about the use of cooperative conflict resolution. Before conflicts over security or interests develop into war, there are many practices that can be utilized for the securing of cooperation and peace. The thrust of the essay is the recommendation of an activist partnership in threatening situations. The Carter negotiations in Haiti persisting even while invasion planes were airborne is symptomatic of the use of conflict resolution to avoid war. The processes of conflict resolution constitute a theory with proven results in themselves and are recommended here but not detailed. Steven Brion-Meisels shared his expertise from school-based conflict resolution. Gary Gunderson offered the Carter Center's experience with alternatives to war. David Steele reflected on his active involvement in mediation and peacemaking in the former Yugoslavia. Edward Long showed that all these known strategies related to the transforming ways of just peacemaking. These strategies fit both the just peacemaking values and the older justifiable war theory that confined any justifiable war to a last resort, implying that imaginative peacemaking had already been exhausted. The many strategies within the conflict resolution options deepen the human possibilities of preventing conflicts from turning into wars.

**9. Acknowledge responsibility for conflict and injustice: Seek repentance and forgiveness.** This principle, developed in essay form by Alan Geyer, drew the most criticism from the assembled group. Like the Tenth Commandment of Moses, "Thou shall not covet," it moves toward the interior realms of humanity and has worldly consequences. There was more agreement on "Acknowledge responsibility for conflict" than on "Seek repentance and forgiveness." In-depth historical knowledge was regarded as vital to peacemaking, and this requires acknowledgment of a nation's contribution to conflicts. In fact, conflict resolution strategies require the discovery and sharing of such knowledge. There was more doubt about the practicality of urging nations to repent and to ask for forgiveness. This seemed too theological to some members of the group for the purposes of just peacemaking principles. It also seemed to characterize prophetic utterance rather than more rational principles for nations. There were many calls for repentance of the nations in the Old Testament but few examples of it as national policy. (Jonah at Nineveh comes to mind as a case of repentance, and there even Jonah was surprised.) The debates revealed some of the tensions in the group between the realists, who tended to use just peacemaking theory within the world we have, and the more idealistic thinkers, who were more bold in expecting transformation of this world and saw the theory as aiding in that transformation. It seems to me that repentance and forgiveness are relevant to international politics and that there are some examples of them in practice that Donald Shriver documents in *An Ethic for Enemies: Forgiveness in Politics*,[49] but I would not regard them as normal expectations of national behavior. After all, the classical realists observed history and saw little repentance and forgiveness, and peace can be achieved without it. Most statespeople are not free to express their self-transcendence of their assigned roles or to confess their own nations' sins in their diplomatic roles.

**10. Encourage grassroots peacemaking and other voluntary associations.** Duane K. Friesen provided the commentary for the affirmation of peace- and justice-oriented voluntary associations. International politics is not just about nation-states. Below the level of the state and beyond the limits of the state exists a vast array of citizen organizations. These organizations assemble the activists and leaders of the "We the people" of the United Nations Charter. These associations provide community for the work of peacemaking and give the work a chance of succeeding.

Nongovernmental associations are growing in power and influence, and they were vital in freeing Eastern Europe and in ending the cold war. Capacities for receiving information and transcending national interest are enriched by transnational associations. People's organizations, including the churches, have capacities for staying with issues beyond particular political administrations. The powerless can find voice in these associations. Mediation possibilities can be nurtured in voluntary associations. Groups outside of government can conceive and foster independent initiatives for nations to adopt. Associations preserve issues and concerns beyond short-range expectations of short-term governmental policy makers. Groups can resist governments when they act against peacemaking. Religious associations, when committed to and active in peacemaking, can nurture transformed souls to work for peacemaking. As Jesus called his followers to organize, so the work of peacemaking calls for organization in community.

## DIVERSIFICATION OF THE
## INTERNATIONAL ACTORS

Another principle is needed to supplement the work of the peacemaking group. For diplomacy to improve, it must include more than the ruling male elites from the various countries. The peace movements have more diversity than the diplomatic corps and foreign policy establishments. Although the ecumenical peacemaking team working on the peacemaking initiatives did not take up this principle, it is a necessary one for Christian conscience. Peacemaking work is too serious to be left just to the men. Without suggesting absolute dichotomies between men and women, it is noted that women in general exhibit less warlike tendencies and more caring tendencies, especially for other women, children, and families. Gender pluralism, like racial, class, and religious pluralism, will enrich all foreign policy teams, and of course the United States as a pluralistic state has great resources to draw on in this regard.

The synthesis of prophetic realism and just peacemaking initiatives prepares us well for our roles as peacemakers, but there is no promise of universal peace in this history. Full shalom will await a transformed nature and history. In our present history we can reduce the number of wars and allow more people to live in peace.

Since the end of the cold war, more than fifty significant wars have occurred or are occurring. Some of these wars have been particularly brutal ethnic and religious clashes in Rwanda, Bosnia, and Sudan. Others have been fought over control of oil resources, as in Kuwait and Iraq. Still others have been associated with the breakdown of political order in the nations of the former Soviet Union. Some of these wars have been fought in primitive contexts, even though conducted with modern arms, whereas others, such as in Ireland and the former Yugoslavia, have been waged by more technologically advanced peoples. It is well to remember that war in many of the forms we know has evolved with our technological civilization.

The technological city magnifies the promises and the threats of human life. Technology reduces the mystery and the ritualized patterns of more primitive life. It turns mysterious creation into disconnected "things" to be manipulated for human purposes. Technology in its developed Western cities overcomes some of the threats to human existence. Slavery, characteristic of the early cities, has been eliminated. Plumbing and medicine reduce threats of plague. Modern agriculture feeds the city and reduces famine to a phenomenon of the poorest two-thirds of the world. Yet industrial pollution, overpopulation, and exhaustion of the earth's resources threaten humanity. Organized war intrinsic to the city threatens to undo modern civilization. Technology so increases the output of the ambiguous being of humanity that in its organized, modern-urban form, it threatens to end humanity.

Lewis Mumford resists claiming that he has proven causal relations among kingship, urban development, human sacrifice, and war. However, he thinks that he has woven the ancient fragmentary sources together to suggest connections. The institution of war rooted in human anxiety seems to have developed along with urban culture. War requires the mass population, the absolute control, the specialization of labor, and the technology that only cities can provide. War, like kingships and urbanization, spread to become established in societies as they developed. Wars receive religious sanction and in fact become institutions of "wholesale ritual sacrifice"[50] replacing animal sacrifice and the symbols of royal sacrifice. As the kings came to command the cities, they achieved potential mobilized armies even if temporarily held in reserve.[51] The city gives to war its potential, and the defense of the city provides a reason to justify war. Here is the fatal flaw of urban life as it organizes itself for mass human slaughter. The city prepares in its achievement its own death, and Mumford believes that beneath all of the modern organization lies the orientation to mass sacrifice.[52]

Accepting that urban life, as well as human personality, has a negative side, even a death-serving impulse, how do we turn to the life-giving impulses? We seek the life-giving human impulses even knowing that most urban civilizations have been destroyed. In the ordinary course of human history, urban centers are razed, much of the population is slaughtered and then new urban centers sometimes arise from the ruins of the old. Technology has reduced the possibilities of renewing life in urban centers if they are subject to modern war. This chapter, grounded in prophetic realism and peacemaking principles, concludes by considering resistance to militarism and extraordinary use of ordinary means of peacemaking.

## Resistance to Militarism

Although peacemaking must be the work of governments, they are often slow to undertake it. Governments tend to rely on military force; war-making has been one of the central functions of government throughout history. Now that total war is so destructive, governments are slow to back away from their military priorities. The very apocalyptic dangers of war encourage them to overarm. One of the major causes of war has been the fear of the military intentions of the other, as Thucydides observed in his history of the wars of ancient Greece. Military expenditures expand governmental functions, military parades show the authority of government, and military alliances may strengthen individuals and interest groups within countries. When military procurements are centralized in socialist countries or in several corporations, as in the United States, the pressures to sacrifice other areas of life to military spending are severe.

Churches and peace organizations, despite some successes, have seen the militarization of the world increase in the twentieth century. Wars in developing countries are common and have consumed millions of lives (12.5 million dead since 1960 according to our estimate) and untold resources. Military expenditures drive countries into debt, reducing standards of living and creating greater conditions of injustice that will, in due course, produce more wars.

Meanwhile, governments engage in more and more of the military practices of arbitrary force, secrecy, censorship, and manipulation of information. Democratic governments that were once relatively open begin to use assassination of political opponents, torture, and starvation to achieve political goals. Chemical weapons threaten to become more frequently used. This extraordinary tendency to increase the military functioning of governments threatens the quality of life and human decency. In secular terms, these developments represent human fear and an absurd overemphasis on weapons. In Christian terms, the arms race, increased killing, and militarization are evil. As the evil comes to be perceived as dominant, it is described as demonic, reflecting the idolatry of weaponry before which societies sacrifice their welfare as well as the worship of money or the god of mammon. Religiously speaking, the gods of Mars and mammon stalk the planet and even invade the churches.

Against organized evil, even if it originated in good motivations, activist Christians must contend. That contention has in the peace movements become known as resistance. Paul Tillich affirmed the necessity of resistance to the suicidal instincts of our political tendencies:

> The increasing and apparently unlimited power of the means of self-destruction in the hands of humanity puts before us the question of the ultimate meaning of this development.
>
> The first point which comes to my mind is the possibility that it is the destiny of historical humanity to be annihilated not by a cosmic event, but by the tensions in his own being and in his own history.
>
> The reaction to this possibility—this is the second point—should be the certainty that the meaning of human history, as well as of everyone's life within it, is not dependent on the time or the way in which history comes to an end. For the meaning of history lies above history.
>
> The third point is that everyone who is aware of the possibility of mankind's self-destruction must resist this possibility to the utmost. For life and history have an eternal dimension and are worthy to be defended against humanity's suicidal instincts which are socially as real as individually.
>
> The fourth point is that the resistance against the suicidal instincts of the human race must be done on all levels, on the political level through negotiations between those who in a tragic involvement force each other into the production of ever stronger means of self-destruction; on the moral level through a reduction of propaganda and an increase in obedience to the truth about oneself and the potential enemy; on the religious level through a sacred serenity and superiority over the preliminary concerns of life, and a new experience and a new expression of the ultimate concern which transcends as well as determines historical existence.
>
> The fifth point is that the resistance against the self-destructive consequences of technical control of nature must be done in acts which unite the religious, moral, and political concern, and which are performed in imaginative wisdom and courage.[53]

The national organizations of the Presbyterian Church, the Methodist Church, and the United Church of Christ have morally rejected the nuclear deterrence doctrine that is the major justification for the ever-expanding development of nuclear terror. The Roman Catholic bishops, although more equivocal than the Methodist bishops or the Presbyterian General Assembly, also condemn the reliance on deterrence. In practice, most local churches have tried both to accept and to reject militarization and nuclear weapons development. The more radical stance of a clear rejection of deepening militarization and nuclear weapons is less frequent in the Christian community, and public action is still the witness of a prophetic vanguard. Demonstrations, civil disobedience, and public statements against the Star Wars program, the School of the Americas, repression in Central America, arms trafficking, nuclear weapons development, and military budget expansion are part of a strategy against militarism. The ethos of the church will tolerate acts of resistance, but it shows little evidence of encouraging them. The peacemaking work will need to find its deeper strength in the extraordinary use of ordinary means.

## Extraordinary Use of Ordinary Means

The Presbyterian Church (U.S.A.) called on its churches to support and stay in solidarity with Christians who in conscience decided to resist the government's policies of making or preparing for war. It chose, in 1988, not to make resistance to militarism or opposition to nuclear warfare preparedness a matter of confessed faith by the entire church. It expects to continue the discussion of whether such opposition should be considered a matter of faith. It is clear, however, in the teaching of the General Assembly for forty years, that increasing militarism is contrary to the Christian's perception of God's will. The church decided in 1988, after discussing resistance to militarism, to make the following recommendation to its membership: "The extraordinary nature of our time demands that the ordinary means of seeking the transformation of political and economic policy is pursued with extraordinary vigor and imagination."[54]

This policy called individual Presbyterians to "strenuous political involvement." It affirmed ongoing General Assembly advocacy of just-peace policies. It did not provide for new programs or resources, but it stressed the urgency of the issues. The political tactic to be employed was not the establishment of new political parties, but the use of existing democratic procedures. Politics was understood both as voting and as the entire process of choosing leaders and policies.

Two other strategies affirmed were the continuation of the campaign to influence *public opinion* and the continuation of efforts to influence *corporate policy*. The concerns about corporate policy reflected actions to encourage corporations to move in directions of greater justice and to turn away from heavy reliance on military procurement and nuclear weapons contracts.

Thus, one of the more activist denominations was encouraged by its highest governing authority to become more active in peacemaking. The preferred methods were politics, influencing of public opinion, and influencing of corporate policy. In evaluating such strategies, it is significant that Presbyterians nationally vote Republican out of preferred party choice, tradition, values, and perceived self-interest. It is unclear whether calling Presbyterians to political activity in the name of peacemaking will do any more than strengthen the Republican Party. Corporate policy has been influenced vis-à-vis investment in South Africa, but whether it is possible to have an impact on military procurement contracts is doubtful. The struggle for public opinion is perhaps the most viable of the three strategies for Christians seeking peacemaking policies. Public opinion, as it did in the case of Nicaragua, can restrain presidential adventurism when opinion is translated into pressure on Congress. The church's primary task here is to teach its membership the implications of the gospel of Christ's peace for governmental policy.[55] The joining of wise interpretations of biblical faith to public policy remains the awesome task of Christian citizens and Christian statespeople. So, the church struggles through, preaching and teaching to interpret the "signs of the times" and to energize Christian people to act out the faith that has been given them. The declaration of itself as a just-peace church during the cold war was a particularly bold act for the United Church of Christ. The policy directions of this denomination reflect the developing just-peacemaking thought edging out reliance on the old Christian debate between just-war perspective and a variety of pacifist perspectives.

In conclusion, the ultimate imperative of love requires penultimate guidelines and practices. In international relations in our time, these guidelines and principles are expressed realistically in the principled initiatives of just peacemaking. At the present moment, with new opportunities on all continents and especially in U.S.–Russian relations, it is a time for courage and hope. This combination of peace thinking, realism, just-peace developments, resistance to militarism, and extraordinary use of ordinary means of peacemaking can lead us into a less threatening and less militarized world.

# Notes

## 1. An Interpretation of Christian Ethics

1. For example, Edward L. Long Jr., *A Survey of Christian Ethics* (New York: Oxford University Press, 1967) and *A Survey of Recent Christian Ethics* (New York: Oxford University Press, 1982).

2. For example, J. Philip Wogaman, *Christian Ethics: A Historical Introduction* (Louisville: Westminster John Knox Press, 1993).

3. Edward L. Long Jr., *To Liberate and Redeem: Moral Reflections on the Biblical Narrative* (Cleveland: The Pilgrim Press, 1997).

4. Ibid., 4.

5. Ibid., 5.

6. Ibid., 8.

7. H. Richard Niebuhr, *The Responsible Self* (New York: Harper & Row, 1963), 50.

8. Ibid., 52.

9. Ibid., 60.

10. Ibid., 65.

11. In the 1960s, I found women students at Vassar to be more enthusiastic about *The Responsible Self* than about the works of any of the other male authors I chose for two semester courses in basic Christian ethics.

12. Ian Barbour, *Ethics in an Age of Technology* (San Francisco: Harper SanFrancisco, 1993).

13. Ibid., 44.

14. Long, *A Survey* (1967).

15. The form of Christian ethics in this book does not fit easily into the philosophical categories of academia. This is attributable in part to the differences between the church and the university and in part to the differences between Jesus and Aristotle. The ethic presented here, although distinctive, is close to a mixed-theory agapism in terms similar to those of William K. Frankena's categories. It is neither pure rule agapism nor pure act agapism, to use Frankena's terms. Reinhold Niebuhr is closer to act agapism, but he has principles. John Calvin is close to rule agapism in his use of the Ten Commandments. See William K. Frankena, *Ethics* (Englewood Cliffs, N.J.: Prentice-Hall, 1963), 42–45.

16. John Calvin, in John T. McNeil, ed., *John Calvin on God and Political Duty* (New York: The Liberal Arts Press, 1950), 62.

17. Paul L. Lehmann, *The Decalogue and a Human Future* (Grand Rapids, Mich.: Eerdmans, 1995).

18. John Witherspoon, *The Works*, I (Edinburgh: J. Ogle, 1815), 303–4.

19. Lehmann, *The Decalogue*, 225.

20. Emil Brunner, *The Divine Imperative*, trans. Olive Wyon (Philadelphia: Westminster Press, 1947), 59.

21. John C. Bennett, *The Radical Imperative* (Philadelphia: Westminster Press, 1975).

## 2. A Particular Love as the Ultimate Imperative

1. Walter Rauschenbusch, *Dare We Be Christians?* (Cleveland: The Pilgrim Press, 1993); originally published 1914.

2. Ibid., 14.

3. Ibid., 30.

4. Walter Rauschenbusch, *Christianity and the Social Crisis* (New York: Harper Torchbooks, 1964); originally published 1907.

5. Walter Rauschenbusch, *A Theology for the Social Gospel* (New York: Macmillan Company, 1917).

6. Rauschenbusch, *Christianity and the Social Crisis*, 67.

7. Ernst Troeltsch, *The Social Teaching of the Christian Churches* (New York: Macmillan Company, 1931).

8. Ibid., vol. 2, 1004–6.

9. Ibid., vol. 1, 54.

10. H. Richard Niebuhr, *Christ and Culture* (New York: Harper & Brothers, 1951).

11. Reinhold Niebuhr, *Does Civilization Need Religion?* (New York: Macmillan Company, 1929).

12. Reinhold Niebuhr, *Man's Nature and His Communities* (New York: Charles Scribner's Sons, 1965).

13. Anders Nygren, *Agape and Eros* (Philadelphia: The Westminster Press, 1953), 737.

14. Ibid., 219.

15. Gene Outka, *Agape: An Ethical Analysis* (New Haven, Conn.: Yale University Press, 1972), 8.

16. Ibid., 9.

17. Ibid., 8.

18. H. Richard Niebuhr, *The Purpose of the Church and Its Ministry* (New York: Harper & Brothers, 1956), 34–36.

19. Outka, *Agape: An Ethical Analysis*, 9.

20. Reinhold Niebuhr, *Love and Justice*, ed. D. B. Robertson (Louisville: Westminster/John Knox Press, 1957), 31. Another major source for Niebuhr's discussion of the height or pinnacle of *agape* as self-sacrifice is Reinhold Niebuhr, *Faith and History* (New York: Charles Scribner's Sons, 1949).

21. Ibid., 220.

22. Ibid., 50.

23. Ibid., 28.

24. Stephen J. Pope finds Outka still working from an individualistic bias in his more recent essay on the love commandment, "Love in Contemporary Christian Ethics," *Journal of Religious Ethics* 23, no. 1 (spring 1995): 167–97.

25. Outka, *Agape: An Ethical Analysis*, 35.

26. Ibid., 43–44.

27. Ibid., 260.

28. Paul Ramsey, *Nine Modern Moralists* (Englewood Cliffs, N.J.: Prentice-Hall, 1962), 7.

29. Sallie McFague, *Models of God: Theology for an Ecological, Nuclear Age* (Philadelphia: Fortress Press, 1987), 149.

30. Barbara Hilkert Andolsen, "Agape in Feminist Ethics," *Journal of Religious Ethics* 9, no. 1 (spring 1981): 69–83.

31. Ibid., 70.

32. Beverly Wildung Harrison, "The Power of Anger in the Work of Love," *Union Seminary Quarterly Review* 36 (Supplementary, 1981): 49.

33. An interesting example is the role of story dominating even the love commandment. See Stanley Hauerwas, "Love's Not All You Need," in *Vision and Virtue* (Notre Dame, Ind.: University of Notre Dame Press, 1981, reprint of 1974), 115. Also see "Rationality and the Christian Story," in *Truthfulness and Tragedy* (Notre Dame, Ind.: University of Notre Dame Press, 1977), 15–81.

34. Stanley Hauerwas, *Dispatches from the Front* (Durham, N.C.: Duke University Press, 1994), 22.

35. Hauerwas, *Vision and Virtue*, 115.

36. Ibid., 119, 113, 116, 117, 126.

37. *The First Catechism of the PC(U.S.A.)*, http://www.pcusa.org.

## 3. Nurtured in Community and Seeking Justice

1. Ernst Troeltsch, *The Social Teaching of the Christian Churches* (New York: Macmillan, 1931).

2. Paul Lehmann, *Ethics in a Christian Context* (New York: Harper & Row, 1963), 45.

3. H. Richard Niebuhr, *Christ and Culture* (New York: Harper & Brothers, 1951).

4. On the discussion of interpretation, see Walter Harrelson, *The Ten Commandments and Human Rights* (Philadelphia: Fortress Press, 1980), and Eduard Nielsen, *The Ten Commandments in New Perspective* (Naperville, Ill.: Alec R. Allenson, 1968).

5. George H. Kehm, *Whose World Is It?* [Louisville: Presbyterian Church (USA) 1991], 14, and George H. Kehm, "The New Story," in *After Nature's Revolt*, ed. Dieter T. Hessel (Minneapolis: Fortress Press, 1992), 92.

6. Quoted in *The Living Pulpit* (Jan.–March, 1993): 28.

7. Ismael Garcia, *Justice in Latin American Theology of Liberation* (Atlanta: John Knox Press, 1987).

8. Ibid., 11.

9. Ibid., 190–93.

10. Ibid., 120.

11. Karen Lebacqz, *Six Theories of Justice* (Minneapolis: Augsburg Publishing House, 1986).

12. Curt Cadorette, *From the Heart of the People: The Theology of Gustavo Gutiérrez* (Oak Park, Ill.: Meyer Stone, 1988).

13. Ibid., 76.

14. Gustavo Gutiérrez, *The Power of the Poor in History* (Maryknoll, N.Y.: Orbis Books, 1983), 14.

15. Gustavo Gutiérrez, *On Job* (Maryknoll, N.Y.: Orbis Books, 1987), 91.

16. Paul Tillich, "Grundlinien des Religiösen Sozialismus," *Blatter für Religiösen Sozialismus*, IV Heft 8/10 (1923). Also, *Gesammelte Werke* (Stuttgart: Evangelischen Verlagswerk, 1962), vol. II. James Luther Adams, ed. and trans., *Political Expectation* (New York: Harper & Row, 1971).

17. Paul Tillich, *Christianity and Society* 8, no. 4 (1943): 10–20.

18. Paul Tillich, *The Socialist Decision*, trans. Franklin Sherman (New York: Harper & Row, 1977).

19. Tillich, *Christianity and Society* 8, no. 4 (1943): 17.

20. Ibid.

21. Tillich, *The Socialist Decision*, 6.

22. Ibid.

23. Ibid., 139.

24. Ibid., 141.

25. See Alistair M. MacLeod, *Paul Tillich: An Essay on the Role of Ontology in His Philosophical Theology* (London: George Allen & Unwin Ltd., 1973).

26. Paul Tillich, *Love, Power, and Justice* (New York/London: Oxford University Press, 1954), 56.

27. Ibid., 62.

28. Ibid., 71.

29. José Porfirio Miranda, *Marx and the Bible* (Maryknoll, N.Y.: Orbis Books, 1974).

30. Karen Lebacqz, *Justice in an Unjust World* (Minneapolis: Augsburg Publishing House, 1987), 159.

31. *Social Action* (October 1968): 53–64.

32. Reinhold Niebuhr quoted Santayana on a "flexible definition of the good" as "the harmony of the whole which does not destroy the vitality of the parts," in Harry R. Davis and Robert C. Good, eds., *Reinhold Niebuhr on Politics* (New York: Charles Scribner's Sons, 1960), 327.

33. Reinhold Niebuhr, "The Problem of a Protestant Social Ethic," *Union Seminary Quarterly Review* XV (November 1959): 5.

34. See Reinhold Niebuhr, "Liberty and Equality," in *Faith and Politics* (New York: George Braziller, 1968), 185–98.

35. See Harlan Beckley, *Passion for Justice* (Louisville: Westminster John Knox Press, 1992).

36. S. I. Benn and R. S. Peters, *Social Principles and the Democratic State* (London: George Allen & Unwin Ltd., 1959).

37. Ibid., 112.

38. John Rawls, "Justice as Fairness," in Peter Laslett and W. G. Runciman, eds., *Philosophy, Politics, and Society* (Oxford: Basil Blackwell, 1962), 132.

39. Rawls's more complete theory of justice expands the argument of "Justice as Fairness." See John Rawls, *A Theory of Justice* (Cambridge: Harvard University Press, 1971).

40. Reinhold Niebuhr's perspective on justice is summarized in Karen Lebacqz, *Six Theories of Justice* (Minneapolis: Augsburg Publishing House, 1986).

41. R. H. Tawney, *Equality* (1931; London: George Allen & Unwin Ltd., 1964).

42. Ibid., 73.

43. G. William Domhoff, *Who Rules America?* (Englewood Cliffs, N.J.: Prentice-Hall, 1967).

44. Thomas R. Dye, *Who's Running America?* (Englewood Cliffs, N.J.: Prentice-Hall, 1974), 236.

45. Larry L. Rasmussen, *Moral Fragments and Moral Community* (Minneapolis: Fortress Press, 1993), 93.

## 4. Loyalty to God

1. Martin Luther, "The Large Catechism," in *Christian Ethics*, ed. Waldo Beach and H. Richard Niebuhr (New York: The Ronald Press Company, 1973), 244–49.

2. Henry Sloane Coffin, *The Ten Commandments* (New York: Harper & Brothers, 1915), 13–29.

3. John Calvin, *Harmony of Exodus, Leviticus, Numbers, Deuteronomy*, in *Calvin's Commentaries* (Grand Rapids, Mich.: Baker Book House, 1979), vol. II, 417–502; vol. III, 5–106.

4. Paul Tillich, *Systematic Theology*, I (Chicago: University of Chicago Press, 1951), 37, 227.

5. See Harrelson, *The Ten Commandments and Human Rights*, 71.

6. Coffin, *The Ten Commandments*, 41.

7. Calvin, *Institutes*, 388.

8. Ibid., 385.

9. See Harrelson, *The Ten Commandments and Human Rights*, 67.

10. Ibid., 72.

11. Ibid., 76.

12. J. J. Stamm, *Le Decalogue* (Neuchâtel: Delachaux et Niestlé, 1959), 44.

13. Hugh G. G. Herklots, *The Ten Commandments and Modern Man* (Fair Lawn, N.J.: Essential Books, Inc., 1958), 56.

14. Martin Luther, "The Large Catechism," in *Christian Ethics*, ed. Waldo Beach and H. Richard Niebuhr (New York: The Ronald Press Company, 1973), 248.

15. See Jan Lochman, *Signposts to Freedom* (Minneapolis: Augsburg, 1982), 56.

16. Joy Davidman, *Smoke on the Mountain* (Philadelphia: Westminster Press, 1953), 48.

17. Atheist states hurry to schedule society so as to exclude Sunday worship and leisure. In Fiji, Christians combined Sabbath freedom with political ambition to rebel against domination by Hindus. In Pittsburgh, Pennsylvania, churches struggle to maintain access to worship in the face of city-government-organized footraces that block streets and deny access to churches on Sunday mornings at customary hours of worship.

18. J. Morgenstern, "Sabbath," *The Interpreter's Dictionary of the Bible* (Nashville: Abingdon Press, 1962), 135–41.

19. Nielsen, *The Ten Commandments in New Perspective*, 82.

20. Harrelson, *The Ten Commandments and Human Rights*, 79.

21. "Der Dekalog enthält kein Gebot zu arbeiten, aber ein Gebot, von der Arbeit zu ruhen." Dietrich Bonhoeffer, *Dein Reich Komme* (Hamburg: Furche-Verlag, 1962), 33.

22. As quoted in Gardiner M. Day, *Old Wine in New Bottles* (New York: Morehouse-Gorham, 1949), 47.

23. M. G. Glazebrook, "Sunday," in James Hastings, ed., *Encyclopedia of Religion and Ethics*, XIII (New York: Charles Scribner's Sons, 1922), 103–11.

24. Karl Barth, *Church Dogmatics*, III, 4 (Edinburgh: T. & T. Clark, 1961), 53.

25. Ibid., 67–72.

26. Exodus 31:14–15.

27. Joseph Kraft, "Washington Insight," *Pittsburgh Post-Gazette*, January 31, 1973.

28. Elliot L. Richardson, "Keep It Local," *New York Times*, January 31, 1973.

29. Eric Schmitt, "Debate on Immigration Bill," *New York Times*, February 26, 1996, 1.

30. Max Weber, *The Protestant Ethic and the Spirit of Capitalism* (New York: Charles Scribner's Sons, 1958).

31. R. H. Tawney, *Religion and the Rise of Capitalism* (New York: Mentor Books, 1947), 206.

32. Simone de Beauvoir, *The Coming of Age* (New York: G. P. Putnam's Sons, 1972), 87.

33. Ibid., 542.

34. Robert Wuthnow, *God and Mammon in America* (New York: The Free Press, 1994).

35. Robert Wuthnow, *Rethinking Materialism: Perspectives on the Spiritual Dimension of Economic Behavior* (Grand Rapids, Mich.: Eerdmans, 1995).

36. David Noel Freedman, *The Unity of the Hebrew Bible* (Ann Arbor: University of Michigan Press, 1991), 24.

## 5. Concern for the Other

1. Harrelson, *The Ten Commandments and Human Rights*, 92.

2. Daniel Callahan, *Setting Limits: Medical Goals in an Aging Society* (New York: Simon & Schuster, 1987).

3. Gordon E. Jackson, ed., *The Ethics of Aging: Church Mission and Practice* (Pittsburgh: Pittsburgh Theological Seminary, 1982).

4. Callahan, *Setting Limits*, 92.

5. John Calvin, *Institutes*, 404.

6. Luther, *Large Catechism*, 254.

7. "Covenant and Creation: Theological Reflections on Contraception and Abortion," *Church and Society* 73, no. 6 (July/August 1983): 58.

8. Lehmann, *The Decalogue and a Human Future*, 166–70.

9. Ibid., 169.

10. Ibid., 171.

11. Robert Shelton, "Biomedical Ethics in Methodist Traditions," *Bioethics Yearbook*, III (Dordrecht: Kluwer Academic Publishers, 1993), 226.

12. Elizabeth Rosenthal, "Panel Tells Albany to Resist Legalizing Assisted Suicide," *New York Times*, May 26, 1969, 11.

13. Lawrence K. Altman, "Quinlan Case Revisited and Yields New Finding," *New York Times*, May 26, 1969, 11.

14. Robert Shelton, "Recent Developments in Medical Ethics in the Methodist Tradition," *Bioethics Yearbook*, I (Dordrecht: Kluwer Academic Publishers, 1991), 145–60.

15. Francis D. Moore, "Prolonging Life, Permitting Life to End," *Harvard Magazine* (July–August, 1995): 46.

16. Timothy Eagan, "No One Rushing in Oregon to Use a New Suicide Law," *New York Times*, March 15, 1998, 14.

17. Lamont Jones, "Life-Ending Acts Unthinkable, Says ICU Nurse," *Pittsburgh Post-Gazette*, May 23, 1996, 14.

18. Byron Spice, "Hastening Death's Hand," *Pittsburgh Post-Gazette*, May 23, 1996, 1.

19. David Noel Freedman, *The Unity of the Hebrew Bible* (Ann Arbor: University of Michigan Press, 1991), 30.

20. Luther, *Large Catechism*, 254.

21. Calvin, *Institutes*, 404.

22. Gardiner Day, *Old Wine in New Bottles* (New York: Morehouse-Gorham Co., 1949), 63.

23. The discussion of justifiable war is an edited version of chapter 5 of my *Christian Realism and Peacemaking* (Nashville: Abingdon Press, 1988), 86–101.

24. Henry Paolucci, ed., *The Political Writings of St. Augustine* (Chicago: Regnery Gateway, 1962), 182.

25. Roland H. Bainton, *Christian Attitudes toward War and Peace* (Nashville/New York: Abingdon Press, 1960), 97. This exposition of Augustine on the just war follows Bainton except on one point. Paul Ramsey has the better of the argument, as he argues that no requirement that the absolute justice reside with one side in a war was suggested by Augustine. Paul Ramsey, *War and the Christian Conscience* (Durham, N.C.: Duke University Press, 1961), 15–33.

26. Herbert A. Deane, *The Political and Social Ideas of St. Augustine* (New York: Columbia University Press, 1963), 159.

27. James T. Johnson, quoted in Donald L. Davidson, *Nuclear Weapons and the American Churches* (Boulder, Colo.: Westview Press, 1983), 5.

28. Ibid.

29. A. P. D'Entreves, ed., *Aquinas: Selected Political Writings* (Oxford: Basil Blackwell, 1965), 159–61.

30. Joseph C. McKenna. "Ethics and War: A Catholic View," *American Political Science Review* (September 1960): 651–52.

31. John Calvin, *Institutes of the Christian Religion*, I (1559), ed. John T. McNeill, trans. Ford Lewis Battles (Philadelphia: Westminster Press, 1960), 404.

32. Ibid., II, 1500.

33. Edward LeRoy Long Jr., *War and Conscience in America* (Philadelphia: Westminster Press, 1968), 24–30.

34. "Winning Peace" (Washington, D.C.: French Embassy, 1983), 9.

35. *In Defense of Creation: The Nuclear Crisis and a Just Peace* (Nashville: Graded Press, 1986), 13.

36. Carl Sagan, "Nuclear War and Climatic Catastrophe: Some Policy Implications," *Foreign Affairs* 62, no. 2 (winter 1983–84), 257–92.

37. James Gleick, "Less Drastic Theory Emerges on Freezing after Nuclear War," *New York Times*, June 22, 1986, Y13.

38. Calvin, *Institutes*, I, 405.

39. "General Synod XV: Pronouncement and Proposal," in *A Just Peace Church*, ed. Susan Thistlethwaite (New York: United Church Press, 1986), 133.

40. Ibid., 7–112.

41. See, for example, Gardiner M. Day, *Old Wine in New Bottles*; Henry Sloane Coffin, *The Ten Commandments*; Joy Davidman, *Smoke on the Mountain*; and Jan Lochman, *Signposts to Freedom*.

42. Kenneth L. Woodward, "Mixed Blessings," *Newsweek*, August 16, 1993, 41.

43. Ibid., 38–44.

44. Rachel Moss, ed., *God's Yes to Sexuality* (London: Collins, 1981), 154–62.

45. Ibid., 158.

46. Joseph Fletcher, *Situation Ethics: The New Morality* (Philadelphia: Westminster Press, 1966).

47. Ibid., 164.

48. Ibid., 164–68.

49. Freedman, *The Unity of the Hebrew Bible*, 28.

50. Brevard S. Childs, *The Book of Exodus* (Philadelphia: The Westminster Press, 1974), 424.

51. Harrelson, *The Ten Commandments and Human Rights*, 135.

52. John Wesley, *Thoughts upon Slavery*, in Warren Thomas Smith, *John Wesley and Slavery* (Nashville: Abingdon Press, 1986), 146.

53. Luther, *Large Catechism*, 257.

54. Calvin, *Institutes*, I, 411.

55. Coffin, *The Ten Commandments*, 163.

56. Stephen G. Bunker, *Underdeveloping the Amazon* (Chicago: University of Chicago Press, 1988); Robert L. Stivers, "The Ancient Forest of the Pacific Northwest: The Moral Debate," *Theology and Public Policy* (fall 1993): 27–48.

57. Roy H. May, *The Poor of the Land: A Christian Case for Land Reform* (Maryknoll, N.Y.: Orbis Books, 1991), 94.

58. Terence R. Anderson, *Walking the Way: Christian Ethics as a Guide* (Toronto: United Church Publishing House, 1993), 274.

59. J. J. Stamm with M. E. Andrew, *The Ten Commandments in Recent Research* (Naperville, Ill.: Alec R. Allenson, 1962), 108.

60. Joe Sexton, "Inquiry Focuses on New York Police Practice of Testifying," *New York Times*, May 7, 1994, 16.

61. Supra, 95, 96.

62. "Moment of Truth," *New York Times*, September 8, 1991, 14.

63. Ibid.

64. "The CIA: Tool or Policy Maker?", *Christianity and Crisis* 26, no. 9 (May 30, 1966): 105.

65. Ernest W. Lefever and Roy Godson, *The CIA and the American Ethic* (Washington, D.C.: Ethics and Public Policy Center, 1979).

66. D'Entreves, *Aquinas*, 159.

67. See Glen H. Stassen, *Just Peacemaking* (Louisville: Westminster John Knox Press, 1992), for a summary of the emerging consensus.

68. See Sam Dillion, *Commandos: The CIA and Nicaragua's Contra Rebels* (New York: Henry Holt, 1991), for some of the recent documentation. The books by Robert Woodward, Victor Marchetti, and John D. Marks survey the corruption from earlier perspectives.

69. David L. Boren and Ernest R. May, *Foreign Affairs* (summer 1992): 52–72.

70. Stansfield Turner, "Intelligence for a New World Order," *Foreign Affairs* (fall 1991): 150.

71. Ibid., 161.

72. Ibid., 153.

73. William Sloane Coffin Jr., *Once to Every Man* (New York: Atheneum, 1977), 89–113.

74. Roy Godson, "Intelligence for the 1990's," n.d.

75. Victor Marchetti and John D. Marks, *The CIA and the Cult of Intelligence* (New York: Dell, 1980).

76. Calvin, *Institutes*, I, 414.

77. Cf. Brevard S. Childs, *The Book of Exodus* (Philadelphia: Westminster Press, 1974), 425–27; Harrelson, *The Ten Commandments and Human Rights*, 148–49; Anthony Phillips, *Ancient Israel's Criminal Law* (Oxford: Basil Blackwell, 1970), 149–52; and Stamm, *The Ten Commandments in Recent Research*, 101–7.

78. Stamm, *The Ten Commandments in Recent Research*, 104.

79. Freedman, *The Unity of the Hebrew Bible*, 34–35.

## 6. Guided in the Spirit of Jesus

1. See Ulrich Luz, *Matthew 1–7: A Commentary* (Minneapolis: Augsburg Press, 1989), 99.

2. Marcus J. Borg, *Meeting Jesus Again for the First Time* (San Francisco: Harper-SanFrancisco, 1994), 69–95.

3. John Dominic Crossan, *Jesus: A Revolutionary Biography* (San Francisco: Harper-SanFrancisco, 1989). Crossan errs in portraying Jesus as a cynic, but his instincts in the direction of seeing him as a philosopher are correct.

4. Ed Sanders is representative of critical biblical scholars who believe that quite a bit of reliable information about Jesus is possible. E. P. Sanders, *The Historical Figure of Jesus* (London: The Penguin Press, 1993).

5. H. Richard Niebuhr, *Christ and Culture* (New York: Harper & Brothers, 1951), 28.

6. H. Richard Niebuhr, *The Purpose of the Church and Its Ministry* (New York: Harper & Row, 1956), 31.

7. Ibid., 57–63.

## 7. Personal and Public Morality

1. Stephen Mott, *Biblical Ethics and Social Change* (New York: Oxford University Press, 1982), 184.

2. Daniel Berrigan, *To Dwell in Peace: An Autobiography* (San Francisco: Harper & Row, 1987), 100.

3. Augustine, *The City of God*, XIV, 1, trans. Marcus Dods (New York: Modern Library, 1950), 441.

4. In George W. Forell, ed., *Christian Social Teachings* (Minneapolis: Augsburg, 1966), 162–63.

5. John Calvin, *Institutes*, II, 1485.

6. Reinhold Niebuhr, *Moral Man and Immoral Society* (New York: Charles Scribner's Sons, 1932), 22.

7. Ibid., 257.

8. Ibid., 267.

9. Ibid., 270–71.

10. Ibid., 273.

11. Reinhold Niebuhr, *The Nature and Destiny of Man*, I (New York: Charles Scribner's Sons, 1941), 208–19.

12. Ibid., 212.

13. Ibid., 214.

14. Reinhold Niebuhr, *Man's Nature and His Communities* (New York: Charles Scribner's Sons, 1965), 22.

15. Ronald H. Stone, *Reinhold Niebuhr: Prophet to Politicians* (Nashville: Abingdon Press, 1972), 84.

16. See Cynthia S. W. Crysdale, "Gilligan and the Ethics of Care: An Update," *Religious Studies Review* (January 1994): 21–28.

## 8. Economic Disparities

1. Paul A. Samuelson, *Economics* (New York: McGraw Hill, 1970), 4.

2. Adam Smith, *The Theory of Moral Sentiments* (Indianapolis: Liberty Classics, 1982), 171.

3. Bob Goudzwaard and Harry deLange, *Beyond Poverty and Influence* (Geneva: WCC Publications, 1995).

4. Max L. Stackhouse, "The Ten Commandments: Economic Implications," in *On Moral Business*, ed. Max L. Stackhouse, Dennis P. McCann, Shirley J. Roels, and Preston Williams (Grand Rapids, Mich.: Eerdmans, 1995), 59–62.

5. James M. Gustafson, *Ethics from a Theocentric Perspective* (Chicago: University of Chicago Press, 1981), 163–64. Paraphrased here.

6. John Calvin, *Harmony of Matthew, Mark, Luke*, II (Grand Rapids, Mich.: Baker Book House, 1979), 143.

7. Ibid.

8. Robert W. Weigand is typical of this popular misconception. Weigand, a professor of marketing at the University of Illinois, wrote: "John Calvin, the sixteenth-century theologian, taught that hard work and an abstemious life brought salvation. These values also bring prosperity." *New York Times*, April 19, 1986, 15.

9. John Calvin, *Calvin: Commentaries*, The Library of Christian Classics, xxiii (Philadelphia: Westminster Press, 1957), 330.

10. Quoted in André Biéler, *The Social Humanism of Calvin* (Richmond, Va.: John Knox Press, 1964), 37.

11. Ibid.

12. Quoted in Benjamin Nelson, *The Idea of Usury* (Chicago: University of Chicago Press, 1969), 78.

13. Ibid, 81.

14. See William C. Innes, *Social Concern in Calvin's Geneva* (Allison Park, Pa.: Pickwick Publications, 1983), 103–20, for an excellent analysis of Calvin's diaconate.

15. Ibid., 152.

16. Quoted in Biéler, *The Social Humanism of Calvin*, 53.

17. Ibid., 52.

18. W. Fred Graham, *The Constructive Revolutionary: John Calvin and His Socio-Economic Impact* (Richmond, Va.: John Knox Press, 1971), 127–44. Graham's discussion of the regulation of commerce in Geneva is the most complete I have found.

19. John Calvin, "Instruction of Faith," in *Great Voices of the Reformation*, ed. Harry Emerson Fosdick (New York: Random House, 1952), 237.

20. Biéler, *The Social Humanism of Calvin*, 63.

21. See Robert L. Heilbroner, *The Worldly Philosophers* (New York: Simon & Schuster, 1972), for a presentation of Smith's eccentricities.

22. Adam Smith, *An Inquiry into the Nature and Causes of the Wealth of Nations* (Indianapolis: Liberty Fund, 1981), 456.

23. Adam Smith, *The Theory of Moral Sentiments* (Indianapolis: Liberty Classics, 1982), 185.

24. Emil Brunner, *The Divine Imperative*, 395.

25. Quoted in John C. Bennett, *The Radical Imperative*, 145.

26. Ibid., 142–64.

27. Barbara Hilkert Andolsen and Mary E. Hunt, in "Professional Resources," *The Annual* (Washington, D.C.: Society of Christian Ethics, 1994), 257–306.

28. Rebecca M. Blank, an economist, has written for the United Church of Christ a useful volume on Christian economic ethics with a wide vision and relationship to the market economy: *Do Justice: Linking Christian Faith and Modern Economic Life* (Cleveland: United Church Press, 1992).

29. Bebb Wheeler Stone, in *Reformed Faith and Economics*, ed. Robert L. Stivers (Lanham, Md.: University Press of America, 1989), 171–82.

30. "Freeing Bonds and Binding Freedom: Reinhold Niebuhr and Feminist Critics on Paternal Dominion and Maternal Constraint," in *The Annual* (Washington, D.C.: Society of Christian Ethics, 1996), 121–43.

31. *Christian Faith and Economic Justice* [Atlanta: Presbyterian Church (U.S.A.), 1984]. The discussion was previously published in Ronald Stone, *Reformed Urban Ethics* (San Francisco: Edwin Mellen Press, 1991), 114–19, 121–28.

32. Reinhold Niebuhr, quoted in *Christian Faith and Economic Justice*, 12.

33. *Toward a Just, Caring, and Dynamic Political Economy* [New York: Advisory Council on Church and Society of Presbyterian Church (U.S.A.), 1985].

34. Lester Thurow, "The Leverage of Our Wealthiest 400," *New York Times*, October 11, 1984.

35. *Toward a Just, Caring, and Dynamic Political Economy*, 37.

36. Several of the papers have been published in Robert L. Stivers, ed., *Reformed Faith and Economics* (Lanham, Md.: University Press of America, 1989).

37. "God's Work in Our Hands: Employment, Community, and Christian Vocation," *Church and Society* (Sept./Oct. 1995): 5–10.

38. *All the Live Long Day: Women and Work* [General Assembly of the Presbyterian Church (U.S.A.), 1988.]

39. *Keeping and Healing the Creation* [Louisville: Presbyterian Church (U.S.A.), 1989].

40. "Restoring Creation for Ecology and Justice," *Church and Society* (July/August 1996).

41. "Hope for a Global Future: Toward Just and Sustainable Human Development," *Church and Society* (Sept./Oct. 1996): 32–54. The full document appears in the minutes of the General Assembly of 1996.

42. "Economic Justice for All: Catholic Social Teaching and the U.S. Economy" (third draft), *Origins* (June 5, 1986).

43. Carol Johnston, "Learning Reformed Theology from the Roman Catholics: The U.S. Pastoral Letter on the Economy," in *Reformed Faith and Economics*, ed. Stivers, 211.

44. John E. Tropman, "The 'Catholic Ethic' vs. The 'Protestant Ethic': Catholic Social Service and the Welfare State," *Journal of Social Thought* (winter 1985): 13–22.

45. R. H. Tawney, *Religion and the Rise of Capitalism* (New York: New American Library of World Literature, 1960).

46. Harold L. Wilensky, "Leftism, Catholicism, and Democratic Corporatism: The Role of Political Parties in Recent Welfare State Development," in *The Development of Welfare States in Europe and America*, ed. Peter Flora and Arnold J. Heidenheimer (New Brunswick, N.J.: Transaction Books, 1981).

47. Tropman, "The 'Catholic Ethic,'" 17.

48. Octavio Paz, *The Labyrinth of Solitude* (New York: Grove Press, 1985), 364, quoted in Tropman, "The 'Catholic Ethic,'" 15. Umberto Eco made a similar point: "In the United States there's a Puritan ethic and a mythology of success. He who is successful is good. In Latin countries, in Catholic countries a successful person is a sinner," quoted in the *New York Times*, December 8, 1988, E7.

49. Cited in James M. McPherson, "Grandchildren of the New Deal," *New York Times Book Review*, September 22, 1996, 15.

## 9. Racism

1. George D. Kelsey, *Racism and the Christian Understanding of Man* (New York: Charles Scribner's Sons, 1965), 19.

2. Nicholas F. Gier, "Sin Color and Skin Color: A Short Look at Racism and Human Nature," in *Abstracts*, American Academy of Religion and Society of Biblical Literature (Atlanta: Scholars Press, 1988), 184.

3. World Council of Churches, "Churches Responding to Racism in the 1980's," 43.

4. The preceding five paragraphs were previously published in Ronald H. Stone, *Reformed Urban Ethics: Case Study of Pittsburgh* (San Francisco: Edwin Mellen Press, 1991), 129–31.

5. Cornel West, *Race Matters* (Boston: Beacon Press, 1993), 75.

6. Peter J. Paris, *The Social Teaching of the Black Churches* (Philadelphia: Fortress Press, 1985).

7. See Gayraud S. Wilmore, *Black and Presbyterian* (Philadelphia: Geneva Press, 1983).

8. An expanded version of this paragraph reflecting the findings of *Racial Justice in the 1980's* [Council on Church and Race of the Presbyterian Church (U.S.A.), n.d.], 3–5, was published in Stone, *Reformed Urban Ethics*, 132–34.

9. The section "Church, Race, and Pittsburgh" is from Stone, *Reformed Urban Ethics*, 134–43.

10. Martin Luther King Jr., *Where Do We Go from Here: Chaos or Community?* (Boston: Beacon Press, 1967), 56.

11. "Civil Disorders 1968," in *Pittsburgh*, ed. Roy Lubove (New York: New Viewpoints, 1976), 237–41.

12. Samuel G. Freedman, "A Voice from the Streets," *New York Times Magazine*, March 12, 1987, 36.

13. Quoted by Jane Blotzer, "The Choice: Poor Job or None," *Pittsburgh Post-Gazette*, December 19, 1988, 1, 6.

14. Ibid., 6.

15. Jovelino Ramos, "Discerning the Racism of the Eighties," *Church and Society* (May/June, 1985), 28–35.

16. Joseph C. Hough Jr., *Black Power and White Protestants* (New York: Oxford University Press, 1968), 218–28.

17. West, *Race Matters*, 63.

18. Ibid., 11.

19. Ibid., 11–12.

20. William Julius Wilson, "Work," *New York Times Magazine*, August 18, 1996, 26–31, 40, 48, 52–54.

## 10. Political Apathy

1. This chapter draws on an edited synthesis of previously published work by Ronald H. Stone, in "Introduction," *Reformed Faith and Politics* (Washington, D.C.: University Press of America, 1983); "Reformed Faith and Politics: A Background Paper" [minutes of the General Assembly of the United Presbyterian Church (USA), 1983], 764–75; "Faith, Politics, and Christian Ethics," in *Reformed Urban Ethics;* and

"Theological Ethics and Political Participation," *Church and Society* (Sept./Oct., 1996): 95–97.

2. Anne Murphy analyzed the problems of the American political system in her essay "New and Old Assumptions about Politics" commissioned for Stone, *Reformed Faith and Politics,* 191–201; and Dorothy Dodge sketched the changes in the U.S. political system in her essay "The Politics of the Eighties," in *Reformed Faith and Politics,* 141–55.

3. Paul Tillich, "Two Roots of Political Thinking," in *The Socialist Decision,* trans. Franklin Sherman (New York: Harper & Row, 1977), 1–10.

4. Ernesto Cardenal, *The Gospel in Solentiname,* vol. 1, trans. Donald D. Walsh (Maryknoll, N.Y.: Orbis Books, 1978).

5. The Reverend Albert C. Winn exposited liberation theology in "The Reformed Tradition and Liberation Theology," in Stone, *Reformed Faith and Politics,* 77–82, and the comments here reflect Winn's work.

6. Gustavo Gutiérrez, *A Theology of Liberation,* trans. Caridad Inda and John Eagleson (Maryknoll, N.Y.: Orbis Books, 1973).

7. Winn, "The Reformed Tradition and Liberation Theology," 83–88.

8. Ibid., 90.

9. The discussion of the fundamentalist approach to politics is dependent on Professor George Marsden's research. See his essay "Understanding Fundamentalist Views of Society," in Stone, *Reformed Faith and Politics,* 65–76.

10. See Peggy L. Shriver, "Piety, Pluralism, and Politics," a descriptive essay on the new Christian right commissioned for Stone, *Reformed Faith and Politics,* 49–63.

11. John C. Bennett, "Church and State in the United States," in Stone, *Reformed Faith and Politics,* 134.

12. *Ethics and the Search for Christian Unity* (Washington, D.C.: United States Catholic Conference, 1981), 27–28.

13. Jane Dempsey Douglass, "Church and State: A Brief Introduction for Contemporary Presbyterians," in Stone, *Reformed Faith and Politics,* 93.

14. H. H. Gerth and Wright Mills, eds., *From Max Weber: Essays in Sociology* (New York: Oxford University Press, 1958), 128.

15. Calvin, *Institutes,* II, p. 1518.

16. David Little, "Legislating Morality: The Role of Religion," in *Christianity and Politics: Catholic and Protestant Perspectives,* ed. Carol Friedley Griffith (Washington, D.C.: Ethics and Public Policy Center, 1981), 39–53.

## 11. Ecological Corruption

1. Ronald H. Stone, "Ethics and Growth," *The South East Asia Journal of Theology* 14, no. 1 (1972): 40–55.

2. Larry Rasmussen, quoted in James A. Nash, "Ethics and Economics—Ecology Dilemma: Toward a Just, Sustainable, and Frugal Future," *Theology and Public Policy* 6, no. 1 (summer 1994): 34. Attributed to Daniel Maguire by Rasmussen.

3. This ambiguous human development is summarized aptly by Stephen Mott, *A Christian Perspective on Political Thought* (Oxford: Oxford University Press, 1993), 107–12.

4. Barbour, *Ethics in an Age of Technology,* xv.

5. Quoted by Dieter T. Hessel, "Now That Animals Can Be Genetically Engineered," in *Ecotheology: Voices from South and North,* ed. David G. Hallman (Maryknoll, N.Y.: Orbis Books, 1994), 293–94.

6. Jaydee Hanson, "The Climate Change Crisis," in *God's Earth, Our Home*, ed. Shantilal P. Bhagat (New York: National Council of Churches, 1994), 1.

7. Barbour, *Ethics in an Age of Technology*, 185. Ronald Bailey, in *Ecoscam* (New York: St. Martin's Press, 1993), argues for a minimalist view of the dangers of global warming.

8. J. E. Lovelock, in *Gaia* (Oxford: Oxford University Press, 1987), 116, 144, is particularly critical of the campaign to prohibit fluorocarbons.

9. Bryant Robey, Shea O. Rutstein, and Leo Morris, "The Fertility Decline in Developing Countries," *Scientific American*, December 1993, 65.

10. Roger D. Stone, *Dreams of Amazonia* (New York: Penguin Books, 1993), 152–53.

11. Ibid, 155.

12. Susanna Hecht and Alexander Cockburn, *The Fate of the Forest* (London: Verso, 1989), 201.

13. Ibid., 208.

14. Jared Diamond, "Portrait of the Biologist as a Young Man," *The New York Review of Books*, Jan. 12, 1995, 18.

15. D. F. Olivier, "'God's Rest: The Core and Leitmotif of a Christian Holistic View of Reality?'" in *Are We Killing God's Earth?*, ed. W. S. Vorster (Pretoria: University of South Africa, 1987), 113–15.

16. J. Ronald Engel, "Sustainable Development: A New Global Ethic," *The Egg: An Eco-Justice Quarterly* (spring 1992): 4.

17. Ibid.

18. "Hope for a Global Future: Toward Just and Sustainable Human Development," *Church and Society* (Sept./Oct. 1996): 32–54.

19. John Cobb, "Sustainability and Community," *The Egg: An Eco-Justice Quarterly* (summer 1992): 8.

20. Quoted in *Sustainable Development, Reformed Faith and U.S. International Economic Policy* [Louisville: Advisory Committee on Social Witness Policy, Presbyterian Church (U.S.A.), 1994], 10.

21. Robert L. Stivers, *The Sustainable Society: Ethics and Economic Growth* (Philadelphia: Westminster Press, 1976).

22. Robert L. Stivers, "The Ancient Forests of the Pacific Northwest: The Moral Debate," *Theology and Public Policy* 5, no. 2 (fall 1993): 27–31.

23. James D. Hudnut-Beumler, "Energy and the Environment," *Church and Society* 81, no. 2 (Nov.–Dec. 1990): 86–87.

24. The "Rio Declaration on Environment and Development" of 1992 represents the acceptance of the term "sustainable development," which dominates the text. This compromise document gives away much more to economic development than to the protection of the environment.

25. Campbell B. Read, "A Survey of the Role of Creation in Divinity Programs" (mimeographed paper, 1993).

26. Hans Küng, *A Global Ethic* (New York: Continuum, 1993), 26.

27. See especially Wesley Granberg-Michaelson, *Redeeming the Creator* (Geneva: WCC Publications, 1992).

28. Dieter T. Hessel, "Spirited Earth Ethics: Cosmological and Covenantal Roots," *Church and Society* (July/August, 1996): 16–36.

29. James M. Gustafson, *A Sense of the Divine* (Cleveland: The Pilgrim Press, 1994).

30. Daniel C. Maguire and Larry L. Rasmussen, *Ethics for a Small Planet* (Albany: State University of New York Press, 1998), 27–31.

31. Ibid., 46.

32. Ibid., 49–51.

33. Ian Barbour, *Ethics in an Age of Technology* (San Francisco: HarperSanFrancisco, 1993).

34. Rasmussen, in *Ethics for a Small Planet*, 120–21.

35. Ibid., 129.

36. Maguire, in *Ethics for a Small Planet*, 10–15.

## 12. Peacemaking

1. Michael W. Doyle, *Ways of War and Peace* (New York: W. W. Norton, 1997).

2. H. Richard Niebuhr, *Christ and Culture* (New York: Harper & Brothers, 1951), 183.

3. Kenneth N. Waltz, *Man, the State, and War: A Theoretical Analysis* (New York: Columbia University Press, 1954), 16–41.

4. Doyle, *Ways of War and Peace*, 49–92.

5. Reinhold Niebuhr, *Moral Man and Immoral Society* (New York: Charles Scribner's Sons, 1932), 83–112.

6. Hans J. Morgenthau, *Politics among Nations: The Struggle for Power and Peace* (New York: Alfred A. Knopf, 1967).

7. Hans J. Morgenthau, *Truth and Power* (London: Pall Mall Press, 1970).

8. Hans J. Morgenthau, "The Influence of Reinhold Niebuhr in American Political Life and Thought," in *Reinhold Niebuhr: A Prophetic Voice in Our Time*, ed. Harold R. Landon (Greenwich, Conn.: Seabury Press, 1962), 109.

9. Eduard Heimann, in *Reinhold Niebuhr: A Prophetic Voice in Our Time*, ed. Landon, 111–12.

10. Reinhold Niebuhr, *Moral Man and Immoral Society*, 122. Emphasis added.

11. "The Ethics of War and Peace in the Nuclear Age," *War/Peace Report* 7 (February 1967): 3.

12. M. Benjamin Mollov, *The Jewish Aspect of the Life and Work of Hans J. Morgenthau* (unpublished dissertation, Bar-Ilan University, 1995), 103.

13. Paul Tillich, *The Socialist Decision*, trans. Franklin Sherman (New York: Harper & Row, 1977), 20–26.

14. Max Weber, *The Sociology of Religion* (Boston: Beacon Press, 1963), 51.

15. Ibid., 58.

16. George Liska, "Morgenthau vs. Machiavelli," in *Truth and Tragedy*, ed. Kenneth Thompson and Robert J. Myers (New Brunswick, N.J.: Transaction Books, 1977).

17. Hans Morgenthau, in "Bernard Johnson's Interview with Hans J. Morgenthau," in *Truth and Tragedy*, ed. Thompson and Myers, 386.

18. Reinhold Niebuhr, "Hans J. Morgenthau: Scientific Man versus Power Politics," in *A Reinhold Niebuhr Reader*, ed. Charles C. Brown (Philadelphia: Trinity Press International, 1992), 147.

19. Morgenthau in *Reinhold Niebuhr*, ed. Landon, 99–104.

20. Morgenthau, *Politics among Nations*, 3–22.

21. Michael Joseph Smith, *Realist Thought from Weber to Kissinger* (Baton Rouge: Louisiana State University Press, 1986), 127, also finds the major difference between Morgenthau and Niebuhr at this point.

22. Ronald H. Stone, "Power and Purpose," in *Realism and Hope* (Washington, D.C.: University Press of America, 1977), 143–58.

23. Ibid. Hans J. Morgenthau himself developed the purposive character of American foreign policy in *The Purpose of American Politics* (New York: Alfred A. Knopf, 1964). Niebuhr also developed the ideological dimension of imperial struggles in *The Structure of Nations and Empires* (New York: Charles Scribner's Sons, 1959).

24. Ronald H. Stone, *Reinhold Niebuhr: Prophet to Politicians* (Nashville: Abingdon Press, 1972), 215.

25. Stanley H. Hoffmann, *Contemporary Theory in International Relations* (Englewood Cliffs, N.J.: Prentice-Hall, 1960), 30.

26. Ibid., 33.

27. Ibid.

28. Ibid., 34.

29. Ibid., 37.

30. For a more developed criticism of Hoffmann on these points, see Ronald H. Stone, "The Realists and Their Critics," *Worldview* 16 (June 1973): 19–23.

31. Despite realism's repeated attempts to sort out the historically contingent from perennial factors, Hoffmann criticizes some of the key concepts as time-bound. For example, in 1995 he repeats his 1960 critique that Morgenthau's concept of "national interest" seemed very time-bound. Stanley H. Hoffmann, "The Political Ethics of International Relations," in *Ethics and International Affairs: A Reader*, ed. Joel H. Rosenthal (Washington, D.C.: Georgetown University Press, 1995), 29.

32. Hans Küng and Karl-Josef Kuschel, *A Global Ethic: The Declaration of the Parliament of the World's Religions* (New York: Continuum, 1993).

33. Joel H. Rosenthal's preface captures the moral commitments of the realists particularly well in *Righteous Realists: Political Realism, Responsible Power, and American Culture in the Nuclear Age* (Baton Rouge: Louisiana State University Press, 1991), xv–xix.

34. Reinhold Niebuhr, *Moral Man and Immoral Society*, 232–33.

35. Reinhold Niebuhr, *Man's Nature and His Communities*, 79.

36. Reinhold Niebuhr, "The King's Chapel and the King's Court," *Christianity and Crisis* 29 (August 4, 1969): 211–12.

37. Ben Hibbs, ed., *White House Sermons* (New York: Harper & Row, 1972).

38. The file of 633 pages is the possession of Ronald H. Stone.

39. Hoffmann, "Political Ethics," 36.

40. Ibid., 35.

41. Ibid., 37.

42. Reinhold Niebuhr and Paul E. Sigmund, *The Democratic Experience: Pasts and Prospects* (New York: Frederick A. Praeger, 1969).

43. Doyle, *Ways of War and Peace*, 285. Doyle summarizes the academic and philosophic insights in chapter 8, "Internationalism: Kant."

44. U.S. National Conference of Catholic Bishops, *The Challenge of Peace* (Washington, D.C.: United States Catholic Conference, 1983), para. 23, p. 12. United Methodist Council of Bishops, *In Defense of Creation* (Nashville: Graded Press, 1986), 13–24. Susan Thistlethwaite, ed., *A Just Peace Church* (New York: United Church Press, 1986), v, 134. General Assembly, *Peacemaking: The Believers Calling* (New York: The General Assembly of the United Presbyterian Church in the U.S.A., 1980), 20. Dana W. Wilbanks and Ronald H. Stone, *Presbyterians and Peacemaking: Are We Now Called to Resistance?* (New York: Advisory Council on Church and Society, 1985), 44.

45. Glen H. Stassen, *Just Peacemaking: Transforming Initiatives for Justice and Peace* (Louisville: Westminster/John Knox Press, 1992), 209–30.

46. Glen H. Stassen, ed., "Just Peacemaking Theory: Papers for Working Conference at the Carter Center, October 11–13, 1996" (Louisville: n.p., 1996).

47. Steven Brion-Meisels, *The Carter Center Chart Papers* (October 14, 1996). Revised and published in Glen Stassen, ed., *Just Peacemaking: Ten Practices for Abolishing War* (Cleveland: The Pilgrim Press, 1998).

48. Stassen, *Just Peacemaking: Transforming Initiatives for Justice and Peace*, 186–87.

49. Donald Shriver, *An Ethic for Enemies: Forgiveness in Politics* (Oxford: Oxford University Press, 1995).

50. Lewis Mumford, *The City in History* (New York: Harcourt, Brace & World, 1961), 42.

51. Ibid., 44.

52. Ibid., 45.

53. Paul Tillich, typed manuscript in Tillich Papers of Andover-Harvard Theological Library, Harvard Divinity School. Quoted with permission by Mutie Tillich Farris, Jan. 1, 1999.

54. The Presbyterian Church (U.S.A.), *Christian Obedience in a Nuclear Age* (1988), 8.

55. A much more complete discussion of these issues and a strategy for the local church are provided in Ronald H. Stone, *Christian Realism and Peacemaking* (Nashville: Abingdon Press, 1988).

# Subject Index

# Scripture Index